Life in Schools

FOURTH EDITION

Life in Schools

An Introduction to Critical Pedagogy in the Foundations of Education

Peter McLaren

University of California, Los Angeles

Boston   New York   San Francisco

Mexico City   Montreal   Toronto   London   Madrid   Munich   Paris

Hong Kong   Singapore   Tokyo   Cape Town   Sydney

Executive Editor and Publisher: *Stephen D. Dragin*
Editorial Assistant: *Barbara Strickland*
Marketing Manager: *Tara Whorf*
Production Editor: *Michelle Limoges*
Production Manager: *Susan Brown*
Editorial Production Service: *Colophon*
Composition and Prepress Buyer: *Linda Cox*
Electronic Composition: *Cabot Computer Services*
Manufacturing Manager: *JoAnne Sweeney*
Cover Administrator: *Kristina Mose-Libon*

For related titles and support materials, visit our online catalog at www.ablongman.com.

Between the time Website information is gathered and then published, it is not unusual for som sites to have closed. Also, the transcription of URLs can result in unintended typographical errors. The publisher would appreciate notification where these occur so that they may be corrected in subsequent editions.

To obtain permission(s) to use material from this work, please submit a written request to Allyn and Bacon, Permissions Department, 75 Arlington Street, Boston, MA 02116 or fax your request to 617-848-7320.

Library of Congress Cataloging-in-Publication Data

McLaren, Peter.
    Life in schools : an introduction to critical pedagogy in the foundations of education / Peter McLaren.—4th ed.
       p. cm.
    Includes bibliographical references and index.
    ISBN 0-205-35118-2 (alk. paper)
    1. Critical pedagogy—United States. 2. Education—Social aspects—United States. 3. Education—United States—Philosophy. 4. Educational equalization—United States. I. Title.
LC196.5.U6 M345 2002
370.11'5—dc21
                                     2002016463

Printed in the United States of America
10 9 8 7 6 5 4 3 2 1   06 05 04 03 02

This book is dedicated to my friend and colleague Henry Giroux and to the memory of Paulo Freire, dear friend and mentor. It is also dedicated to my wife Jenny, my daughter Laura and my son-in-law Marcelo, my son Jon, and to the memory of James Montgomerie and Jake Dale. I also wish to dedicate this book to Joe Kincheloe and Donald Macedo. And now in this fourth edition, I will add two more names to this list, my daughter-in-law Julie and my granddaughter Aubrey.

CONTENTS

FOREWORD TO THE FOURTH EDITION

We live in dangerous times. The world runs amok as global carpetbaggers looking to become the world's latest centillionaires take advantage of the results of increasing rights for business owners worldwide—privatization, budget cuts, and labor "flexibility"—due to the engineered absence of government constraint on the production, distribution, and consumption of goods and services brought about by global neo-liberal economy policies. Stacking the shelves of Planet Mall with goods shaped for designer lifestyles becomes the operative strategy. Following in the wake of pushcart, no-frills, bootstrap capitalism, is the cultural flotsam and jetsam produced by the Starbucking and Wal-Marting of the global landscape, as the tyranny of the market ruthlessly subjects labor to its regulatory forces of social and cultural reproduction in the unsustainable precincts of the capitalist market.

Under the tutelage of neoliberialism's economic engineers, Milton Friedman and Friedrich Von Hayek, the 1980s and 1990s became a showcase for an orchestrated conservative and right-wing backlash against the civil rights of working-class minority groups, immigrants, women, and children. Recently in the United States we have witnessed a series of democratic "victories" for proponents of propositions 21, 209, and 227 in California, propositions aimed at welfare "reform" and managed "care" as well as increasing the executions of criminals and massively expanding the prison industry.

It is not surprising that the privatization of health care, dwindling social services for the poor, and rumors of the marriage between Social Security and Wall Street coincide with the stagnation of wage growth and declining economic prosperity for most working-class men, women, and children. These recent trends are also associated with the shrinking middle class in the United States. Given such a scenario, democracy seems perilously out of reach. Indeed, the frontiers of human freedom are being pushed back as "free" market forces are being pushed forward. As I write this preface, the United States has engaged in what William S. Cohen, former Secretary of Defense, has called an "American Holy War" against terrorism. As we carry out this Holy War against the despicable acts of terror inflicted upon innocent victims, it is unclear if U.S. politicians and corporate leaders will begin to address the root causes of wars that can be traced to global capitalism's greatest export: violence against the poor.

In the last twenty years, the United States has bombed Libya, Grenada, Panama, Somalia, Haiti, Afghanistan, Sudan, Iraq, and Yugoslavia, all poor countries where the majority of the population is dark-skinned. Are these the necessary acts of defenders of world freedom? Are these necessary unilateral acts of "lesser evil" that protect the world from greater threats to freedom and democracy? Are there other ways to bring peace and social justice to the planet? Can terrorism be fought through education? Can militant religious fundamentalism attached to any religion be resisted and transformed through dialogue and debate before it spawns the kind of violence recently witnessed in Washington or New York? It is in the context of these questions that the work of Peter McLaren acquires both national and international significance.

McLaren's unorthodox writing style (that has led Joe Kincheloe to call McLaren "The Poet Laureate of the Educational Left"), his fearless "in your face" rhetorical strategies, and his anti-establishment physical appearance make McLaren an easy target in the largely conservative field of education. He is also a visible target for careerist leftist educators more interested in building their own radical empires than in liberating students from capitalist social arrangements. McLaren has been criticized by narrow-minded educators for everything from using an arcane, elitist language that is designed to communicate only with other intellectuals and to frustrate the classroom practitioner in the process, to being unnecessarily theoretical, to being insensitively critical of white people—and even to lacking humility because he revealed his tattoo of Che Guevara in one of his authors' photos in a recent book (which shows just how low educational criticism can sink). Right-wing ideologues like David Horowitz and Larry Elder have attacked him on the radio, and yet his work continues to inspire growing numbers of teachers, scholars, and political activists across the United States. To appreciate McLaren's work it is important to move beyond facile dismissals such as these and deal with the concepts he introduces and adumbrates. The reader will be well repaid for his or her effort.

Cries from the Corridor

Twenty years after its publication, Peter McLaren's *Cries from the Corridor* (1980) remains by far one of the most influential ethnographic studies to have emerged from the early 1980s literature on schooling. *Cries from the Corridor* is a collection of diaries written between 1973 and 1979, during a period when McLaren was a schoolteacher at Driftwood Public School in the Jane-Finch Corridor, a six square block area with a large concentration of West Indian immigrant families.

Along with Paul Willis's groundbreaking ethnographic study of the working-class culture of high school students in England, *Learning to Labor* (1977), and Paul Corrigan's *Schooling the Smash Street Kids* (1979), McLaren's *Cries from the Corridor* is an original contribution to the field of critical ethnography that documents the everyday life experiences of inner-city school children in Toronto, Canada. It was a precursor to McLaren's highly acclaimed full-length ethnographic study, *Schooling as a Ritual Performance* (1986). Teaching in the 1970s, at the height of the post-Second World War economic boom, McLaren offered through his diaries a rare glimpse into the little-known world of teaching and learning experiences of working-class immigrant students. When McLaren's unorthodox teaching style and leftist politics provoked his university not to renew his teaching contract in 1985, he took up a professorship in the United States at the invitation of radical educational scholar Henry Giroux. Because McLaren became highly critical of *Cries from the Corridor* (for reasons that he will explain throughout this book), one of McLaren's first projects upon his arrival to the United States was to integrate the diaries of *Cries from the Corridor* (1980) into a longer and more theoretically informed education textbook which he titled *Life in Schools* (1989). By drawing upon the life experiences of his Canadian students, McLaren masterfully brings into the foreground the fundamental contradictions of capitalist schooling in the larger North American context (see Bowles & Gintis, 1976). In essence, *Life in Schools* captures the darker side of capitalism by showing how, in McLaren's view, democracy fails to live up to its promise.

To McLaren's surprise, *Cries from the Corridor* (1980) had become a best-selling book in Canada. The book's success generated an unparalleled measure of public controversy and debate among educators, scholars, and policymakers both in North America and abroad. It is also to McLaren's credit that he listened to the critics of his books: not only Marxists, but also the very community members about whom he wrote. He incorporated what he learned into the pages of *Life in Schools* (1987). McLaren's key insight was that he had not provided a socio-political context for readers so that they could make critical sense of what he was writing about. Without such a context, readers could easily "blame the victims" of McLaren's story. That McLaren had the foresight and courage to address the limitations of his first book is a testament to his commitment as a critical scholar.

Twenty Years after *Cries from the Corridor*

Today, educators do not need to skim through the pages of Marxist journals or books to convince themselves that class polarization and antagonisms in both the United States and Canada has accelerated over the past two decades. A recent article by Matthew Bishop (2001) in one of the leading business magazines, *The Economist*, a staunch defender of capitalism, offers mind-numbing data on the growing upward redistribution of wealth. According to the article, there are 7.2 million people today who have minimum "investable assets" of $1 million compared to 5.2 million back in 1997. These 7.2 million millionaires possess one-third of the world's wealth. Or take another example of a recent article in the same magazine which reports:

> Never in the history of human wealth-creation has so much been pocketed so quickly by so many. The United States now boasts 300 billionaires and 5 million millionaires, with Silicon Valley adding 64 new millionaires every day. Nine million Americans have household incomes above $100,000 a year, up from just 2 million in 1982. If Great Britain was the first country to produce a mass middle class, the United States is the first country to produce a mass of upper class. (2000, p. 42)

With the injection of free trade agreements such as NAFTA and GATT, the globalization of capital has accelerated what can be described as the "Beirutization" of Toronto's suburban areas. Pockets of neighborhoods plagued by poverty have mushroomed at an astonishing pace. Elaine Carey (2001, June 9) of the *Toronto Star* reports that the poverty rate in over 100 neighborhoods in the metropolitan Toronto area has climbed to 30%. Even more disturbing is that in a number of areas the poverty rate has ballooned to 60%.

It is no secret that the 1994 North American Free Trade Agreement shifted manufacturing jobs and industries from Canadian suburbs such as North York to the *maquiladoras* that have mushroomed in northern Mexico's border towns where labor costs are merely a fraction when compared to Canada. The devastating impact of neoliberal social and economic policies in Canada are cause for great concern. To give just one example, between 1987 and 1995, Toronto's manufacturing sector shrank from 23.7% to 18.7% (Carey, 2001). During the same eight years, 85 out of the 481 industries (or 20% of industries and factories) in the city either relocated or were forced to close down.

Moreover, Elaine Carey (2001) reports that since the paralyzing recession that Canada experienced in 1991, poverty in the metropolitan Toronto area has grown by an astounding 67%. In addition, one out of every four adults and one out of every three children lives below the poverty line. The average income of poor families in Toronto is 14,800 Canadian dollars. And while it may be the case that between 1996 and 1998 family incomes in the poorest neighborhoods increased by 4.3%, nevertheless, this increase was only after a sharp 23.6% decline in income between 1992 and 1996. In comparison, during the same period, the income of wealthy families grew by 19%. To put things into perspective, the average income of families in wealthy neighborhoods was four times as much as families in poor neighborhoods. Since 1995, the loss of manufacturing jobs along with a 22% decline in social services and welfare programs have contributed to the growing inequality and class polarization. The same can be said of conditions throughout the United States.

Against overwhelming odds, and faced with poverty and violence on a daily basis, the Jane-Finch Corridor remains one of the most culturally diverse and vibrant communities in Canada. More than 72 languages and dialects are spoken by immigrants from 115 countries. Today most immigrants in the Jane-Finch Corridor are from East-Asian origins: Sri Lankans, East Indians, Tamils, and Pakistanis. Driftwood Public School, where McLaren once taught in the 1970s, has a culturally and linguistically diverse student population of over 700 students.

Life after Schools:
Towards a Revolutionary Critical Pedagogy

Why does *Life in Schools* remain pertinent to current educational practices in schools? What lessons can educators learn from reading *Life in Schools*? Why is McLaren's ethnographic study read over and over again by generations of teachers and social activists from all walks of life? Why do students in Latin America find such a powerful resonance reading the Spanish and Portuguese translations of the book? Why should teachers be concerned with the political economy of schooling in an age that has witnessed the triumph of globalized capital? More importantly, why should teachers be concerned with the exploitation of labor by capital when they have never seriously considered any alternative? How can teachers resist the dominant ideology? How can teachers develop a critical ideology? How can they recognize the decisive role they play in the ensuing battle between labor and capital? These are a few of the pressing issues that McLaren raises in *Life in Schools*.

Like that of his friend and mentor, Paulo Freire, McLaren's revolutionary criti-cal pedagogy is a project that is closely aligned with revolutionary struggles that seek to end economic exploitation, political domination, and cultural dependency. Its main objective is to build a new, more humane, and just society. The revolutionary critical pedagogy of Peter McLaren is immersed in a dialectical method of teaching. It begins with students' experiences (practice), and builds upon those experiences by helping them to develop a more critical, structural, and scientific understanding of their daily lives in relation to the lives of others and the institutional, cultural, and social media-tions that structure these relations (theory). Finally, it helps students to take strategic action based on a new and deeper understanding (practice). McLaren contends that the role of educators is not so much to offer their students dogmatic or pre-cut an-swers to social, economic, and political problems, as to encourage and provoke stu-dents to question and to make problematic existing social injustices.

McLaren's primary aim is to arm teachers with a critical vernacular in order to help them recognize social class as an objective social relation. He challenges teachers to develop a working-class consciousness in order to gain an awareness that, as intel-lectual workers, their class interests are tied to working-class struggles. And while teachers may participate unwillingly in the reproduction of class relations (pedagogi-cally), they can resist and challenge capitalist schooling by empowering their students with a critical ideology and a set of political strategies designed to challenge the rule of capital. McLaren also helps students understand racism, sexism, and homophobia in the context of the current class-divided society.

McLaren's revolutionary critical pedagogy is, first and foremost, informed by a "class-conscious ideology." It accentuates the class dynamics of capitalist social rela-tions by elucidating how social classes are inherently antagonistic. Not only does McLaren's (2000) revolutionary critical pedagogy identify social classes as the main forces in society, but it also underscores the fact that classes are essentially "diametri-cally opposed" to one another (Mantsios, 1998).

For McLaren, the objective of revolutionary critical pedagogy is to disrupt and challenge bourgeois knowledge by utilizing critical knowledge that is *transformative* as opposed to *reproductive*, that is *empowering* as opposed to *oppressing*. McLaren passion-ately believes that part of the pedagogical task of critical educators has to be linked to the larger social and political struggle (both at the local and global arena) for achiev-ing *economic democracy*, *human rights*, and *social justice*.

To undress the existing contradictions between democracy and capitalism, McLaren's revolutionary critical pedagogy places political education at the forefront of pedagogical struggles. He calls upon teachers to engage their students into discus-sion on a wide range of topics from cultural oppression to "class exploitation." McLaren identifies critical educators as those who transform their classrooms into political spaces, whereby students analyze and question how race, class, and gender relations are lived and experienced. Critical educators raise further questions such as: Who has class power? How is class power exercised to establish class domination? How is class power employed to reproduce and maintain class privileges? What ac-tions must be taken to challenge class oppression? And finally, how is class oppression related to and implicated in racism, sexism, and homophobia? McLaren believes that these questions have the potential to stimulate, to broaden, and to foster teachers' as well as their students' understanding of class society. It can also encourage students and teachers to investigate and raise questions that are no less urgent today: What are the necessary social conditions for developing a revolutionary praxis? Under what social and political circumstances can workers develop a revolutionary consciousness? How can workers and students recognize and confront their own labor power as alienated labor?

Too often, teacher education programs fail to engage student teachers in discussions about class exploitation and oppression. Under most scenarios, class power is sanitized and its powerful effect on the life chances of working-class students is made invisible. As Paul Lauter (1998) has cogently expressed:

> Class . . . remains that unaddressed member of that now-famous trio "race, gender, class." Over the last two decades, there has been far more widespread acknowledgment of and open discussion of race and gender in the classroom, while class has generally remained the silenced subject. In fact, in classrooms, people have seemed afraid to talk about class. They often don't know [how] to acknowledge economic difference and economic privilege—with their entourage of conflicting social and cultural forms.

Regrettably, many progressive teacher education programs continue to insulate and divorce the causes of cultural, racial, and gender oppression from class oppression. As a result, the struggle for social justice oftentimes is reduced to a truncated reformist strategy that fails, in the main, to challenge and to expose the mechanisms responsible for reproducing capitalist hegemony. In stark contrast to liberal and progressive educationalists who espouse "social reform," McLaren's critical pedagogy has a broader political vision that is not limited to *social justice education*. Rather, his pedagogical praxis is driven by the struggle for *economic democracy* as the foundation of liberation, a democracy that can flourish only when capitalist social relations of production are abolished. McLaren is not satisfied with mere social reform. Of course, this is not to claim that social reform is not desirable. But for McLaren, social reform must be channeled and directed towards a broader vision of a revolutionary praxis of social transformation that leads to a socialist alternative.

Teachers have often complained that critical pedagogy is too theoretical or abstract to have any concrete applications inside their classrooms. In most cases, teachers have used their personal experiences to guide their pedagogical practices in the classroom. However, as critical pedagogists have frequently explained, experience alone fails to offer an accurate account of how teachers are positioned in relation to one another and how they are situated within the social relations of production. This is because experience is mediated through the process of commodity production. Thus, teachers need to incorporate critical theory to inform their pedagogical practices. As Cyril Smith (1996) notes:

> Theory is a form of thinking which reflects that inhuman shell in which our lives are covered, taking it for granted that humanity can never escape. Marx's struggle for communist revolution is centered on revealing this imprisonment, allowing us to regard it from a human standpoint and to find a way out. Instead of "seeking science

in his mind" and presenting a theory, Marx wanted to free our consciousness from these shackles. It is that insight which must be recaptured if communism is to be regenerated. (p. 136)

In short, many critical pedagogists would argue that logical and rational thinking is central in grasping and penetrating what Marx has referred to as the "thing in itself."

The underlying message throughout McLaren's book is loud and clear. McLaren believes that revolutionary critical pedagogy must avoid resigning pedagogical struggles to the mere abrogation of class exploitation. Instead it must anchor itself in the emancipation of humanity from class society. Guided by a revolutionary praxis, the main objective of revolutionary pedagogy is not merely *economic equalization*, but *human realization* and de-alienation of labor from the chains of capital (Eagleton, 1999).

McLaren lays out the foundational principles of a renewed and retooled approach to revolutionary critical pedagogy that parallels the five pillars of popular education which has been articulated by Deborah Brandt (1991). First, revolutionary critical pedagogy must be a *collective process* that involves utilizing Freirian dialogical learning approach. Second, revolutionary critical pedagogy has to be *critical*; that is, by locating the underlying causes of class exploitation and economic oppression within the social, political, and economic infrastructure of capitalist social relations of production. Third, revolutionary critical pedagogy is profoundly *systematic* in the sense that it is guided by Marx's dialectical method of inquiry, which begins with the "real concrete" circumstances of the oppressed masses and moves towards a classification, conceptualization, analysis, and breaking down of the concrete social world into units of abstractions to get at the essence of social phenomena. Next, it reconstructs and makes the social world intelligible by transforming and translating theory into concrete social and political action. Fourth, revolutionary critical pedagogy should be *participatory*, involving building coalitions among community members, grassroots movements, church organizations, and labor unions. Finally, revolutionary critical pedagogy needs to be a *creative process* by incorporating elements of popular culture (i.e., drama, music, oral history, narratives) as educational tools to politicize and revolutionize working-class consciousness.

Teachers and Neoliberal Globalization

Why should teachers be concerned with the impact of the global economy? Why should teachers be troubled with the growing class polarization and the *maquiladorization* of the United States economy? What lasting impact, if any, will the persistent wave of attacks by the forces on the Right have on the working conditions of teachers? More importantly, are teachers immune from the devastating impact of the globalization of capital and the neoliberalization of the markets? Should teachers join workers and resist the corporatization and privatization of schools? Clearly, the answer to these questions and others will depend largely on how teachers perceive their role in the on-going battles between labor and capital. What is clear is that, as wage earners, and like much of the rest of the working-class, teachers are forced to endure the assaults of the Right on the welfare state as well as other public institutions. Recent strikes by teachers in Philadelphia, Buffalo, New York, and Detroit are a compelling testament to the fact that teachers, much like workers in other sectors of the economy, are exploited by capital.

In 1999, faced with similar threats by Michigan laws which outlaw strikes, 7,700 teachers in Detroit went on strike. Teachers objected to a number of new proposals made by the school district: lengthening of the school day from seven to eight-and-a-half hours, tying merit-pay to test scores, closing down and replacing "non-performing" schools with charter schools, and privatizing school services such as custodial services, food, transportation, and building maintenance by contracting them out to non-unionized workers.

September 2000. Three thousand eight hundred teachers in Buffalo go on strike and rally against large class sizes, deteriorating school buildings, insufficient teaching staff, and lack of basic school supplies. Similar to teachers in Philadelphia and Detroit, teachers in Buffalo risked losing their jobs by the Taylor Law, which prohibits teachers to go on strike.

October 27, 2000. At the risk of losing their teaching certification and pension plans by Pennsylvania state laws which prohibit public employees to strike, 21,000 teachers in Philadelphia defied the anti-strike laws and voiced their opposition to the decisions made by the school board to extend the school day and reduce teachers' health benefits. In addition, teachers protested against the replacement of salary increases by a two-tier pay system including merit pay for new teachers.

November 16, 2000. Ten thousand teachers in New York City, the nation's largest school district, go on strike. Teachers objected to a new school district plan which involved implementing a four-tier salary structure, replacing wage increases with merit pay, eliminating the tenure system and replacing it with renewable teaching contracts, and, finally, making it easier to hire and fire teachers.

Faced with the growing low-skill, low-wage service economy in the United States, Marxist educationalists place the ideological and political conflicts over public education in context of the larger social struggles between labor and capital. They believe that Right-wing attacks on public education are ideologically aligned with the neo-liberal social and economic policies that support corporate anorexia: downsizing, outsourcing, and flexible rearrangements of labor markets. Furthermore, Marxist educationalists place the politics of educational privatization within the broader context of the reorganization of property relations, capital accumulation, and the intensification of competition among transnational corporations.

Looking Forward

In *The Communist Manifesto* (1848), Karl Marx and Frederick Engels briefly discussed the relationship between social class and education. In their critique of the bourgeois nature of pedagogy, they raised questions that are no less urgent today than they were a century and a half-ago: "And is not your education also determined by society? By the social conditions under which you educate, by the direct or indirect intervention of society, through schools . . . ?" For Marx and Engels, education is "determined" by capitalism's class structure. This does not imply that they endorsed an economistic interpretation of educational practices or believed that education is reducible to economic relations. Rather, Marx and Engels asserted that education is determined by the "social conditions" that are imposed upon it (i.e., the mode of production).

Marx and Engels further noted that: "The Communists have not invented society's impact on education; they merely change its character, they wrest education from the influence of a ruling class." The aim of revolutionaries such as Marx and Engels was not only to emancipate education from the influence of *the* ruling class (i.e., capitalist class), but also from the influence of *all* social classes. Yet, as they further expounded, this task can only be accomplished when class society is abolished altogether. In other words, democratic schooling is only possible when the influence of social class (in particular, an end to private property relations) on schooling and education is abolished altogether. McLaren believes that the essential struggle that faces educators today finds a parallel in the address given by Marx and Engels to the Central Committee of the Communist League in 1850 in London. Here they proclaimed that class struggle and proletarian hegemony is not limited to the "alteration of private property but only its annihilation, not the smoothing over of class antagonisms but the abolition of classes, not the improvement of existing society, but the foundation of a new one" (cited in Tucker, 1975, p. 505).

What might constitute the main pillars of a revamped, retooled, and reinvigorated Marxist pedagogy? What can Marxist educational theory offer educators in the wake of the dictatorship of the financial markets where, in the words of Robert Went (2000), the "invisible hand" of the market is mercilessly and ruthlessly strangling millions of working-class men, women, and children? How do we liberate creative human powers and capacities from their inhumane form, namely capital? These are some of the questions that McLaren's revolutionary politics is at pains to answer.

McLaren holds that critical pedagogy must renew its commitment to emancipate humanity from its own inhumanity. For Marxist educationalists, the challenge of critical pedagogy should be intimately linked to the following questions: What does it mean to be human? How can we live humanely? What actions or steps must be taken to be able to live humanely? McLaren believes that these questions, along with others, can be answered in the course of revolutionizing educational practices in the context of class struggle.

How can teachers recognize the important role they play in the battle between labor and capital? How can they develop a working-class ideology? As McLaren explains, part of the answer to these questions will depend upon the ability of teachers to become class conscious and to recognize class as an objective social relation. To become critical educators, McLaren argues that teachers need to develop class-consciousness and to recognize that, as workers, their class interests are linked to working-class struggles. Struggles that are linked to anti-racist, anti-sexist, and anti-homophobic social practices. And while it is true that teachers take part in reproducing class relations (pedagogically), they can utilize their pedagogical skills and expertise to resist and to challenge capitalist schooling.

Undoubtedly, McLaren's *Life in Schools* remains a source of hope and inspiration for thousands of educators worldwide who are engaged in class struggle within public schools. The time has come for educators across the nation to engage McLaren's revolutionary critical pedagogy with a renewed interest and sense of urgency. While McLaren's voice without doubt comes under increasing attack by reactionary ideologies and ideologues, his message only becomes more vital and important in these troubled and dangerous times.

Ramin Farahmandpur
Los Angeles, California

REFERENCES

Bishop, M. (2001, June 16). The new wealth of nations: A survey of the rich. *The Economist*, Vol. 259, No. 8226, p. 5.

Bowles, S., and Gintis, H. (1976). *Schooling in capitalist America: Educational reform and the contradictions of economic life*. New York: Basic Books.

Brandt, D. (1991). *To change this house: Popular education under Sandinistas*. Toronto: Between the Lines.

Carey, E. (2001, June 9). The new face of poverty. *Toronto Star*, News, Sec. B1.

Corrigan, P. (1979). *Schooling the smash street kids*. London: Macmillan.

The Country-club Vote. (2000, May 20). *The Economist*, Vol. 355, No. 8171, p. 5.

Eagleton, T. (1999). *Marx*. New York: Routledge.

Lauter, P. (1998). Interview with Paul Lauter by Leo Parascondola. [Online]. *Workplace: The Journal for Academic Labor*, Vol. 1, No. 2. Available at: http://www.workplace-gsc.com/workplace2/lauter.html

Mantsios, G. (1998). What does labor stand for? In G. Mantsios (Ed.), *A new labor movement for the new century* (pp. 44–64). New York: Monthly Review Press.

Marx, K., and Engels, F. (1848; 1998). *The Communist Manifesto*. New York: Monthly Review Press.

McLaren, P. (1980). *Cries from the corridor: The new suburban ghettos*. Toronto: Methuen Publications.

McLaren, P. (1986). *Schooling as a ritual performance: Towards a political economy of educational symbols and gestures*. London and New York: Routledge.

McLaren, P. (1989). *Life in schools: An introduction to critical pedagogy in the foundations of education*. New York: Longman.

McLaren, P. (2000). *Che Guevara, Paulo Freire, and the pedagogy of revolution*. Boulder, CO: Rowman & Littlefield.

Smith, C. (1996). *Marx at the Millennium*. London and Chicago: Pluto Press.

Tucker, R. C. (Ed.). (1978). *The Marx-Engels reader* (2nd ed.). New York and London: W. W. Norton & Company.

Went, R. (2000). *Globalization: Neoliberal challenge, radical responses*. London and Sterling, VA: Pluto Press.

Willis, P. (1977). *Learning to labor*. Farnborough, England: Saxon House.

FOREWORD TO THE THIRD EDITION

The English title of the book, *Life in Schools*, reveals the author's professed revolutionary process. It subverts the common pedagogical order. This order proposes putting school into life. It understands school as the place where learning and the appropriation of the accumulated knowledge of a society or culture takes place, enabling a flourishing later in life. But this order does not ask about life, does not question the conditions within which life is realized; it does not propose transforming life. The method assumed by Peter McLaren, which comes from the critical theory of education, inverts the order. It wants to take life into the school, life with all its dynamics and contradictions, with its economic basis and thus with its class dimension, with its political support and thus with its relationship to structures of power, with its gender marks and thus with all the singularities and conflicts related to the masculine and the feminine, with its subjacent ideology and thus with a sense of life and the world that is hidden behind lifestyles.

Yet, we could still broaden the horizon and understand life within the cosmogenesis, the beginning of which can be traced to 15 billion years ago when the first singularity occurred with the Big Bang. We could then perceive life as the greatest miracle of all within the evolutionary process, which finds its major expression on Earth as a live superbeing, Gaia, that walks, thinks, loves, creates schools, dreams, and dialogues with the Ultimate Reality, and in human beings as sons and daughters of Earth. These perspectives are implicit in the fundamental intuition of this book.

The author arrived at this vision in the same way that Latin American liberation theology and Paulo Freire's pedagogy of the oppressed did, by co-existing with peripheral, impoverished, and excluded populations. The pedagogical project is created in order to place their lives inside the classroom and to employ knowledge and transformation as weapons to change the world. From the perspective of the social location of the condemned on Earth, it becomes clear that knowledge alone, as intended by the school, does not transform life. Only the conversion of knowledge into action can transform life. This concretely defines the meaning of practice: the dialectic movement between the conversion of transformative action into knowledge and the conversion of knowledge into transformative action.

This transformation not only changes life, but also the subject, making these subjects free beings able to think their individual and social praxis, articulating the local with the global, extracting from life experiences and from the various knowledges about life a strategic direction for their life projects. Only a praxiological education such as this one enables and forms human beings who are capable of administering a socio-cosmic democracy, one that acts in solidarity with nature, a very much needed democracy in today's world, both in technologically developed

*Translated by Walter de Oliveira, Maria Beatriz A. P. Santana, and Cesar Rossatto. Foreword used by permission of Editora Artes Médicas Sul Ltda., Porto Alegre, Brasil.

countries and in those countries seeking their own sustainability. The author has many friends in Brazil. For many Brazilians engaged in the construction of a quotidian citizenry, based on critical, participant and creative persons, in formal schools, and in all educational processes occurring in communities and in organized society, this book will be affirming. The book is a stimulus to Brazilian pedagogy, which for more than 40 years has been trying to become more innovative and become a path to liberation, while it searches, pedagogically and critically, to make of the shapeless masses a free, united, ludic people, a people open to the dimensions of a changing world. With this book, Peter McLaren shows himself as a comrade in the path of reclaiming and constructing what is most excellent and mysterious in human beings: their ability to protect against a world of oppressions, their will for creation and their determination to seek those paths that nurture the new.

Leonardo Boff
Rio de Janeiro, Brazil

FOREWORD TO THE SECOND EDITION

In April of 1992, many white Americans were surprised by what they perceived to be a violent overreaction by the black and Latino communities of Los Angeles to the acquittal of police officers for the beating of Rodney King. Many students I spoke with, although skeptical of media interpretation of the rebellion, still floundered for an alternative analysis. Like most mainstream media coverage, their questions tended to be limited to the beating and acquittal itself, decontextualizing these acts from the history of relations between African Americans and white-controlled police forces and vigilante groups. They also decontextualized what happened from the growing poverty and hopelessness in many large urban areas as jobs have been exported to Third World nations and as white middle- and upper-class communities have reinforced their own physical and social distance from urban poor people. They tended to view the aftermath of the acquittal as a self-contained event, taking place in a particular time and location that has little connection with their own world.

The discourse most readily available to students, as well as to the wider society, questions the motives and morals of individuals, placing everyone on a fictitious equal plane that is buttressed by the words "equal opportunity," "democracy," "progress," and "individualism." How can educators engage students in a process of analyzing social issues with reference to unequal and unethical social structures and processes that they see every day but have learned to take for granted? And how can educators do this in a way that affirms students' ability to grasp concepts, while at the same time challenging them to place particular events in a wider context?

Critical pedagogy directs educators toward a teaching process that does this but that often enmeshes us in an ethical and pedagogical dilemma. Critical pedagogy is about power and empowerment. Although this assertion may seem straightforward, in the classroom it often plays itself out in contradictory ways. On the one hand, the critical educator invites students to construct their own analysis of social phenomena and to appropriate for themselves the process of theory-building. But on the other hand, the critical educator wants students to situate social phenomena in broader structural relationships and to ask questions, such as who benefits from these relationships, how are unequal relationships being reproduced, and how do individuals interpret their situatedness in a system of unequal economic, racial, and gendered relations? For some students, these kinds of questions support their own analysis of social phenomena; for others, they do not. In the latter case, the critical educator often finds herself or himself caught in a dilemma: how to support students' questioning and meaning-making while at the same time teaching students to critique power relations that contextualize schools and place limits on lives.

Life in Schools offers the critical educator an excellent resource for addressing precisely this dilemma. In the first half of the text, readers travel with Peter McLaren through four years of teaching in the inner city, by way of a journal he kept. Although the journal does not pretend to be a repository of systematically collected ethnographic data, it does provide a wealth of relatively uninterpreted vignettes of the

students, the school, and McLaren's experiences. I say "relatively uninterpreted" because McLaren did decide what to write about and what not to write about. Nevertheless, the journal is extensive enough to present a rich picture, and one that readily
connects with my own experiences in inner-city schools, as well as that of many other
educators.

The journal invites students to ask questions and begin to theorize about conditions of life in schools that serve poor students and racial and ethnic minority students. It provides a concrete referent around which students can begin to generate
interpretations and analyses of why youth tend to leave school prepared to follow in
their parents' footsteps despite the rhetoric of schools serving as avenues for social
mobility. A class might stick to analysis of the experiences in the journal itself, or explore local and current experiences in urban areas that are similar to those recorded in
the journal.

In the next section of the text, students then engage with McLaren in his own
analysis of schooling, which was written several years after the journal. Here, the text
stretches students to consider life in schools through the theoretical framework of
critical pedagogy and to ask how teachers can engage children in inner-city schools in
ways that actually empower them to gain more control over their own lives. After introducing students to the main concepts of critical pedagogy, McLaren uses it to analyze the content of the journal and, more broadly, the failure of most inner-city
schools (and other urban institutions) and to suggest a vision for doing schooling
differently.

Excellent teachers grow, their analysis of issues expands, and their vision for the
possible becomes richer. The final section of *Life in Schools* presents Peter McLaren's
most recent reading of his own journal and earlier analysis of ideas. Over a period of
years, he grapples with a broader array of issues and theoretical perspectives. Here, he
critiques his own earlier thinking and recasts and extends issues raised in the journal
through a critical postmodern perspective. In so doing, he challenges students to
think, grow, and allow themselves to self-reflect and self-critique, just as he did. Some
students will be tempted to target their criticisms solely toward McLaren, but by
making himself vulnerable, he directs their questions back to them and challenges
them to examine their own ideas.

Students need not agree with McLaren, but they must engage with him. The
text, in fact, welcomes their engagement, and presents them with multiple layers of
analysis. *Life in Schools* is not bounded by its cover. The text also invites the critical
educator to apply additional theoretical analyses that interrogate unequal power relations, to the issues raised by the journal, such as postcolonialism and socialist feminism. *Life in Schools* offers a rare opportunity for students, critical educators, and a
leading educational theorist to dialogue, disagree, question, and stretch each other's
thinking and action around ethical issues involving schooling and democracy in a
capitalistic, patriarchal, and racist society.

Christine Sleeter
University of Wisconsin—Parkside

FOREWORD TO THE
FIRST EDITION

Life in Schools brilliantly combines theory and practice. McLaren integrates a moving description of his own teaching experiences with an analysis of current social problems and a clear, understandable statement of a theory that allows us to analyze and formulate solutions to modern educational problems.

The centerpiece of the book is McLaren's autobiographical journal—the narrative of a teacher struggling to make a difference in the lives of children of immigrant and minority group parents stuck in the netherworld of the economic and social underclass. These children constitute the major social problem for American public schools in the 1980s and 1990s. The new immigrant population of the 1980s confronts educators once again, as did the immigrant population of the early twentieth century, with the task of teaching children from a variety of cultural, language, and socioeconomic backgrounds. At the same time, other groups of students seem destined to join the permanent underclass, of which sociologists include a growing segment of the United States population.* McLaren provides both a powerful portrayal of his students and his efforts to reach them, and a theoretical context in which to begin thinking about the challenges they represent.

Critical theory is one of the most important methods available to us for understanding modern social problems. Applied to education, critical theory helps students and teachers understand the political, social, and economic issues underlying classroom practices and the social world of the school, and it points the way to possible solutions. In *Life in Schools*, Peter McLaren makes critical theory accessible and understandable to the reader by applying its methods of analysis to his vivid description of school life.

Life in Schools is a thought-provoking introduction to the real world of modern schools, to the social problems confronting educators, and to a theory that provides both insight and hope.

Joel Spring
University of Cincinnati

*Isabel Wilkerson, "New Studies Zeroing in on Poorest of the Poor," *New York Times*, vol. CXXXVII, No. 47,359 (December 20, 1987), p. 26.

IN MEMORIAM

Paulo Freire died May 2, 1997.

Born Paulo Reglus Neves Freire on September 19, 1921, in Recife, in the northeast of Brazil, he became a legendary figure in the field of education. A courageous scholar, a social activist, and a cultural worker admired for his integrity and humility, Freire became internationally renowned for developing an anti-imperialist and anticapitalist literacy praxis employed by progressive educators throughout the world.

Freire joined the faculty of law at the Universidade do Recife in his early twenties but his work at the Social Service of Industry and his participation in the Movement for Popular Culture of Recife helped to motivate him to devote his energies to the area of adult literacy. He abandoned his work as a lawyer shortly after his first case in order to study the relationships among pupils, teachers, and parents in working-class communities in the northeast of Brazil. As director of the Extension Service of the University of Recife, Freire began to work with new methods in teaching adult literacy. In 1962 in the town of Angicos in Rio Grande do Norte, Freire's approach to literacy helped three hundred rural farm workers learn to read and write in 45 days. The literacy worker, by living communally with groups of peasants and workers, was able to identify generative words according to their phonetic value, syllabic length, social meaning, and relevance to the workers. These generative words represented the lived reality of the workers. Each word was associated with issues related to existential questions about life and the social factors that determined the economic conditions of everyday existence. Themes were then generated from these words, such as "wages" or "government," that were then codified and decodified by groups of workers and teachers known as "cultural circles." Reading and writing thus became grounded in the lived experiences of peasants and workers and resulted in a process of ideological struggle and revolutionary praxis—or conscientization. Workers and peasants were able to transform their "culture of silence" and become collective agents of social and political change. This success marked the beginning of what was to become a legendary approach in education.

In 1963, Freire was invited by President João Goulart and by the Minister of Education, Paulo de Tarso Santos, to rethink adult literacy programs on a national basis. In 1964, 20,000 cultural circles were designed to assist two million illiterate workers. However, this work was brazenly interrupted in 1964, when a right-wing military coup overthrew Goulart's democratically elected government. Freire was accused of preaching communism and was arrested. He was imprisoned by the military government for 70 days, and exiled for his work as director of the national literacy campaign. According to Freire's leading biographer, Moâçir Gadotti (one of the founding members of the Partido dos Trabalhadores [Workers Party] and Freire's chief of cabinet in the administration of São Paulo's Municipal Secretariat of

Education), the Brazilian military considered Freire to be "an international subversive," "a traitor to Christ and the Brazilian people," and accused him of developing a teaching method "similar to that of Stalin, Hitler, Perón, and Mussolini." He was furthermore accused of trying to turn Brazil into a "bolshevik country" (Gadotti, 1994).

Freire's 16 years of exile were tumultuous and productive times: a five-year stay in Chile as a UNESCO consultant with the Research and Training Institute for Agrarian Reform; an appointment in 1969 to Harvard University's Center of Educational and Developmental Studies associated with the Center for Studies in Development and Social Change; a move to Geneva, Switzerland, in 1970 as consultant to the Office of Education of the World Council of Churches, where he developed literacy programs for Tanzania and Guinea-Bissau that focused on the re-Africanization of their countries; the development of literacy programs in some postrevolutionary former Portuguese colonies such as Angola and Mozambique motivated by Freire's personal sympathy for Amilcar Cabral's Movimento Popular Liberaçaõ de Angola (Popular Movement for the Liberation of Angola), Frente de Liberaçaõ de Moccambique (Mozambique Liberation Front), and Partido Africans para Independencia da Ginea-Bissau e Cabo Verde (African Party for the Independence of Guinea-Bissau and Cabo Verde); assisting the governments of Peru and Nicaragua with their literacy campaigns; the establishment of the Institute of Cultural Action in Geneva in 1971; a brief return to Chile after Salvador Allende was assassinated in 1973, an act that provoked General Pinochet to declare Freire a subversive; participating in literacy work in São Tomé and Principe from 1975 to 1979; a brief visit to Brazil under political amnesty in 1979; and his final return to Brazil in 1980 to teach at the Pontificia Universidade Catolica de São Paulo and the Universidade de Campinas in São Paulo. These events were accompanied by numerous works, most notably *Pedagogy of the Oppressed, Cultural Action for Freedom*, and *Pedagogy in Process: Letters to Guinea-Bissau*. Freire would go on to undertake literacy work in Australia, Italy, Angola, the Fiji Islands, and numerous other countries throughout the world.

In São Paulo, Freire witnessed growing resistance to the military government such as the 1978 and 1979 strikes by the metalworkers of São Bernardo (an industrial region of São Paulo) and he joined the socialist democratic Workers Party that was formed in 1979. When the Workers Party won the 1989 municipal elections in São Paulo, Mayor Luiza Erundina appointed Freire municipal secretariat of education for São Paulo, a position he held until 1991. During his tenure as secretariat, Freire continued his radical agenda of literacy reform for the people of São Paulo. Under Freire's guidance, the secretariat of education set up a literacy program for young people called MOVA-SP (Literacy Movement in the City of São Paulo) that contributed to strengthening popular movements and creating alliances between civil society and the state. Freire also created the "projeto de interdisciplinaridade" that attempted to create collective work through a decentralization of power and the fostering of school autonomy and the reconstruction of the curriculum around community issues.

Based on a recognition of the cultural underpinnings of folk traditions and the importance of the collective construction of knowledge, Freire's literacy programs for disempowered peasants are now employed in countries all over the world. By linking the categories of history, politics, economics, and class to the concepts of culture and power, Freire managed to develop both a language of critique and a language of hope that work conjointly and dialectically and that have proven successful in helping generations of disenfranchised peoples to liberate themselves.

Freire's pedagogy of the oppressed is a clarion call to unhinge established structures of capitalist exploitation. With a liberating pedagogy such as Freire's, educators and cultural workers in the United States and elsewhere—both male and female, and from different ethnic locations—have an opportunity to engage in a global struggle for transforming existing relations of power and privilege in the service of greater social justice and human freedom. Influenced by the writings of Leszek Kolakowski, Karel Kosik, Eric Fromm, Antonio Gramsci, Karl Mannheim, Teilhard de Chardin, Franz Fanon, Albert Memmi, Lev Vygotsky, Amilcar Cabral, and the Christian Personalism theory of Tristiande Atiade and Emanuel Mounier (not to mention the classic works of Hegel, Marx, Rousseau, and Dewey), Freire's pedagogy was antiauthoritarian, dialogical and interactive, and put power into the hands of students. Most important, Freirean pedagogy put social and political analysis of everyday life at the center of the curriculum.

What is remarkable about Freire's work is that it continues to be vigorously engaged by scholars in numerous disciplines: literary theory, composition, philosophy, ethnography, political science, sociology, teacher education, theology, and so on. He has given the word "educator" a new meaning, inflecting the term to embrace multiple perspectives—border intellectual, social activist, critical researcher, moral agent, radical philosopher, and political revolutionary. To a greater extent than any other educator of this century, Freire was able to develop a pedagogy of resistance to oppression. More than this, he lived what he taught. His life is the story of courage, hardship, perseverance, and unyielding belief in the power of love.

Freire's pedagogy of the oppressed helped me as young man to unlearn my privilege as a white, Anglo male and to "decolonize" my own perspectives as an educator teaching in the industrialized West. I first began reading Freire after five years of teaching in an inner-city school in my hometown of Toronto, in my native Canada. In trying to analyze my inner-city teaching experiences once I had left the classroom to pursue graduate studies, Freire's work helped me both to recognize and to name my own complicity in the oppression that I was trying to help my students resist. In other words, Freire's writings helped me to unlearn the influences of my liberal heritage that positions so many white teachers as "missionaries" among the disenfranchised. Freire's work has further helped me to recognize how the system of education is situated within a discourse and legacy of imperialism, patriarchy, and Eurocentrism. More important, Freire's work was able to help me develop counterhegemonic strategies and tactics of urban educational reform. This project is a difficult one, especially for many white, male educators who want to make a difference in the metropolitan contexts of contemporary urban schooling. It is also a difficult lesson for teachers and prospective teachers who come from the ranks of the privileged. Of course, Freire acknowledged that decolonization was a project that knows no endpoint, no final closure. It is a lifetime struggle that requires insight, honesty, compassion, a willingness to brush one's personal history against the grain of "naive consciousness" or commonsense understanding.

In 1996, I was honored to share the platform with Paulo and Augusto Boal (who developed the "theater of the oppressed" based on Freire's work) at the Rose Theater in Omaha, Nebraska. It was the first time the three of us had made a presentation together. Paulo was remarkable during our dialogue with the audience, fielding questions with an extraordinary intellectual agility. What struck me most about Paulo was his humility and generosity. He was kind enough to help translate a speech I gave at the Pontifica Universidade Catolica de São Paulo, when the official translator experienced difficulty. The week after his unexpected death, Freire was scheduled to attend a ceremony in Cuba where Fidel Castro was to present him with a major award for his contribution to education. According to his friends, this was to be the most important award of Freire's life. Shortly before his death, Freire was reported to have said something to this effect: "I could never think of education without love and that is why I think I am an educator, first of all because I feel love . . ." As Marcia Moraes, who teaches in Rio de Janeiro State University and who was a friend of Freire's, remarked to me recently: "Freire is not leaving the struggle, he has merely changed his location."

We will miss him.

REFERENCES

Gadotti, Moãçir (1994). *Reading Paulo Freire.* Albany, NY: State University of New York Press.

Peter McLaren and Peter Leonard (1993). *Paulo Freire: A Critical Encounter.* New York and London, Routledge.

Peter McLaren and Colin Lankshear (1994). *Politics of Liberation: Paths from Freire.* New York and London: Routledge.

Marcia Moraes, personal communication, Rio de Janiero.

PREFACE

Life in Schools is the story of my reinvention as an educator, from a liberal humanist who pressed the necessity of reform to a Marxist humanist who advocates a revolutionary praxis. This book is an attempt to bring together two worlds that the poet William Blake once called "songs of innocence" and "songs of experience." Within the context of this writing, these worlds represent, respectively, the intuitive, practical knowledge of the beginning classroom teacher and the domain of critical educational theory. I bring them together in this book to shed a more critical light on the issue of why working-class students generally don't succeed in school, despite the efforts of well-meaning and enthusiastic educators and teachers. The tradition of critical pedagogy, out of which grew the challenge of this book, represents an approach to schooling that is committed to the imperatives of empowering students and transforming the larger social order in the interests of justice and equality. My central task is to develop a language through which educators and others can unravel and comprehend the relationship among schooling, the wider capitalist social relations which inform it, and the historically constructed needs and competencies that students bring to schools.

Every book constitutes for its author a struggle with the past; each page testifies to a place somewhere in the writer's own granular and sedimented history. This book represents for me a particular crossroads in time, an historical juncture in which I remain poised pedagogically between the innocence and naiveté of a young man's sudden introduction to teaching and the reflections of a social theorist privileged with the power of hindsight and research. *Life in Schools* is an attempt to reconstruct a set of past experiences in the light of my current research efforts, in order to give some pedagogical hope to the tension they embody and the story they tell. This "J'accuse," aimed at the custodians of empire, is a story about rage and hope, about injustice in the disguise of democracy, about pain and despair, and about the joy of collective solidarity.

The story begins in 1980, with the publication of the journal documenting my teaching experiences in an inner-city elementary school in Toronto's Jane-Finch Corridor. The book became a controversial bestseller in Canada in the wake of heated public debate. Like so many public school teachers, I survived the classroom by drawing upon a mixture of practical knowledge and relatively untutored pedagogical instinct. This got me through five years of teaching and under the circumstances I felt that I had fared quite well. But a troublesome feeling that I had not made a real difference in the chances of my students to acquire a qualitatively better future began to shadow my personal and intellectual life. With few theoretical resources to help me better understand my students, their families, and the nature of the schooling process, I had failed to see how they were related to the larger socioeconomic context and technologies of power of the wider society. I was blind to the most damaging effects of exercising my professional duties among the children of the disaffected, the disadvantaged, the disenfranchised, the dispossessed. I let slip an important chance to develop a pedagogy that would have been more effective in both empowering my students and transforming conditions in the existing community.

My purpose in publishing my journal was neither to create scholarly discourse for an academic audience, nor to transform schools into communities of risk and resistance; quite simply, my purpose was to draw public attention to the social conditions of the disaffected students who lived in the nearby public housing units under terribly oppressive circumstances. I also wanted to address the immediate needs of inner-city teachers, many of whom felt desperate and helpless in their overcrowded classrooms, which lacked both necessary material resources and an ethos conducive to learning.

Unfortunately, I couldn't then avail myself of the conceptual tools that might have given my journal a necessary theoretical depth. I had little or no familiarity with the tradition of critical pedagogy and the writings of Paulo Freire, Henry Giroux, Glenn Rikowski, Dave Hill, Mike Cole, Paula Allman, Peter Mayo, Donaldo Macedo, Roger Simon, Joel Spring, Paul Willis, Tom Popkewitz, and others. But I did have an important story to tell of the lives and struggles of children. In the triumphal manner of a young frontier-style muckraker, I set off an educational debate through the publication of my classroom diary. My immediate goal in publishing my journal was not to embrace despair but rather to convince school board members to decrease the pupil-teacher ratio, to develop new programs that were more sensitive to the needs and experiences of disaffected students, and to funnel more curriculum resources and equipment into inner-city schools. As it turned out, the board felt pressured enough to transfer a few hundred thousand dollars into the schools in my area, thanks in part to the efforts of the Canadian media, who reported the contents of my book on a national scale, and to the growing advocacy of grass roots groups and popular constituencies who took full advantage of the publicity brought on by the efforts of investigative journalists and by the publication of my journal. But the real roots of the problems remained inexorably entangled in the everyday lives of the students and their families. Once the publicity ceased, the Board of Education reneged on its plan for school reform.

Since the journal's publication, I have grown increasingly dissatisfied with my attempt to understand and communicate my classroom experiences. My journal was primarily description, without a theoretical framework that could help the reader better understand the conditions I was attempting to portray. On the advice of a prominent journalist, I had reluctantly removed the few theoretical insights that I had initially included in the early drafts of the manuscript. My theoretical formulations—which admittedly were, at the time, crude stabs in the dark—"slowed down" what was otherwise a good "crisp" read; forget theories, I was advised, and let the vignettes "speak for themselves." In those days, that advice sounded almost profound. After all, who was I to impose an analysis or set of recommendations on the lived culture of the disadvantaged?

I realize now that observations of events—whether in the classroom or the laboratory—*never* speak for themselves. Every description is ideologically loaded, codified, and intertextually related to larger interpretive contexts, not to mention capitalist relations of production. Nothing that can be observed or named is ideologically neutral or innocent. No thoughts, ideas, or theories are transparent, autonomous, or free floating; to say that they are is a middle-class mystification and fleabitten fairytale that seeks to disguise the social interests being served. Ideas are always and necessarily tied to particular interests and enciphered in particular relations of power, and tied to particular power/knowledge configurations. Absolutely nothing is of unmediated availability to human consciousness. To "know" anything is always an effect of power/knowledge relationships. The crucial question is: Who has the power to make some forms of knowledge more legitimate than others? By failing to set my classroom journal within a critical theoretical context, I could not adequately reveal how power and knowledge work in the interests of the capitalist class over the working class. Consequently, I ran the risk of allowing readers to reinforce their stereotypes of what schooling was like in the "blackboard jungle" and what constituted the behavior of economically disadvantaged students. I also was in danger of portraying impoverished communities as crucibles of violence and hatred, devoid of humanity and dignity. This book is an attempt to provide the reader with the necessary theoretical framework for initiating a critical interpretation of the classroom episodes included in the journal.

I tried to convey in the journal both my concern for my students and their strength and perseverance in the face of their oppression. Looking back from my present vantage point, however, I see the author of that journal as a young, liberal teacher both fascinated by and fearful of the marginalized, the disaffected, the disenfranchised, and the indigent—fascinated because their poverty and behavior seemed to be born of defiance rather than despair; and fearful because their anger, pain, and hate had clearly been constructed out of the neglect and greed of a democratic society. The full horror of the situation struck me only when I realized that my students were essentially spitting in the eye of a ruling ideology, and in many ways I represented that eye.

The perspective of that young journal writer represents one moment in my understanding of inner-city teaching. It is a moment that defines a pedagogy I now largely reject. That moment has now been put in context by an excursion into the theory of schooling's "deep structure," from which I have drawn a new theoretical figuration. The project that began as *Cries from the Corridor* has now become part of a larger work which provides a critical analysis of schooling and classroom culture from the perspective of the labor/capital dialectical contradiction.

Shortly after the publication of the journal I left teaching to enroll in graduate studies. In my attempt to understand how schooling "really" works, I was soon struck by the range of sociological theories that explained how schools can and do disempower, delegitimate, and disconfirm the lives of disadvantaged students. I discovered as well that schools operate through a "hidden curriculum" that incarcerates students in the "semiotics of power" and works against the success of racial minorities, women, and the poor. Yet I was also made aware of how schools could work in emancipatory ways to empower students to accomplish, in the words of Paulo Freire, "reading the word and reading the world." This book does not attempt to answer fully the question of *how* to construct a critical pedagogy within the constraints of an educational system whose character and structure are firmly established by the state. Rather, this book asks: *Why* is a critical pedagogy so necessary? Part of the answer is that mainstream pedagogies generally avoid or attempt to obscure the question that should be central to education: What is the relationship between what we do in the classroom and our effort to build a better society?

Apart from the obvious need for a theoretical introduction to critical pedagogy, it has occurred to me that educators are rarely encouraged to seek connections that would link their personal brand of pedagogy to wider social processes, structures, and issues. One of the purposes for writing this book has been to respond to the failure of North American education to provide prospective teachers with the critical skills, conceptual means, and moral imperatives to analyze critically the goals of schooling. This book attempts to present ways of understanding schooling in terms generally unfamiliar to teachers and prospective teachers. The terminology and frames of reference that I shall be using are drawn from an educational tradition known as critical pedagogy. The book is organized with the intention of introducing readers to some general perspectives that make up this tradition while at the same time providing them with an opportunity to make informed decisions regarding the overall purposes and day-to-day realities of schooling in the United States. More specifically, the problem this book attempts to address is how critical educators can create a language that enables teachers to examine the role that schooling plays in joining knowledge and power to capitalist social relations of production. Critical pedagogy is designed to serve the purpose of both empowering teachers and teaching for empowerment. I have tried to deepen the notion of "empowerment" by connecting it to the Marxist humanist tradition. Within this perspective, classroom social relations and cultural formations are seen as intersecting fields of struggle, and the contradictory character of teaching as it currently defines the nature of teacher work, everyday classroom life, and the purpose of schooling is subjected to more critical forms of analysis.

Part One documents the nature of the present crisis in schooling and society in this country. It does so from the perspective of a renewed engagement with Marxist theory and praxis. Part Two attempts to present the day-to-day struggles of teachers and students in an inner-city school through the inclusion of sections of my elementary school journal. In Part Three, I offer a broad overview of the tradition of critical pedagogy and introduce you to an array of general terms associated with the critical educational tradition. Since many of the terms and theoretical formulations within this tradition are presently being debated, refined, and extended, I discuss only the more fundamental categories, and only in the briefest possible fashion. This fits well with the purpose of this book, which is to provide those of you who are virtually unacquainted with critical pedagogy or the critical social sciences with an overview of some of the more basic socio-pedagogical formulations. After reading this part, you are encouraged to return to the journal in Part Two in order to reevaluate my experiences as a beginning teacher. I also encourage you to consider the classroom journal and new theoretical categories in terms of your own experiences as teachers and as students. Some questions have been provided at the end of Part Three to help you get started. Part Four presents additional categories and theoretical perspectives from the critical tradition and concludes with a short essay on the role of the teacher as social agent. Part Five provides a unique context for furthering the analysis of critical pedagogy with respect to my more recent analyses of schooling and social and political struggles. It's central thesis deals with the abolition of whiteness.

The purpose of the book is to provide a theoretical framework that will enable readers to interrogate critically my own ideological formation as a white Anglo male and a middle-class teacher. Reading my journal after so many years is always a painful experience, especially when I see my early development as a teacher as complicitous in the reproduction of dominant systems of intelligibility and social relations of capitalist production that position minorities and working-class students and parents in relations of subordination.

This book is an invitation to interrogate the liberal humanist discourse of progressive and well-intentioned teachers—including my own early teaching practices—and uncover its complicity in dominant myths about people of color and working-class people from a new, critical perspective. This perspective is the result of my work in critical pedagogy over the last twenty years. This new perspective appears in Parts One, Three, and Four of the book, and it is greatly extended in the new Part Five.

I hope that this book might prove to be not just a book *about* education, but an *educational book* that will promote an understanding of teaching in cultural, political, and ethical terms. This book will have failed if it merely presents an alternative or opposing view and does not provoke you to begin to examine seriously the assumptions that underlie your own teaching. I do not pretend that this book represents a scholarly advancement of the fundamental issues in critical pedagogy. If my book serves its purpose as an introductory text, then it should leave you with a desire to move beyond the theoretical parameters that I have constructed within these pages.

Acknowledgments

I am grateful to Henry Giroux for graciously permitting me to include throughout this book ideas from his research as well as sections from our co-authored works. I want to make clear at the outset that many of the perspectives presented in the first edition were inspired by his writings, especially *Theory and Resistance in Education*, *Education Under Siege* (with Stanley Aronowitz), *Teachers as Intellectuals: A Critical Pedagogy for Practical Learning*, and *Schooling and the Struggle for Public Life: Critical Pedagogy in the Modern Age*. I would be remiss if I failed to credit him for developing many of the categories and concepts used in this work. I would also like to thank him for his spirited encouragement and critical support, and for providing me with perceptive lines of inquiry that I might otherwise have overlooked. I especially want to thank him for providing me with comradeship and shelter during a time of exile and for being such a good friend and colleague. I am grateful, too, for the friendship and support of Jeanne Brady, whose work as a mother and educator offers concrete evidence that critical pedagogy can empower the lives of young people. I am deeply grateful to Jenny McLaren, whose unyielding support for this project was truly a labor of love. Her intelligence and strength are a continual source of inspiration. I wish to thank Methuen Publications (Canada) and PaperJacks (Canada) for their assistance in reprinting Part Two of this book, which appeared in Canada under the title *Cries from the Corridor: The New Suburban Ghettos*. I should mention that I have edited sections of *Cries from the Corridor* for reasons of length and style and in so doing I trust that I have not shifted the original context of the book nor altered the meaning of the diary entries.

I owe a debt of thanks to the editors of the following journals who have agreed to let me print material from previous publications: *The Harvard Educational Review, Metropolitan Education, Philosophy and Social Criticism, Boston University Journal of Education, Educational Policy, Insights, Canadian Woman Studies, Educational Studies, The Canadian Journal of Sociology, The Ontario Public School Teachers' Federation News, Social Education, Review of Education, Educational Foundations, The University of Toronto Review*, and *Educational Theory*.

David Llewellyn and Nikki Raeburn deserve acknowledgment for their editorial suggestions and advice. David Llewellyn provided me with excellent editorial assistance from the very outset of this project and deserves a heartfelt thanks, especially with respect to the revised format of *Cries from the Corridor*. A thanks also to Richard Smith and Anna Zantiotis, my good friends from Australia, and to Stanley Aronowitz. I want to express my gratitude to Lourdes Lugo Lopez, whose work with the Puerto Rican community, and whose courage and intelligence, inspire hope and faith in the struggle for liberation. Richard Quantz and the late Laurie McDade, friends and colleagues at the Center for Education and Cultural Studies, and Donaldo Macedo of the Department of English, University of Massachusetts, were sources of wisdom throughout the project. Khaula Murtadha and Marcia Moraes gave me critical advice. Rhonda Hammer's intelligent suggestions were welcome, as were those of Gary McCarron. I greatly appreciate the efforts of Beth Eldridge and Tammy Huntsman, who corrected proofs of the original version. I want to add a special note of gratitude to Joel Spring and Naomi Silverman for encouraging me to undertake this project and for seeing it through to its completion. Their critical comments greatly helped improve the volume. Thanks to Naomi Silverman too for encouraging me to undertake a second edition of *Life in Schools* and for offering some initial suggestions. I want also to thank Ginny Blanford of Longman for her excellent editing of the first edition, which helped make some very complex ideas clearer and more accessible. The second edition required the coordinated efforts of a number of people. I am especially grateful for the assistance of Linda Moser, Ginny Blanford, Mary Bucher Fisher, and Jude Patterson. I would like to thank Jan Kettlewell and Nelda Cambron-McCabe for creating a welcome atmosphere at the School of Education and Allied Professions at Miami University of Ohio for those who wish to undertake critical work in education. I would like to thank my undergraduate and graduate students for their reactions to drafts of this book, and for making the initial suggestion that an introductory text on critical pedagogy be made available for classroom study. I should mention too, that Barry Kanpol's sage suggestions have been invaluable. I want to thank Arianne Weber of Addison Wesley Longman for her guidance and support in getting the third edition of *Life in Schools* into production. I also want to thank Sonia Nieto for providing me with some criticisms of my work. Dennis Carlson deserves thanks for his many insights into the politics of urban schooling.

There are many other individuals whose work has provided me with ideas and insights. I want to thank Siebren Miedema, Alicia de Alba, Christie Sleeter, Rudolfo Chávez Chávez, Carl Boggs, Herman Garciá, Gert Biesta, Adriana Puiggrós, Jeannie Oakes, Edgar Gonzalez, Ira Shor, Bertha Orozco Fuentes, Nize Maria Campos Pellanda, Tom Popkewitz, Mike Peters, Nick Burbules, Jim Giarelli, John Novak, Bill Pinar, Tom Oldenski, Ramin Farahmandpur, Glenn Rikowski, Helen Raduntz, Ruth Rikowski, Dave Hill, Mike Cole, Gregory Martin, Donna Houston, Manuel Espinoza, Cindy Cruz, Noah de Lissovoy, Sandy Grande, Sonny San Juan, Carl Boggs, Doug Kellner, José Solís Jordán, Mike Apple, Michelle Fine, Stanley Aronowitz, Joe Kincheloe, Shirley Steinberg, Valerie Scatamburlo-D'Annibale, Antonia Darder, Barbara Flores, Cameron McCarthy, Warren Crinchlow, Jim Banks, Carl Grant, Phil Carspecken, Bill Tierney, Jeannie Oakes, Mike Rose, Daniel Schugerensky, Alfredo Artiles, Doug Kellner, Cathy Walsh, Kris Gutiérrez, Concepcíon Valadez, Bernardo Gallegos, Colin Lankshear, Don Dippo, David Theo Goldberg, Cesar Rossatto, Ana Dinerstein, Seehwa Cho, Paula Allman, Cheong Huh, Peter Mayo, Shahrzad Mojab, Mashhood Rizvi, John Holst, Marc Pruyn, Luis Huerta-Charles, Carmel Borg, Michele Knobel, Lou Mirón, Ilan Gur-ze'ev, Janette Habashi, Linda Rogers, Mike Pavel, Terri Patchen, Epi Amoo-Adare, Anna Kornbluh, Slavoj Zizek, Stephen May, Peter Roberts, Norm Denzin, Grant Banfield, Pepi Leistyna, Estanislao Antelo, Hector Alvarez, Jill Pinkney-Pastrana, Rick Allen, Henry Trueba, Silvia Serra, Gustavo Fischman, Danny Solorzano, Juan Muñoz, Antonia Darder, Rudy Torres, Carlos Tejeda, Stephen Nathan Haymes, Zeus Leonardo, and Paulo Freire. The following reviewers provided many helpful suggestions and ideas: William De La Torre, California State University, Northridge; Anne Wescott Dodd, Bates College; Louise E. Fleming, Ashland University; Felipe V. Gomez, University of Minnesota; W. Thomas Jamison, Appalachian State University; Jeff Liles; John Marciano, SUNY Cortland; Wendy M. Kropid, University of Wisconsin, Superior; Sandra M. Stokes, University of Wisconsin, Green Bay; Bonnie Fisher, College of St. Catherine, St. Paul, MN; Gwendolyn C. Webb-Johnson, University of Texas at Austin; DJ Chandler, University of Southern Florida; and Erin McNamara Horrat, Temple University. Of course, I take full responsibility for what appears within these pages.

I should note I have tried to use the term "Latinos" rather than "Hispanics" wherever possible for reasons made clear in the text. However, when reporting on other researchers' work, this was not always possible. I have also used the term "minority" while recognizing people of color are in the minority only in North America. I have talked about "Anglo Americans" as a counterpart to "Latin Americans" while recognizing "Americans" as a term meaning people from the Western hemisphere rather than solely from the United States. I use the term "Third World" while recognizing it cannot be employed monolithically since characteristics associated with Third World countries are proliferating in many so-called "First World" contexts. Gracias Memo por darme espacio en tu fantástico Café-Café, lugar para escribir esta nueva edición, gracias por tu visíon política y por ser tan Zapatista.

Life in Schools

PART ONE

Reflections on Life in Schools
Forging a New Beginning in an Age of Political Deceit and Imperial Grandeur

The weapon of criticism cannot, of course, replace criticism of the weapon, material force must be overthrown by material force; but theory also becomes a material force as soon as it has gripped the masses.

—Karl Marx

A liberal sees a beggar on the street and says the system is not working. A Marxist sees a beggar on the street and says it is.

—Bill Livant

When I feed the poor, they call me a saint. When I ask why they are poor, they call me a communist.

—Brazilian Bishop Dom Helder Camara

Of all the modern economic theories, the economic system of Karl Marx is founded on moral principles, while capitalism is concerned with only gain and profitability. Marxism is concerned with the distribution of wealth on an equal basis and the equitable utilization of the means of production. It is also concerned with the fate of the working classes—that is the majority—as well as with the fate of those who are underprivileged and in need; and Marxism cares about the victims of minority-imposed exploitation. For these reasons the system appeals to me, and it seems fair. . . . The failure of the regime in the Soviet Union was, for me, not the failure of Marxism but the failure of totalitarianism. For this reason, I think of myself as half-Marxist and half-Buddhist.

—the Dalai Lama

Introduction

I am pleased that the editors of Allyn and Bacon have invited me to publish yet another edition of *Life in Schools*. I will not hesitate to share with readers my genuine surprise that *Life in Schools* still continues to be widely used as a textbook in schools of education throughout North America, nearly fifteen years after it first appeared. When I initially proposed the text to various publishers throughout the United States, the general response to my prospectus was that it would never fly in a conservative field such as education, especially in a country like the United States, which is widely committed to capitalist principles and practices. The prospect of *Life in Schools* being placed with a major textbook publisher looked grim. That it was a book absent of treacly paeans to the Founding Fathers, munificent advice on how to foster the entrepreneurial spirit, directions on how to narrow the digital divide, and the usual piquant advice on how teachers can raise standardized test scores in their classrooms apparently was not the issue. It was not a question of the book lacking in relevant content. It was clearly a question of the book proposing a specific type of analysis of educational issues usually dealt with in foundations of education classes. Foundations of education textbooks written from a critical perspective were virtually nonexistent in the 1980s. It wasn't exactly a strong selling point that *Life in Schools* was created for the purpose of challenging race, class, and gender privileges within North America's dominant capitalist society.

After pitching a prospectus for the book to various mainstream publishing houses, with no success, I felt sure that *Life in Schools* was destined to be published by an alternative press—not a bad thing in itself, mind you—but a move that would surely have restricted significantly the size of its readership and thus its potential to make a political impact on the field of teacher education. Henry Giroux offered his support for the book, which captured the attention of astute editors aware of Giroux's growing national reputation for hard-edged educational analysis. Fortunately I was to discover a progressive and fearless editor in Naomi Silverman, and a political ally in renowned educational historian Joel Spring. They both convinced Longman, Inc. (who eventually published the first three editions), that the text was a political necessity and that, despite its potential for political controversy, it would hold its own in the marketplace.

Yet even with the success and critical acclaim that *Life in Schools* has enjoyed, I admit that with the launching of each new edition, I steady myself for the likely reality it will be the final one to see print. Not because I consider the ideas discussed in the book to be conceptually outdated, but because my politics have become more progressively radical with each new edition. And with few exceptions (with *Life in Schools* appearing to be one of them), radical politics and teacher education textbooks do not have an untroubled history or one of longevity.

Those who are familiar with some of my other recent books, or who have happened to notice the progressive radicalization of my politics, surely will not be surprised by this new introduction and other additions. I have in no way concealed the fact that what is currently underwriting my larger project of educational reform is nothing less than what Marx referred to as a total social revolution. How is this so different from my position in the last three editions? My educational project has always supported an emancipatory politics, certainly. I have always taken a stand against the abuses of capitalism, the practice of tracking, institutionalized racism and sexism, economic and cultural imperialism, and homophobia, and, to the best of my ability, have attempted to redress asymmetrical relations of power and privilege wherever and whenever they have crossed my pedagogical path (or other paths as well). For the last two decades, I have vigorously challenged the conservative position that the breakdown of our schools can be directly traced to a lack of Judeo-Christian family values, a lack of professionalism among teachers, or a lack of ability on the part of economically disadvantaged students, even though such a position mounted in the most reactionary precincts of the dominant ideology is so stupefying that even addressing it is giving it too much credibility. Shifting away from a left postmodernism, my emphasis over the last six years has been on developing forms of revolutionary praxis and transformation rather than on the politics of reform, although "reform" efforts can be good places to start a social revolution.

It is important to keep in mind that this edition of *Life in Schools* is not meant to be an elegiac homage to revolutionary socialism as much as an anti-elegy to capital and a challenge to educators to strive for forms of associated labor outside of the social factory or social universe of capital. As Ellen Meiksins Wood makes clear, it is undeniably and tragically the case that today "the imperatives of the market will not allow capital to prosper without depressing the conditions of great multitudes of people and degrading the environment throughout the world" (1999, p. 121). With the associated pressures of competition, accumulation, and exploitation imposed by more developed capitalist economies and leading to a general crisis of overcapacity, it is plain even to the nonspecialist that "the attempt to achieve material prosperity according to capitalist principles is increasingly likely to bring with it only the negative side of the capitalist contradiction, its dispossession and destruction without its material benefits—certainly for the vast majority" (1999, p. 121).

This is a particularly difficult time to call for rethinking the role that the United States plays in the global division of labor. The recent events of mind-shattering and gut-wrenching dimensions, the sudden unfolding apocalyptic nightmare that saw death and destruction unleashed upon thousands of innocent and unsuspecting victims in Washington, D.C., and New York City such that the gates of hell appeared to have been blown open, have made it difficult for many United States citizens to comprehend why their familiar world has suddenly turned upside down. Critical or revolutionary pedagogy, as I use the term throughout this book, takes a strong position against terrorism. Acts of terrorism can be as backward and horrific as acts of capitalist-driven imperialism and in no circumstances can they be justified (Hudis, 2001). At the same time, the cruelly imposed carnage from the repugnant and immoral terrorist attacks witnessed recently on the World Trade Center and the Pentagon must not be used by reactionary forces in the United States government and media to turn public sentiment against critics of social injustice. Nor must critics of U.S. capitalism, and I count myself as one of them, simply list all the horrible acts of imperialism engaged in historically by the United States—a long and bloody list, to be sure—as evidence of or a rationale for why these terrorist acts occurred. They occurred without reason, demand, or proclamation (Hudis, 2001). These acts were not acts against U.S. capitalism, imperialism, or injustice, but were demonic crimes against working people.

For instance, hundreds of workers from all over Latin America and the Caribbean were killed in the attacks, including those who worked at Windows on the World, in the office cafeterias, for cleaning services, and for delivery companies, and little media attention has so far been paid to them (Anderson, 2001, p. 1). And while we can gain a deeper understanding of the roots of terrorism by recognizing how the United States and other imperialist states are implicated in a long history of crimes against the oppressed throughout the world—including military interventions in post–Cold War theaters—this history in no way justifies the terrorist attacks. To take a "chickens come home to roost" position is morally reprehensible and politically undialectical. The attacks of September 11 were propelled by reactionary religious fundamentalist ideology that represents only a small fanatical minority of followers of Islam. As Edward Said remarks, "No cause, no God, no abstract idea can justify the mass slaughter of innocents, most particularly when only a small group of people are in charge of such actions and feel themselves to represent the cause without having a real mandate to do so" (2001, p. 2). Even as Bush moves toward the creation of a permanent war, progressive leftist educators need to meet the challenge of moving beyond a reactionary anti-Americanism insofar as this misconceives the task ahead; that is, insofar as it abstracts away the root of imperialism: capital, especially in its monopoly form. As Peter Hudis (2002) importantly remarks, imperialism is an outgrowth of a state-monopoly capitalism writ large on the world stage. It surely extends beyond the talons of the American Eagle. At the same time we must oppose in the United States the senseless xenophobic statism, militarism, erosion of civil liberties, and quest for permanent and indiscriminant military interventions overseas within the fracture zones of geo-political instability that have followed in the wake of the attacks, all of which can only have unsalutary consequences for world peace. This is particularly crucial, especially in light of another of Said's trenchant observations— that "bombing senseless civilians with F-16s and helicopter gunships has the same structure and effect as more conventional nationalistic terror" (2001, p. 2). This is not taking an "against America" stand but taking a stand for the rights of working-class citizens throughout the world who labor at the behest of the capitalist class.

At a time when media pundits and high-level government leaders are calling for more blood to be spilled in the name of democracy and freedom, and are clamoring for the killing of people who are not even directly involved in the terrorist attacks, we need to join together in a renewed commitment to global justice. At a time when popular syndicated columnists are calling for military crusades in the name of Christianity, we should be renewing our efforts to fight against a new breed of fascism. When Ann Coulter, contributing editor for the *National Review*, shrieks in her online column, "We should invade their countries, kill their leaders and convert them to Christianity" (2001), we know that this is far from an isolated, crackpot sentiment. Isn't this sentiment as ideologically repugnant and politically shameful as Pat Buchanan's demonization of America's foreign-born, who allegedly threaten the safety of "real" Americans? In his frenzied attempt to claim the United States for white Christians, he appeals to his Catholic faith. In his book, *The Death of the West*

(2002), he oozes admiration for Protestant and Catholic monarchs of old who had the "courage" to burn heretics and draw and quarter them at the Tyburn tree. As critical educators we are faced with a new sense of urgency in our fight to create social justice on a global scale, establishing what Karl Marx called a "positive humanism" (Hudis, 2001).

Our values and attitudes as "Americans" have been shaped by the corporate mass media that function largely as the guard dogs of corporate capitalist ideology. Today, Fox Television is growing in popularity throughout the country. When you take a look at the political commentary on Fox, it is enough to create splinters along your spinal column.

Fox Television commentator Bill O'Reilly, his mind rarely burdened by a dialectical thought, berates with autocratic homilies those few guests he invites on his show who dare offer an explanation for the events of September 11. He enjoys sparing his audiences insight, and lifting from them the burden of comprehension, preferring instead a spectacle of self-congratulatory belligerence and Stygian anger. The majesty of O'Reilly's self-regard is propped up by a stubborn conviction that unsupported opinions presented in a mean-spirited fashion are preferable to complex analysis. Proud of his simple patriotic (i.e., war-mongering) advice to kill the enemy because the enemy is evil, he admonishes anyone offering critical analysis as giving evil credibility and as comforting our enemies. On a September 17 segment of his show, *O'Reilly Factor*, our "no-spin" host Bill put forth a plan for action if the Taliban did not hand over bin Laden:

> If they don't, the U.S. should bomb the Afghan infrastructure to rubble—the airport, the power plants, their water facilities, and the roads. This is a very primitive country. And taking out their ability to exist day to day will not be hard. Remember, the people of any country are ultimately responsible for the government they have. The Germans were responsible for Hitler. The Afghans are responsible for the Taliban. We should not target civilians. But if they don't rise up against this criminal government, they starve, period. (Hart, 2001, p. 8)

O'Reilly also went on to say that the infrastructure of Iraq "must be destroyed and the population made to endure yet another round of intense pain" (Hart, 2001, p. 8). He also disembarrassed himself from any humanitarian sentiments by calling for the destruction of Libya's airports and the mining of its harbors, crying: "Let them eat sand" (Hart, 2001, p. 8). There is no spectacle of suddenly vanishing competence here, for his reasoning is as inexorably puerile as it is predictable. It is the journalistic equivalent of gunboat diplomacy. He is effectively asking for millions more Iraqi children and civilians to die at the hands of the United States (as if the United States-imposed sanctions have not killed enough), not to mention the millions of civilian casualties that would result from the kind of utter destruction of the infrastructure that he so perversely calls for. So savage was O'Reilly's call for acts of terror to be rained down on Afghan civilians by the U.S. military, one wonders if he received his political education in the caves of Lascaux. We have heard this kind of advice before. It is underwritten by the same logic that informs the Taliban's advice to their own followers. It is the logic of fascism, only this time it is *our fascism* sweetened and made more palatable by the nationalist arrogance and righteous indignation betrayed by O'Reilly and those of his stamp.

One of the primary ideological vehicles of the new totalitarianism is Fox News. Owned by Rupert Murdoch, Fox News is rapidly gaining a wide and committed audience on the basis of its appeal to right-wing male viewers. Its political catechism is spiked with testosterone and rage and gives ballast to the logic of transnational capitalism and U.S. militarism. James Wolcott aptly describes this gang as the "Viagra posse":

> Relatively subdued in the first weeks after September 11, Chris Matthews, Geraldo Rivera, and the Viagra posse of Fox News refilled their gasbags and began taking turns on Mussolini's balcony to exhort the mob, their frog glands swelling like Dizzy Gillespie's cheeks. Agitating for the insertion of ground troops, hothead hosts and like-minded guests (many of them retired military officers now getting a chance to coach from the sidelines) scoffed at the over-reliance on airpower before doing a nimble backflip and complaining that we weren't bombing enough, or in the right spots. Frustrated, indignant, and irate over the patty-cake pace of the Afghan campaign (talk shows serve strong coffee in the greenrooms), these masters of Stratego escalated their rhetorical heat as if hoping the bombing campaign would follow their lead, sounding riled enough to storm the fighter cockpit and get the job done themselves if these gutless wonders wouldn't. (2001, p. 54)

The corporate media have driven out any hope for even left-liberal news coverage or commentary. Labeled as "leftist" pundits, the likes of Sam Donaldson, Cokie Roberts, George Stephanopoulos, Bill Press, Michael Kinsley, Bob Beckel, Margaret Carlson, Al Hunt, Mark Shields, David Broder, Juan Williams, and Susan Estrich are paraded before the American public as an attempt to balance right-wingers such as Limbaugh, Buckley, Novak, McLaughlin, Buchanan, Robertson, Liddy, and North. The truth is that the so-called "leftists" are, at their most extreme, "centrists" and, more often than not, tilt politically to the right. With no leftist representation in the mainstream media, the U.S. public is literally being ideologically massaged by opinions and positions that serve the corporate capitalist elite. The myth of the liberal media talked about so much by right-wing pundits is simply a lie (*Extra!* July/August, 1998).

While publishers in Alabama are stamping 40,000 biology textbooks with warning stickers, reminding students that evolution is a controversial theory they should question, and while President Bush pushes for faith-based programs (what he calls "armies of compassion") to provide social services, and for tax breaks and other benefits for religious charities that would entitle them to be the recipients of billions of dollars of government funding, and while Christian talk-show hosts prone to lachrymose sermons on the goodness of America continue to bless the war on terrorism "in Jesus' name," one realizes that the United States functions as a covert theocracy.

Those disappointed that the apocalypse was not ushered in at the millennium's end are making up for it in their razor-edged celebration of the war on terror. History has been split down the middle as if it had been sliced by a Taliban cane soaked in water. On the one side, modernity houses the transnational ruling class, whose dreams remain unbounded, rewinding time. On the other side, the transnational working-class takes refuge in modernity's refuse heap of time unravelled and dreams dehydrated. Understanding how this mighty division has been prepared by capital is the skeleton key that unlocks the bone yard of reason where truth can be found amidst the charred ruins of civilizations past and those yet to come.

It comes as no surprise that the American Council of Trustees and Alumni (founded by Lynne V. Cheney) has released a report condemning the response of many university professors to the September 11 attacks (ACTA claims Senator Joseph Lieberman as a co-founder but Lieberman says he was only a supporter). Titled "Defending Civilization: How Our Universities Are Failing America, and What Can Be Done About It," the report itemizes 117 incidents that allegedly reveal a treasonous refusal of the professoriate to defend civilization and a stubborn willingness to give comfort to its adversaries through statements of moral relativism and opposition to the U.S. war effort. In other words, some professors have the gall to be critical of Bush's war on terrorism. Comments condemned in the report included the following: "We have to learn to use courage for peace instead of war"; "war created people like Osama bin Laden, and more war will create more people like him"; "it is from the desperate, angry, and bereaved that these suicide pilots came"; and "We must acknowledge our role in helping to create monsters in the world, find ways to contain these monsters without hurting more innocent people, and then redefine our role in the world." These comments were uttered, respectively, by an Oberlin freshman; former U.S. ambassador at large to Russia, Strobe Talbott, currently at Yale; and Arun Gandhi, the grandson of Mahatma Gandhi, speaking to a crowd at UNC in Chapel Hill (see Scigliano, 2001). ACTA lashed out at a Penn State vice provost for telling a faculty member that his web page advocating military action against terrorists was "insensitive and perhaps even intimidating." The faculty member in question had quoted and endorsed an editorial by Leonard Peikoff of the Ayn Rand Institute that read: "We must now use our unsurpassed military to destroy all branches of the Iranian and Afghani governments, regardless of the suffering and death this will bring to many innocents caught in the line of fire" (Scigliano, 2001, p. 16).

It is striking to witness how terrorism is sanctioned and condemned, and by whom. In 1990, George Bush Sr. released from house arrest the notorious Orlando Bosch, after Bosch had served two years for illegally entering the United States. Government officials in the United States believed that Bosch was involved in the bombing of a Cuban civilian airliner that killed 73 people, and the Justice Department linked him to at least 30 acts of sabotage. The *New York Times* called Bosch "one of the hemisphere's most notorious terrorists." It turns out that Bush's son, Jeb, who was at the time a Republican leader trying to curry favor with Miami's anti-Castro Cubans, had lobbied for Bosch's release (Bortfeld and Naureckas, 2001).

At a time when Marxist social theory seems destined for the political dustbin, it is needed more than ever to help us understand the forces and relations that now shape our national and international destinies. I am committed to the belief that critical/revolutionary pedagogy can help to bring about a global society where events of September 11, 2001 are less likely to occur. Like many freedom-loving U.S. citizens, I long for a world unsullied by violence, terror, scarcity, and alienation and am committed to efforts that will make such a world possible. That is why I am committed to critical pedagogy. Critical pedagogy is a politics of understanding and action, an act of knowing that attempts to situate everyday life in a larger geo-political context, with the goal of fostering regional collective self-responsibility, large-scale ecumene, and international worker solidarity. It will require putting aside stereotypes of leftists as "collaborators" with the enemy, as nonpatriots, as bleeding-hearted naysayers bent on selling out the country under the banner of political correctness. It will require the abandonment of cardboard cutout images of radicals as bad guys, and feminists as extremists; equally it will require leftists to jettison their blanket-thinking about those who disagree with them. It will require the courage to examine social and political contradictions, even—and no doubt especially—those that govern mainstream United States social policies and practices. It means that leftists will have to be more attentive to opposing political positions, and listen carefully to arguments put forward by conservatives and libertarians alike. Students need to analyze various positions and to make judgments based on the caliber of arguments put forward.

Given this daunting global scenario, it is important that educators ask the following: Is there a viable socialist alternative to capitalism? What would a world without wage labor be like? Without living labor being subsumed by dead labor? Without the extraction of surplus value and the exploitation that accompanies it? While I have always fought for the redistribution of economic resources, I have not always sufficiently challenged the processes that have undergirded them. To examine critically the relationship between education and the globalization of capital has never before been so urgent, even as drooling, pro-capitalist ideologues, drunk on the idea of a world unzipped, spread-eagled, and helpless against their corporate assaults, dance their pathetic jigs over the grave of Marx and pronounce capitalism as civilization's potent savior. Even though global capitalism has forced proletariats of developing nations a choice between starvation and malnutrition, or between the prostitution of their labor-power and resistance against their capitalist pimps, many among the educational left in the United States have chosen to retreat, to lick their wounds in hiding, or to take refuge in the rag-and-bone shop of postmodern theory where they can mount their vainglorious assaults on consumer culture with little opposition from the eagle-eyed guardians of capital. Or else they have taken refuge in a hollowed-out sociology of knowledge where they can carp about the politics of the New Right without offering a genuine challenge to the rule of capital.

It is thus perfectly understandable if somewhat disquieting that the field of critical pedagogy has become so institutionally vulgarized and domesticated. In many instances, it has been reduced to a bourgeoisified version of its original incarnation in the works of Paulo Freire and others. The highly contentious field of critical pedagogy and radical education is currently marked by internecine debate, personal attacks, and pseudo-radicalism, and the acrimony with which critical educators attack each other nowadays is surpassed only by the passion with which they band together in order to defend their turf and their academic status. Leftist educationalists have displayed everything from a rancorous juvenilia where even well-known pundits decry the call for class struggle as merely romantic rhetoric, to calls for a "détente" with the right, even to a sinkhole sanctimoniousness where criticism of one's personal appearance, such as displaying a tattoo in an author's photo, is put forward as evidence of a serious character flaw.

Postmodern theory (often in the guise of a trade union leftism) has, of late, become the favored terrain upon which to launch their cultural revolution. Here the revolution is largely a textual one, reduced to waging war against the literary canon and other forms of discursive authority but leaving the concrete world of laboring subjects largely on its own. Willie Thompson observes that "the response of the left to the postmodern condition, if such it may be termed, has tended to retreat into a form of hermetic analysis divorced from much purchase on reality, a stance greatly reinforced by the collapse of the Eastern bloc, the environmental crisis and the real or imagined discredit of Marxism whether as a mode of analysis or as a guide to action" (1997, p. 218).

Why is it that the demise of state communism in Eastern Europe in the 1980s and 1990s has received more attention in the United States media than the crisis of capitalism in the so-called Western democracies? Part of the answer is, of course, the collapse of Western enlightenment ideologies. Carl Boggs traces the depoliticization of public discourse to the collapse of modern political ideologies tied to the Enlightenment tradition (liberalism, socialism, Communism, nationalism). He writes:

> Tied to the nation-state and to the failures or contradictions of 20th-century governing regimes, such ideologies have lost their legitimating power not to mention their capacity to inspire mass mobilization. They offer few insightful analyses of present-day social reality or compelling visions of the future. Globalization subverts classical liberalism with its emphasis on individualism, democratic participation and human progress through industrial development; nationalism with its fixation on the nation-state; socialism with its inability to carry out basic redistributive programs or address environmental concerns; and Communism with its attraction to the command model and its failure (like others) to resist incursions of the world market. These ideologies, obliterated by an expanding neoliberal consensus serving the interests of global corporate elites, cannot fully come to grips with vast changes in the system of production and consumption, class and power relations, labor and popular culture. Nor can they offer much in the way of political inspiration—witness their nearly total absence from discourses surrounding the anti-WTO campaigns of the past few years or, for that matter, the language of most contemporary social movements. (2001, p. 307)

I would argue that Boggs is only partially correct in his otherwise perspicacious assessment. There are numerous schools of Marxist analysis that are well-equipped to provide a rigorous analysis of the globalization phenomena. Regardless of the school of radical criticism to which one steadfastly proclaims allegiance, the defense of communism has had durable ideological and political consequences. But it is important to realize that communism failed not because in principle it is unworkable but because its fundamental principles and practices were ruthlessly betrayed. While communist countries were often ridiculed in the West as an iron container for mindless collectivism, and a stock symbol of everything loathsome about political ideology and organization, what often went unremarked in the Western media was the more reductionist, vulgar, and domesticated form of collectivism that occurs under capitalism, where individuals are reduced to their labor-power, to reified containers of living capital, and where entire populations are over-coded as consumer citizens in a continuous reaffirmation of profits over people. But Boggs is correct when he asserts that leftist ideologies have been all but written out of the script by today's anti-capitalist crusaders. The attacks against capitalism have brought into relief its tendential invisibility. When, in January 2001, Colin Powell announced that "other systems do not work" (cited in Boggs, 2001, p. 313), he lapsed into a form of motivated amnesia when he failed to note that they do not work because the U.S. does not permit them to work; when he bragged that "We are going to show a vision to the world of the value system of America," he studiously avoided mentioning that such a vision is supported by the most powerful military apparatus in human history. Powell's "value system of America" has little to offer those who refuse to kneel before Capital's God of Profit.

Negatively impacted by the waning of Marx's theoretical leverage upon radical educators, much of the motivated advocacy of current left discourse does little more than call for altering already existing economic arrangements, and thus unwittingly placing the oppressed and the oppressors on the same ontological level. It is important for left educators to realize that, despite the worsening economic conditions around the world, brought about by a new virulent "capitalism with the gloves off," the ascendant ideologies of the right are not embedded in immovable institutions although they happen at this present moment to be blessed by political success. They can be overcome and transformed. But the tactics won't be the same as those used by the Bolsheviks in their valiant siege of the Winter Palace. Nor will they be purely discursive tactics, either, even though it is true that, as Marx put it, ideas in the hands of the masses ready to receive them can have a powerful effect on history.

Relaunching left educational theory on the foam of postmodern theory is an enfeebled strategy that, at best, can buy the left some time in order to create more substantive educational correlatives to an anti-bourgeois, anti-capitalist politics. Capital cannot be defanged by a postmodern feint of the head, followed by a post-Marxist left hook aimed at the solar plexus of corporate greed. What is needed is a knockout punch that will send capitalism sprawling through the ropes. The problem is that poststructuralist and postmodern theorists in the field of education have largely diffused capitalism and imperialism as an ever-present danger. They have done this while experimenting with terminology and syntax and partaking in a scholastic ritual in which, to use the words of R. U. Sirius, "language tries to see how far it can crawl up its own ass" (2002, p. 44).

Barbara Foley notes that while CIA recruitment is on the increase, in the academy we seem to be experiencing exciting and progressive developments of a different sort: namely, the number of canon-busting scholars and poststructuralist theorists is also on the increase. According to these theorists, "polysemous subversion waits everywhere in ambush" (2001, p. 201), and there exists "a tendency to find subversion under every textual bush" (2001, p. 206). These scholars see oppositional practices in every conceivable trope, conceit, catachresis, and stylistic intervention. Capitalism and imperialism can supposedly be brought down by voguish apostasy and deconstructive brigandism directed against bourgeois ideology. Foley writes that "if it is true not only that marginalized texts subvert the established canon, but also that canonical texts subvert the traditional and conservative ideologies that they seem to endorse, then bourgeois ideology—at least when embodied in literary texts—really poses no sort of threat at all. It self-destructs when touched—or, at least, when touched by the poststructuralist critic or pedagogue" (2001, p. 206). I am not arguing that textual subversion is unimportant. I am trying to make a case for making pedagogical and curricular practices a form of class politics against the tyranny of neoliberalism, within the orbit of a larger anti-corporate, anti-globalization program and direct-action politics.

As an opponent to democracy and social justice, capitalism's ability to disguise its connection to reactionary politics is greater today than ever before. Bertell Ollman makes an important point when he writes:

So long as capitalism hides its real relations behind its appearances, its underlying processes behind its surface events, class struggle behind class collaboration, and its potential for an egalitarian order behind the present in-egalitarian one—so long will Marxism be needed to uncover the true situation. And the capitalists and their "intellectual handmaidens" who insist that "it's time to bury Karl Marx." Well, Cacus, too, had an interest in keeping people from finding out what went on in his cave. (2001, p. 162)

Ellen Meiksins Wood has identified on the vast landscape of global economic relations what she calls "a new kind of imperialism." She uses this term to refer to "the spread of market imperatives (with the help of international capitalist agencies like the World Bank and the IMF) [that] has compelled farmers in the third world to replace agricultural self-sufficiency with specialization in cash crops for the global market" (1999, p. 118). Of course, as Wood further notes, not even if workers owned the means of production would the market suddenly disappear. On the contrary, asserts Wood:

Once the market is established as an economic "discipline" or "regulator," once economic actors become market dependent for the conditions of their own reproduction, even workers who own the means of production, individually or collectively, will be obliged to respond to the market's imperatives—to compete and accumulate, to let "uncompetetive" enterprises and workers go to the wall, and to exploit themselves . . . wherever market imperatives regulate the economy and govern social reproduction, there will be no escape from exploitation. There can, in other words, be no such thing as a truly "social" or democratic market, let alone "market socialism." (1999, p. 119)

One could say, after Warren Montag, that the doctrines of market socialism represent "a creature with the head of Hayek and the heart of Rawls" (2001, p. 198). Many progressive educators defend the poor and powerless today by opining that those most excluded in today's social order—*los olvidados*—inhabit rich and vibrant cultures and the curriculum should build upon the varied cultures of the poor in order to affirm their many and formidable strengths. This is only part of the answer, surely. Celebrating the inexhaustible richness of the social life of the poor should not be an excuse to ignore their economic plight. At the same time, even as we underscore how capitalism is able to appropriate workers' struggles and instrumentalize and integrate them into the structured hierarchies of the dominant culture, we underestimate the creativity and democratic instincts of the great masses of the poor at our own peril. For those who advocate a tightly administered vanguard party of intellectuals to "co-ordinate" the struggle ahead, I would remind them of the powerful potential for workers to self-organize at the point of production.

This is not to say that the role of a vanguard party is hopelessly anachronistic or wrongheaded, especially when facing the somnabulisms of the present; the point is that even if such a party were to play a role in the struggle ahead, it should be a role that respects the autonomy and self-activity of the poor. Please do not mistake this for a clarion call for spontaneity, but rather an attempt to reinvigorate working-class struggle and to reaffirm workers as the primary agent of anti-capitalist struggle. We saw the fecundating effects of such struggles in the establishment of the soviets and the German and Hungarian workers councils. Here it is important to remember that not only does dead labor (capital) shape living labor (the labor-power of the workers) but we do have moments when labor evolves from living labor to become a revolutionary subject capable of negating capital (see Cleaver, 2000).

My *métier* in this fourth edition of *Life in Schools* is not to provide more updated statistics to show how economic and educational conditions are worsening for both teachers and students under current attempts to re-Reaganize U.S. politics and turn the country into a garrison state. Statistical evidence is often a weak antidote to ignorance especially when the janiform sentinels of the dominant culture exercise their legitimizing frameworks of interpretation in ways that deliberately spin the facts and statistics one way or another. Rather, my efforts are directed to pitching a modest class-oriented counterplot to capitalism's false narrative of hope, to explore the cracks and fissures of capitalist society hidden beneath its decorous sublimity, as well as strategically to place conceptual sticks of dynamite in the rotting pillars of its foundations. It is also designed to present in summary fashion a language of critical analysis gleaned from the left social science tradition. *Life in Schools* is designed as an introductory approach to education—mainly philosophical in tenor and temper—if one considers, after Raya Dunayevskaya (2002), that philosophy generally consists in making explicit what is only implicit in the objective movement of history. In a way, you could describe it as an attempt to force reality to surrender to a more emancipatory vision of democratic social life, a life only made possible by the elimination of capitalist social relations. But reality does not surrender without a struggle, often protracted, and usually bloody.

Revolutionary philosophy is labor-intensive and takes years to develop. It is a deliberate, lifelong journey with no guarantees. In embarking on such a journey, I have ventured into the realm of abstract thought, believing, with Marx, that abstractions can help one understand in a powerful way the concreteness of social life. It is through dialectical thinking that one can best grasp the contradictions of everyday life (i.e., why so much misery exists within capitalist democracies; why there exists racial, class, and gender hierarchies; why freedom has become an empty signifier often used to justify imperialism and war).

I have always believed—and still do—that it is the responsibility and challenge of the educator to make the link for herself between the "macro" socio-economic domain of social life and the microsocial relations found within the agitated fabric of school classrooms. Critical educators can offer up their experiences, and can do their best to provide the lineaments of a theoretical framework with which to analyze those—and other—experiences, including the experiences of their students. More important, critical educators can provide scientific concepts from the vast lexicon of Marxist theory and offer some direction on how to apply them to an analysis of schooling. In working with such concepts it is important that the student not downgrade or gloss over the significance of the antagonisms between capital and labor.

As the Salvadoreano poet Roque Dalton proclaimed, we are not fashioned by words alone. Marx himself reminds us that we are fashioned in and through history, by conditions not entirely of our own making. We are the products of systems of mediation—dialectical contradictions spawned by the social relation known as capital as well as cultural representations, social formations, and institutional relations, all of which contribute to the objective conditions of possibility for our human development. Critical pedagogy works at, in, and through all of these levels in order to create conditions for the development of freely associated human beings whose relationships are not overpopulated by the intentions of Western capitalists; whose dreams, desires, and needs are not circumscribed by the necessity of capital to reproduce itself; whose sense of purpose is not nurtured in the womb of necessity; and whose subjectivities are not fashioned by the social relations of production that rely upon the reduction of human identity to that of value production through commodification.

Millions from aggrieved populations worldwide stand witness to the law-governed process of exploitation known as capital accumulation, to the ravages of un-even development called "progress," and to the practice of imperialism in new guises called "globalization." Exploitation is not an aberrant deviation but a constituent and durable form of capitalist democracy itself. Capitalism constitutes the absolute nega-tion of humanity, personhood, and freedom and, as such, represents the limit of the logic of domination. But this absolute limit needs to be transformed into its opposite by what Dunayevskaya calls (after Hegel and Marx) the negation of the negation. This she refers to as absolute negativity, which becomes the condition of possibility for revolutionary consciousness and the basis for the affirmation of freedom at its highest level as a form of revolutionary humanism. The famous author of *Marx's Con-cept of Man*, Erich Fromm, reveals revolutionary humanism to be at the center of Marx's philosophy: "Marx's aim was that of the spiritual emancipation of man, of his liberation from the chains of economic determination, of restituting him in his hu-man wholeness, of enabling him to find unity and harmony with his fellow man and with Nature" (2000, p. 3).

Yet many schools of education today offer little more than lukewarm courses on popular culture, watered-down versions of critical theory, or "lite" versions of postmodern theory as the calculable basis for pedagogical transgression. In my mind, the more conservative versions of postmodern theory provide the gastric juices neces-sary to make the world of capitalist exploitation easier to digest and to reduce dissent mainly to matters of style and taste. By wrapping transgression in the hot salsa of avant-gardism, postmodern theory challenges capitalist cultural formations through the dizzying experience of decentering representations that are presumed to be ontologically secure, or by finding refuge in weird intersections of meaning or unex-pected detours of syntax, or in the radical dislocation of sign systems. There is cer-tainly nothing wrong with these challenges in themselves; but they offer little from which to mount the kind of struggle necessary to bring an end to the rule of capital.

Those who are interested in my more mature radical thinking about education along Marxist lines will perhaps want to read another of my more recent books, such as *Che Guevara, Paulo Freire, and the Pedagogy of Revolution* (2000). Those who are dis-appointed with the more Marxist turn in my work no doubt will try to sell this text-book back to the college or university bookstore at the end of the semester.

When I finished writing my book about Che Guevara and Paulo Freire, a friend of mine and compañero in the struggle for social justice—himself a well-known radi-cal scholar—told me that my move to an unapologetic Marxist position undeniably would cause my readership demonstrably to shrink. Yet my Che/Freire book contin-ues to be read by wider and more enthusiastic audiences than many of my other, less Marxist books. This to me reflects perhaps a new fomenting social consciousness among today's North American youth, signaled most dramatically by the recent protests against the World Trade Organization in Seattle, Quebec City, and Genoa. I'm not suggesting that young people today can't be found palavering happily with their friends in front of mind-numbing television game shows, but I am more convinced than ever that the dialectical contradictions and internal relations of capitalism are becoming more glaring and less accepted by young people as an historical inevitability. They know that capitalism brooks no opposition to its imperialist demands.

While the language of Marxism may have been thrust willy-nilly into the trash can of educational scholarship, Marx's ideas and commitment to forging a society free of exploitation are alive and well. And even though Marxist discourse may be the language informing the politics of no more than a handful of these valiant young protesters, it is likely that, when stripped of its Cold War propaganda that has doomed its reception in North America, Marxist analysis is likely to be more readily engaged by growing numbers of young social activists. When its full analytic potential is recognized, it could very well begin to resonate with many young people today. I am talking about the same young people who rail against corporations and their private armies hacking out profits in developing countries; who condemn the transnational biotech corporations exploiting the genetic wealth of, for example, the Montes Azules Biosphere Reserve in the Chiapas rainforest of the Selva Lacandona, Mexico, where local indigenous farmers are taken to court by transnational corporations who accuse them of violating their property rights; who challenge the violence of the oil companies such as Shell (the Anglo-Dutch giant) that financed the Abacha regime's reign of terror in Nigeria and that led to the hanging of internationally known writer and environmental activist Ken Saro-Wiwa and eight of his Ogoni compatriots in November, 1995; and who oppose many of the recent military operations by NATO—the attack dogs of the advanced capitalist nations.

I am also referring to young people who are fed up with the political charlatanry of the Democrats and the Republicans. Most recently, they have become enraged by the Supreme Court, in its per curiam majority ruling on December 12, 2000, in which it thus became a knowing surrogate for George W. Bush and Republican Party interests and then shamelessly—and possibly treasonously—defended the action by arguing that it was intended to preserve "the fundamental right" to vote (Bugliosi, 2001; see also Kellner, 2001). The Supreme Court effectively stole the election from the American people, even though it hypocritically embraced the equal protection clause. How could conservatives embrace equal protection, claiming that different recount standards in Florida counties amounted to unequal protection? According to Bugliosi, only because no Congress ever imagined enacting a statute making it a crime to steal a presidential election did the five justices of the Supreme Court escape going to prison for their felonious conduct. The recent presidential election provides an excellent opportunity for young people to explore the contradictions and contestations around the issue of how politics is conducted at the highest levels of government.

Young people don't profit very much from talk shows debating Bill Clinton's serial adultery or George W. Bush's past alcohol and alleged cocaine use. More important issues to discuss and debate as critical citizens include the ramifications of Clinton's NAFTA free trade initiative and its effects on the poor in developing nations, and Bush's complicity with big business. More important than learning from the scandal-hungry media about George W. Bush's despicable imitation of Karla Fay Tucker, when he mockingly whimpered "Please don't kill me!" before ordering her execution, is a critical analysis of both his foreign policies (especially in light of the recent terrorist attacks and his militarization of the global economy) and domestic policies (that some argue have turned back the clock on civil rights, women's rights, labor conditions, and the environment).

But the popular media only reluctantly criticizes Bush (or any sitting president) for his major policy initiatives and offers little substantive analysis of them from a left-ist perspective. Before the terrorist attacks, they preferred to gossip about his personal life rather than to challenge his fundamental capitalist principles (challenging his capitalist principles is even less likely at the present moment as the country unites behind him for war). While it is of historical interest to note that as a managing part-ner of Brown Brothers Harimon, Prescott Bush, the grandfather of George W. Bush, was a major supplier of economic support to the Nazi Regime of Adolph Hitler from 1934 to 1940, the fact that IBM as well as other U.S. corporations also played a vital role in the functioning of the Nazi war machine through its German subsidaries has far greater political significance for understanding the history of United States capi-talism. IBM supplied the Nazis with billions of punch cards that were used by sorting and tabulating machines leased and serviced by IBM, machines that helped to facili-tate the massacre of the Jews (Black, 2001). In addition, the German subsidiaries of Ford and General Motors used slave labor to help produce thousands of tanks and trucks for Hitler's military forces. This, of course, is singularly illustrative of the logic of capital. This is how capital works. Today such a logic is rarely traced historically in terms of United States complicity, or challenged in the mainstream media, let alone the public schools.

When I look at the young activists of today, I see courageous and forward-look-ing individuals rethinking the meaning of freedom. They are collectively recognizing that within a capitalist economy, freedom is really a counterfeit term. People have the freedom to starve if they cannot find work or if they refuse the most demeaning job. These young people have figured out that the only free cheese in a capitalist society is in the mousetrap. Ollman deftly captures this sentiment when he writes:

> Freedom to be left alone to starve, to freeze, to remain ignorant can't really be free-dom. For freedom to be worthy of the sacrifices made in its name, it must include something of the real life conditions that enable people to do what they want as well as the fact that no one is actively keeping them from doing it. But let's not forget the counterfeit [sense of the] term, if only to learn who benefits from this deception and how they have managed to fool us for so long. (2001, p. 57)

In other words, poor people do not have the freedom to buy goods that they cannot afford. Ollman asks: "[C]an workers choose to sell their labor power for a de-cent wage to employers who don't want it or are only willing to pay half that amount to get it? Rather than focusing on the moment of choice, it is the unequal conditions in which people make their choices and which narrowly prescribe what can be chosen that should get our attention" (2001, p. 62).

Today there are millions of potential workers who want to be exploited as work-ers. They are screaming to the corporations: "Please exploit us!" But capitalism derisively refuses them because it does not need them. They comprise capital's new reserve army who have been demoted to the rank of "unworthy, even of exploitation." The point here is that so many well-intentioned and progressive educators still talk about the struggle for social justice in terms of resource and income distribution. This position does not take as its point of departure the necessary struggle for a class-free society, and it thus reproduces the very capitalist social relations that have become the object of criticism. In addition, social class is often reduced to cultural experiences, assumptions, and attitudes, rather than understood as how one is positioned within the social relations of production and the larger social division of labor. The reduction of social class to cultural capital or "sharing the wealth" tacitly endorses the notion that there exists somewhere the good capitalist with compassion, with a heart. Yet how is it possible to exercise a "good heart" except in a limited sense when the very nature of capitalism stipulates that the cost of living labor be cut, and that the capitalist must undertake a relentless drive for value and more value?

Anti-capitalist struggle is not enough to produce the type of new beginnings necessary to bring about a society that does not merely reproduce fundamental class antagonisms in the name of some revolutionary movement or principle. What is needed, of course, is a struggle that moves beyond simply opposing capitalism and the crapulent depression that it inflicts upon its subjects, and that creates the revolutionary new beginnings for freely associated and mental labor that transcends the separation of manual and mental labor and hierarchical social relations. This demands a transformation of human relations at the point of production, between men and women and between various ethnic groups as part of a larger revolution in permanence (Hudis, 2001). In a world in which 100 million people are unemployed, you can count on the presence of disaffection and anger. Does it matter that in the United States there are free elections, if the lives of the working class do not improve?

Another problem with well-intentioned progressive educators occurs when those from the metropolitan centers of the developed West are roundly admonished for trying to speak for or about the subaltern subject. Apparently, one should not try to represent the "other." Marx is often criticized for trying to represent the world for and on behalf of the proletariat. While I agree that it is wrong for anyone to arrogate to themselves a position that claims to represent the last word on any social relation or circumstance, I take issue with the blanket admonition that we should not attempt to represent the world as a people struggling to rebuild it. To my mind this avoids the question of how we can represent ourselves collectively to ourselves and to others. The challenge, it seems to me, is to analyze the social and cultural relations that both permit us to and prohibit us from representing ourselves to ourselves and to others for the purpose of creating active and collective alliances against capital.

What needs to be understood by the broader public in general, and by educators in particular, is that within the context of the globalization of capital, military, trade, and energy interests are so intertwined that they are often virtually indistinguishable from each other. Consider the recent case of the Bush administration's Plan Colombia. The International Monetary Fund and the World Trade Organization has put pressure on the Colombian government to cut the public-sector budget and sell off government-operated services and companies. This has resulted in massive layoffs and cuts in public funding for healthcare, and pensions. The money saved (more accurately, stolen from the poor) is used to pay off the government's debts to foreign banks and lending institutions, which will make the country much more attractive to foreign investors. The Bush administration's multibillion dollar aid to Colombia (the third-largest recipient of U.S. military aid in the world) ostensibly was put into place in order to suppress cocaine production, but that money—as the Bush administration rightly knows—is used by right-wing paramilitary groups (such as United Self-Defense Groups) in their assassination attempts of trade union leaders.

Approximately two hundred trade union leaders have been murdered over the last several years. Of course, U.S. aid is merely a "cover" for the cheap extraction and sale of coal to the United States. (Coal has been encouraged for greater use in U.S. power plants, and I wonder if it is a coincidence that Bush comes from the state that is the biggest consumer of coal, whereas Cheney comes from the state that is its largest producer.) Colombian coal mines are owned by U.S. multinational corporations such as Drummond Co., Inc., based in Birmingham, Alabama.

That the history of both communist regimes and advanced capitalist democracies have been marked by unspeakable horrors is something that should escape no alert student of world history. For me, the issue at hand is not to defend the historical regimes that called themselves communist (most of them, after all, were highly bureaucratized forms of state capitalism) but to awaken in the reader a commitment to transform the world into something that transcends the current forms of capitalist exploitation that today is nearly everywhere. (To blame the totalitarianism of the former Soviet Union on Marxism is tantamount to blaming the Spanish Inquisition on the Sermon on the Mount.) Such a commitment to total social revolution cannot be made solely on the basis of shared experiences or emotional sentiment but must include a scientific analysis of global capitalism and its workings throughout world history. For many of you, such a commitment will hinge on the question of whether or not capitalism can be transformed into a social relation that can promote and bring about social justice and emancipation from oppression and exploitation. I, for one, do not think such a society can be created within the social logic and social relations of capitalism, although it is certainly true that the transition to socialism that must be undertaken can be glimpsed within the contradictions of capitalism. What Manning Marable expresses here in relation to the struggle of Black people is what I would affirm in relation to all oppressed peoples:

> I remain convinced that Black people as a group will never achieve the historical objectives of their long struggle for freedom within the political economy of capitalism. Capitalism has shown the remarkable ability to mutate into various social formations and types of state rule, but its essentially oppressive character, grounded in the continuing dynamics of capital accumulation and the exploitation of labor power, remains the same. The U.S. capitalist state, in the final analysis, will never be cajoled or persuaded to reform itself through appeals of moral suasion. Fundamental change will require a massive democratic resistance movement largely from below and anchored in the working class and among oppressed minority groups. (2000, xxxviii)

Here we need to reject the benign expectations reflected by progressives who maintain a dream of a quasi-capitalism and semi-socialism, a type of "third way" détente between Marx and the market that is called the social market or market socialism. The dream of a "people's capitalism" is wrongheaded, although try telling that to those countries suffering from underdevelopment and anxious to join the cultural economic order of the developed West. A recent issue of *The Black Panther*, speaking from the position of "revolutionary and scientific intercommunalism," describes the current phenomena of globalization or globalism as "reactionary intercommunalism":

> Not unlike its predecessors, "capitalist free trade" [under which African Slavery had its birth and official sanction], modern globalism is a force without morals, simply seeking new supermarkets and new ways of exploiting the world's natural resources and the labor of the people. This new global phenomenon [so-called modern "globalism" or "globalization"] has its roots in the very nature of the capitalist economic system; it is this fact that must cause rational minds to have serious concerns over the prospects for human life, or for that matter, any future life on this earth. The origins of capitalism, we must never forget, are found, first, in the "extermination" of the indigenous peoples of color in many parts of the so-called "underdeveloped world" [particularly the "Third World" in Asia, Africa, and what is now known as Mexico, Central and South America]; and, second, in the African Slave Trade and the "theft" of billions of dollars of "free labor" [paid in francs, pounds, marks, etc.], and outright theft of the gold, silver, and other precious stones found in these Third World lands. It is an indisputable historical fact that, literally, hundreds of millions of "people of color" were sacrificed to the God of Profits, a "god" who continues to be worshipped by those who believe in the virtue, vitality, and continued viability of the "free flow of trade and finance" of the capitalist economic system. (2000, p. 24)

Once hymned as the source of salvation for the world, and the concrete foundation of all democracy-building, capitalism has managed to triumph in its many stages of crisis, including the crisis-ridden moment of its current incarnation, and to trump the odds against its survival, but not without world-shaking consequences. Only recently, the lives of millions of people have been pulverized by the destruction of Russia's economy, the meltdown of the economies of the "Asian Tigers," and the bankruptcies of Mexico and Brazil. And we could go on to talk about more recent economic catastrophes, like those of Turkey and Argentina. But you can rest assured that the capitalist class has managed to survive without a scratch. Today, there is little talk of throwing communists and socialists into the suffocating gyres of Hell's eternal fire, because they are all presumed to be residing there already. Satan's sphincter is presumably packed tight with the undigested remains of Marx, Lenin, Rosa Luxemburg, and the whole rotten lot of Reds.

Here in the U.S., media propaganda against communism and socialism has been so prevalent and pervasive, there is not much chance that their founding ideas will survive in the public archive with much credibility. The stage was already set by 1960 (with no small help from Senator Joe McCarthy) when John Wayne starred in *The Alamo*. Wayne represented *The Alamo* as the battle between democracy (the Texans) and communism (the Mexicans). In the publicity for the film, written by Wayne himself, he expressed a desire to "sell America to countries threatened with Communist domination . . . [and] put new heart and faith into all the world's free people" (cited in Floyd, 2001, p. 109). The battle against communism has been won. Which isn't to say that NATO's billion-dollar-a-day war machine isn't being conscripted into battle from time to time against "rogue" nations—from the Soviet Union and Nicaragua to Iraq or Yugoslavia—to ensure genocide as the fateful consequence for any developing nation bold enough to pursue an economic alternative to free market capitalism (McMurtry, 2000). That is, when the United States doesn't decide to "go it alone," unilaterally, as it did in Afghanistan (with some back-up from England).

Make no mistake about it, the logical of capital is as pernicious as it is deceptive. Sometimes, however, it becomes so flagrantly arrogant and self-exculpating that it exercises itself in full view of the public, capitalism *à la* full Monty. But putting itself out in front of the public in all of its naked corruptness has done little to foment opposition against it. In fact, what this often does is to naturalize its inevitability. Let's take a few recent examples. Philip Morris, the second largest food company in the world and the world's largest cigarette maker, recently distributed a report in the Czech Republic that constituted an unvarnished illustration of the logic of capital. The report stated, with a bold arrogance destined to backfire, that 22,000 smokers saved the Czech government 30 million dollars in 1999 by dying early, because their deaths reduced costs for health care, pensions, and housing for those decrepit Czech citizens in their post-productive years (Holley, 2001). The report was intended to garner support for the indirect positive effect of smoking on public finances. The report pointed out that when the impact on government finances of all smoking-related costs was taken into account (i.e., when smoking-related costs, savings, and tax revenues were added together), the result was a net positive effect of $152 million in 1999. The subtext of the report was that smoking was a reliable way for the state to rid itself of seniors who were draining the economy. What state bureaucracy could resist such an alluring formula? To the shock of the Philip Morris executives, there was worldwide outrage in response to their report. But not surprisingly, there was little challenge to the rule of capital that underlay the logic of the report.

I would like to present another close-to-the-bone example of how the logic of capital works. Even though the United States is just coming off its biggest economic expansion in over a century, hospital care for all but the extremely wealthy is diminishing. Patients are stacked in hospital corridors today like so many cans of sardines. People arriving in ambulances are being turned away from emergency rooms. Peter Gosselin of the *Los Angeles Times* writes: "Medical specialists generally agree that a key force behind the current crisis is an effort by business and government to let market forces streamline the nation's huge and expensive health care system" (2001, A8). As managed care companies discourage money-losing emergency room use by refusing to pay for most visits, human lives are being left to the vagaries of the market. While industry critics claim that hospitals have closed beds to cut costs and devote resources to lucrative, easier-to-manage elective surgery patients, they fail to address the fundamental workings of capital that spins the drive-wheel of the health care industry.

This illustrates a point that I have consistently tried to make in my work over the years: that United States citizens have been sold a false god in the mystical marketplace. Their veneration of the market is gathering hubris worthy of a blood-soaked Greek tragedy. Money that should go to the provision of medical services ends up being "floated" on the international markets, making CEOs and their companies very rich (CEOs can afford private health care) and devastating the working-class. This is what I mean when I argue that money is being taken from the poor to give to the rich. But Marx foreshadowed this in the first volume of *Capital*—that the labor-capital relation is grounded in the subsumption of living labor (people) to abstract labor (the extraction of surplus value).

Bear with me for one more glaring example of the contradictory logic of capitalism and capitalist democracy. Capitalist democracy usually takes the position of supporting religious freedom. Government leaders have often denounced, for instance, China's suppression of a mystic group known as Falun Gong, that bases its practices on a brand of *qigong* exercises that promotes strong physical health and well-being, and that has been mustering a sustained challenge to Communist rule in China. In March, Republican Senator Jesse Helms hosted the annual Heritage Foundation "International Religious Freedom Award" and presented it to Li Hongzhi, founder of Falun Gong (*Workers Vanguard*, 2001). At first blush this would seem to contradict actions that we have come to associate with the Helmsman from Hell: his winning of the election against black opponent, Harvey Gant, with an ad playing to racist white fear—the so-called "white hands" ad, in which a white man's hands crumple a rejected job application while a voice-over intones, "You needed that job . . . but they had to give it to a minority"; his description of the University of North Carolina as "the University of Negroes and Communists"; his reference to Black civil rights activists as "Communists and sex perverts"; his commentaries on civil rights protests that maintained that "The Negro cannot count forever on the kind of restraint that's thus far left him free to clog the streets, disrupt traffic, and interfere with other men's rights"; his statement that "Crime rates and irresponsibility among Negroes are a fact of life which must be faced"; his remarks that homosexuality is "degenerate," and that homosexuals are "weak, morally sick wretches"; his routine opposition to AIDS research funding; or his singing of "Dixie" in an elevator to Carol Moseley-Braun, the first African American woman elected to the Senate, bragging, "I'm going to make her cry. I'm going to sing Dixie until she cries" (Fairness and Accuracy in Media, 2001).

The championing of Li by someone like Helms might seem a bit strange, given that Helms and the Heritage Foundation support, in the main, conservative Christian beliefs and practices, and given that Li claims that he can fly, that fox and weasel spirits take over human souls, that an ancient two-billion-year-old civilization practiced Falun Gong and built nuclear reactors, and that Li claims to be able to install telekinetically in the abdomen of his followers the "Dharma Wheel" that gathers vital "qi" energy and throws off bad karma. Yet the support by Helms and The Heritage Foundation for Falun Gong makes more sense when you realize that it serves to destabilize China's population while affirming the hateful principles associated with the extreme Christian Right. Falun Gong denounces interracial marriage as degenerate, claims that heaven excludes persons of mixed blood, condemns homosexuality, attacks the theory of evolution, challenges sexual freedom, and is hostile to women's rights.

Popular preacher Jerry Falwell also condemns feminism, homosexuality, and the theory of evolution. In fact, Falwell reported on a television program that the terrorist attacks in New York and Washington were caused by feminists, homosexuals, the American Civil Liberties Union, and the People for the American Way who, in trying to secularize the United States, have brought about God's wrath, provoking a capitalist heterosexual God to allow the enemies of America to punish it. Falwell's comments have been rightly compared to militant Islamic fundamentalist rhetoric, situating him as an ideological twin of groups like the Taliban.

Good, honest, conscientious citizens who share an active participation in the political, cultural, and economic life of the United States, while often well-intentioned, nevertheless unconsciously bolster the status quo by operating in ideological fields powered by unquestioned assumptions about capitalism, and its relationship to freedom and democracy. This is because, by participating uncritically in the same bourgeois discourse field and partaking of shared symbols and rituals of everyday life, their "citizenship" practices fail to break out of the very ideological—and recidivist—integument that protects them. Under cover of the American flag and expressions of patriotism, they operate from narrow ideological fields.

A similar process is at work in some of the positions taken up by the postmodern avant-garde. Their counter-cultural criticism often masks an aristocratic radicalism underwritten by a liberal affective politics that rarely challenges the capitalist system as a whole. In fact, its rhetorical emphasis on property-related atomistic individualism fortifies the central elements of a liberal bourgeois humanism. Regrettably, such a position remains overly hospitable to existing social relations of production. It provides ballast for the worst elements of chauvinistic nationalism and reigning mechanisms of social hierarchization. Furthermore, it often champions a politics of individual volition peddled by neo-liberal overworlders and their global carpetbagger accomplices. Certain versions of postmodern criticism comport with the type of intellectual high-mindedness that is modulated through the *embourgeoisement* of academic parvenues bent on stirring up the system without fundamentally changing it. What I am trying to emphasize here is lucidly captured by the distinction Ollman makes between a reform that can lead to a revolutionary upsurge or a reform that can prevent one. He is worth quoting at length on this distinction.

> Real reforms involve changes that improve people's lives (always worth doing), while leaving the main problems of society untouched and the relations between classes as is. Every reform also has important contradictory effects on the class struggle. By demonstrating the flexibility of the ruling class and its supposed concern for the well being of ordinary people, reforms make the system appear more legitimate and hence more acceptable in the eyes of the many. On the other hand, the struggle for reform, when successful—the ruling class seldom makes reforms on its own initiative—builds up the self-confidence of the oppressed and leaves them with the organizational and other means needed to intensify the struggle over other matters. Depending on which effect is dominant, a given reform may help to preempt a revolutionary upsurge or serve as a key part of it. (2001, p. 166)

All of this should not lead to gasping, forehead-clutching astonishment, especially when you consider how brazenly the U.S. media has moved to the right, despite the protestations by conservatives that the media is dangerously overpopulated by liberal ideology. Commentators who identify themselves as "left" often display a moderate "right" political ideology, a move that is calibrated to preclude a truly oppositional politics. As a result, Marxist analysis—especially in the very conservative field of education—is viewed as part of the lunatic extreme. Is it any wonder why the rank-and-file teacher doesn't cotton to class analysis and is particularly susceptible to the drive-by theorizing of right-wing talk show hosts? Most average U.S. citizens see through the semantic legerdemain of the slippery pro-capitalist politician (is there any other kind today?). The problem is that there are few credible alternatives to the status quo politics that infect most of the country (Kincheloe, 1998).

István Mészáros (2001) has argued that capitalism's functional division of labor is horizontal and is *potentially* liberating because it partakes of a socially viable universality—the harmonization of the universal development of the productive forces with the all-around abilities and potentialities of freely associated individuals. However, it is the vertical dimension of capitalism and its hierarchical division of labor that constitutes capital's "reproductive horizon" and "command structure" ensuring that living labor is subsumed by dead labor and that capital's productive developments remain containable by the imperative of surplus labor accumulation. This results in the structural/hierarchical subordination of labor to capital. In other words, this creates a permanent structural crisis within capitalism in contrast to what some believe are only periodic, conjunctural crises. Marxists recognize that as powerful as this system has become, it does not exclude the possibility of inworming it, virusing it, and opening it up to various strategies of socialist contestation.

Revolutionary critical educators maintain that neoliberal ideology as it applies to schooling is often given ballast by poststructuralist-postmodernist/deconstructive approaches to educational reform because many of these approaches refuse to challenge the rule of capital and the social relations of production at the basis of the capitalist state. Neoliberalism ("capitalism with the gloves off" or "socialism for the rich") refers to a corporate domination of society that supports state enforcement of the unregulated market, engages in the oppression of nonmarket forces and anti-market policies, guts free public services, eliminates social subsidies, offers limitless concessions to transnational corporations, enthrones a neomercantilist public policy agenda, establishes the market as the patron of educational reform, and permits private interests to control most of social life in the pursuit of profits for the few (i.e., through lowering taxes on the wealthy, scrapping environmental regulations, and dismantling public education and social welfare programs). It is undeniably one of the most dangerous politics that we face today.

Neoliberal free market economics—the purpose of which is to avoid stasis and keep businesses in healthy flux—functions as a type of binding arbitration, legitimizing a host of questionable practices and outcomes: deregulation, unrestricted access to consumer markets, downsizing, outsourcing, flexible arrangements of labor, intensification of competition among transnational corporations, increasing centralization of economic and political power, and finally, widening class polarization.

As Dave Hill and Mike Cole (2001) have noted, neoliberalism advocates a number of pro-capitalist positions: that the state privatize ownership of the means of production, including private sector involvement in welfare, social, educational, and other state services (such as the prison industry); sell labor-power for the purposes of creating a "flexible" and poorly regulated labor market; advance a corporate managerialist model for state services; allow the needs of the economy to dictate the principal aims of school education; suppress the teaching of oppositional and critical thought that would challenge the rule of capital; support a curriculum and pedagogy that produces compliant, pro-capitalist workers; and ensure that schooling and education carry out the ideological and economic reproduction that benefits the ruling class. Of course, the business agenda for schools can be seen in growing public-private partnerships, the burgeoning business sponsorships for schools, business "mentoring," and corporatization of the curriculum (McLaren and Farahmandpur, 1999a, 1999b), and calls for national standards, regular national tests, voucher systems, accountability schemes, financial incentives for high performance schools, and "quality control" of teaching. Schools are encouraged to provide better "value for money" and must seek to learn from the entrepreneurial world of business or risk going into receivership. In short, neoliberal educational policy operates from the premise that education is primarily a sub-sector of the economy.

My approach to understanding the relationship between capitalism and schooling and the struggle for socialism is premised upon Marx's value theory of labor as developed by British Marxist educationalist Glenn Rikowski and others (see Cole, Hill, McLaren, and Rikowski, 2001, Raduntz, 1999; and Allman, 2001). Following Marx, Rikowski notes that labor is the source of all value in capitalist society. Capital relies for its very existence on the generation of surplus value—that is, value over-and-above necessary labor. Surplus value is over-and-above that which is represented by the value of labor-power. In other words, when a worker works beyond what is necessary to ensure his or her survival, then that worker is generating surplus value for the capitalist. Surplus value rests upon our labor-power or our capacity to labor (our skills, knowledges, physical abilities, work skills, and social skills). Labor-power—our capacity to labor—takes the form of "human capital" in capitalist society. It has reality only within the individual agent. Thus, labor-power is a distinctly *human force*. The worker is the active subject of production. He or she is necessary for the creation of surplus-value. He or she provides through living labor the skills, innovation, and cooperation upon which capital relies to enhance surplus value and to ensure its reproduction. Thus, by its very nature, labor-power cannot exist apart from the laborer.

Labor-power is what Rikowski (2000, 2001a, 2001b) describes as the primordial "cell" form of social energy within capital's social universe. Labor-power is a special kind of commodity whose use value possesses the possibility of being transformed into a source of value. It constitutes value in a unique manner as the special living commodity that possesses the capacity to generate more value—that is, surplus value—than is required to maintain its social existence as labor-power. In other words, surplus value is possible because labor-power expends more labor-time than is necessary for its maintenance. It rests upon the socially necessary labor-time required to produce any use value under conditions normal for a given society. This presupposes labor-power as the socially average.

The value of labor-power is represented by the wage. The key point here is that while the labor-power that the worker expends beyond the labor necessary for her maintenance creates no value for her, it does create value for the capitalist: *surplus value*. Education and training are what Rikowski refers to as processes of labor-power production. They are, in Rikowski's view, a sub-species of relative surplus value production (the raising of worker productivity so that necessary labor is reduced) that leads to a relative increase in surplus labor-time and hence surplus value. Human capital development is necessary for capitalist societies to reproduce themselves and to create more surplus value. The core of capitalism can thus be undressed by exploring the contradictory nature of the use value and exchange value of labor-power. Harry Cleaver notes:

> The use-value of labor-power, as Marx shows . . . is its ability to work and to produce value and surplus value. Its exchange-value is the value the working class gets in return for its sale. The use-value and exchange-value of labor-power are clearly contradictory because labor-power can only be exchange-value for the working class (because it has no means of production) and not use-value. Yet the same labor-power does have use-value for the capitalists who buy it and put it to work. (2000, p. 98)

Let's rehearse here what Rikowski and others, like Helen Raduntz (1999), have said, because it is important for the reader to grasp this process. Capital does not move on its own accord, but rather the mental and physical capabilities of workers enable these movements through their expression in labor. Labor-power is the substance of value or the "cell form" of value. The act of laboring enables labor-power (the movements or motion of capital) to be transformed into surplus value. Labor-power ensures the maintenance of the social universe of capital but also constitutes capital's weakest link. Social agents have to transform labor-power into labor and in order for surplus value to occur, workers must be forced and coaxed and coerced to produce more value than covers their subsistence that defines socially necessary labor. Ironically, labor-power has, within capitalist society, generated its own master: capital.

Labor-power enhancement creates more value and surplus value when workers are educated so that they can work harder, faster, and more efficiently. Teachers can disrupt the capitalist class relation by teaching about social justice. Insofar as schooling is premised upon generating the living commodity of labor-power, that fuel for the furnace of living labor upon which the entire social universe of capital depends, it can become a foundation for human resistance. In other words, labor-power can be incorporated only so far. Workers, as the sources of labor-power, can engage in acts of refusing alienating work and delinking labor from capital's value form. As Dyer-Witheford argues: "Capital, a relation of general commodification predicated on the wage relation, needs labor. But labor does not need capital. Labor can dispense with the wage, and with capitalism, and find different ways to organize its own creative energies: it is potentially *autonomous*" (1999, p. 68, italics original).

The labor-capital relation is not a symmetrical one. As Mészáros notes, "That means in the most important respect that while capital's dependency on labor is *absolute*—in that capital is absolutely nothing without labor, which it must permanently exploit—labor's dependency on capital is *relative, historically created and historically surmountable*" (2001, pp. 76–77, italics original). This means that an alternative socialist metabolic order outside the social universe of capital can—and must—be struggled for.

Revolutionary Marxists believe that the best way to transcend the brutal and barbaric limits to human liberation set by capital are through practical mass movements centered around class struggle. But today the clarion cry of class struggle is spurned by the bourgeois left as politically fanciful and reads to many as an advertisement for a B-movie. The liberal left is less interested in class struggle than in making capitalism more "compassionate" to the needs of the poor, as if this were truly possible within the capitalist law of value.

Unhesitatingly embraced by liberals is a concern to bring about social justice. This is certainly to be applauded. However, too often such a struggle is antiseptically cleaved from the project of transforming capitalist social relations. When somebody tries to make the case for class struggle among liberals who fervently believe that capitalism is preferable to socialism or—god forbid—communism, people react as if a bad odor has just entered the room. I am not arguing that people should not have concerns about socialism or communism. After all, much horror has occurred under regimes that called themselves communist. We are arguing that capitalism is not inevitable and that the struggle for socialism is not finished. Perhaps today this struggle is more urgent than at any other time in human history. Socialism is no longer a homogeneous struggle but, as Dunayevskaya (2002) elaborates, must involve coalition-building and international working-class collaboration in struggles against global capitalism. Such a politics is one of difference and inclusion, but a politics whose center of gravity is the struggle for alternatives to capital.

In the face of such a contemporary intensification of global capitalist relations and permanent structural crisis (rather than a shift in the nature of capital itself), we need to develop a critical pedagogy capable of engaging everyday life as lived in its midst. We need, in other words, to face capital down. This means acknowledging global capital's structurally determined inability to share power with the oppressed, its implication in racist, sexist, and homophobic relations, its functional relationship to xenophobic nationalism, and its tendency towards empire. It means acknowledging the educational left's dependency on the very object of its negation: capital. It means struggling to develop a lateral, polycentric concept of anti-capitalist alliances-in-diversity to slow down capitalism's metabolic movement—with the eventual aim of shutting it down completely. It means looking for an educational philosophy that is designed to resist the "capitalization" of subjectivity, a pedagogy that I have called, after Paula Allman, revolutionary critical pedagogy.

Classroom reality is not seamless but agonistic, conflictual, antinomic, and paradoxical. One rule of thumb that accompanies me into every classroom is to respect the wide variety of experiences that students bring with them into the classroom, experiences often linked to widely divergent backgrounds, and to interactions with others that are gendered, shaped by social class, and racialized. What makes experiences especially important is not how generically interesting they are, or how awe-inspiring they happen to be—or traumatic, for that matter—but how people interpret their experiences and grapple with their complex meanings. There are many languages through which human beings can come to better understand and transform their experiences, but critical pedagogy, as I see it, must commit itself to the language of citical theory and Marxist analysis.

There are many schools of Marxist thought, and many languages of Marxist theory, so this is not as easy a challenge as it might first appear. In my own approach to critical pedagogy, students are challenged to read their experiences against Marxist-humanist theories of alienation and exploitation and to consider Marxist-humanist alternatives to capitalism. I am not saying other theoretical languages should be avoided, which would be absurd. Surely there are many other critical languages that are worthwhile and important. I am saying that Marxist theory should play a central role in critical pedagogy. Because *Life in Schools* was written before I came to fully embrace a Marxist-humanist perspective, I would advise students to read my more recent books if they find themselves motivated to deepen their grasp of critical pedagogy after reading *Life in Schools*. Does this admission make *Life in Schools* hopelessly outdated? Far from it. While it endorses a wide range of radical perspectives rather than specifically focussing on Marxist analysis, it covers a lot of ground that I believe will be indispensable for helping students engage the crucial kinds of issues addressed above.

My establishing connections between Marxist concepts and personal or collective experience is no substitute for readers making those connections for themselves. Students need to be provided with ways of analyzing their own histories and the cultural politics in which they are embedded from the vantage point of the forces, relations, and practices that mediate them. Again, these include economic structures, social relations of production, cultural representations, social formations, and institutional arrangements.

How do these systems of mediation advance or foreshorten human capacities? How do they influence forms of social organization? How do they further the radicalization of subjectivity and produce critical consciousness? After all, these systems of mediation are not self-evident or transparent. They appear to us in disguised patterns and relations that function to "pull the strings" of our family relationships, our peer group relations, our relationship to the commercial media, our teachers, our community values, etc. These systems, the machinations exercised by them, the interests that they serve, and the hierarchies that they privilege don't work in a mechanical fashion but produce us "dialectically." We need to recognize this process of dialectical fashioning and be equipped to interrogate its complex functioning (see Ollman, 1998b). Students and teachers both need to analyze their experiences and to move beyond the relativism of "holding an opinion" by understanding how such opinions and viewpoints are situated historically in larger belief systems and worldviews. Such viewpoints should be challenged for their coherence, and tested against other viewpoints in ways that help students deepen their dialectical understanding of everyday life both inside and outside the classroom. As Marx says, the educators themselves need to be educated. This means taking seriously Marx's conviction that the people can be subjects of history, creating a new society.

Revolutionary Critical Pedagogy[1]

What I would like to do in the remainder of this discussion is to reflect upon concrete pedagogical practice, with the understanding that I will not provide a blueprint for doing critical pedagogy (which goes against the entire principle of critical pedagogy) but rather provide some "talking points" for approaching the nuts and bolts of critical praxis. What should be obvious here is that revolutionary pedagogy makes no claim to political neutrality. Raya Dunayevskaya makes a good point when she writes that "distinct from the alleged neutrality claimed by non-Marxist interpretations of capitalism, Marxists openly state that their interpretations lead to a transformation of existing society, holding that their objectivity, far from excluding subjectivity, is proven by the subject, i.e., the proletariat, becoming the 'gravedigger of capitalism' because that is both force and reason of the opposite to capitalist exploitation" (1978, p. 355).

For instance, in the recent United Nations Special Session on Children, the United States has aligned itself against the European Union, the British Commonwealth, Scandinavia, and much of Africa, and has joined forces with Sudan, Libya, Iran, and Pakistan in its call for "traditional values." The United States has taken a position against raising the minimum age for recruiting soldiers to 18, and against sex education. The U.S. wants to limit information on reproductive health, to teach abstinence as the sole form of preventing premarital pregnancy, and generally to move away from the conditions set forth in the Convention on the Rights of the Child. The current attempt by the United States to roll back earlier international agreements on minors' rights and access to health education and services is one that needs to be engaged and debated among teachers. Why? Because this is a part of the "macrostructure" that impacts issues of educational policy, curriculum, and accountability.

Critical pedagogy eschews any approach to pedagogy that would reduce it to the teaching of narrow thinking-skills in isolation from the contentious debates and contexts in which such skills are employed. Critical pedagogy has been sterilized, vulgarized, and domesticated and purged of its theoretical depth and insight (see McLaren, 1998b). I operate from the premise that all thoughts, acts, and relations are political in the ideological sense. Politics is omnipresent: all categories and criteriologies, classifications and architectonics, bifurcations and invocations, insights and intoxications are political. I reject those who admonish: "If everything is political, then nothing is political." The question raised by this approach to the relationship between the formation of consciousness and capitalism is this: If capitalism continues to expand uncontested by stealthily hiding its practices of exploitation in the shadow of the crisis of world capitalism, and if it proceeds, as it has always done, to harness working-class subjectivity to the yolk of capitalist development, then how is it possible to put into pedagogical practice a critical subjectivity capable of contesting this relationship, and, further, to develop forms of subjectivity outside the social factory of capital? Teachers can purchase any number of educational kits or bags of tricks from educational freemarketeers and corporate investors committed to the "businessification" and privatization of education. But reducing teaching to a tool box of prepackaged lessons does little to bring into dialectical relief the underlying logic of capitalist social life grounded in the internal relations or dialectical contradictions inherent in the labor-capital relation.

We are not talking here just about opening up discussions in classrooms to a wide array of diverse and conflicting perspectives (although the more perspectives the better). You can have all kinds of discussions in classrooms without coming a flea-hop closer to genuine dialogue. How can you have a genuine dialogue when the discourse of socialism is systematically excluded? It is crucial not to mistake "turn-taking" for genuine dialogue, or to believe that getting all the opposing positions out on the table is the same thing as being able to make a coherent argument that supports your position, while at the same time considering other positions. You can't simply have a "pick-and-mix" approach, but need to genuinely hear the opposing positions, and consider them in light of their coherence, their contradictions or lack thereof, and their ability to hold up to rational challenge. Ideological differences do not resolve themselves when placed in the correct organizational framework. Conceptual problems can't be sorted out with correct classroom arrangements. In addition to providing a welcoming classroom environment where students can discuss their life experiences, we should give them an opportunity to acquire a dialectical consideration of social life.

Here a Marxist dialectical approach is crucial. I don't believe that Marxist dialectics is a form of Hegelian mysticism. Nor do I believe that Marxist dialectics is only useful for understanding the bourgeois political science of the nineteenth century. Whereas Hegel viewed the idea as the *demiurgos* of the real world and the real world as an illusion, Marx saw the ideal as the material world as reflected in the human mind and transformed into forms of thought. Hence, Marx regarded dialectics as the self-movement of the objective world; in other words, he recognized the rational kernel within the mystical shell of the Hegelian dialectic. My approach to critical pedagogy is to try to understand in a dialectical fashion how students and teachers have become formed by capitalist social relations—that is, by capital as a social form (when market imperatives set the terms of social reproduction). How can the very fundamentals of existence be subjected to the requirements of profit? To my mind, an historical materialist approach is essential in making these connections.

Not everyone who benefits from participating in a critique of the many and often baleful contradictions of capitalism can be found in the sociology of education or critical pedagogy seminar room. But for those of us who have the opportunity to spend time there in a dynamic, engaging, and productive fashion, there are methodological concerns that should be addressed. What teachers learn in their academic programs should be shared with their own students. What teachers learn about society, culture, the politics of curricula, the relationship between media formations and ideological configurations, the relationship between theory and practice, and so forth can be employed in lessons in their own classrooms, with necessary adjustments for the various grade levels, and other conditions.

This stipulates that teachers need to acquire some kind of critical education themselves, something not always available—or only offered in a limited sense—in graduate programs in education. Broadly speaking, this requires that they learn enduringly from works of critical social theorists to analyze the objective conditions that are responsible for the creation of everyday life in all of its myriad social manifestations. For instance, teachers could be challenged productively by the following questions: How is value produced in capitalist societies? What is the relationship between value and labor? What is the role of labor-power (human labor, living labor) in the current emphasis on educational standards, monetary rewards for successful schools, the current stress on accountability, and the push towards a national curriculum? Why do social classes exist? What forces, relations, and determinations have come together to produce them? What does this have to say about living in a meritocracy? How are racial and gender formations linked to the production of social classes? How does the production of meaning through media apparatuses establish and sustain relations of domination? What is the relationship between symbolic forms and rituals of everyday life, and the production of value within capitalist society? While social

classes constitute a primary axis of inequality, what other forms of inequality and exploitation exist, such as relations between nation states and blocs of nation states?
How do different social classes represent themselves to themselves through various
forms of symbolic representation? How do they represent their interests and their
aims and aspirations to themselves as well as to other social groups? How are these
symbolic forms—these modalities of communication and means of representation—
themselves constitutive of social life and involved in helping to sustain and reproduce
social relations produced by the accumulation of surplus value within capitalism?

While it is important to make available to teachers methodological approaches
such as social-historical analysis that, upon employing them in a rigorous manner,
will help teachers to reconstruct the social and historical conditions surrounding the
production, circulation, and reception of symbolic forms (see Thompson, 1990), it is
also crucial that teachers engage in the kind of historical materialist analysis developed within the Marxist tradition so that they can see how the production of consciousness works gear-in-gear with capitalist social relations. Symbolic formations
need to be analyzed in their spatio-temporal settings, within certain fields of interaction, and in the context of social institutions and structures so that teachers have a
greater sense of how meanings are inscribed, encoded, decoded, transmitted, de-
ployed, circulated, and received in the arena of everyday social relations.

In addition to this type of discourse analysis, it is crucial that teachers be able to
articulate their site of self-discovery by uncovering the network of relations that situates themselves in the context of class confrontation, alienated labor, and exploitation
as the private appropriation of surplus value. And while it remains important to acknowledge that bourgeois practices do have some progressive aspects to them, we
nevertheless need to recognize the far-flung and problematic nature of the United
States' corporate reach across the hemispheres. As a mode of resistance, I am inspired
by the principle of internationalism. Marx and Engels enunciated such a principle
when they wrote about how a people that oppresses other peoples cannot itself be
free. It should be remembered here that Marxism is a guide to action, not a set of
metaphysical dogmas; more specifically it is a guide for creating the conditions of possibility for revolutionary action where collective struggle becomes a means for discov-
ering new apertures through which insights can be generated, theories constructed,
and strategies mobilized for the purpose of popular emancipation and empowerment.

Glenn Rikowski has pointed out that many educationalists who analyze social
class focus too narrowly on issues of stratification and social inequality and in the process literally abandon the notion of working-class struggle. I am using the term "class
struggle" after Rikowski (2001b), as a social relation between labor and capital. It is
one of the phenomena integral to the existence of capitalist society, "an element of
the constitution of a world struggle" (2001b, p. 1) that exists everywhere in capitalist
society. Education is a key process in "the generation of the capital relation." Education "links the chains that bind our souls to capital." It is one of the ropes comprising
the ring in which the combat between labor and capital takes place, a fight that uti-
lizes fists of fury, a clash that powers contemporary history: "the class struggle"
(2001b, p. 2). Schools therefore act as vital supports for, and developers of, the class
relation, "the violent capital-labor relation that is at the core of capitalist society and
development" (2001b, p. 19). As De Angelis remarks:

Education is crucial for capital if it wants to rely on a strategy of continuous displacement of the class composition. An educated worker in today's paradigm is a worker who is able to adapt—who is able to take over one job one day and another job the next day—who is engaged in life-long learning as a continuous process, which means updating their skills to suit the market. That is essential to maintain social cohesion in a context in which there is continuous displacement of the class composition of what kind of work is done. (2000, p. 10)

I share Glenn Rikowski's perspective that the class relation *is* the capital-labor relation that forms the "violent dialectic" that generates all value. Class struggle is born out of the antagonistic relation between capital and labor. In fact, Rikowski argues that class struggle occurs *intersubjectively* as well as collectively as a clash of contradictory forces and drives within the social totality. Rikowski notes that

the class relation *runs through our personhood*. It is internal to us; we *are* labor, and we *are* capital. We are social beings incorporating antithetical social drives and forces. This fact sets off contradictions within our lives, and their solution can only come from the disintegration of ourselves as both capital and labor and our emergence as a new, non-capitalised life-form. (2001b, p. 20)

This split within capital-labor itself is founded on the issue of whether labor produces value directly or labor-power.

In sum, class struggle has to be linked to the relation internal to all labor, the split or rift within labor as a form of social existence within capitalist society. Class struggle is implicated in the tragic truism that labor creates its own opposite (capital) that comes to dominate it. The issue of class struggle needs to be approached from the perspective of *a critique of capital and its value form of labor*. As Ebert argues: "*Globalization begins with the commodification of labor-power itself*—when human labor becomes a commodity like all other commodities and is exchanged for wages. The commodification of labor is the condition of possibility for 'profit'" (2001, 397, italics original).

Recognizing the "class character" of education in capitalist schooling, and advocating a "socialist reorganization of capitalist society" (Krupskaya, 1985) are two fundamental principles of a revolutionary critical pedagogy. Following Marx (1973), I would argue that it is imperative that teachers recognize the contradictions of "free" and "universal" education in bourgeois society and question how education can be "equal" for all social classes. Education can never be "free" or "equal" as long as there exist social classes. I believe that the education and instruction of working-class students must be linked to productive labor and also to social production. Thus, I envision a revolutionary critical pedagogy that pivots around a number of key linkages: the production of critical knowledge and productive work; the organization and management of critical knowledge and the organization and management of production; and the utilization of critical knowledge for productive consumption (Krupskaya, 1985).[2]

Furthermore, the severing of workers from the products of their labor under the capitalist mode of production *mirrors in a number of basic instances the separation of the production and consumption of knowledge among students*. For instance, in public schools today, theoretical knowledge is seldom linked to labor practices. Our vision of a revolutionary critical pedagogy, in contrast, consists of teaching students how knowledge is related historically, culturally, and institutionally to the process of production and consumption.

Revolutionary critical pedagogy, in my view, should focus on problematizing the production of value through the work experience. This should include, but not be limited to, *four relations* that lie at the center of the work experience in U.S. society. Marx described these four relations as constituting what he termed "alienation." These are summarized by Ollman as follows:

> 1) the relation between the individual and his/her productive activity, in which others determine how it is done, under what conditions, at what speed, and for what wage or salary, and even if and when it is to begin and end; 2) the relation between the individual and the product of that activity, in which others control and use the product for their own purposes (making something does not confer any right to use what one has made); 3) the relation between the individual and other people, particularly, with those who control both one's productive activity and its products, where each side pursues their own interests without considering the effects of their own actions on the other (mutual indifference and competition become the characteristic forms of human interaction); and 4) the relation between the individual and the species, or with what it means to be a human being. (2001, p. 111)

Capitalist production and consumption constitutes a totality of interconnected social relations that can be divided into productive and unproductive consumption. While productive consumption satisfies the physical, spiritual, and social needs of individuals, unproductive consumption (its antithesis) appropriates and transforms the surplus value of labor into capital. Thus, it is imperative that teachers and students question how knowledge is produced and ask the following: Who produces it? How is it appropriated? Who consumes it? How is it consumed? Revolutionary critical pedagogy gives analytical priority to the struggle between labor and capital, to the relationship between the forces of production and the means of production, and to the relationship between nature and society.

Revolutionary praxis is brought about by approaching Marxism not as an inert body of ideas for contemplation but as a motive force for remaking society, not as some form of autotelic or noumenal freedom arrived at by transcending contingent interests and imparting an eternal value, but rather as a means of giving material force to ideas through collective revolutionary action both in and on the world. Theory and practice symmetrically evoke the two contrasting tensions between labor and capital. Praxis, on the other hand, is theory in motion, the dialectic between matter and consciousness, between social being and subjectivity. I am using revolutionary praxis as a term that refers to "the unity of theory and practice of class struggle" (San Juan, 1995, p. 67). As such, it becomes "the locus of synthesizing form and content, thought and action" (1995, p. 67).

The Retreat of Democracy

We inhabit a perilous course in history in which democracy is in retreat. Many of the gains made during previous decades in social and educational reform have been abandoned or at the very least have demonstrably waned. Not only have we sadly

Moments in America

Every 35 seconds an infant is born into poverty.

Every 2 minutes an infant is born to a mother who received late or no prenatal care.

Every 2 minutes an infant is born at low birthweight (less than 5 pounds, 8 ounces).

Every 11 minutes an infant is born at very low birthweight (less than 3 pounds, 8 ounces).

Every 14 minutes an infant dies in the first year of life.

Every 31 seconds an infant is born to an unmarried mother.

Every 55 seconds an infant is born to a mother who is not a high school graduate.

Every 21 seconds a 15- to 19-year-old woman becomes sexually active for the first time.

Every 32 seconds a 15- to 19-year-old woman becomes pregnant.

Every 64 seconds an infant is born to a teenage mother.

Every 5 minutes an infant is born to a teenage mother who already had a child.

Every 74 seconds a 15- to 19-year-old woman has an abortion.

Every 14 hours a child younger than 5 is murdered.

Every 5 hours a 15- to 19-year-old is murdered.

Every 2 hours a 20- to 24-year-old is murdered.

Every 2 seconds of the school day a public school student is suspended.

Every 4 seconds of the school day a public school student is corporally punished.

Every 10 seconds of the school day a student drops out of school.

Source: Children's Defense Fund, *The State of America's Children 1991*, Washington, D.C., p. 5.

witnessed the delegitimization of the egalitarian impulses of the last two decades, but we have seen an inordinate stress placed on career motivation and school/business partnerships in efforts to link youth to the corporate imperatives of the international marketplace.

In this age of historical amnesia, endlessly deferred hope, and a retreat from civil rights, the concepts of social struggle and civic courage have congealed around politically accommodating forms of liberal humanism and an ideological shift toward the conservative New Right and a neo-liberal political agenda. As the pillars of our democratic temple wobble in current reactionary winds, we can only glimpse through the cracks of history an uncertain future.

The civil rights marches in Selma, Alabama, and other parts of the South, and the fight for day-care programs and community schools, now seem consigned to a museum of memories, historical artifacts of a strange and uncomfortable past. Little has been accomplished beyond the palliative to build upon the democratization of our schools and to ensure the welfare of our nation's youth. Freedom and equality have become dust-covered relics in history's warehouse. Since the aborted cultural revolution of the 1960s, we seem more like curators of old dreams, archivists of history who arrange the past in glass-enclosed dioramas. We have turned into disembodied repositories of reformist visions, shelved in moments of cynical despair, rather than active agents of new communities of risk and resistance.

It is symptomatic of the present crisis that a new public philosophy has emerged along with the rise of the new Christian Right, a philosophy whose moral charter celebrates the virtues of the nuclear family, defends at all costs America's God-fearing cultural tradition, and interprets world events according to a literal reading of the Bible; this burgeoning revival of "born again" Christianity—especially the televangelistic variety—represents a jingoism of the spirit whose lay equivalents include the hyper-patriotism of "resurgent America," the importance of the patriarchal family as the Promethean embodiment of a righteous lifestyle, the militia mentality of Jeffersonian Communitarianism, the prevailing rhetoric about consensus enemies such as Iraq and Cuba (and Bush's new "axis of evil"), and the moral terrorism of shuttle diplomacy. The ideological conservatism of the New Christian Right enshrines a masqueraded version of the Christian faith, a parody of its originating source, a form of tyrannical surrogacy whose dogmatic intolerance of feminists, gays, radicals, and non-Christians has militantly invaded what could ideally be a considerate, compassionate, and loving community of faith.

The ideological shift that characterizes schooling in the last fifteen years has hardly been subtle. We need only witness attempts in the mid-1980s by New Right reformists to construct an unproblematic view of history in which schools are called upon to assume their roles as the gatekeepers of society by passing on the great tradition of old-fashioned "republican virtues" embodied, for example, in books such as the McGuffey readers and in the old Latin classics curriculum. In fact, the image of the public school put forward by exponents of the New Right approximates a mixture of the fundamentalist Sunday school, company store, and "old West" museum. The dominating logic of this agenda is bolstered by arguments put forward by individuals such as Gary L. Bauer, former Undersecretary of Education under George Bush the elder, who blames America's "youthful fling with self-indulgence" during the 1960s and 1970s for the current malaise in American Society. This argument is less than convincing when promulgated by representatives of a government that was sabotaging governments in Central America, trading in arms with Iran, and eroding the call for civic courage and critical citizenship in our public schools.

Today's students have inherited an age in which liberty and democracy are in retreat. (The fact that George W. Bush's administration has hired or appointed many of his father's Iran/contra schemers and lawbreakers—Elliott Abrams, John

Poindexter, Otto Reich, John Negroponte—is a sad testament to the pursuit of free-dom and democracy.) Ironically, existing criticisms of schooling and the agenda for educational reform themselves constitute part of this retreat. On the one hand, neoconservatives have defined the school as an adjunct of the labor market, and subset of the economy, couching their analysis in the technocratic language of human capital theory. On the other hand, liberals have provided a more comprehensive critique of schooling, but so far have been incapable of addressing the major problems that schools face within a race-, class-, and gender-divided society. The resulting prescriptions for school reform are severely restricted to forms of bourgeois reformism disembarrassed of a concerted critique of capitalism.

In the present rush toward accountability schemes, corporate management pedagogies, and state-mandated curricula, an ominous silence exists regarding the ways in which new attempts to streamline teaching represent an attack on both the democratic possibilities of schooling and the very conditions that make critical teaching possible.

Framed in the language of hypernationalism and neo-liberal economics, the current conservative attack on schools represents, in large part, a truncation of the democratic vision. Underlying the new reform proposals set forth by the recent coalition of conservatives and liberals is an attack on schools for producing a wide-ranging series of national crises, ranging in scope from the growing trade deficit to the breakdown of family morality. Not only does such an attack misconstrue the responsibility schools have for wider economic and social problems, but it is characteristic of a dangerous ideological shift that has been taking place regarding the role that schools should play in relation to the wider society.

At the heart of the ideological shift is an attempt to define academic success almost exclusively in terms of capital accumulation and the logic of the marketplace. The authors of the "blue ribbon" committee reports have cast their recommendations in a language that reflects the resurgence of chauvinistic patriotism and have reformulated their goals along elitist lines. In doing so, they have attempted to eliminate a social concern for nurturing a critical and committed citizenry. They have passively surrendered educational reform to a fetishism of procedure rather than demonstrating a concern with emancipatory social goals. Furthermore, the increasing adoption of management-type pedagogies has resulted in policy proposals that promote the deskilling of teachers and the creation of a technocratic rationality in which planning and conception are removed from implementation, and the dominant model of the teacher becomes that of the technician or white-collar clerk. At the same time, the model of the school has been transformed, in Giroux's terms, into that of the "company store." In general, the new efficiency-smart and conservative-minded discourse encourages schools to define themselves essentially as service institutions charged with the task of providing students with the requisite labor-power capacities to enable them to find a place within the corporate hierarchy.

This New Right ideology of school reform provides only a sterile and truncated range of discourses and conceptions that undermines what it means to be a critical citizen. Under the logic of the reforms, students are taught to link citizenship to the profit imperative and to the norms of market relations and brokerage politics wherein the vested interests of the individual, the corporation, or one's country are always valued over the collective interests of humanity to live in a world unburdened by scarcity. Rarely is the concept of profit maximization considered immoral, even when it is discovered to be at the expense of the poor or minority groups, or, further afield, at the expense of the social and educational development of Central American and Third World populations. Absent from this discourse is any recognition of the importance of viewing schools as sites for social transformation and emancipation, as places where students are educated not only to be critical thinkers, but also to view the world as a place where their actions might make a difference.

Social problems in the United States weigh most heavily on minority groups, women, and the poor, but do not end there. Middle-class, suburban youth are also caught in a dilemma: They are children of the baby boom coming of age in a stagnating economy. Brought up in a televised world of self-interest and greed based on the principle that commodities buy happiness, and where schools are a full partner in the sales pitch, these young people experience a dilemma cogently expressed by Ralph Larkin:

> (Middle-class) students experience a two-fold alienation: from adult society wherein lies the power, and from each other as invidious competition and mobility undercut authenticity and understanding of each other. They are isolated as a class and as monadic individuals. Most lives are characterized by lack of depth: in their family ties, friendships, skills, and commitment to any organizations. They live at the surface, fearful yet desirous of what might happen should they "bust out" of their not quite Edenic existence ... [they] are terrorized by their fears. Their impotence and timidity generates self-hate and despair. . . . (1979, p. 210)

In other words, these students do not recognize their own self-repression and suppression by the dominant capitalist society, and in our vitiated learning environments they are not provided with the requisite theoretical constructs to help them understand why they feel as badly as they do. Because teachers lack a critical pedagogy, these students are not provided with the ability to think critically, a skill that would enable them to better understand why their lives have been reduced to feelings of meaninglessness, randomness, and alienation and why the capitalist class tries to accommodate them to the paucity of their lives. Consequently the culture continues to run amuck, degrading the process of labor, encouraging volatile commodity consumption, and maintaining the market mechanism as the basis for the distribution of wealth and status, all of which work to impoverish the psychic life of our youth and contribute to the degradation of everyday life.

The Five Faces of Oppression

As educators and cultural workers, we need to recognize the various manifestations of oppression as they affect the lives of millions of North Americans. Iris Marion Young (1992) offers a detailed typology of oppression that is worth summarizing. She argues, rightly in my view, that the meaning of oppression has shifted from the practice of colonial domination and conquest. That is, it can no longer be simply thought to be an evil perpetuated by others, as the exercise of tyranny by a ruling group. Young has substantially redefined the term to designate "the everyday practices of a well-intentioned liberal society" and "systemic and structural phenomena that are not necessarily the result of the intentions of a tyrant." In other words, "oppressions are systematically reproduced in major economic, political, and cultural institutions" and are part of the basic fabric of social life. In Young's view, oppression can exist even in the absence of overt discrimination, the latter term referring to an individualist concept that links discrimination to an identifiable agent. Oppression is related to "unconscious assumptions and reactions of well-meaning people in ordinary interactions, media and cultural stereotypes, and structural features of bureaucratic hierarchy and market mechanisms, in short, the normal ongoing processes of everyday life." Although I would situate oppression more centrally than Young does in the social relations of capitalist production, her analysis repays close consideration.

Oppression disempowers groups—and here Young warns us not to think of groups simply as aggregates in which group membership is linked to a simple set of attributes. Rather, group membership means that one finds oneself as a member of a group in the sense that one's identity "is defined in relation to how others identify him or her, and they do so in terms of groups that always already have specific attributes, stereotypes, and norms associated with them, in reference to which a person's identity will be formed." The oppression of a group does not mean that there is a correlating oppressor group, which is not to suggest that individual persons do not intentionally harm others.

Young explicates what she refers to as "five faces of oppression" that affect groups such as women, blacks, Chicanos, Puerto Ricans, most Spanish-speaking Americans, Native Americans, Jews, lesbians, gay men, Arabs, Asians, old people, working-class people, poor people, and physically or mentally disabled people.

Exploitation

Exploitation, notes Young, is a form of domination in which the labor of working-class groups is transferred to benefit the wealthy, reproducing and causing class division and relations of inequality. For instance, women are exploited as wage workers and also in the sphere of domestic labors; additionally, women suffer forms of gender exploitation in the workplace and within the structure of patriarchy. Race, as well as class and gender, is also a structure of oppression. Blacks and Latinos are oppressed by capitalist superexploitation due to the segmented labor market in which skilled, high-paying, and unionized jobs are reserved primarily for whites.

Marginalization

Marginalization refers to groups who constitute the growing underclass of people who suffer severe material deprivation and are confined to lives of unemployment and "expelled from useful participation in social life." Often marginalized groups are racially marked, and this includes groups both in Third World and in Western capitalist countries—"blacks or Indians in Latin America, blacks, East Indians, Eastern Europeans or North Africans in Europe." Marginalized people are often positioned by the dominant culture in relations of dependency where they are excluded from equal citizenship rights. Even if they are materially comfortable, these groups may be oppressed on the basis of their marginal status, for instance, senior citizens who suffer from feelings of uselessness, boredom, and lack of self-worth.

Powerlessness

Powerlessness deals with structures of social division, such as social status. More specifically, powerlessness "describes the lives of people who have little or no work autonomy, exercise little creativity or judgement in their work, have no technical expertise or authority, express themselves awkwardly, especially in public or bureaucratic settings, and do not command respect." Young here refers to the cultures of professionals and nonprofessionals, which, of course, are linked to the division between mental and manual labor. She specifically refers to the norms of respectability in our society and the ways in which such norms privilege "professional" dress, speech, tastes, and demeanor—and the way this privilege appears in the dynamics of racism and sexism.

Cultural Imperialism

Cultural imperialism, according to Young, refers to "the universalization of one group's experience and culture and its establishment as the norm." The dominant cultural group exercises its power by bringing other groups under the measure of its domination. Consequently, the dominant groups construct the differences of subordinate groups as lack and negation in relation to their privileging norms. For instance, "the difference of women from men, Native Americans or Africans from Europeans, Jews from Christians, homosexuals from heterosexuals, or workers from professionals becomes reconstructed as deviance and inferiority." Victims of cultural imperialism live their oppression by viewing themselves from the perspective of the way others view them: a phenomenon known as "double consciousness." Young writes:

> The dominant culture's stereotyped, marked, and inferiorized images of the group must be internalized by group members at least to the degree that they are forced to react to behaviors of others that express or are influenced by those images. . . . This consciousness is double because the oppressed subject refuses to coincide with these devalued, objectified, stereotyped visions of herself or himself. The subject desires recognition as human, capable of activity, full of hope and possibility, but receives from the dominant culture only the judgement that he or she is different, marked, or inferior. (p. 192)

Cultural imperialism, notes Young, is the paradoxical experience of being invisible while simultaneously being positioned as different. It is the process of being defined by both dominant and subordinate cultures.

Violence

Oppression involves the fear of systematic and legitimized violence. For instance, systematic violence is directed at members of particular groups simply because members belong to those specific groups. Young notes that in U.S. society women, blacks, Asians, Arabs, gay men, and lesbians live under threats of xenophobic, random, and unprovoked attacks, as do Jews, Puerto Ricans, Chicanos, and other Spanish-speaking Americans who inhabit certain regions. This form of violence is also legitimate because most white people find it a common occurrence and do little to punish the offenders. In my view, this could clearly be seen in the Rodney King beating by the Los Angeles police in 1992.

Finally, I would like to draw attention to a pressing concern of Americans both within and outside the educational system: illiteracy. In his book *Illiterate America*, Jonathan Kozol (1985) presents us with one of the most comprehensive assessments of this crippling condition:

> Twenty-five million American adults cannot read the poison warnings on a can of pesticide, a letter from their child's teacher, or the front page of a daily paper. An additional 35 million read only at a level which is less than equal to the full survival needs of our society. Together, these 60 million people represent more than one third of the entire adult population. The largest numbers of illiterate adults are white, native-born Americans. In proportion to population, however, the figures are higher for blacks and Hispanics than for whites. Sixteen percent of white adults, 44 percent of blacks, and 56 percent of Hispanic citizens are functional or marginal illiterates. Figures for the younger generation of black adults are increasing. Forty-seven percent of all black seventeen-year-olds are functionally illiterate. That figure is expected to climb by 1990.
>
> Fifteen percent of recent graduates of urban high schools read less than sixth grade level. One million teenage children between twelve and seventeen cannot read above the third grade level. Eighty-five percent of juveniles who come before the courts are functionally illiterate. Of 8 million unemployed adults, 4 to 6 million lack the skills to be retrained for high tech jobs. The United States ranks forty-ninth among 158 member nations of the U.N. in its literacy level. (pp. 4–5)

For U.S. citizens besieged by the relentless logic of consumerism and privatization, it is no wonder that illiteracy thrives as a means of resisting, escaping, or refusing to be part of the cultural nightmare. What is needed to meet the crisis of literacy is a critical literacy that frames reading and writing in terms of moral and political decision making. Literacy in this view is not linked to learning to read advertisements and becoming better consumers, or escaping into the pages of romance novels or spy thrillers; critical literacy links language competency to acquiring analytical skills that empower individuals to challenge the status quo.

It is difficult to perceive the full significance of the social crisis I have tried to portray in the preceding pages, for it demonstrates that history does not represent some linear progressive continuum headed toward equality and the steady enrichment and enhancement of human life; it is not a teleological unfolding of some metaphysical plan, the "essence" of which is material, spiritual, moral, or ethical progress. It is not the presence of linear reason in linear time but is, in fact, contingent upon particular regimes of truth operating in a class-divided society. As a society, we are caught between an imminent sense of destruction and an inability to acknowledge it.

The grim reality of the present situation is that the United States continues to be disfigured by class exploitation and sexual and racial inequality. Shadowed by the logic of nihilism, violence has become the purifying aesthetic to growing right-wing militant factions who wish to purge North America of blacks, Asians, Arabs, and Jews. Such xenophobia is but one of the consequences of a deteriorating society based on the accumulation of surplus value from its exploited workers, a society that has allowed a pathological and destructive structuring of social relations to occur. These relations have been heightened in recent years by the resurgence of fundamentalist evangelism and the revitalization trends of the New Right. In the words of Richard Sennet, "Lacking in America is any sense that the nation is a collectivity of difference, that the human community might indeed be enriched by the experience of the Other, of that which cannot be rendered transparent" (1987, p. 44).

It has long been known that poverty (linked to the division of labor via the extraction of surplus value from workers by capitalists) is a major factor in determining the success of students at school. It is perhaps the greatest predictor of academic success in this country, which makes it disturbing to learn that in 1988, only 25 percent of three- and four-year-olds with family incomes of less than $10,000 a year were enrolled in a preschool program. Yet 56 percent of those with family incomes of $35,000 or more were enrolled. More than one-third of all children in families headed by someone younger than thirty are living in poverty. The Bush administration suppressed a 1989 White House Task Force report on infant mortality that reported that 10,000 of the 40,000 infant deaths in 1988 in the U.S. could have been averted and 10,000 of those 40,000 left disabled could have been spared by applying current knowledge. Of course, the mortality rate of black infants was more than double that of white infants in 1988. By February 1990, 2000 or more cases of AIDS had been diagnosed in children younger than 13 years of age, while it is expected that there is double that amount of HIV-infected children younger than 13 years.

It is estimated that one in seven teens currently has a sexually transmitted disease. In the age group of 15 to 19, the average gonorrhea rate in black males is about fifteen times that of their white counterparts, while the rate for black females of that age is about ten times the white rate.

Suicide—not homicide—is the second leading cause of death among young white males aged 15 to 24. Add to this the fact that 2.4 million children were abused or neglected in 1989.

Of course, the answer to this epidemic of neglect is not to blame the victims— heaping abuse on the disadvantaged in our society and blaming them for not being able to create better conditions for their children. White people often look condescendingly toward people of color who find it difficult to earn a living and provide decent conditions for their children in a white supremacist capitalist democracy. In fact, a recent report in *Extra!* (1992) notes that white people begin leaving a neighborhood when the percentage of African Americans reaches about 8 percent—even when the African Americans are from the same socioeconomic class. The unemployment rate for black workers in 1990 was 176 percent greater than that of white workers.

Although I think it is fair to say that people of color—especially African Americans and Latinos—are living in a state of siege in this country, I am not suggesting that white readers paralyze themselves with self-hatred because of this state of affairs. However, I do ask that they begin to unlearn their white privilege and as teachers begin to address the urgent social issues that face the country.

One recent social issue whose urgency cannot be denied nor should be ignored is the Los Angeles uprising of May 1992. The killing and looting and burning of buildings that took place during this event have received much media attention, most of it directed at the gang involvement and random violence that took place after the Rodney King verdict. When the Los Angeles police officers who were videotaped beating motorist Rodney King were initially acquitted by an all-white jury, parts of Los Angeles erupted into the worst urban violence since the Watts rebellion in the 1960s. The media and "media analysts" largely attributed the blame to black and Latino street gangs who used the verdict to take advantage of the tension generated in the black community and eventually to exploit it through acts of arson and looting.

Yet this "analysis" largely ignored the context surrounding the uprising, which deals with police racism and the plight of black and Latino people across the United States. As Mike Davis notes, the Los Angeles uprising was, in part, a result of the systematic harassment and repression of black youth for decades (Katz and Smith, 1992). The media reports generally ignored the shooting of fifteen-year-old Latasha Harlin, who was shot from behind by a Korean shopkeeper after an argument over an orange juice. Latasha Harlin's head was blown off and the shopkeeper was fined $500 by a white judge and sentenced to 400 hours of community service. Just prior to this incident, a black postman was sentenced to six months in jail for shooting a dog.

As Davis points out, the Los Angeles uprising was truly multiethnic and involved African Americans, Mexican immigrants, and Central Americans, and as many Latinos as African Americans were killed while looting by the police and National Guard. The rebellion consisted of homogeneously younger youths than in the Watts uprising and also included middle-class blacks since the L.A.P.D. policies have criminalized black youth, regardless of their socioeconomic status. This oppression by the police helped to make gang membership a more natural form of resistance. The Crips and the Bloods and the Florentia gang—the biggest Mexican gang of the East Side—are now talking about the unity of all the oppressed. But as Davis also notes, the real problem is the racism and the erosion of minimum-wage jobs through declining demand and business relocation to Mexico.

Los Angeles has been turned into a type of Third World city by neo-liberal economic policies that exploit the poor and "outsource" businesses to countries where workers are forced to labor for lower wages and fewer benefits. But unlike a real Third World city it is unable to create squatter settlements and survival economies. Davis notes that the choice for youth now is "between blow-drying rich people's lawns or joining gangs" (Katz and Smith, 1992). In the face of structural unemployment and deindustrialization, gangs have become a compensatory social structure and, notes Davis, "surrogate families." It's the Mexicans, Salvadorans, and Guatemalans who are the most vulnerable to ravages of the depression, and it's not surprising that on Christmas Eve, 1992, 20,000 Latinos turned up downtown to wait all night for a blanket and a turkey. During the day, they waited in line for day labor in the slave markets.

Of course, we are not simply talking about conditions in Los Angeles. In Detroit, Malice Green was pulled from a parked car by the police. A black man, Green was savagely beaten by a white male officer in the face, chest, and stomach. Part of his scalp was torn off by a police officer wielding a flashlight like a golf club. After fourteen blows to Green's head, an officer stepped on Green's neck as he was handcuffed. Green died from blunt-force trauma to the head.

We are still seeing the afterglow of what Davis has termed "an American urban Intifada."

We live in dangerous times, a time in which many college freshmen think it's "cool" to agree ideologically with Rush Limbaugh and to be a fan of Bill O'Reilly or the other media pundits on the Fox-TV network. To be fascist and singularly untutored in the political economy of ideas has never been in such fashion. Rarely are the political consequences of such allegiances thought through. This is one of tragedies of contemporary schooling.

Although we fight hard not to admit it, the capitalist economy is unravelling worldwide. Walter Benjamin's "angel of history" continues to gaze through clouds of despair—not to mention a disintegrated ozone layer—at a continent whose potential is greater now than ever before for unleashing worldwide catastrophe. Recent U.S. military actions in Afghanistan and the U.S. support for Colombia's brutal military regime are warnings to any country of what they can expect if they threaten U.S. economic interests.[3]

In an era of falling profitability and production, where each percentage point increase in the unemployment rate brings 318 additional suicides, and a 2 percent increase in the mortality rate brings a 5 to 6 percent increase in homicides, a 5 percent rise in imprisonments, a 3 to 4 percent increase in first admissions to mental hospitals, and a 5 to 6 percent increase in infant mortality rates, consumer culture grabs at the grotesque and the decadent (Cohen and Rogers, p. 29). Images of garish and vulgar commodities litter both print and electronic media, creating an ethos of possessive and atomistic individualism, a debilitating privatization, and self-seeking careerism that shunts aside the imperative to analyze existing social conditions and oppressive relations of power and privilege and to eliminate exploitation. Instead, these images reinforce a consumerist ideology characterized by the belief that the quality of everyday life is irrevocably enhanced through the continual creation of material wealth. Silicon Valley's apostles of technology and efficiency, backed by Sun Belt entrepreneurs, parade their wares as functional imperatives for modern survival, while questions of social justice and human struggle seem more and more peripheral to the commodity culture. Failing to consider how our dreams, desires, and actions have been manufactured and socially conditioned, we remain instead in the thrall of consumerist ethics. We are living collectively the American nightmare, Death of a Salesman, and like Willy Loman we are realizing that the exchange value of dead labor is empty hope. We seem to accept the belief that present conditions have arisen out of democratic necessity, as a prerequisite for our fetishistic quest for the best of all possible worlds. Inequality and poverty are the prices we must pay for freedom. What is so hypocritical in all of this is that right-wing politicians, posing as populists looking out for the little guy against the Washington liberals who are wasting the taxpayers' money on excessive social programs, are really loyal servants of the corporate elite who economically cripple those little guys the so-called populists purport to defend.

In reality, progress has become the scourge of history, an attack on human freedom, as the profound illogic of the times runs frictionless and free. Those who wish to build a society free from the din and carnage of war find it hardly comforting that many key figures in today's burgeoning New Right—including high-ranking government and military figures—harbor sweet cravings for Armageddon, use the Bible as the chronometer of history, and ascribe to a variation of "imminent rapture/holocaust" in which the "purifying violence" of nuclear war is perceived as part of God's plan. (Of course, true believers will be instantly teleported to heaven by Jesus in the sky, just before the apocalyptic showdown.) (Jones and Sheppard, 1986). This is the reverse mirror image of the Taliban's logic of jihad. A logic well known to Attorney General John Ashcroft, among others.

Rampant illiteracy, growing dropout rates among the poor, and a dramatic increase in classroom violence and despair exemplify the plight of today's students and teachers. As we fail to consider the possibility of practical political action or to exercise our abilities to intervene in the world, our dreams glide over the domain of ethics and continue to be manufactured in a culture of unchallenged consumer hype and moral destruction. Today more than ever before we need a pedagogical theory that is able to counter the New Right's excoriating attack on schooling, which argues that the moral vocabulary of critical pedagogy must be expunged as leftist or socialistic. The repeated assaults of reactionary ideologies, whether they are carried to us through school bashing, arms scandals, gun-running diplomacy, or television preachers hungry for corporate power, have normalized greed, the right to be racist, the logic of self-interest, a desire for private gain, and a hatred for conscientious dissent. As the dark and ambivalent wings of history beat about the stage of our present era, where hope is held hostage, where our political leaders follow the corporate logic of Enron executives while decrying its outcomes, where justice is lashed to the altar of capital accumulation, and where the good works of our collective citizenry have been effaced by despair, we desperately need a new vision of what education should mean.

For teachers, this means that we must begin candidly and critically to face our society's complicity in the roots and structures of inequality and injustice. It means, too, that as teachers we must face our own culpability in the reproduction of inequality in our teaching, and that we must strive to develop a pedagogy equipped to provide both intellectual and moral resistance to oppression, one that extends the concept of pedagogy beyond the mere transmission of knowledge and skills and the concept of morality beyond interpersonal relations. Pedagogy in this instance must be linked to class struggle and the politics of liberation. This is what critical pedagogy is all about.

The Corporate Assault on Education

We have entered the age of the corporatization and businessification of education. As capital insinuates itself over the vast terrain of the globe, it is not surprising that the United States is leading the charge toward the privatizing of public education. Nor is it surprising that standardized testing is being pushed, that test publishers are scrambling to boost their revenues, and that educational publishers in the testing business are experiencing economic windfalls.

George W. Bush's administration has strong links with the publishing giant, McGraw-Hill. In fact, the friendship between the McGraws and the Bushes dates back to the 1930s (Metcalf, 2002). Harold McGraw, Jr., sits on the national grant advisory and founding board of the Barbara Bush Foundation for Family Literacy. When George W. Bush was governor of Texas, he used many McGraw-Hill authors to develop the reading curriculum for Texas schoolchildren (Metcalf, 2002). McGraw-Hill touted a phonics-based reading program that was supported by the Bush administration (Metcalf, 2002). Not surprisingly, McGraw-Hill gained a dominant share of Texas's profitable textbook marketplace. But between fiscal years 1995 and 2001, spending for adult education was cut by half and there was a two-thirds decline in spending for professional development (Gluckman, 2002). Yet, in that same time period, spending on tests more than tripled (Gluckman, 2002).

The same pattern is repeating itself in the George W. Bush White House administration. The National Reading Panel (assembled by Congress in the late 1990s) advocates systemic instruction in phonemic awareness and a skills-based, phonics approach. (Remember, you need textbooks to teach phonics, and McGraw-Hill textbooks are the ones most recommended.) The National Reading Panel has hired a powerful Washington public relations firm, Widmeyer Communications, to promote Open Court, a signature McGraw-Hill literacy product, as well as DISTAR, another literacy product. They are increasingly being adopted by school boards across the country, with little scientific evidence backing them up (Gluckman, 2002).

Today the creation and scoring of K–12 tests is a multimillion dollar industry. Businesses are predictably emphasizing "output" in their workers, and business-based management techniques are increasingly being adopted in schools. The business model that drives the U.S. classroom requires frequent and efficient testing. The K–12 standardized testing industry generates sales of about 1.5 billion dollars a year. One of its major corporate players is National Computer Systems, recently purchased by Pearson, a British media conglomerate that owns *The Financial Times*, *The Penguin Group*, *Pearson Education*, and some television production companies. National Computer Systems and other test production firms are not government regulated (Gluckman, 2002).

It used to be the case that scholars of psychometrics wrote tests of basic skills as in the case of classic K–12 tests, the Stanford Achievement Test and the Iowa Test of Basic Skills. But today, publishing employees more often than not write the tests, and errors have become routine (Gluckman, 2000). Gluckman notes that:

In 16 states, testing contractors had made significant errors in scoring or results analysis. In 1999, scoring errors by CTB/McGraw-Hill affected schools across the country: In New York City, 9,000 students were mistakenly ordered to go to summer school, and principals and district superintendents across the city—along with Schools Chancellor Rudy Crew—lost their jobs; in Nevada, elementary schools were mistakenly labeled "inadequate." In the spring of 2000, thanks to scoring errors by NCS, a number of Minnesota high-school seniors had their diplomas withheld. And last year in Massachusetts, where Harcourt has run the state-wide testing program since 2000, students themselves found errors in several questions on the high-stakes Massachusetts Comprehensive Assessment System (MCAS) tests. (2002, p. 35)

In view of the the Code of Fair Testing Practices, many educators and psychometricians agree that using a single test score to make a high-stakes determination represents an ethical abuse. For instance, a single test score should not be used to determine high-school graduation or to fire teachers. Yet test-makers continue to create customized statewide tests, even if they know in advance these tests will be misused.

Gluckman notes that standardized testing can compromise classroom instruction as teachers put aside their regular curricla, includes important work such as literature and social studies, in order to prepare for tests. Gluckman points out that this practice goes against the grain of current research that "shows that small schools are more effective and that interdisciplinary approaches to subject matter and heterogeneous grouping of students can enhance learning" (2002, p. 37). In his classic book, *The Case against Standardized Testing*, Alfie Kohn writes:

> Standardized tests, as we've seen, tend to measure the temporary acquisition of facts and skills, including the skill of test-taking itself, more than genuine understanding. To that extent, the fact that more such tests are likely to be used and emphasized in schools with higher percentages of minority students predictably results in poorer-quality teaching in such schools. The use of high-stakes strategy only underscores the preoccupation with these tests and, as a result, accelerates a reliance on direct instruction techniques and endless practice tests. (2000, p. 37)

When we want to examine how ideology is used by the capitalist class as a mode of social control, we often look first to Texas to see what is happening there. In 1990, Texas began an extensive testing program called the Texas Assessment of Academic Skills (TAAS) that is mandated for all students in grades three through eight, plus grade ten. Now Texas is implementing standardized end-of-course tests for high school biology, algebra, and U.S. history (Gluckman, 2002). Of course, such tests limit the amount of time that can be allotted to discussing critical social issues. It serves as an effective policing device—an ideological prophylactic—for keeping oppositional discourses and practices out of the classroom. But consider some of the other effects of high-stakes testing in general. Amy Gluckman writes that a number of studies, many of them commissioned by the Civil Rights Project at Harvard University, have documented negative impacts of high-stakes testing on classroom instruction, student and teacher morale, and drop-out rates. In Texas, for instance,

Drop-out rates among African-American and Latino students have risen since high-stakes testing began. There is even some evidence that students who pass the TAAS test and graduate actually demonstrate poorer writing skills when they arrive at college than did their peers a few years earlier, before high-stakes testing. (2002, p. 36)

The new stress on "collaboration" between teacher unions and local school administrators that is touted by some progressive educators as the way to bring schools into a social justice focus is fatally constrained by the unwillingness of many administrators to fight against high-stakes standardized testing, because school success is overwhelmingly framed by how well students perform on standardized tests. Such a collaboration must jettison its shared support of teacher accountability and standardized testing and gain control of the fundamental resources needed by schools, such as textbooks, smaller classes, and increased teacher salaries.

It is not uncommon these days to see school buses in certain states covered with advertisements for Burger King and Wendy's, fast-food chain restaurants. It has become fashionable for elementary schoolchildren to carry books wrapped in free book covers plastered with ads for Kellogg's Pop-Tarts and Fox-TV personalities. School districts have granted Coca-Cola and Pepsi exclusive contracts to sell their products in schools. In health education classes students are taught nutrition by the Hershey Corporation that includes a discussion on the important place of chocolate in a balanced diet. A classroom business course teaches students to value work by exploring how McDonald's restaurants are operated and what skills are needed to become a successful McDonald's manager, and provides instructions on how to apply for a job at McDonald's. Ecological and environmental education now involves students learning ecology from a "Life of an Ant" poster sponsored by Skittles candy and an environmental curriculum video produced by Shell Oil that concentrates on the virtues of the external combustion engine.

In the wake of the widespread corporate assault on public schooling, social justice educators face the insurmountable challenge of educating and preparing students for critical citizenship. I will present here in broad strokes a number of fundamental steps teachers can take in preparing students to become critically literate. I locate critical literacy in a broader framework that I refer to as the development of critical citizenship.

A major step in preparing students to become critically literate is not only to provide them with meaningful learning experiences (i.e., through the use of numerical literacy, computer literacy, cultural literacy, and critical literacy skills), but also to validate and legitimate the experiences that students bring into the classroom from their everyday lives. Student experiences can be linked to a theme-based curriculum designed to facilitate economic literacy, media literacy, eco-literacy, consumer literacy, and other literacies linked to current social and educational policies motored by unregulated global capitalism.

Secondly, social justice educators can offer students a "language of critique" and a "language of possibility," so that they can conceptualize, analyze, theorize, and critically reflect upon their experiences. Radical educator Henry Giroux uses the term "language of critique" to refer to developing a theoretical vocabulary and a set of analytical skills drawn from mainly the disciplines of sociology, critical theory, and cultural studies. The term "language of possibility" refers to developing a vision of a better world by bringing theory into practice (praxis). In other words, it refers to using new sets of analytical skills from the social sciences to interrogate and transform the social conditions that have socially, culturally, and historically produced one's individual and collective experiences.

The recognition of the dialectical unity between theory and practice, and action and reflection, is a third step social justice educators can undertake to empower students. Here we make a crucial distinction between *reflection* and *critical reflection*. While the former is related to students' awareness of their concrete social and economic circumstances, the latter deals with the investigation of their social location *in* the world as well as their relationship *with* the world. Paulo Freire, the Brazilian critical educator, refers to this as a "radical form of being," which he associates with "beings that not only know, but know that they know."

Bringing Theory into the Streets

This brings us to the action dimension of critical literacy—what Ramin Farahmandpur and I refer to as *praxis-oriented pedagogy* (McLaren and Farahmandpur, 1999a; 1999b; 2000). Praxis-oriented pedagogy bridges the gap between critical knowledge and social practice. This involves bringing theory into the streets. It includes organizing and mobilizing students, parents, and teachers at the community level, and linking their struggles to larger national and international struggles.

Given the pivotal role that critical literacy can play in the warp and weft of the daily lives of students, a question that many social justice educators raise has to do with the concrete applications of critical literacy in their classrooms. For example, as Ramin Farahmandpur and I have argued, social justice educators can incorporate economic literacy as part of teaching critical literacy. A useful resource guide in teaching economic literacy is Rick Ayers' *Studs Terkel's Working: A Teaching Guide* (2001) used in conjunction with Studs Terkel's nationally acclaimed book, *Working* (1972). Terkel's book is an ethnographic account of the lives of working men and women. In his book, Terkel interviews workers about job security, workplace safety, economic opportunity, and whether or not they find personal fulfillment and meaning in the work they perform.

Following the ideas developed by Terkel, teachers can direct students in interviewing family members, friends, and people who make up their local neighborhood. Students investigate not only the types of jobs that exist in their community, but also the workplace conditions that exist, including terms of employment, salary ranges, and medical and dental benefits. Students can communicate through the internet with other students undertaking similar projects who live in neighborhoods with widely divergent socioeconomic conditions. They can then link job conditions to related socio-political issues affecting their communities. In Los Angeles they might include complications arising from anti-immigrant government initiatives; racial profiling by the police; the treatment of the homeless; slave labor in sweatshops; and the political education of undocumented immigrants. These conditions can then be traced to economic initiatives put forward by both Democrats and Republicans at both state and federal levels. Students can then analyze these initiatives in the light of competing economic philosophies (i.e., socialist, green, reform). Students can also interview the "owners" as well as the "producers" of the various businesses that exist in their neighborhoods and raise issues that affect people's working and non-working lives.

This activity and variations thereof can encourage students to link local issues with the wider arena of social life. Students will most likely raise a number of critical questions: Why is there a shortage of community centers in some neighborhoods and not in others? How can public transportation be made more accessible? Why is there a large police presence in some communities for the purpose of repression and other, more benign forms of police presence in the gated communities for the purpose of protection? Why is there a larger concentration of liquor stores in African-American communities and virtually none in other communities populated by white and middle-class residents?

Here, classroom teaching can be a dialectical approach to knowledge. Comments by Dunayevskaya help underscore such an approach when she writes:

> As Marx put it in his Theses on Feuerbach: "The educators themselves must be educated." This requires that (1) some of the lectures be given "from below," not only to give the students "experience," but so that the teachers can learn; and (2) where possible, at least one of the lectures (say on the class struggle), be made "in the field" either by a tour of a factory or visit to a picket line. (There is sure to be one somewhere if eyes and ears are turned to the production line.) As for learning from students, it is not only a question of the dialectical principle Hegel articulated, that "Error is a dynamic of truth," but also a fact that even when a student commits errors, the teacher can discern where his or her presentation failed to communicate; failure to project an idea is every bit as wrong as failure to "know." (1978, p. 355)

Dunayevskaya additionally notes that

> Methodology, then, must be a new beginning, that is, a projection of future study and action so that no one, teacher or student, should feel that teaching has "ended" when the last lecture of the course is delivered. Everyone must experience the lifeblood of the dialectic-continuity, a continuity that arises daily from the objective situation, both in the class struggles at the point of production, and through every layer of society. (1978, p. 356)

Preparing students for critical citizenship through critical literacy deepens the roots of democracy by encouraging students actively to participate in public discourses and debates over social, economic, and political issues that affect everyday life in their own and neighboring communities. In this way, students can acquire the pedagogical courage and moral responsibility to participate in democratic life as critical social agents, transforming themselves into authors of their own histories rather than being written off as the passive victims of history. In this regard, we would do well to remember the manifest possibilities offered by the creation of a socialist society, including those of education. Ollman writes:

Throughout social society, in education but also at work and at play, special efforts will be made to counter selfishness and the fear of what is different, and to promote the values of cooperation and mutual concern. With people participating in making the key decisions that effect [sic] their varied activities, products, and social relations, alienation—with its accompanying feelings of disconnectedness and powerlessness—will gradually give way to feelings of empowerment and a deep sense of belonging to a single human community. In the process, freedom, equality, and democracy, all the noble ideals that capitalism (to its credit) first set out, and then (to its shame) proceeded to undermine and distort, will finally become actual descriptions of our life together in society. (2001, p. 154)

We look forward to a world in which the accumulation of expropriated surplus value is no longer the motor of development, where individuals' capacities are nurtured by collective solidarity, where schools are able to fire our transformative power as living, breathing subjects of history, where in the end we may be able to achieve post-capitalist ways of being.

I always have been proud to be a teacher, and to have been given the opportunity to work with students both as an elementary and middle-school teacher, as well as a university professor. My own role as a student is one that I unashamedly continue to occupy in every arena of social life. I have been blessed with the opportunity to travel to many countries and to continue my education, both here and in Latin America, Southeast Asia, and Europe. What I continue to realize is that the struggle against social injustice does not stop at the classroom door, but is never-ending and continues during every waking minute, in every single day, in every situation that calls for human engagement, for trust, for solidarity, for respect, for peace, and for a willingness to make concepts, principles, and ideas our weapons—and not bombs and missiles—in the ongoing class struggle.

Over the last decade and a half, *Life in Schools* has enjoyed a wide readership. As with any widely read book, it has received—justly or unjustly—its share of criticism. Why does the book contain a challenging theoretical language? Why are my discussions filled with so many abstractions? Why am I so critical of white folks, especially since I am officially designated as a white person? Why do I now embrace a revolutionary socialist politics?

There are, of course, countless other questions that have been raised in the wake of the publication of *Life in Schools* (and no doubt will be raised in conjunction with this new fourth edition). While not attempting to answer these charges in any detailed way, partly because to do justice to these questions would take another book, I am able to make the following preliminary remarks. I believe that teachers have been swindled into accepting a number of specious notions: that they are primarily "practitioners" rather than what Antonio Gramsci called "organic intellectuals"; that theory largely is unrelated to practice; and that theoretical discourse is primarily the select preserve of ivory tower intellectuals. Of course, those who occupy positions of power in our capitalist society don't want teachers to have a firm grasp of political and sociological theory, especially its Marxist, feminist, and post-colonial variants. Such a theoretical understanding, if embraced by a significant number of teachers, could have a devastatingly debilitating effect in dislodging the powerful and the privileged from the top of the capitalist hierarchy. Ideas can exert a powerful material effect. The ruling-class would prefer that teachers think about practice using ideologically domesticated sound-bytes supplied by supposedly politically disinterested mainstream journalists or occupy a pedagogical discourse ideologically tinged by right-wing television or radio talk-show hosts; not surprisingly, I have been denounced by a handful of them as a self-hating white man or as a subversive boogeyman out to destroy democracy.

What is important to understand is that within revolutionary critical pedagogy, theory and practice occupy a dialectical relationship in the interests of social justice. However, in most schools of education, they are violently sundered apart so they may be considered as two separate entities. A transformative classroom practice demands a revolutionary theory. As I mentioned earlier, experiences never speak for themselves, and are never self-evident or transparent. We need a rigorous critical theory so that we can better interpret, understand, and transform our everyday experiences. Enough said.

I grew up in a working-class neighborhood until my father landed a job as a manager of a major electronics firm, and consequently, my formative years were spent mainly in lower-middle-class surroundings. I was the first member of my immediate family to go to university. My early teaching experiences were colored largely by an ignorance of how my subjectivity was shaped, and how my teaching practices were implicated in wider social relations linked to the forces and relations of capitalist production. One never fully unlearns one's privilege; it is a lifetime of struggle. But it is a struggle that must be waged, regardless of whether a complete victory is ever possible. In a homage to Freire in her important new book, *Reinventing Paulo Freire: A Pedagogy of Love*, Antonia Darder writes:

> In keeping with your wish, we must now carry on. We must continue to struggle over meanings, make sense of capitalist relations of production, critique the devastating impact of "globalization," champion education within the larger political project of liberation, refuse apolitical theories that veil injustice, and uncompromisingly confront issues of economic restructuring, class and gender equalities, and the racialization of populations around the globe. And all this we must do with as much scientific specificity as the quickening of our hearts. (2002, p. 257)

My supporting an anti-racist pedagogy has little to do with being a self-hating white man, as some reactionary pundits have asserted, and more to do with recognizing that the process of unlearning white privilege is an ongoing project that can never be abandoned. And while I subscribe to the teachings of the new abolitionists who call for the abolition of the white race, I need to clarify what I mean when I say that the white race must be abolished. Marxist-humanism rejects terrorism and violence. Abolishing the white race means, in the way that I am articulating it, unlearning white privilege and ceasing to identify with a fictitious white race invented in seventeenth-century colonial Virgina (see Ignatiev and Garvey, 1996; and Roediger, 1994).

I have no problem personally identifying with my Canadian ancestors who tilled the fields of farms near the St. Lawrence River. In fact, I share a great deal of pride in identifying with certain accomplishments of my Canadian, Scottish, English, and

Irish working-class ancestors. My background is filled with a rich cultural heritage. Yet I would never think of identifying myself as part of the white race, which saw its historical beginnings in the racist plantocracy of slave owners in colonial Virginia. There is nothing to be gained with identifying with the white race, and everything to lose. All humanity and decency is lost in seeing oneself as part of a larger "white race." This is because identifying with the white race justifies occupying a social position historically predicated on the destruction of those whom one names as non-white. It is a denial of both the subjectivity and historicity of the Other. If this seems an extreme position, then tell that to those who routinely gather at places across the United States such as the Shack, a north Anaheim, California, rock club that features special rock concerts for neo-Nazis and in celebration of the white race, where kids as young as 10 jump on stage sieg-heiling Hitler.

I am aware that this new introduction raises more issues than it answers. Paulo Freire always said that critical pedagogy is about problem posing, not supplying stock answers. And finding the right answers are based upon asking the right questions. I believe that the questions I have raised throughout this new edition of *Life in Schools* are the right ones to raise at this current moment in our political history, and that in raising them I have deepened reader engagement with critical pedagogy and its larger political agenda of creating a society freed from exploitation. I am proud to be part of the tradition of radical educators and activists in the United States. To challenge the social arrangements of capitalist exploitation has always been a worthy goal. It is uwise to mistake this as anti-Americanism, for to dismiss it as such is to denigrate the history of working-class struggle that permeates U.S. history.

As is my custom, when I am not traveling, I write drafts of my books and articles in the local coffee shop near my home off Sunset Boulevard in Los Angeles. The coffee shop I have been frequenting for the last three years is one of those oh-my-god-let's-do-lunch-make-me-an-offer-excuse-me-that's-Tom-Cruise-on-my- cellphone-get-me-a-silicone-birthday-present-or-an-Armani-suit-I-drive-a-Ferrarri-I-can-get-you-into-the-Sky-Bar-if-you-can't-promote-my-career-then-get-out-of-my-way cof-fee shops on Sunset Boulevard. Trying to engage the other customers—the writers, herbologists, pagan universalists, New Age workshop and retreat addicts, conspiracy theorists, urban developers, film agents, slackers, hackers, Wiccan spiritualists, ferals, media industry imposters, neo-shamans, scientologists, whole brainers, real movie stars, and wannabe movie stars who also frequent the coffee shop—in a conversation about socialism is about as easy as trying to organize the residents of Beverly Hills to combat Swiss banks.

The fetishization of everyday life into a series of commodities that displays "who you are" has helped to hypostasize capitalism as a natural force that serves those worthy or cunning enough to become rich. As difficult as it may be to combat this "natural force," I often engage the locals in conversations about politics and praxis. And while some are mollified that I dare to criticize capitalism, let alone advocate for a socialist alternative, and while cynicism about any form of social organization runs strong, I am surprised to find that many of them share points of agreement with me. While lifestyle consumption is their *modus vivandi*, there is a growing weariness with what, for many of them, has been a world of empty promises and endless disappointment.

Los Angeles is the homeless capital of the United States. In L.A., on any night, 50,000 to 80,000 people spend the night on the county streets. On rare occasions at the coffee shop you might see a homeless person sitting cheek-by-jowl with a character actor you recognize but can't put a name to, discussing the state of the economy. More likely than not, you'll see a spectacle of wealth. It is hard not to notice that Los Angeles is a city with people who have and who like to display enormous wealth. In fact, Los Angeles has more high-income households than anywhere in the United States. In the most luxurious part of the city—Beverly Hills—the area code is 91210. Eight-four percent of the inhabitants of this area code are white. One of the most poverty-stricken areas of Los Angeles is South-Central. The area code there is 90059 (see Cooper, 2000). Forty-eight percent of the population who can be reached at this area code are African American and 51 percent are Latino(a). For those who are toiling in the sweatshops on the Eastside, or who are trying to survive the mean streets of South-Central, even to some of the locals at the coffee shop on Sunset Boulevard, the promises made by capitalism to most Americans appear remote and almost surreal. It is difficult to make the case to many of the young people who live in the 90059 area code that history is not written for them in advance, or that it can change direction. But what is the direction their history should take? Toward a 91210 area code? Or toward a new social universe where area codes no longer serve as demarcation lines that separate people on the basis of social class or race?

It is in these boulevards of broken dreams and streets of despair and desperation where critical pedagogy can make a difference, where history can dramatically change course, where revolutionary beginnings can take root. And where a new society free from the constraints of the old can be won.

ENDNOTES

1. I have borrowed the concept of "revolutionary critical pedagogy" from Paula Allman (2001).

2. I am referring here to reports that have played a major role in shaping educational policy at both the national and local levels. These include: The National Commission on Excellence in Education, *A Nation at Risk: The Imperative for Educational Reform* (Washington, DC: GPO, 1983); Task Force on Education for Economic Growth, Education Commission of the States, *Action for Excellence: A Comprehensive Plan to Improve Our Nation's Schools* (Denver: Education Commission of the United States, 1983); The Twentieth Century Fund Task Force on Federal Elementary and Secondary Education Policy, *Making the Grade* (New York: The Twentieth Century Fund, 1983); Carnegie Corporation, *Education and Economic Progress: Toward a National Education Policy* (New York: 1983); and Carnegie Forum of Education and the Economy, *A Nation Prepared: Teachers for the 21st Century* (Hyattsville, MD: 1986). Also considered are other recent reports on teacher education reform: The National Commission for Excellence in Teacher Education, *A Call for Change in Teacher Education* (Washington, DC: American Association of Colleges in Teacher Education, 1985); C. Emily Feistritzer, *The Making of a Teacher* (Washington, DC: National Center for Education Information, 1984); *Tomorrow's Teachers: A Report of the Holmes Group* (East Lansing, MI: Holmes Group, Inc., 1986); and Francis A. Maher and Charles H. Rathbone, "Teacher Education and Feminist Theory: Some Implications for Practice," *American Journal of Education* 101 (1986): 214–235. For an analysis of many of these reports see Catherine Cornbleth, "Ritual and Rationality in Teacher Education Reform," *Educational Researcher* 15 (4), (April, 1986): 5–14.

3. For an expanded analysis of the events of September 11, see my two articles (in press) in *Cultural Studies/Critical Methodologies*.

REFERENCES

Allman, Paula. (2001). *Critical Education Against Global Capital: Karl Marx and Revolutionary Critical Education*. Westport, CT: Bergin & Garvey.

Anderson, Karen. (2001). Immigrant Victims of the WTC Attack. *NACLA Report on the Americas*. Vol. XXXV, no. 3, pp. 1–2, 4

Ayers, Rick. (2001). *Studs Terkel's Working: A Teaching Guide*. New York: The New Press.

Bacon, David. (2001). "Blood for Coal." *LA Weekly*. Aug. 24–30, Vol. 23, no. 40, pp. 32–33.

Black, Edwin. (2001). *IBM and the Holocaust: The Strategic Alliance Between Nazi Germany and America's Most Powerful Corporation*. London: Little Brown Publishers.

Boggs, Carl. (2000). *The End of Politics: Corporate Power and the Decline of the Public Sphere*. New York: The Guilford Press.

Boggs, Carl. (2001). "Economic Globalization and Political Atrophy." *Democracy & Nature*. Vol. 7, no. 2, pp. 303–316.

Bortfeld, Joey, and Naureckas, Jim. (2001). *Extra!* (June) Vol. 14, no. 3, p. 14.

Buchanan, Patrick (2002). *The Death of the West: How Dying Populations and Immigrant Invasions Imperil Our Country and Civilization*. New York: St. Martin's.

Bugliosi, Vincent. (2001). *The Betrayal of America: How the Supreme Court Undermined the Constitution and Chose Our President*. New York: Thunder's Mouth Press/Nation Books.

Cleaver, Harry. (2000). *Reading Capital Politically*. Leeds: Antitheses and Edinburgh: AK Press.

Cohen, Joshua, and Rogers, Joel. (1983). *On Democracy: Toward a Transformation of American Society*. Middlesex, England and New York: Penguin Books.

Cole, Mike. (1998). "Globalization, Modernization and Competitiveness: A Critique of the New Labour Project in Education." *International Studies in Sociology of Education*. 8(3): 315–332.

Cole, Mike, Hill, Dave, McLaren, Peter, and Rikowski, Glenn. (2001). *Red Chalk: On Schooling, Capitalism & Politics*. London: Tufnell Press.

Cooper, Marc. (2000). "The Two Worlds of Los Angeles." http://past.thenation.com/issue/000821/0821cooper.shtml.

Coulter, Ann. (2001). "This is War." *National Review Online*. Sept. 13. *http://www.nationalreview.com/coulter/coulter091301.shtml*

Darder, Antonia. (2002). *Reinventing Paulo Freire: A Pedagogy of Love*. Boulder, CO: Westview Press.

De Angelis, Massimo. (2000, July). "Enclosure and Integration." *Workers' Liberty*. No. 63, pp. 9–10.

Dunayevskaya, Raya. (1978). "From Raya Dunayevskaya." In Theodore Mills Norton, and Bertell Ollman, eds., *Studies in Socialist Pedagogy*. New York and London: Monthly Review Press, pp. 354–356.

Dunayevskaya, Raya. (2002). *The Power of Negativity*. Boulder, CO: Lexington Press.

Dyer-Witheford, Nick. (1999). *Cyber-Marx: Cycles and Circuets of Struggle in High-Technology Capitalism*. Urbana and Chicago: University of Illinois Press.

Ebert, Teresa. (2001). "Globalization, Internationalism, and the Class Politics of Cynical Reason." *Nature, Society, and Thought*. 12(4): 389–410.

Extra! (1998). Vol. 11, no. 4 (July/August).

Fairness and Accuracy in Reporting Media Analysis, Critiques, and News Reports. "Media Downplay Bigotry of Jesse Helms." August 31, 2001. FAIR-L <FAIR-L@FAIR.ORG>

"Falun Gong: Force for Revolution in China." *Workers Vanguard*. No. 762 (2001), pp. 4–5, 14–15.

Floyd, Kevin. (2001). "Closing the (Heterosexual) Frontier: Midnight Cowboy as National Allegory." *Science & Society*. Vol. 65, no. 1, Spring, pp. 99–130.

Foley, Barbara. (2001). "Subversion and Oppositionality in the Academy." In Henry A. Giroux and Kostas Myrsiades, eds., *Beyond the Corporate University: Culture and Pedagogy in the New Millennium*. Boulder, CO: Rowman & Littlefield Publishers, Inc., pp. 195–211.

Freire, Paulo. (1978). *Pedagogy as Process: The Letters to Guinea-Bissau*. Trans. C. St. John Hunter. New York: The Seabury Press.

Fromm, Erich (2000). *Marx's Concept of Man*. New York: Continuum.

Giroux, Henry, and McLaren, Peter. (1997). "Paulo Freire, Postmodernism and the Utopian Imagination: A Blochian Reading." In J. O. Daniel and T. Moylan, eds., *Not Yet: Reconsidering Ernst Bloch*. London and New York: Verso Press, pp. 138–162.

Gluckman, Amy. (2002). Testing . . . Testing . . . One, Two, Three: The Commercial Side of the Standarized-Testing Boom. *Dollars & Sense*. Vol. 239 (January/February), pp. 32–37.

Gosselin, Peter G. (2001). "Amid Nationwide Prosperity, ERs See a Growing Emergency." *Los Angeles Times*. Aug. 6, pp. 1, 8.

Gramsci, Antonio. (1971). *Selection from the Prison Notebooks*, edited and translated by Q. Hoare and G. N. Smith. London: Lawrence & Wishart.

Hart, Peter. (2001). No Spin Zone? *Extra!* Vol. 14, no. 6 (December), p. 8.

Hart, Peter, and Ackerman, Seth. (2001). Patriotism and Censorship. *Extra!* Vol. 14, no. 6 (December), pp. 6–9.

Hill, Dave, and Cole, Mike. (2001). "Social Class." In D. Hill and Mike Cole, eds., *Schooling and Equality: Fact, Concept and Policy*. London: Kogan Page.

Holley, David. (2001). "Philip Morris Angers Czechs with Tobacco Toll Report." *Los Angeles Times*, Aug. 5, pp. 1, 9.

Hudis, Peter. (2001). Terrorism, Bush's Retaliation Show Inhumanity of Class Society. *News & Letters*. Vol. 46, no. 8 (October), pp. 1, 10–11.

Hudis, Peter. (2002). The Power of Negativity in Today's Search for a Way to Transform Reality. Presentation to Expanded Resident Editorial Board of Jan. 20, 2002. Chicago: *News & Letters*.

Ignatiev, Noel, and Garvey, John. (1996). *Race Traitor*. New York and London: Routlege.

Jones, Lawrence, and Sheppard, Gerald. (1986). On Reagan, Prophecy, and Nuclear War. *Old Westbury Review*, 2(Fall), pp. 9–22.

Katz, Cindi, and Smith, Neil. (1992). L.A. Intifada: Interview with Mike Davis. *Social Text*, 33, pp. 19–33.

Kellner, Doug. (2001). September 11, Terror War, and Blowback. Manuscript.

Kellner, Doug. (in press). *Grand Theft 2000*. Boulder, CO: Rowman and Littlefield Publishers.

Kincheloe, Joe. (1998). *How Do We Tell the Workers? The Socioeconomic Foundations of Work and Vocational Education*. Boulder, CO: Westview Press.

Kohn, Alfie. (2000). *The Case Against Standardized Testing: Raising the Scores, Ruining the Schools*. Portsmouth, NH: Heinemann.

Kozol, Jonathan. (1985). *Illiterate America*. Garden City, New York: Anchor Press, Doubleday.

Krupskaya, N. (1985). *On Labour-Oriented Education and Instruction*. Moscow: Progressive Publishers.

Larkin, Ralph W. (1979). *Suburban Youth in Cultural Crisis*. New York: Oxford University Press.

Marable, Manning. (2000). *How Capitalism Underdeveloped Black America*. Cambridge, MA: South End Press.

Marx, Karl. (1973). *Critique of the Gotha Program*. New York: International Publishers.

Marx, Karl. (1977). *Capital: A Critique of Political Economy: Vol. 1*. Trans. B. Fowkes. New York: Vintage Books.

McLaren, Peter. (1995). *Critical Pedagogy and Predatory Culture: Oppositional Politics in a Postmodern Era*. London and New York: Routledge.

McLaren, Peter. (1997). *Revolutionary Multiculturalism: Pedagogies of Dissent for the New Millennium*. Boulder, CO: Westview Press.

McLaren, Peter. (1998b). "Revolutionary pedagogy in post-revolutionary times: Rethinking the political economy of critical education." *Educational Theory*. 48(4): 431–462.

McLaren, Peter. (2000). *Che Guevara, Paulo Freire, and the Pedagogy of Revolution*. Boulder, CO: Rowman & Littlefield.

McLaren, Peter, and Farahmandpur, Ramin. (1999a). "Critical Pedagogy, Postmodernism, and the Retreat from Class: Towards a Contraband Pedagogy." *Theoria*. No. 93, pp. 83–115.

McLaren, Peter, and Farahmandpur, Ramin. (1999b). "Critical Multiculturalism and Globalization. Some Implications for a Politics of Resistance." *Journal of Curriculum Theorizing*. 15(3): 27–46.

McLaren, Peter, and Farahmandpur, Ramin. (2000). "Reconsidering Marx in post-Marxist times: A requiem for postmodernism?" *Educational Researcher*. 29(3): 25–33.

McMurtry, John. (1998). *Unequal Freedoms: The Global Market as an Ethical System*. West Hartford, CT: Kumarian Press.

McMurtry, John. (1999). *The Cancer Stage of Capitalism*. London: Pluto Press.

McMurtry, John. (2000). "A Failed Global Experiment: The Truth About the U.S. Economic Model." *Comer*. 12(7): 10–11.

Mészáros, István. (1995). *Beyond Capital.* New York: Monthly Review Press.

Mészáros, István. (2001). *Socialism or Barbarism.* New York: Monthly Review Press.

Metcalf, Stephen. (2002). Reading Between the Lines. *The Nation*, Vol. 274, no. 3, pp. 18–22.

Modern Globalism Is "Reactionary Intercommunalism." *The Black Panther.* Vol. 1, no. 7, Autumn, 2000, pp. 1, 24.

Montag, Warren. (2001). From the Standpoint of the Multitude: A Review of Insurgencies by Antonio Negri. *Historical Materialism*, Vol. 9 (winter): pp. 196–204.

Ollman, Bertell. (2001). *How to Take an Exam and Remake the World.* Montreal: Black Rose Books.

Ollman, Bertell. (1998b). "Why Dialectics? Why now?" *Science and Society.* 62(3): 338–357.

Raduntz, Helen. (1999). "A Marxian Critique of Teachers' Work in an Era of Capitalist Globalization." A paper presented at the AARE-NZARE Conference, Melbourne, Victoria, November-December.

"The Power of Negativity in Today's Freedom Struggles." *News & Letters*, Aug.–Sept. 2001, pp. 1, 5–8.

Rikowski, Glenn. (2000). "Messing with the Explosive Commodity: School Improvement, Educational Research and Labor-power in the Era of Global Capitalism." A paper prepared for the Symposium on "If We Aren't Pursuing Improvement, What Are We Doing?" British Educational Research Association Conference 2000, Cardiff University, Wales. 7 Sept., Session 3.4.

Rikowski, Glenn. (2001a). *The Battle in Seattle: Its Significance for Education.* London: Tufnell Press.

Rikowski, Glenn. (2001b). "After the Manuscript Broke Off: Thoughts on Marx, Social Class and Education." A paper prepared for the British Sociological Association, Education Study Group Meeting, King's College London, 23 June.

Roediger, David. (1994). *Towards the Abolition of Whiteness.* London and New York: Verso.

Said, Edward. *The Observer.* Sunday, Sept. 16, 2001. Londonhttp://www.observer.co.uk/comnet/story/0,6903,552764,00.html

San Juan, Jr., Epifanio. (1988). *Ruptures, Schism, Interventions: Cultural Revolution in the Third World.* Manila, Philippines: De La Salle University Press.

San Juan, Jr., Epifanio. (1995). *Hegemony and Strategies of Transgression: Essays in Cultural Studies and Comparative Literature.* Albany, NY: State University of New York Press.

Scigliano, Eric. (2001). Naming—and Un-naming—Names. *The Nation.* Vol. 273, no. 22 (December 31), p. 16.

Sennett, Richard. (1987). A Republic of Souls. *Harper's* (July).

Sirius, R. U. (2000). Diss Belief. *LA Weekly.* Vol. 24, no. 16, p. 44.

A Statement from the National Editorial Board of News and Letters Committees, 2001. newsandletters.org

Terkel, Studs. (1972). *Working.* New York: Pantheon Books.

Thompson, John B. (1990). *Ideology and Modern Culture.* Stanford, CA: Stanford University Press.

Thompson, Willie. (1997). *The Left in History: Revolution and Reform in Twentieth-Century Politics.* London: Pluto Press.

Wolcott, James. (2001). Terror on the Dotted Line. *Vanity Fair.* January, pp. 50–55.

Wood, Ellen Meiksins. (1999). *The Origin of Capitalism.* New York: Monthly Review Press.

Young, Iris Marion. (1992). Five Faces of Oppression. In Thomas E. Wartenberg (Ed.). *Rethinking Power.* Albany, New York: State University of New York Press, pp. 174–195.

PART TWO

Cries from the Corridor
Teaching in the Suburban Ghetto

Introduction

The section that follows presents a number of incidents from my four years of teaching elementary school in one of Toronto's "inner-city" suburbs known as the Jane-Finch Corridor. I have changed the names of students, parents, and teachers and have occasionally constructed composite descriptions to further protect their identities.

Some readers may object to my shifting context from a critique of schooling and society in the United States to an inner-city school in Canada. I would argue that the disadvantaged students of whom I speak, and the teachers who work with them, face daily struggles in the classroom that do not recognize the national boundaries between the United States and Canada. The agony of this situation, in fact, is that it not only spans the border between the United States and Canada, but also occurs in a variety of settings—cities, towns, suburbs, and rural areas. The struggles of many Canadian teachers are similar to the struggles of teachers in the Bronx and Harlem, in Roxbury and Watts, and in Youngstown and Cedar Rapids. They are experiences shared by teachers across the United States. They speak to common conditions faced by teachers and students in many of our industrialized nations, and they represent a collective challenge to the teaching profession and to the youth who make up our future citizenry.

The appropriateness of incorporating my Canadian journal in this volume has been favorably gauged by reactions I have received from audiences in the United States, including inner-city teachers and graduate students (many of whom teach full-time in inner-city schools), colleagues in colleges of education, and parents from a wide variety of ethnic backgrounds. There are certainly differences between teaching in Canada and in the United States, but these are far outweighed by the similarities. The overwhelming response has been that the experiences and conditions reflected in my journal do resemble those of many teachers who work in inner-city schools in the United States. In both countries teachers are faced with overcrowded classrooms, large immigrant populations, outmoded pedagogical theories, stifling bureaucratic demands, top-down centralization of control, management by be-havioral objectives, a distrust of teachers' abilities and judgment in the classroom which has led to the effective deskilling of teachers, insufficient funding and resources, tracking measures and a hidden curriculum that favor certain groups over others on the basis of race, class, and gender—the list goes on and on. Ghetto schools across the continent are similar to the one I describe. Even in the rural classrooms of the Midwest I see faces of despair—the Appalachian poor from the trailer parks and surrounding farmlands side by side with struggling blacks, Latinos, and other minorities. And here, as elsewhere, the schools are ill-equipped to meet their needs.

I would like to be clear that the purpose of reproducing my elementary class-room journal is not to illustrate what critical pedagogy is all about—that will be discussed in Parts Three, Four, and Five. The purpose of the journal is to provide you with some insights into school life as it is lived by students and teachers. These insights are presented from the perspective of a novice teacher unfamiliar with the theories discussed in Part One and in later sections of this book.

This section of the book is the most problematic for me since reading it from the perspective of a critical theorist confronts me with my own ideological and pedagogical shortcomings; it places me face-to-face with my own situatedness as a young teacher in discourses that unconsciously worked against my own emancipatory intention. It is painful for me to read many of these vignettes because I recognize that I was not immune to many of the criticisms that I now lay at the feet of unjust schooling practices and the workings of a racist, sexist, and culturally imperialistic social formation. I recognize that in many of the diary entries the white, Anglo, patriarchal, and liberal humanist discourses and the Euro-American missionary zeal that I now harshly criticize actually undergirded my own early teaching practices. Of course, I don't want to condemn all of my efforts, many of which did attempt to challenge (although with limited success) existing social cultural and institutional practices that worked against children of the poor and powerless. I present the reader with this diary in order to reveal my beginning experiences as a teacher. My lack of critical consciousness is laid bare, warts, boils, and all. I invite the reader to analyze these experiences in light of the perspectives offered that follow my diary and the Marxist perspective that I sketch out in the new introduction. I do not ask the reader to celebrate unqualifiedly my efforts or to criticize them before reading the sections that follow. It is the theoretical sections that follow the diary that I hope will provide a framework for understanding and analyzing my teaching practices.

Part of my plan in this book is to invite you to become a more critically engaged theorist after being introduced to the concepts in Parts Three, Four, and Five.

The Corridor Kids

"Teach in an inner-city school! You're completely crazy," a friend warned me. "You'll ruin your career!"

I was taken aback. "What do you mean 'ruin my career'?"

"When you've decided you've had enough, and apply for a job in a better area, you'll be labeled an 'inner-city' teacher. Once you've been pigeon-holed as teaching mainly immigrant kids, you've had it. Be smart—get out before you get in."

But I wanted to work with inner-city kids and jobs were scarce.

The Jane-Finch Corridor is a six-square block area in the city of North York, a suburb just outside downtown Toronto, Canada. In 1970, there were twenty-one high-rise apartment buildings, and a population of 34,000. By 1975, there were fifty-nine high-rises (with four more under construction) and a population of 60,000. Thirty-eight thousand people are crammed into a two-square-mile area around the intersection of Jane Street and Finch Avenue. About 25,750 of them are nineteen years old and under. Many live in the nearly 3,000 income-assisted housing units. Twenty-two percent of the apartment buildings are government subsidized. Approximately 30 percent of the residents are black, and many are new immigrants with low-paying jobs or no jobs at all. There is a substantial West Indian population, and large numbers of Italian- and Spanish-speaking peoples.

Although the Jane-Finch Corridor is technically a suburb, it shares many demographic characteristics with the inner-city: large numbers of single-parent families, low incomes, a high juvenile delinquency rate, constant turnover in population, government-subsidized housing, high-density high-rise buildings. When we think of inner cities, we tend to visualize the ghettos of the big cities—New York, Chicago, Detroit—with their garbage-strewn streets and smashed windows, derelicts lying in doorways, and whole sections deserted in the flight to the suburbs. These same suburbs, however, frequently produce new high-rise ghettos, and behind their facades of order and containment, conditions are beginning to parallel those horrors left behind in the cities. There is crime and vandalism and racial tension. Police form "beat patrols" and special "youth squads." Shopping malls spring up like fungi at every intersection, replacing neighborhoods with sterile parking lots.

The Jane-Finch Corridor lacks the cohesive presence of established cultural forms such as local bars, clubs, and church organizations, which would give the community a collective solidarity. Given the hard economic times, ethnicity often works as a divisive force, exacerbating community conflict in the area among East Indians, West Indians, Italians, Asians, and Caucasians. Although each group bears traces of its own sociopolitical and cultural history within its ethnic sensibility, each has become part of a social order that incorporates grave disparities in wealth between oppressed groups and groups within the dominant culture. To a large extent they are lost in the tapestry of the larger society—subjugated threads, tied tightly in an historical pattern of racism and oppression.

One is immediately struck by the vast sweep of shopping malls, parking lots, fields thick with hydroelectric towers, and row upon row of housing units. Bowling alleys and movie theatres are relatively scarce, and the recreational center unofficially reserves special nights for "blacks only" and "whites only."

There is an intergenerational continuity with respect to jobs and labor, which means that many working-class students in the area are slotted through the schooling process for working-class jobs in the nearby stores, factories, or fast food outlets.

Youths drink beer, smoke dope, shoot craps long into the night; they sometimes vandalize property and break into homes.

And they come to school. . . .

1966. At seventeen, I followed world events on my parents' old RCA Victor TV. For me, as for many Canadians, the world barely existed north of the 49th parallel. It had been an interesting year: President Johnson ordered the first major bombing raids against North Vietnam; Mariner 4 transmitted the first pictures from Mars; Malcolm X was gunned down at the Audubon Ballroom in New York City; Cesar Chavez voted against Delano, California, grape growers; Queen Elizabeth made each Beatle a member of the Order of the British Empire for bringing home the megabucks from the United States and the colonies; electrical failure blacked out the Northeastern states, causing a sudden boom in the birth rate.

I rarely ventured beyond the confines of what was considered "normal" for a straight-laced kid growing up in the protective custody of the Suburban Dream. My T-shirts were so white that they rivaled Tide commercials. I had tennis shoes that squeaked. Strapped to my Austin Mini was a roof rack for the surfboard I was always talking about buying but never did.

Secretly, however, I felt entombed in a world of routine banality, guilty for thinking thoughts darker than my beige chinos. My life was drifting laterally, waiting for something to happen. Anything. The future looked predictable and grim until the day I met Zeke.

That was the summer of 1966, after which the comforting veneer on my horizon was forever scraped away. He was sitting on a street curb under a willow tree, reading a Jack Kerouac novel. Beside him were a half-empty bottle of ninety-five cent wine and a huge battery radio. Zeke sat there with a Zen asceticism, stoically ignoring the passing traffic—a placid image despite his shock of neon red hair, electrical yellow shirt, navy blue industrial overalls, bottle-green rubber hipwaders supported by fuchsia suspenders, and wine-stained moustache.

I had seen him around the school. Everybody knew about Zeke. His eccentricity was strapped on like a codpiece; incessantly he stalked and challenged our cozy conventions.

For reasons I didn't yet understand, I wanted to know him.

When he noticed my gawking at him, he shifted from the lotus position and surveyed me intently through a homemade pair of glasses—like the x-ray glasses they used to advertise on the backs of Marvel comic books. As I approached him, he removed the glasses, stood up slowly, and stretched his arms. He was extremely tall, about six-four, and slightly Neanderthal. Brilliant red hair, a broad forehead, and fierce, tufted eyebrows dominated his other features: his eyes sanguine, grey-green, strange; his skin pockmarked and leathery. Though his appearance was imbued with confidence and just the slightest trace of haughtiness, he had an aura of premature decay, as though he were someone who had lived well beyond his nineteen years—an Ancient Mariner of Suburban Sidewalks.

"Have you read Pynchon?" he asked, holding up a tattered copy of *V.*

"I don't know him," I admitted.

"How about Genet? You must read *Our Lady of the Flowers.*"

"I'm not into Catholic literature," I shrugged.

"Well," he said, breaking into a beatific grin. "I can see you're uneducated. We'll just have to do something about that."

Zeke was my first nonconformist, part scoundrel, part saint. He taught me Greek dancing in the evenings, which we practiced for hours, guzzling back ouzo to a scratchy recording of the theme from *Zorba the Greek*. In the fifties, he would have been a coffee-cup anarchist, reading his poetry in espresso bars or smoke-filled taverns, accompanied by bongos, double-drums, and a real live black person in Cuban shades playing stand-up bass.

Zeke lent me dozens of books filled with strange antics and antiheroes—*Catch 22, The Gingerman, On the Road, One Flew over the Cuckoos' Nest*, and the poetry of Francois Villon. I began putting aside my homework. Each day I carried to school a copy of *Finnegan's Wake*, which I propped open in the cafeteria, trying hard to appear engrossed in the pages. Zeke considered pretension a fine art. He also valued the art of conversation. Even a brief discussion with Zeke was taking a chance on having your brain wrenched. He rarely talked *with* you—more often *at* you, trying to rearrange your thinking patterns in new ways. It could be a painful—or exhilarating—experience.

Though harassed on all sides by well-furnished, split-level suburban dormitories, manicured lawns, and parks with tennis courts, Zeke's place was my Greenwich Village, North Beach, Telegraph Hill, or Left Bank.

Bored by school, Zeke still attended regularly. For him, school was a stage—a burlesque ramp where he could intellectually strut his stuff. He liked to show up his English teachers—especially when it came to drama criticism—and put everyone on with his crazy antics. He both enraged and enchanted the staff by arriving late for class one day dressed in a black velvet opera cape with pearl buttons, wing collar, and large plump cravat, clutching his latest manuscript in a tattered manila envelope. A gilded walking stick hung from the crook of his arm. His cape billowing behind him, he swept into geometry class and gallantly saluted the teachers with a click of his hobnailed boots.

I had met no one like Zeke. His off-beat brilliance and Rabelaisian worldview helped allay the anomie and restlessness of a suburban youth growing up in the electronic age, whose body and spirit had been put on hold by the morals of the industrial age. Zeke belonged to a different world. He was always excited, his voice rising, hands waving in a state of continual incandescence. Zeke educated my senses, derailing the boredom of my daily existence, stirring me from my comfortable emotional anesthesia.

I soon found it impossible to keep up with my studies. It was too easy to put down a book or put off an assignment for the excitement of Zeke's company or of entering the renegade world to which Zeke had given me access. By comparison, school often seemed like an irrelevant intrusion that obstructed rather than furthered my education.

During the sixties, Toronto's Yorkville counterculture provided me with a strange and often bizarre reality. The maze of streets graced by old brownstone homes, the artists' lofts, the rooming houses, the cafes, the head shops populated with what sociologists referred to as "alienated youth," comprised what was, in a manner of speaking, my classroom away from school. I would often observe the street life from the Penny Farthing Cafe, a volume of Kafka or Beckett under my left arm and a walking stick hung from the crook of my right.

The perennial street crowd spanned all backgrounds; their movement was based not on social class but on the ethos of a generation. Poor kids from Cabbagetown and rich kids from Rosedale dealt dope on the street corners in jeans and army fatigues; preppie girls threw away their knee socks and kilts to roam the streets in jeans, copies of *The Prophet* clutched in their hands; weekenders from Upper Canada College donned sandals, leather vests, and green felt Robin Hood caps and gamboled to Jimi Hendrix and the Doors in between algebra assignments; Kresge cashiers were transformed into beautiful and mysterious Midnight Madonnas, wrapped in shroudlike medieval gowns, silver jewelry adorning their Pre-Raphaelite hair.

I spent considerable time with a variety of colorful and creative individuals whose lives bounced paradoxically between expressive rituals of emancipation and pathological rituals of self-destruction. Drugs became a part of many lives. For many, drugs seemed to serve as a symbolic medium to penetrate the contradictions between freedom and constraint in a society nourished by the myth that progress through technology is the only objective reality. Timothy Leary, the high priest of LSD, handed me a note at a concert: DIPLOMA, it read. YOU ARE NOW FREE.

I took a room downtown with Zeke and enrolled at the University of Toronto in 1968. Zeke made our "digs" a center of Dionysian excess. I often returned from class to find the record player blaring and the room a carnival of strangers: pushers, hookers, poster-makers, poets, mystics, draftdodgers, mimes, speed freaks, junkies, aesthetes, revolutionaries, jugglers, body builders, gardeners, go-go dancers, and university professors.

At sixteen I had ruled out ever working for a large corporation. My father had just turned fifty when the new owners of the electronics firm for which he was general manager decided to let go all executives over forty-five. I watched my father try one low-paying job after another; severe bouts of asthma and emphysema finally forced him into retirement and an early death. After that, I vowed always to stay clear of the business world. I began to read Marx, Gramsci, Sartre, Lenin, Trotsky, and Marcuse. Something was fermenting inside of me.

During my senior year of high school, I had become disillusioned with lessons that seemed boring and pointless. I would imagine myself standing in front of a class and teaching the most impassioned lesson possible. With the arrogance of innocence and the inspiration of Zeke, I was sure I could become the consummate teacher.

I graduated from the university in the early seventies, hung up my love beads and my beloved fatigue jacket, festooned over the years with slogans and handstitched doves, and enrolled in Teachers' College.

My first job was in a wealthy village outside Toronto. Although I liked the students and enjoyed teaching, I felt expendable. These students, already favored with wealth and social power, would probably get by in the world in spite of their teachers; their affluent background almost assured them success in the system. I wanted to save working-class kids. Also, I wanted to enroll in graduate school in Toronto. My wife encouraged me to look for a job in the inner city. "That's where you'll feel most needed," she said. I handed in my resignation and began job hunting.

My new principal told me he thought I'd made the right choice. He welcomed me to the ranks of inner-city teachers, leading me into his office saying. "Just call me Fred." I relaxed immediately.

In his mid-forties, he had a disarming grin and a thick shock of grey hair that looked strangely out of character. The button on his shirt read "I'm the boss." It was clear that the button was a joke. "The excellent grades I see in your Teachers' College report won't matter much here in the jungle," he began. "This is the real world." He leaned over the desk. "I only have one criterion for hiring new teachers. Every kid in this school, and I mean each one, has the right to be loved. No matter how difficult the kid is, no matter how he or she drives you batty from the very first day . . . give them all the love and affection you can. When it feels too impossible, come and see me and we'll talk. All right, Peter? Now good luck, and we'll see you in the morning."

I left his office with a good feeling. I later learned that he was somewhat of a folk legend in the city. As the "hugging principal," he had a high success rate in creating an atmosphere of trust between teachers and students.

My tour of the school was conducted by Fred's secretary, who filled me in on all the latest school gossip as she led me past various classrooms, sketching portraits of the teachers inside. Usually, the reports were favorable, but there was always at least one complaint per teacher. When she remarked, "He always sends two of his kids down to the office with a pile of stencils to be run off late in the afternoon, when I'm busiest," I considered it a warning.

Later I ventured into the staff room. Several teachers were crammed into the tiny room, dutifully cleaning up the lunch dishes. A teacher was swearing at the broken Coke machine; it had just eaten several quarters. "How do they manage to break into our staff room and screw up our Coke machine?" he complained. "I thought the caretaker locked up after we leave!" He kicked the machine several times before finally giving up.

I introduced myself.

"We heard you were coming!" answered a voice near the sink. A big, rugged-looking man came over and introduced himself as the vice-principal, Rod. I shook his hand, which was still dripping with dishwater. "I suppose you'll manage just fine," he said, as he looked me over. "You've got youth on your side at least . . . doesn't he, John?" An elderly gentleman with a friendly smile came over and gave me a pat on the shoulder. "Watch out for John," the vice-principal warned. "He's one of those health nuts!"

"Just keep yourself in shape and you'll survive, young man. Look how long I've lasted, and I've been at this game for over forty years!"

"Got any trade secrets?" I asked.

John grinned. "Sure! B-6!"

"B-6?" Suddenly, I felt stupid.

"B-6! Vitamin B-6! Good for the nerves, you know!"

I was hired to replace a teacher who couldn't handle the pressure. Her class comprised seventeen grade five students, and nineteen grade sixes, ranging in age from eleven to thirteen. This was a "regular" class, as opposed to "special" classes for kids with severe learning problems. As in most of the classes, a third of the students were black, most of them from the West Indies.

They certainly hadn't accepted the teacher I was hired to replace. On one of her last days, all thirty-six students walked into her gym class, faced the far wall with their backs toward her, and refused to move. Several of the kids spit against the wall to punctuate their protest. I wasn't told why the kids were upset, and I decided not to ask.

My classroom was in a "portable" building, about fifty feet from the main building. It resembled one of those units you see in a documentary film from World War II (prefabricated, a year old, and beginning to decay).

The inside of the portable was cold and lifeless and looked more like a funeral parlor than a classroom. An old-fashioned roller blind filtered the winter sun, shining a dead green light over the empty desks. There was only one picture on the wall: a washed out, glue-streaked poster advocating dental hygiene. The girl on the poster had freckles and a pigtail and the boy was wearing a brushcut. It could have sold as an antique at a fleamarket. In comparison with the furniture in the main building, the desks and chairs of my portable looked like they had been scrounged from some storage warehouse for junked school furniture of the 1940s. Desks were hacked and gouged, while the wobbly chairs were often equipped with only three legs. The green blackboard was in such poor condition that you almost had to chisel letters onto it.

I can't recall many details from my first morning of actually working with my kids. I tried to ignore their individual differences and treat them as one giant, uniform mass. I felt that if I lumped them into a single personality, I would be less overwhelmed.

Things went reasonably well during the first part of the morning (that is, if failing to remember most of what happened is synonymous with success). I was riding much too high to pay close attention to what I was doing. But when the first recess bell sounded, I received my inner-city initiation.

There was a concussive sound of glass breaking. Every window on the north side of my portable was smashed, simultaneously. The rest of the day I remember well. I had to teach it in my woolen toque and Hudson's Bay blanket coat, while the kids murmured and laughed with nervous excitement, crouching next to the heat vents, which to their delight squeaked loudly. "Hey, this is neat!" one of the kids yelled.

1   The Frontiers of Despair

Monday, January 3

The first day I started my initial lesson on "People and Society" by asking the kids what they wanted and expected from the course. Silence.

"Okay," I continued, undismayed, "let's try it this way. How many of you are interested in what goes on in the world today—the problems, the politics, the environment, the media, the job market—that sort of thing?"

Nothing. Blank eyes.

"Well," I went on, determined, with more than a small measure of arrogance, "I'm giving you kids the chance to choose the topic for yourselves. Can you hear me over there? What will it be?! Pollution? War? More rights for kids? How about some ideas for projects you want to do?"

No cheers. No boos. Not even a yawn.

I was almost shouting now in frustration. "What is it with you kids, anyway? If you can't think for yourselves, you might as well join the army where there are plenty of orders and few decisions."

Nothing.

Great, I thought to myself. *This is going nowhere.* Maybe I'm expecting too much. Just when I thought everybody had been sworn to a conspiracy of silence, a kid wearing a Maple Leaf hockey sweater raised his hand. I felt like hugging him and called on him eagerly.

He wanted to know why I wore a beard.

Friday, January 7

I eagerly awaited picking up my mail from my personal mailbox during my first trip to the office.

Once inside the office, I saw a student lying on the bench. His knees we raised to his chest, his arms holding them tight; he looked like a pale fetus. A second glance revealed a glint of metal protruding from behind one of his ears. I looked closer. There was a heavy steel dart lodged just above his ear.

The boy responsible for throwing the dart was sitting in the vice-principal's office.

Apparently feeling no remorse, the kid remarked to a teacher who was watching: "He's just lucky I didn't hit him where I was aimin' for!" There were no abject tears.

I stuck my head through the door to get a better view. His feet up on the vice-principal's desk, and his face split by an enormous yawn, he bellowed. "Who are you, sucker? Are you new? You want a dart in your head? Hahaha . . . !"

Tuesday, January 11

The first day I was posted inside the main building on stair duty, they hit me from above. Ten or more kids spitting in unison. From the highest platform of the stairwell, the gobs of saliva picked up velocity by the time they reached my head. And if I looked up to identify the owners, my face would offer an even more tempting target. I could feel my hair growing damp as I descended.

I gathered together some of the teachers and formed a plan. Some of us stood under stairwells at each recess, trying to inveigle the spit-kings to reappear, while other teachers crouched hidden, ready to surprise them.

We weren't able to catch them in the act. I began wearing a washable broad-rimmed hat.

Friday, January 14

Levon arrived in the class this morning after recess—a transfer from another inner-city school.

Just before lunch, he was hit on the head by a flying book. I decided he could use a Band-Aid.

"Sanjay," I called out. "Will you please take Levon to the nurse's office?"

"Sanjay couldn't find his asshole with a roadmap," Duke interjected.

"I'll take him there," Winston volunteered.

"No! I will!" Spinner blurted out.

"Let me sir, please!" Taiwo insisted.

Before long, half the class marched out of the portable.

"It didn't need no Band-Aid," Levon said when he returned with the others after only fifteen minutes.

About two hours later, he complained of an upset stomach and asked if somebody could show him to the nurse's office.

"But half the class took you there just a few hours ago," I reminded him. "Have you forgotten where it is already?"

"Oh, ya," Levon said with a wry smile on his lips. "That was only to show me the best place to grab a quick smoke."

Tuesday, January 18

One of the more colorful characters around the school is a twelve-year-old named Buddy. Hated and feared—sometimes loved—Buddy literally runs the school, a role he plays with the virtuosity of an artist. He is a master technician when it comes to creating his own image. At a moment's notice he can become Lover, Fighter, Revenger, Champion of Freedom, King of the Sidewalks, or Defender of the Dance. Everything and everyone is a point of reference for his act.

The kids in the school accord Buddy demigod rank. When he walks down the corridor and says "Move over!" the kids move, fast! His voice is rarely loud, but it has a way of slicing through the air like cold steel.

The teachers treat Buddy with a subtle deference. Any attempt at confrontation makes them nervous. He's only twelve, but he can immobilize you with a glance, quickening the breath, causing the heart to pound.

Some of the teachers have no compunctions about treating kids roughly, if they have to. Yet Buddy could panic a whole school full of teachers. There are even warnings over the public address system when he's out of control. He is ours, and for a variety of technical reasons, we keep him in school instead of tossing him out onto the unsuspecting world. We contain him, but we are all afraid of him.

Buddy has an aggravating habit of fingering marbles, a bit like Captain Queeg in *The Caine Mutiny*. He rolls them unconsciously between his thumb and fingers like worry beads, sometimes shaking them fiercely in a loosely clenched palm as a rattle-snake-like warning that he is about to strike.

Buddy is allowed to "float." Floaters roam the halls at will and are ignored as long as they don't leave the school building. To qualify as a floater, you have to be incorrigible, but in a soft, almost understated way. You have to conceal your violent behavior, saving it for strategic showdowns. Otherwise, the administration would send you away, to the "outside" or to another school.

Buddy spends most of the day wandering the halls with another floater called Puppy (so named because he's the youngest in his family). Buddy and Puppy spend their time window-shopping different classrooms for interesting things to do, always finding ways of breaking the monotony. They visit classrooms which have attractive girls, or they take karate lessons from the caretaker, or they catch a drag in the washroom.

Fred warned us that Buddy might appear unexpectedly in our classrooms. We were encouraged—coached—to respond in a highly positive way to any friendly gestures he might make. If you were lucky, Buddy would soon tire of you and float off somewhere else.

When you were teaching a class, it was unnerving to see Buddy pause at your doorway. He wore black boots, colorful dashikis, tight black cords. The flared bottoms of his pants had been lengthened numerous times. He was big and getting bigger. His muscular build made him a star attraction, and he seemed to walk an inch off the ground to the beat of an invisible tune. He was always in motion, often gesturing lewdly to Puppy. The first iron-clad rule when Buddy showed up was to appear to be in the middle of a boring lesson. The second rule: Never turn on your record player—he tracked down music like a bloodhound—as long as there was music, he'd hang around.

When he wasn't floating, Buddy was in a special program for slow learners called a "developmental" class. Mr. Bailey, a good natured Welshman, ran it. Buddy's floating embarrassed him, and he decided to boost his reputation by trying to win Buddy back into the class for at least one day a week. Giving him more responsibility might be just the thing. Once, Mr. Bailey decided to try leaving Buddy in charge of the class while he left to run off some stencils—a last-ditch attempt by a desperate teacher to give Buddy a feeling of self-worth. It was a risky venture, and when Mr. Bailey returned the first thing he noticed was the blood on a student's swollen lip.

Once I thought that I could keep Buddy away with the raw force of purely negative emotion. Whenever I caught him standing outside my door, I would dilate my nostrils or curl my lips ever so slightly—just enough for him to pick up my hostility and leave.

But Buddy was a master of the unspoken. He talked with his eyes, or by moistening his lips, or casually mopping his brow. His favorite gesture was to yawn loudly. Today, when I dilated and curled, he walked to the front of the room and picked his rear end nonchalantly. The class howled.

He also ran a protection racket. He would walk up to a kid in a corridor and say "Hey dude, how ya doin'?" Then his lackeys would grab the kid from behind and drag him into the nearest washroom. Once inside, they would threaten to rearrange an arm, leg, or a face unless money was "donated" to Buddy the next day. In the case of small children, Buddy insisted they bring him the green pieces of paper that mommy kept in her purse.

In a month or so, Buddy's empire confiscated well over a hundred dollars. By then the police had been called in to halt the racket.

"Where do you live?" one of the cops demanded of Buddy as they hauled him away. "We'll take you home."

Buddy smiled, then slowly pursed his lips. "Take me to Nova Scotia."

Thursday, January 20

Ruth is exceptionally tall and good-looking. Her expression reminds me of a thin Elvis. She's always raising her hand to be excused. When I asked her why she had to go to the bathroom so often, she told me it was due to "personal problems."

When I asked her if she had seen a doctor about the problem, she said no, it was a "women's problem," and to "mind my own business!" I replied that doctors knew all about "women's problems," that many doctors are women.

I sent her down to see the school nurse. It appeared that Ruth was pregnant.

Monday, January 24

Duke stands out in class. He wears black boots, tight pants, and a shiny, red calypso shirt. Sometimes an old porkpie hat is balanced precariously on his black mountain of hair. If he feels like it, he'll come into class wearing a woolen beret. Sometimes he tucks the beret into the epaulet of his safari jacket and salutes the flag in mock respect. He is what his schoolmates refer to as a "classic dude."

During the first week, Duke kept silent, sometimes catnapping at his desk. Occasionally he'd shift his body around to check out the room.

Today I got fed up with his sleeping during a lesson I'd worked particularly hard to prepare. I asked the kid next to him to wake Duke up. The kid touched him on the shoulder gingerly, as if he were disarming a bomb.

Suddenly Duke shot up from his chair, shouting: "Jesus! Don't do that, man, or I'll break your ass!" He was out the door in an instant.

I didn't see him until the end of the day. He said he fell asleep on the park bench.

Wednesday, January 26

From the beginning of the year it was obvious that Barry worshipped Duke as a hero.

He admired his fighting ability—and was equally terrified of it. He toadied to Duke, fussing around him, running errands for him.

His admiration shot up as he watched Duke fight Sam. Duke hooked Sam with a left, then staggered him with a haymaker. Sam's mouth filled with blood, and he spit out bits of teeth.

Duke was a serious street-fighter, the star attraction for the school's would-be pugilists.

One day Duke turned on Barry. It was for no apparent reason, other than a lark—something to amuse Duke's other followers.

"The best way to teach you how to fight is to beat the shit out of you. Right?" Duke said, leering at Barry.

Barry cowered in terror. "Come on, Duke! Please!"

Duke walked closer to him.

"Stay back, Duke! Please! Just tell me what to do!" Barry pleaded in a plaintive, pitiful whine.

Duke drew his arm back slowly, his fist clenched. He stood inches from Barry, ready to let fly.

"*I'll* do it for you, Duke! Here, *I'll* do it!" Barry screamed. Suddenly he grabbed his metal lunchbox, raised it over his head, then brought it down hard on his skull. There was a loud *crack*. He hit himself several times, until his lunchbox was hopelessly battered and blood trickled down his forehead.

"Okay, Duke? Okay?" Barry yelled.

Delirious and in tears, he found me in my classroom, and told me what happened.

Duke remarked that he didn't even throw a punch and still did all that damage.

"He did it all to himself, man," Duke said, when I questioned him. "He's some kind of nut."

Monday, January 31

Everybody called Francine "Muscle Lady." When she flexed her eleven-year-old's biceps, eyeballs popped. Boys became jealous.

Muscle Lady wore a Superman tee shirt to school with a plastic tiger's tooth hung from a piece of thread around her neck. She always wore jeans with the legs turned up over her cowboy boots. When she walked by, you identified her by the sound of the clicking tacks she shoved into the heels of her boots.

Muscle Lady loved to fight—boys especially. But boys didn't want anything to do with her outside of having sex with somebody that tough. It was not only painful but humiliating when Muscle Lady had you pinned by the neck with her boot, then bragged to the onlookers, "Should I cut off his balls?" If the crowd gave a "thumbs down" (which it usually did), Muscle Lady had been known grind down her heel.

The word was out: If Muscle Lady has your nuts in her sights, wear your steel hockey cup to school.

Tuesday, February 1

I was green: suffered from naivete and cultural myopia.

I obtained an 8mm movie about World War II from a United Church clergyman. I had no idea where he got it, but I jumped at using it with my class.

The film was overpowering. One section in particular, featuring Nazi war atrocities, revealed the terrible legacy of the Holocaust. All that I told the students was that the film was about war, and that it was real footage—not actors playing roles.

As they watched the film, I watched their expressions. I waited expectantly for the sequence that showed Nazis carting dead bodies toward an open grave. I had no idea what the kids were thinking. Finally, the long unusual silence shattered when a student cried out: "Stop the film!"

I felt that the film had done its work: These children, now and hereafter, would understand the horrors of war.

I switched off the projector, ready to open up a discussion on the brutality of war. But the same voice in the darkness snapped: "Turn the film backward. Show that last part again. Did you see the arm falling off that body? Let's see it again!"

Wednesday, February 2

It was the end of another boring school day. Duke, the tough dude, sauntered through the teachers' parking lot, sipping on a Coke, and smoking. His after-school stroll often became the occasion for an impromptu gathering of his followers. Hordes of students would sometimes trail behind him, shouting "Hey, Duke!" or rhythmically chanting his name: "Duke . . . Duke . . ." Even teachers hailed him. His manner was always engaging, familiar: "Hiya pal. Whaddya say, baby?"

Everybody gathered around him, always careful not to crowd him.

"Hey, Duke!"

"Who ya punched out lately?"

"Hey Duke, whose pants you been into this week?"

Today Duke was ordered off the school property for a few days: He had cracked a kindergarten kid in the face with his fist, pushed him headfirst into the fence. Then he had stomped on his face.

When Fred phoned to explain that Duke could not return to the schoolyard, his older sister answered. She promised she'd take care of him and keep him inside, but as soon as he walked through the door, she told him to get lost.

So he decided to wander down to the bicycle paths and torment some of the kindergarten kids there. Many passed that way after school. He caught two boys who were running home and tripped them, pinching their ears. He tried to pull their pants down, taunting them in a whining voice: "Daddy's goin' to give ya a beatin'! Do what the daddy says! Be good little boys, and daddy won't beat ya no more!" Resistant students were slammed to the ground. When Duke's mother returned home from work and heard what had happened, she waited for him with her hairbrush.

The next day, the parents of the injured children reported Duke; the incident was investigated. He was suspended from school for a week, and his mother was given the name of a social agency she should contact.

When he returned to school, he was met as if he were an exiled king who had finally returned to lead his people into battle.

"Hey, Duke baby!"

"Whaddya say!"

"Hey hey, the man is back!"

Monday, February 7

My teaching methods don't seem to be going over as well as I'd hoped; a lot of the kids are resistant to my lessons. I can't believe how defiant of authority these kids are—and they're only grades five and six! When I decided to swallow a little of my pride and ask for help, I went to see Fred.

"My lessons don't seem to be capturing the kids' attention," I told him, "even though they're right out of the latest books and programs available."

Fred laced his fingers behind his head, leaning back in his chair. "Peter, you know that even the most up-to-date textbooks are still only textbooks. Mostly our texts have middle-class settings that are irrelevant to our kids. Try some role-playing. It's a good technique with our kids. They like to act out situations. Ham it up, then see what you get."

The next day I proposed the idea to my class. Tina and Sandra volunteered at once to improvise a skit.

"What do you want to do it on?" I asked, noting happily how eager they seemed.

"Let's pretend I'm the husband," Tina suggested, "and this classroom is our apartment, and Sandra is my wife."

"Okay," Sandra agreed.

"I've just got home from work, and I find out you drank my case of beer. But you were supposd to do all the housework, see? Now you gotta explain why you didn't do no housework, and why you're drunk. Ready?"

As the rest of the class watched intently, Tina walked out of the room. She closed the door behind her, then knocked loudly. Sandra answered the door wearing a scowl on her face, pretending to be drunk. Tina stepped into the room, her arms held out in greeting.

"I'm home, honey," she called, trying to embrace a resistant Sandra. "I'm so glad to come home to a clean house for a change!" She paused, looking around. "What are my clothes doing on the sofa? Your breath stinks of booze!" Tina pretended to shout, without really raising her voice. "Why are last night's dishes still piled in the sink? I oughta slap you silly."

"Why dontchya go to the track tonight?" Sandra mumbled, slurring her words. "Lemme alone. There's a good program on TV, and I don't wanna be disturbed."

"Disturb you! Why would I wanna do that?" quipped Tina. "Looks like nobody has disturbed you yet today! Why should I be different? Jus look at all those beer bottles on the floor! Get dressed and pick up this mess and fix me somethin' to eat. Go on—move it!"

"Make it yourself!" Sandra snapped.

At this point, Tina was pretending to pick up the empty bottles and throw them away. "Jus' look at this place! It's a pig sty!"

With that remark, Sandra pretended to hit Tina on the head with a beer bottle. Tina responded by fighting right back, faking slaps at Sandra and screaming, "You good-for-nothin' drunk! Why'd I marry you in the first place?"

Thursday, February 10

Kids often reveal a bizarre sense of humor—they enjoy trying to make teachers retch with sick jokes and peculiar antics. I understood all that; I'd met lots of adults at parties who enjoyed doing exactly the same things. That's why I didn't think twice about Barry's jokes. I'd heard similar ones before.

For example, Barry would stroll into the classroom and ask me: "What do ya get when you take the wings off a fly?"

Before I could reply, he'd shoot back: "A walk, stupid! Hahaha!"

He once asked me: "What goes ha-ha clunk?"

"Don't know, Barry. What?"

"A man laughing his head off! Hahahaha!"

I almost started to appreciate Barry's sense of humor until a reliable source informed me that, after school, Barry sometimes strangled cats.

Friday, February 11

Duke removed his winter coat and threw it on his desk. He was shirtless, dressed in overalls. He slumped down in his chair, munching on a sandwich.

At Teachers' College they told us to lay down the rules on the very first day and stick to them.

"There's no eating in the room, so put away the sandwich."

Duke shut his eyes, nodded his head knowingly, and said softly (but not so softly that I couldn't hear), "It figures."

But he didn't leave it at that. "I ain't had breakfast, so I'm just fillin' up early on my lunch." He studied my reaction with cool disdain.

I looked at him angrily. He went on eating.

"What do you mean?" I asked, uneasily, annoyed that he'd triggered off such a strong reaction in me. What was really bothering me was that I didn't know if he was putting me on or not. Maybe he *was* being sincere.

"Just gimme two seconds," he promised, his mouth crammed with salami. "There . . . only one bite left," he mumbled, chewing hungrily. Then he smiled: "All gone! Now what was so bad about that?"

I closed my eyes, shook my head, indicating that I wasn't to be questioned further. There was an uneasy silence.

"Listen," I said, putting an end to the awkward moment. "It's all right."

He looked at me, then nodded impertinently. "Thanks, man. You can relax now, right?"

By the end of the day an eerie, engulfing sense of panic swept over me.

"What the hell are you doing here?" That was the question a voice in my head kept repeating.

I crossed the parking lot quickly, anxious to get home. Several kids who were playing on the roof of my van jumped off as soon as I approached. For a few minutes I just sat inside, staring through the windshield at the steel-gray sky, the windswept gray high-rises towering in the distance. Everything seemed a mixture of white and black or in between—not a spot of color in the entire landscape. The moon's surface probably had more charm than this.

When I reached home I was greeted by my nine-year-old stepdaughter, Laura, her eyes blinking happily behind a pair of fluorescent cardboard glasses.

"How was school today?" I asked.

"Just great, dad!" she exclaimed. "Everybody got to make a pair of these glasses in art. The teacher bought all the material."

I nodded, then asked her, "How do the kids in your class behave?"

"Everybody does what the teacher tells them to, pretty well. Nobody even talks in class without the teacher's permission."

"Nobody even talks," I echoed blankly.

Laura groaned. "You're acting funny these days, Dad."

That evening I fell asleep at the kitchen table. Laura claims she saved me from drowning in my soup. Somehow, Jenny managed to drag me to bed.

Monday, February 14

Teaching for a year in junior high school in a wealthy neighborhood had been relatively problem free; disciplinary problems were few. My teaching style had been calm and friendly, and I rarely had reason to lose my temper. In a very short time, I realized that my present school was another matter entirely. I would have to change my approach, since the kids either ignored me completely or else went to the other extreme, continually interrupting my lessons. Soon I was shouting, trying to get my lessons heard over the din. I threatened kids with after-school work or detentions if they didn't settle down.

But I found it repulsive to act "the heavy." The kids sensed my authoritarian image was merely a tactic, and called my bluff. When a class enjoys wearing down the patience of its teacher, all that is necessary is a hint that the teacher is out of control. Then the students move in for the kill.

Since my attempts at control were backfiring, I decided to try another approach. I did a John Wayne in *The Green Berets*, pacing in front of the class and barking orders:

"Sit up straight and tall!"

"Tuck in that shirt!"

"Eyes front!"

I didn't quite make it as the hard-boiled drill instructor, berating the kids into subservience on the theory that a good soldier obeys on reflex. That method got a few laughs, but not much else.

Sometimes I tried being a tough but kindly TV detective: "Get those lessons done, kids, on accounta they're an important part of growin' up!"

"Reading will keep you off the streets, outta trouble, and outta the slammer!"

The kids sensed I was strange.

Tuesday, February 15

After the class returned from gym, I asked them what improvements they'd like to see me make in the classroom.

"You ain't gonna leave the room like that bitch had it?" Duke asked, cocking his head to one side.

"What was wrong with the room?"

"We didn't like the set-up!" he barked back. "We didn't like havin' no spare time! It was always work."

Levon stood up and walked to the back of the room, with a ruler stuck out of his open fly. "We wanna teacher with big boobs!"

Marianne, one of my West Indian girls, rose out of her chair. "We wants a black teacher!"

"A black teacher with big boobs!" Levon cut in.

"Naa!" someone else cried. "Who wants a fuzz-top for a teacher?"

"When are we gonna play floor hockey?"

"What about field trips?"

"Can we play records in class?"

For the rest of the day, I was swamped with questions. For me, the questions themselves were part of the solution. The kids were coming out of their shells, testing me out, airing some of their frustrations.

Any reasonable suggestion, I made a note of, and tried to do something about.

It was too early to know what they made of me, but I was confident that with time, they would grow to respect me.

Wednesday, February 16

Duke and Al paired off cautiously. From an upper window, I saw what looked like the entire school population in the main yard, surrounding the two fighters. The crowd was bouyant and talkative. Students jerked, twisted, strained in gleeful anticipation of the bout. I started at once for the stairs.

The shouting got louder and louder, the excitement feeding on itself, swelling with hoots and whistles.

"Kill him!"

"Break the sonofabitch's balls!"

"Punch his eyes out!"

Fever-pitch wails burst through the yard. Drops of bright red blood spattered the pavement.

Duke's foot shot out in a blur. Al coughed and gagged, dropping to his knees. "Ya goddam motherfucker!"

Smooth as a cobra, Duke took a short step forward. "Fuckin' nigger bastard!" A lightning kick to the solar plexus. The crowd screamed for more blood . . . my commands to stop were lost in the roar.

This time Al fell screaming on his side. A hard kick in the ribs as he tried to raise himself up. Another. Four kicks to the head. Al's eyes rolled up. To break up the fight, I plowed my way through the eager crowd.

Thursday, February 17

I don't like looking out the windows of my portable. The view is too bleak: an inner ring of identical bungalows, an outer perimeter of ugly high-rises. The small park near the school serves as only a partial buffer against the impersonal, almost anonymous, surroundings.

During roll call, I realized that over half my class had the same address—a large government-subsidized building nicknamed "The Jungle" by some teachers. Only one student lived in a "regular" house, and only a few lived in the public complex of townhouses.

I asked my kids what they did with their free time.

"Play in the laundromat until the super kicks us out."

"Go to the arcade at Food City."

"Ride the elevator."

"Me and Buddy," Levon offered eagerly, "watch the teenagers screw each other in the basement."

Fred once mentioned to me, "The only thing worse than being poor is being poor in the suburbs."

Friday, February 18

Nearby is a Catholic school that the kids call St. Welfare. One morning last week, Levon crawled through a hole in the fence and crept up to a window. He watched the students going through the morning's opening exercises, and when he finally showed up in *my* class, he described them in detail.

"The whole class started to pray all at once to this cross on the wall. But there were some guys at the back of the room who were playin' with hockey cards—the teacher didn't see 'em 'cause her eyes was closed. Hey, sir. Why don't the Catholic teachers pray with their eyes open?" He grinned, and scratched his head. "Anyway, sir, how come them Catholic kids get to talk to God, and we don't?"

Levon's last remark caught me a bit off guard. I quietly retreated to my desk, stalling for time.

"Well . . ." I hesitated, "we don't say prayers in class because this is a public school, and kids come here belonging to different religions. Some people have different ideas about God, and some people don't believe in God at all."

Levon looked puzzled, but he shrugged. "Who cares about talkin' to God, anyway? I heard this story from a lady in my buildin' that God was born in barn, with a bunch of cows and donkeys, and she says He slept on some straw on the floor. Is God really on welfare?"

Monday, February 21

When I was teaching junior high, I had set foot in the principal's office only once. I had been put on the carpet because I had allowed some of my students to call me by my first name.

Fred's office, on the other hand, was a place where I spent considerably more time—but for different reasons. Fred kept his office open so teachers could use it whenever it was free.

Because Fred did most of his paperwork in the staff room, teachers could use his office for phone calls, or help themselves to the stacks of educational books and journals he stashed in a big box in the corner marked "Free." He had also replaced the standard-issue grey desk with a pine coffee table, as well as replacing his chrome and vinyl chair with a Boston rocker. One wall of his office was entirely devoted to children's art.

Teachers often went to his office simply to relax.

The vice-principal's office was right next door. Rod had the same open-door policy, but he spent more time in his office, so it wasn't as available to the teachers.

Today when I stepped inside Rod's office to use the phone, I found him sitting in his chair, calmly holding a struggling black kid.

"Would you mind watching this guy for me while I go get a coffee? I'm bushed. He went berserk in Mrs. Rogers' room. Just make sure he doesn't get out the door."

After Rod left, the kid simply smiled and quietly sat down in a chair in the corner of the office. I sat down in Rod's chair, picked up a magazine, and started skimming pages, the phone call temporarily delayed.

Without warning, I was knocked right out of my chair by a blow from behind. I looked up from the floor to see the kid standing over me waving a hockey stick!

I got to my knees, propping myself up on the arm of the chair, but before I made it to my feet the kid yanked the chair away, and I fell back on the floor.

"Vanilla trash," the kid snarled, and ran out the door.

Rod came back into his office a few minutes later to find me alone, tucking my shirt in and rubbing my sore, throbbing neck.

"Let me guess," Rod said. "You let him escape."

Tuesday, February 22

Each day the buildup in my mailbox grew. Curriculum materials, surveys, advertisements for curriculum materials, and surveys to establish an advertising policy. Subject guidelines, policy guidelines, guidelines for guidelines—it seemed endless.

At first, in my naivete, I thought everything was important and actually read it all. Somehow the educational system was nourished by all these forms and papers. However, I soon realized that I'd receive something worthwhile no more than once a week. Teachers, I learned, referred to mailbox buildup as "Administrivia."

One day, feeling particularly wretched, I simply picked up the latest pile of papers and dumped them all into the wastebasket.

"Hey," a seasoned veteran exclaimed, "you'd make a great principal."

Thursday, February 24

In spite of the fact that Ricky got on my nerves, I wouldn't call his parents for help when he got into trouble.

It was too possible that what Ricky said was true . . . that when his parents heard he had done something wrong, they strapped him on top of the dining room table and, taking turns with a belt, beat him.

Friday, February 25

Kids called Marianne "Big Mama."

She was a giant of a girl with the most beautiful braids I had ever seen. The top of her head looked like a black patch-work quilt with white stitching. Her mother had given her a button which she wore proudly. It read: "Kid for Rent (cheap)."

She became a legend one day by giving Duke an unprecedented defeat by knocking him off his feet with a swoop of her huge hand, and then sitting on his chest until he almost turned blue.

There was little sexual stereotyping in my class.

Saturday, February 26

Jenny and I decided to do some shopping at a plaza in the corridor.

Packed into the Miracle Mart, Food City, and Dominion stores were Italian mothers in black kerchiefs, West Indian families in matching dashikis, teenagers chasing each other through the aisles, and scores of young kids at the pinball machines.

As we were going out I spotted four of my students hanging out in the parking lot. Duke and Jackson were wobbling and slurring their words. Dave was sneezing violently, and Lisa was laughing, hiding her face. Duke had a smaller, frightened kid backed into a corner, cold-bloodedly trying to provoke a fight. They all look very high on something.

"Is this what you kids do on weekends?" I asked, giving the frightened kid a chance to run away.

"We're not *kids* on the weekend," Jackson said. "On the weekend, we're the Dukes!"

Tuesday, March 1

The teachers were all crowded around a notice posted on the staff bulletin board. It was the new yard duty schedule, still smelling from duplicating fluid. Because I had been hired in midyear, my name hadn't appeared on the first list. That oversight had now, unfortunately, been corrected.

Yard duty meant the entire school population at once—more than six hundred crowded together at recess in a mass of swirling bodies.

Near the main entrance, a group of kids huddled under a blanket, trying to walk in unison. They managed to make this giant insect move only a few feet at a time before they tripped all over each other's legs. Across the yard, a group of kids stood around the drinking fountain. A tiny kindergarten kid was pushed against the metal water faucet.

I ran across the yard, but was too late. I had two girls from my class take the kid to the office to have his bleeding gums looked after. Meanwhile, kids played marbles or made bets on which way baseball cards flung against the wall would land.

A kid with a frantic look led me to the other side of the yard where I found a little six-year-old girl tied to the fence. She was being swatted across the legs by an older boy armed with a tree branch. When I grabbed the boy, he sneered defiantly, "Whatta ya doin'! Eh? She's my sister, ya know! I can do what the fuck I like with her!" and then he took off like a rocket. I untied her, and my two girls led her inside the school.

When the bell sounded, I thanked God.

Thursday, March 3

When I return home from work I usually go directly into the den and close the door. I prefer not to talk to anyone. I had halfheartedly started working on a series of children's stories that were about the real world as opposed to the world of magic and make-believe, but after about an hour that depressed me, too. My one outlet is playing a bottleneck guitar after some of the Delta blues artists who played out of the Mississippi region in the early 1920s. It gives me a tremendous emotional release.

Monday, March 7

After a few weeks of trying to teach my kids according to the Ministry guidelines and the approaches I had been taught in my teacher training, I knew that I would either have to change my entire approach or sacrifice my stomach. My health had been suffering. I continually caught colds, had dizzy spells, stomach cramps. I sometimes threw up in the staff washroom after a hard day.

I decided to enroll in a master's program in education, even if it was only part-time. For two evenings a week I would study the sociology of poverty, as well as child management.

Fred was glad that I showed concern, but he disagreed with my strategy: "You *already* know these kids are poor," he told me patiently. "You *already* know most of them come from single-parent families, and you *already* know that a great majority of them are beaten up at home. So what's a university course going to teach you?"

Wednesday, March 9

I was anxious to get some ideas about teaching from the rest of the staff, and I looked forward to our lunchtime conversations in the staff room.

The room itself was starting to look interesting. Some of the teachers were re-decorating it, trying to achieve a coffeehouse atmosphere. Hieronymous Bosch prints hung on the walls, and the shell of an old radio was placed over the intercom speaker. The librarian fitted the tables with plastic checkered tablecloths, and volunteers (kids included) brought in empty wine bottles to hold candles. One teacher described it as "creating a buffer."

This afternoon I took a seat beside a teacher I hadn't seen before. She introduced herself as a supply teacher who had been working the area for a while. I was struck by how much she looked the caricature of the spinster teacher: hair in a bun, horn-rimmed glasses, worn tweed jacket. She reminded me of the middle-aged women I saw in church when I was a child. "How do you like being an inner-city teacher?" she asked.

"Things are getting easier," I replied. "I'm doing a lot of reading . . . trying to discover some new ideas. By the way, what kind of approaches do *you* use with the kids? Maybe we can exchange ideas."

She cleared her throat, looking down at her lunch, smiling. "There *is* one thing that I find helps me make it through the day," she said softly.

"Yes?"

"I never talk about the kids during lunch."

Thursday, March 10

Jabeka had a pile of letters on her desk that her mother asked her to mail, three of which were addressed to relatives in Spanish Town, Jamaica.

"Have you been back to visit since you've come to Canada?" I asked her.

"Are you kidding, Mr. McLaren?" she replied. "My father is in Jamaica and no way do I want to see him. My mother don't want to see him, no way. Ever since we came here, my dad don't bother callin' us. He never writes no letters, or calls collect on the phone—not even Christmas."

"How long have you been away from your father?"

"Five years. I got a stepdad now. He's got two kids who live with his other wife next to Food City. His wife's got a boyfriend named Mr. Jimmy who's got three kids. Mr. Jimmy buys all the best food for his own kids."

"What does your real father do in Jamaica?" I asked, trying to maintain casual tone.

"He lives with his girlfriend. I gots two other brothers there, but they don't live with my dad. They lives with my grandmother—you know, my dad's mother."

"So you never see your other brothers?"

"Last time I was in Jamaica, and then me and my mother moved away went to visit my grandmother and she told me to go back to where I belong."

"Where was that, Jabeka?"

"How the hell am I supposed to know? With my mother, I guess."

"So your parents split up before you came to Canada?"

"Yah. I still want to visit my dad sometimes. He likes me more than his girl-friend because when we was coming back from shopping he told his girlfriend to get off his motorcycle, and he put me on the back."

"Do you have any other brothers and sisters living with you?"

"I got a younger brother and a younger sister. I don't know if they come from my real dad, but my mom says they're my brothers. My stepdad and my mom just made a baby, but it's not born yet."

"Are you glad you came to Canada, Jabeka?"

"Yah," she replied. "We never had colored TV in Spanish Town."

Monday, March 14

During recess, Spinner and Duke, opponents in ball hockey, started to argue over whether or not to allow a last-minute goal. Duke decided to settle the issue by crack-ing Spinner in the mouth. Spinner reeled backwards, knees buckling. Duke kicked him in the groin as he fell.

His moans were heard by the teacher on yard duty, and he was taken to the hospital with a bleeding penis.

Spinner's mother showed up at the school later that afternoon. "Show me Duke!" she demanded.

A tiny kid wearing a mass of dreadlocks said, "There!" and pointed to the open gym doors. After taking a huge drag on her cigarette, Spinner's mother suddenly bolted down the corridor after Duke.

I ran to stop her.

She caught up to Duke in time to drag him to the floor and punch him. I man-aged to get between them. Then I calmed Spinner's mom down. Duke hadn't been injured.

"He got what was coming to him!" she told me triumphantly.

Rod took Spinner's mother into the office, and I turned to Duke. "How're you feeling?" I asked him.

"Okay," Duke said, panting. "Okay. Nothin's busted. Shee-it! What a suck that Spinner is—sendin' his momma over to take care of his own business."

Tuesday, March 15

An announcement came over the public address system regarding a potluck luncheon for the teachers.

"Potluck, eh?" Ricky mused. "What's you bringin', sir?"

"Pot or hash?" Duke called out.

"My brother's got some dynamite Colombian at home! You want some?" Spin-ner volunteered.

Wednesday, March 16

The lunch bell sounded.

Children exploded from the doors and poured into the halls. Unresolved arguments that had accumulated during the morning were now settled with fists. The air was thick with screams, shouts, and well-chosen obscenities. A contingent of teachers and lunchroom supervisors waded through tiny human walls, challenging kids who refused to leave the halls. "I gotta wait for my mom!" "My teacher said I don't got to leave!" "I gotta wait for my little sister!" The excuses sounded convincing.

Kids screamed louder and louder while balls, paper airplanes, and plastic hockey pucks flew through the air.

A teacher with hair swarming over her head, her kids swarming over her classroom, ran out the door in tears. "Damn these kids! I can't take it!"

Mothers met their children in the halls to conduct them safely home. From the schoolyard could be heard do-wah medleys in sweet, piercing falsettos.

Finally weary, overtaxed teachers retreated to the staff room and quickly shut the door behind them.

Thursday, March 17

Buddy tore madly around the yard, pummeling everyone he passed on the back with a windmill series of quick blows. When the terrified kids fled, he stood in the middle of the empty corridor and threw impressive jabs at his shadow. He was celebrating new boxing gloves—initiating them, breaking them in. For Buddy, all the world was a ring.

It was my duty to tell him that gloves were not allowed in school. I figured he'd tell me where to get off. What he casually said was, "If you want me to stop, you gotta go me a few rounds first. I'll bring my brother's pair this afternoon."

At the end of the day, kids of all ages poured into my room. Buddy was the last to enter. I figured it couldn't be too bad. After all, I stood six feet and weighed 165 pounds. Buddy was a twelve-year-old kid, even if he was big for his age.

Applause accompanied his entrance. Even members of my own class cheered him; they had a right to protect themselves after school.

Buddy began wrenching his neck back and forth in an impressive limbering-up ritual. We tied on our gloves; everyone waited in suspense.

Suddenly he rushed me, almost bowling me over. I threw a jab to keep him back. Then I stood ready, and we began to box.

"You can do better than that, McLaren!"

"Come on, Buddy—move it."

"Hit 'em in the nuts."

"You're okay, man."

After the first few rounds I was tiring noticeably, while Buddy grew strong and more confident. I wasn't trying to land solid punches, but Buddy was determined to knock me out.

I finally ended the match gracefully by saying I had to leave and get a course. Buddy stood perspiring, in a classic boxing stance. He accepted my decision to stop the fight and walked over. "You put on a pretty good show, man," he said, not too confidentially, so everyone would hear. "Of course, I coulda decked you anytime, but I don't want you to look like a dummy in front of your kids."

Friday, March 18

In Teachers' College, budding young professionals were guaranteed at least one fool-proof lesson. It would always work, no matter who the kids or what the class. In moments of desperation this lesson could turn a would-be disaster in a fantastic success. Or so the theory went.

In a moment of panic, I decided to haul out my sure-fire lesson. I wrote two sentences on a piece of paper—an opening and a closing sentence. The students were directed to fill in the story by contributing one sentence, then passing the paper to the next student.

My opening sentence was: "I wish I had more friends like the ones I met last summer." The closing sentence: "It was the most exciting vacation I ever had."

It seemed to be working. The kids were getting into it, and the class quieted down, with a few giggles and knee slapping.

The finished product read:

I wish I had more friends like the ones I met last summer. I met a girl in a bikini. She had big tits. Don't write so dirty, Duke. Shut up Tina, and let him write what he feels like. I put my hands on her big knockers and squeezed them. We necked a lot. She felt my giant cock. Change the subject. Then we went into my cottage. . . .

Monday, March 28

"Let's have art this afternoon, Mr. McLaren!"

"Yah. We want art!"

"Well, we've got some math to do this afternoon. Perhaps after we're finished with that. . . ."

"We wanna naked model . . . one with really big tits that stick out to here!"

". . . and lots of fuzzy hair down here!"

"You guys are sick! Is that all you think about?"

"Shut up Sandra! All you think about is naked boys!"

"Barry's a fag. He thinks about naked boys, too!"

"Fuck you, you stupid morons!"

"Let's keep the language clean, okay? Can we drop this naked model business and get on with the math lesson!"

"Wash out your mouth, Barry! You said fuck about a hundred times today!"

"Fuck off!"

"A hundred and one."

"Hey, sir. Barry's got the tail of a cat tied to the aerial of his bike!"

"It's a raccoon's tail! I bought it at the store!"

"Sir! Let's have floor hockey instead!"

"I hates floor hockey!"

"We don't want you girls! Hey, sir! Let the girls play skippin' or something, but let us play floor hockey!"

"There will be no playing anything until we finish our math!"

"Kids should be allowed to choose sometimes. You said so!"

"Yah! You never let us have fun—real fun!"

"Okay, okay. What does 'real fun' mean?"

"If we wanna go somewheres, the creek or somethin', then you should let us. . . ."

"Duke just wants to finger Sandra!"

"You're dead! After school you're gonna get two black eyes, and you're gonna swallow your teeth, you smartass!"

"Hold it, Duke! Settle down, okay? Open your books to the math review on page 51."

"Wait a minute! I ain't gots no pencil!"

"That's because you used it to jab that little kid at recess and the teacher took it off you!"

"Get lost. . . ."

"Here, you can use my pencil."

"Thanks, sir! Hey look! I stole the teacher's pencil!"

"Can I turn on the radio during art?"

"Quietly, yes . . . quietly. But first, our math!"

"Hey Sandra, get up on the desk and take off your shirt!"

"Shaddup! Why don't you get up there and whip out your prick?"

"Question number one! You've got three minutes!"

"Hey, I need to go to the bathroom! Stop the test! If I don't go now, I'm gonna shit my pants!"

"Let's draw his shit!"

"Yah, I wanna draw his turds!"

"Anybody who doesn't finish this test gets a note to take home and get signed!"

"Sir! Can I have a note, please! I love notes!"

"Me too! I wanna note sayin' I'm bad!"

"Everybody line up for bad notes!"

"Hurry up Levon! Whip down those pants and shit on your desk! I wanna draw your stinky plops."

"Hey! Gimme back my math book!"

"Cut out the crap."

"This is boring."

Tuesday, March 29

Levon's father stumbled through the door and took a chair. He wore a faded blue tee shirt which had "Unemployed With Dignity" stenciled across the chest. After examining the room, he asked me where the washroom was.

"The boys' john is around the corner," I said.

On his way out, he turned and said, "You don't really buy beer, you know. You rent it."

On his return, I showed him a short story his son had written a week earlier. It began:

> It was so nice out, I decided to leave it out all day. I didn't feel like going to school, so I stayed home and watched the Flintstones on TV.

It ended:

> Life is like a prick. When it's hard you get fucked. When it's soft you can't beat it.

Levon's dad cracked a smile. "Takes right after his old man, don't he?"

Wednesday, March 30

I asked the class to act out what they watched on television.

Vince did a beautiful number on the evangelical TV shows by having the host of the program repeat the words "Praise the Lord!" while he made a move on one of his voluptuous guests.

Frank and Sanjay did a put-on of two cops busting a group of dissident youths for smoking pot. Then the two cops took it home for themselves.

Hamlin, a frustrated new student, made up a character he called Super Student, who went through the school socking malefactors and bumbling, bigoted, short-sighted teachers.

But in my opinion, the best was Tina's portrayal of a movie starlet. She emerged clad in a scintillating red smock, with a matching hat and scarf. She tossed aside her hat, unwound her scarf, and dropped her smock to reveal two enormous breasts, which resulted from the strategic insertion of two soccer balls under her sweater.

Tina also had another ball thrust up her back, which she described as her "spare boob—it'll start a new trend in Hollywood!"

Thursday, March 31

There was a loud knock at the door. Spinner answered it, and was almost bowled over by Mark's mother as the stormed up to my desk.

"Gimme Mark," she demanded.

Mark slumped down in his seat, peering timidly over the edge of his desk.

"Mark," I said, "you'd better go with your mother."

No sooner had Mark walked to the front of the room than his mother had him pinned to the blackboard.

"Who was it, Mark?" she ordered.

"I don't know. Lemme go." Mark pleaded.

"Not until you tell me the name of the kid that beat you up and took my twenty dollars. You stupid jerk. Why'd ya tell him you had twenty bucks on you for?"

"I don't know," Mark whined.

By now the whole class was quietly watching. Dave, another West Indian kid, asked: "Was he black?"

"No, he was goddam honkey white," Mark answered, head down.

"You goddam well pick him out of some class. Mr. McLaren, I'm taking Mark for a walk aroun' the school." She half-dragged him out of the room.

Mark found the kid in a grade six class. He still had ten dollars in his pocket. Mark's mom took the kid by the scruff of the neck, and hauled him to Fred's office.

Later, she returned Mark to class.

"I don't know what you're gonna do with this one," she said. "Sometimes he can get so stupid, he don't know whether to fart or turn blue."

Monday, April 4

Burt always seemed to know what was troubling me, even though I tried to keep my problems to myself.

He could tell if I didn't get enough sleep the night before, whether or not I was feeling rotten, or if I wasn't getting along with a particular staff member that day. Burt seemed to possess some special capacity for reading people's minds.

For example, today Burt blurted out: "Mr. McLaren's in a good mood today. That's 'cause Spinner hasn't shown up yet. Mr. McLaren can't stand the way Spinner snaps his gum when he chews. Right, Mr. McLaren?" He grinned. And continued. "You hate Spinner's buck teeth, too—dontchya, Mr. McLaren? You think they make him look like a donkey. Am I right? I'm right, ain't I, sir?" He refused to stop. "Mr. McLaren's probably prayin' right now that Spinner's sick, and not just late for class. Hey, Mr. McLaren. You got both fingers crossed?"

They were.

Tuesday, April 12

After school, over a cigarette and coffee, Fred filled me in on a bit of his background.

He had been hired here as principal after serving four years in another inner-city school in the west end. It was there that he gained his reputation as an innovative principal. Articles were written about him, and he was invited on several TV talk shows to speak about his philosophy of reaching kids through improving their self-concept.

The main reason he had put so much effort into his previous school was because his wife had died prior to the appointment, and he'd tried to lose himself in his work.

Teachers were so devoted to Fred's method that they involved themselves in group therapy sessions, and often stayed until eight or nine in the evening working out new programs for the kids. "Several marriages suffered badly," he told me. "Teachers seldom made it home to see their spouses before bedtime."

When the former principal here retired, the staff had decided they wanted a definite say in who would be chosen to succeed him. They formed a committee and approached the Board, offering a list of qualities the new principal should possess.

After all, a school in the Jane-Finch Corridor had special needs, and a special person was needed to help fill them as principal.

When the staff heard that Fred was available, they called a staff meeting to decide if he would be suitable. Except for a few teachers who preferred a more authoritarian type, the majority agreed they liked Fred's philosophy.

He was hired in September, four months before he hired me.

"At our first staff meeting," he told me, "the teachers told me they wanted me to do here what I had done at my former school. I told them about my wife dying, and that was one of the reasons I had put everything I had into my work. I also explained that since that time I had remarried, and my wife was expecting a baby soon. I knew I wouldn't be able to give as much as I had previously, but I promised I'd do my best to bring a better program into the school."

Thursday, April 14

During art, Donnie drew a picture of Sharon squeezing her breasts and squirting great jets of milk into the air, and then left the drawing on Sharon's desk, waiting for her reaction.

She reddened, gritting her teeth. Crouching low, she charged and split open Donnie's cheek with a head-butt. Her eyes widened when she saw the sight of blood.

Donnie stemmed the flow with his shirt tail and retreated to his desk. I sent him down to the nurse.

"Stupid prick!" Sharon hollered. "The dummy don't even know ya gotta be pregnant before you squirt milk!"

Friday, April 15

After teaching in the area for a few months, I was aware of what the environment could do to the kids. Every so often I would see new kids with impeccable records turn into sad, battered little things. It was the particularly meek and timid child that drew my sympathy.

Such a child was Hari, a miniature bespectacled Mahatma. On his second day he walked timidly up to my desk. "Sir, some girls in the other class beat me up after school."

I knew he would have a tough time.

But Hari got the break he deserved. His father bought him a motorcycle tee shirt, black polyethylene boots, and a Leatherette jacket with lots of zippers and studs. It's a very effective disguise.

Monday, April 18

Before I started teaching, I assumed any hyperactive students would be in special classes; I had no idea there would be so many in my "ordinary" classroom.

John, a fellow teacher, told me that children in the area were particularly under-nourished, and that could not be disputed. He thought they probably were suffering from allergic reactions to the food dyes in all the junk food they ate. He also warned me that the fluorescent lights installed in every classroom affected behavior, making kids jumpy, making them lose control. "Shut off those lights. Keep your blinds wide open," he advised, looking up from his latest copy of *Prevention* magazine.

I found his admonition of fluorescent lighting eccentric, to say the least, but I was desperate enough to try anything. I usually kept my venetian blinds angled downwards, to shut out the view; the slightest opening would distract the class.

Today I threw caution to the wind and opened them as far as I could. From the open windows long shafts of honey-colored sunlight fell across the children's faces, highlighting the faint cloud of chalk dust, bathing the room in a golden haze. The children's faces appeared almost angelic.

After about ten minutes of peace, Duke decided to go on "scrap patrol," drag-ging the wastepaper basket around the room, collecting all the paper that had fallen on the floor. Then, like a bulldozer out of control, he crashed his way through a row of desks, elbowing kids along the way. Sally tried to avoid him, only to fall backward in her chair. Then Robbie and Sharon, ignoring all the commotion, sauntered up to the blackboard, each trying to outdo the other a graffiti competition.

Clutching at their groins, Levon and Frank asked me if they could be excused. They ran out, giggling, to the main building, not bothering to wait for an answer.

Duke must have noticed the grimace on my face, because he bounded to my desk with a puzzled look on his face. "Hey, sir . . . what's with you?"

I gave natural light a chance for the next few hours, but then the kids began throwing things out the open windows.

One of the teachers was delighted to bring this to Fred's attention. He sug-gested it would be a good idea to keep my blinds closed in the future—natural light notwithstanding.

Friday, April 22

At my previous school, I remember the boasts of the staff I overheard during lunchtime:

"One girl in my grade eight class is already working on advanced calculus."

"One of mine already has a firm grasp of quantum physics."

"I have a student who will be the next Emily Carr."

Whereas the bragging of inner-city teachers was of a different nature:

"Three kids in my class have been to court this year for vandalism."

"One of my girls was so hard to handle it took three of us, including Fred."

"Two of my students shot at each other with .22s from the balconies of their apartments, and say they'll shoot me if I hassle them."

They often painted the most dismal picture possible of their students, compet-ing over who had the toughest kids, the worst problems; it was their red badge of courage.

Monday, April 25

Rod asked me if I'd mind taking over the lunch-hour duty; the regular supervisor was off sick. "You're pretty good with the kids," he said. With that remark, I was able to chalk up my first compliment of the year. He explained that the students were given half an hour to eat, and then were led, by me, outside to be supervised during play in the schoolyard.

The kids were already eating when I arrived. The place was in an uproar; food was spread all over: pop, Twinkies, chocolate pudding, Oreo cream wafers, brownies, hot dogs, peach pits, salami rinds, bread crumbs, potato chips, cheesies.

I took my place at the supervisor's desk, watching quietly. There was as much food trading going on as food eating. Right away one kid tried to trade me his bologna sandwich for my ham-on-a-kaiser, saying his cost twice as much.

Every so often I ducked flying baseball cards. Music blared mysteriously from a car parked across the street, the kids tapping their feet to it. And I swear every kid took his empty lunch bag, blew it up, and popped it with a bang!

A little boy wearing a sea-island shirt and wire-framed sunglasses stood up and danced "the robot" for a group of clapping girls, dreadlocks flapping.

At the half-hour mark, I told the kids it was time to go outside. Sandwich wrappings flew everywhere in the delicate stampede out the door.

Once outside, I heard screams coming from the sand pit. A big red-headed kid had tied a piece of glass to the end of a broken hockey stick and was gleefully charging a terrified pack of fleeing behinds. He held a garbage-pail lid as a shield, and wore an inverted plastic funnel as a helmet. I took the weapon from this miniature Don Quixote, which he didn't like at all.

"Gimme back my spear, you son-of-a-bitch."

"Sorry, weapons aren't allowed on school property," I said crisply.

"Hand it over or I'll break your ass, man."

I pried the glass off the end of the stick, and threw it over the fence.

"You're new here," the kid drawled, "ain't ya, turkey?"

That afternoon, as I was pulling out of the school parking lot, I glanced down at the dashboard. The eight-track stereo I kept locked in my car was missing.

Wednesday, April 27

Duke and his mom and dad had moved down to the Jane-Finch area from a mining community in northern Ontario. The only work the father managed to find lasted merely six weeks. Soon after, he packed it in and headed back up north; Duke and his mother stayed behind.

"No way I'm heading back up north," she told me today during an interview, a tremor of irritation in her voice. "There's nothing up there. The city is where you make it. Everybody knows that. I'm looking for a job as a keypunch operator. If I can get that, well it won't be easy, but maybe we'll finally move out of this dump. I don't like the gang that Duke's been hanging around with. I don't like what's happenin'."

I mentioned that Duke was settling down a little—I wanted to give her some relief. Underneath the brave exterior, she seemed worried.

"I don't like the way Duke picks on kids. I think he's reacting to the way the bigger kids pick on him. Do you really think he's getting better?"

She candidly admitted how frustrated she was, stuck in a government-subsidized building, a single parent, out of work. . . . She was feeling stagnant, dormant, even though she was in her prime years.

She found herself weeping in the elevator one day. From crying she went to drinking, gulping tranquilizers, and sometimes "running away, leaving Duke alone in the apartment all night." She felt anger against a society that didn't seem to care about her or her son. "Christ, Mr. McLaren, I don't know what I'll do."

Instead of going home directly tonight, I decided I needed to calm down. I took a stroll along the boardwalk by the lake, at the foot of my street. I thought about Duke and his mother. Then, partially restored by the sky and water, I turned toward home.

Thursday, April 28

The lunchroom, created with the intention of serving as a buffer against the hectic classroom, was not always immune to intrusions from the outside world. Just as I was digging into a plate of steaming spaghetti from the nearby Italian restaurant, a gaunt, pock-marked teenager walked into the lunchroom and sat down next to me.

"Are you Ruth's teacher? I'm Jeff—her brother."

I put my fork down. "That's me. How's Ruth been? She's missed most the week and—"

"Don't know where the hell she is," Jeff said, taking a hand-rolled cigarette from a flat tobacco tin, lighting it.

"What do you mean?"

"Mom took off with Ruth this weekend and said she ain't coming back. My dad figures that maybe mom called you at school. He sent me here to find out."

"I haven't heard a thing." By now, I'd lost my appetite. "Are you sure she won't come back? I mean—has this sort of thing happened before?"

"Mom's always yakkin' about leavin' and takin' Ruth with her if the old man don't get a job. But she's never had the guts."

"If she notifies the school where she is," I said slowly, "the information must be kept confidential. Sorry."

"Ya? Well . . . okay." He rose to his feet and thrust his hands into his back pockets. "Because when the old man catches up with her, he'll kick her ass into tomorrow."

"And what does that mean?" I asked apprehensively.

He cocked a thin, dark eyebrow. "You'll find out."

After he left, I asked the secretary to let me know if she receives a letter from another school requesting Ruth's records.

Monday, May 2

Teachers often miss the obvious, even when it stares them in the face every day.

The school year was almost over when I noticed that, with very few exceptions, Tina was absent every Monday. I mentioned it to a parent volunteer who lived on the same block as Tina. She looked surprised: "You mean you don't know why Tina misses school on Mondays?"

"No."

"It's the same thing every Monday night," she explained. "Her mother makes her stay home to look after her baby brother during the day. That way it's easier for her mother to sleep all day long. She wants to rest up for the late night session of Bingo."

Well, that seemed like a pretty weak reason to keep a child out of school. I cornered Tina's mother during parent interviews. She was reluctant at first, but eventually she admitted the truth.

"What's one day a week, Mr. McLaren? You tell me. Tina can always make up her school work. Just keep her in the next day, after school." She kept raising and lowering her arm, drawing my attention to the fact it was in a cast. "I'm supposed to feel guilty about keepin' my daughter home one day a week? You gotta be kidding. How can I afford a baby-sitter? On a lousy Mother's Allowance check I can hardly make the rent. Come on, Mr. McLaren. What's one lousy day a week if Tina makes up for it the next day? Just a drop in the bucket. Look, I got problems. Life ain't easy. My boyfriend's one of them sadists you know."

The more she went on, the worse I felt.

"It was my birthday a few days ago. And he walks in Friday night with no present. No card, no flowers, no chocolates. And the worst part was that I kept remindin' him that my birthday was Friday.

"I started yellin' and screamin'. I called him a creep for comin' home drunk on my birthday. He never even wished me a happy birthday!"

She shook her fist angrily. "Then he tells me he's got me a birthday present. I don't believe him. So he walks up the stairs to where I'm standin', and I'm still mad at him, so he yells 'Here's your birthday present!' and throws me down the stairs!" Which explained the cast.

Tuesday, May 10

Sophie wore a limp wreath of straws, strung together from thread picked off the frayed edges of the classroom carpet. On her tee shirt was printed "Children Are People Too." Her body was bent, emaciated. She walked with her arms held protectively across her necklace, as if it were an amulet that would keep her from harm.

"I saw Sophie's dad in the elevator last night," Mark suddenly announced to the class. "He was drunk. I know, 'cause I seen lotsa drunk people before, and when he got out, he fell on the floor."

"You're lyin'!" Sophie yelled.

"Sophie's 'welfare,'" Duke taunted. "Your dad's always drunk, ain't he, Sophie?"

"He is not!" cried Sophie. "My dad's sick, that's all! He gots the flu!"

"Then how come his breath stinks?" Duke chimed in, contemptuously. "I was there, too." A flurry of giggles and sniggling passed through the class.

"He wasn't drunk." Sophie shouted, desperate. "Shut your face!"

"Okay! Okay!" I shouted. "Enough!"

Sophie was already running for the door. Duke reached out and grabbed at her straw necklace as she raced by, breaking it.

"Welfare!" he screamed, as she slammed the door.

Thursday, May 12

Over dinner, I started blaming the entire universe for the problems I was encountering at school: parents, the school system, the government, the decline of the West. I'm becoming quite a cynic. I miss the days when I was a young student radical who really believed society could be changed, poverty abolished and everyone given an equal chance to make something worth while of their lives.

Was education a middle-class pablum which, upon ingestion, socialized into uniform amorphous lumps? It was obvious my kids couldn't fit into the system, so the most obvious solution was to make the system more accommodating to "culturally and economically disadvantaged kids."

"You're putting an educational Band-Aid over a major social wound," Jenny told me, "when what is really needed is drastic surgery."

I nodded. "But the only people who are empowered to perform the surgery are in top administrative positions, too far away from the scene."

"Become a political activist then," Jenny suggested, winking.

"Maybe I should," I laughed. "I could go out and try to abolish poverty and scream about the injustices of the system. Then they might listen enough to give me an executive position on the School Board and ask me to invent a more advanced attendance sheet!"

Friday, May 13

During "news," Dan told the class how his baby sister was run over by car. She was running across the street to fetch an order of french fries for her mother.

He vividly described how the blood dripped onto the road from her broken nose, and the cut on her head, and the ambulance taking so long to arrive. "I saw her in the hospital today," he told us. "That's why I wasn't here this mornin'. My sister's disconscious and talks in her sleep. She talks funny—real slow and shaky like."

"Hey, man, she's drunk," Levon cracked. "What'd she drink—vodka or whiskey?"

"Maybe she was smokin' pot," Duke added.

"Hey . . . wow!" Jackson said, excited. "I gotta tell my mom. She really likes gory stories."

"Tell us about the blood."

By this time I had marched to the front of the room. "Hold it. I don't think Dan finds his sister being hit by a car that exciting."

"Yah, you guys!" Burt shouted, backing me up. "If you guys find it so neat, why don't you go play on the highway. Go up on the 401 and play in traffic."

"You guys are gross," Sandra exclaimed. "I wouldn't wanna watch somebody gettin' run over."

"News is over," I announced.

Dan walked over to his desk slowly, as if he were measuring each step. He took his seat, put his head down.

"Hey, Dan," Al said, placing his hand on Dan's shoulder. "Keep us posted, eh?"

Monday, May 16

Jabeka sidled up to Marlene's desk and solemnly stated: "You know, Marlene, I don't never wanna get married." She usually didn't initiate conversations.

"How come?" Marlene asked.

"You gotta make meals, do the washin', and do whatever the man says. You gotta do the wash on Friday night or Saturday, 'cause the laundromat's closed on Sundays."

"You don't have to do all that. You and your husband could take turns. I want to get married when I grow up."

"How come?" It was Jabeka's turn to ask.

"When you gots to pay the rent," Marlene replied smugly, "your husband can pay half."

"My mom's got to do everythin' in our house," Jabeka mused. "And she don't like it. Besides, men drinks too much. When they die, you gotta pay a lot of money for their funeral. My grandmother forgots to sign this paper so that the government would pay for my grandfather. He died because he drunk too much, so my grandmother had to pay for buryin' him—I member she was real mad. I didn't like my grandfather, he was always drunk. The only time I liked him was at Christmas, when he gave me five dollars."

"Maybe you'll marry a man who don't drinks."

"My mom says that they all drinks too much. Yesterday my mom told me she might get divorced from my dad."

Friday, May 20

The mild weather was my salvation. I took the kids outside to explore the creek at the back of the school. It was ideal for them—they could run around and shout and work off the excess aggression they had built up. When they cooled off, they eagerly started the science experiments I had planned.

Duke decided to find a crayfish and write a brief description of it as his project. Unfortunately for the crayfish, his description included a drawing of its insides, which he explored after cutting the crayfish open.

Some of the kids removed their shoes and socks and waded in the creek. That was hazardous, unless you were wearing horseshoes, because of the broken glass and cans and other garbage accumulated over the years. I had to keep a sharp eye on them, warning them away from dangerous areas.

I've started to take my kids outside for more than just science lessons. We enjoy it out there. We set up a little shelter behind some trees, and it becomes our classroom on warm afternoons. We bring our books, papers, and pencils with us. The kids use stones as paperweights on windy days to hold their papers in place. Back in class, they decorate the stones, painting them in marvelous colors.

Tuesday, May 24

Max was the school psychologist. He usually showed up on Tuesdays to assess students who had been referred to him by their teachers.

He had read my referral form for a new kid named Matthew, and wanted to see him in a classroom setting. I slipped Max into the back of the room, and the class went on as usual.

Matthew sat at his desk, tapping a book with his pen. His whole body involved. He shook up and down in a jumping-jack motion, a strange dance in time with the pen taps. The taps were growing louder and louder. He turned and looked at Max. Then he went back to tapping his book—only this time added some obscene gestures to his act. Matthew's mannerisms were starting to make Max look uncomfortable.

Suddenly Matthew stopped his book-tapping and took three casual steps toward the middle of the room. Then he wildly attacked his desk, pushing it the corner and turning it completely over, spilling its guts on the floor: pens, pencils, books, binders, loose paper, magic markers I had been searching for for weeks, crayons. . . .

I rushed over to Matthew and grabbed him under the arm. Then I quickly escorted him outside, telling him to stay by the door until he cooled off.

Max agreed to test Matthew. "Once the results are in, though," he tonelessly, "it may take him years to be placed. There are already so many on the waiting list. The system can't absorb them all. Maybe if Matthew's parents were better off and had some pull with the Board. . . ."

On my way out the door tonight, the school secretary told me we'd received a request for Ruth's records from a small, rural school in Alberta.

Friday, May 27

Clad in a pin-stripe suit, plaid vest, and fingering the looping chain of his pocket watch, Fred entered his office, waved me a hello, and slumped down in his Boston rocker.

It was very early in the morning, but already a third of the student body had poured into the library where Dean, the librarian, had set up a special program for kids whose parents worked the early morning shift.

Fingers loosely laced behind his head, Fred kicked off both shoes in motion, resting his stocking feet on the pine coffee table. He picked up the phone and mumbled a message to his secretary around an unlit cigar.

A tiny girl in tattered overalls and a baseball cap so large that it almost hid her face timidly knocked on the office door. Fred welcomed her in with a broad grin.

Slowly, almost reluctantly, she removed her hat, revealing a mass of dreadlocks that she fingered nervously.

"Who did your hair?" Fred asked, smiling approvingly.

"My auntie," she replied, giving Fred a quick, sideways glance.

"Well then, tell your auntie she did a great job, because you look terrific."

The girl's head snapped up and her eyes widened. A smile broke across her face. She rushed across the room and planted a kiss on Fred's forehead. He responded by giving her a long, extended hug.

"She comes in every morning before class," Fred winked, "just to get a hug."

The sincerity of Fred's affection for the kids was obvious. I sometimes wondered whether I was living up to his standards, being only too aware of my lack of love for certain students. Even when I tried looking at the positive side of a particular student's character—Duke's, for instance—I found it extremely difficult to let go of my hostile feelings. Only an affection that was honest and spontaneous would have any effect.

Thursday, June 2

Duke bumper-hitched a ride on my van so many times that today, as I was about to drive off for lunch, I got out and asked him to join me for a hamburger. My suggestion threw him, but after a few seconds he said, "Sure, man, as long as you're buyin'."

Around the other kids Duke was aggressive and hard, but often with me he was a completely different person. He talked about missing his dad, spoke eagerly of his plans for a newspaper route. With the money he saved up from his job, he would be able to travel to see his dad—although he admitted sadly that his dad never wrote him or his mom.

Duke and I agreed to have more excursions for hamburgers, but from now on, he says, he'll pay for his own.

Monday, June 6

"Wanna know somethin', sir?" Jabeka asked out of the blue.

"Sure. What's on your mind?"

"My stepdad went to Jamaica last night for good. He wants me to go with him, but I didn't want to. So he took my brother instead."

"Why's your stepdad leaving?"

"My mom don't like him no more. Me either. You know, when he buys us clothes they're always old, and they tear easy. When they go in the washin' machine, they shrinks."

"Is that all?"

"No, sir. When I was a little baby he changed my diapers and treated me real rough."

"Can you remember that far back, Jabeka?"

"Well, my mom told me."

"What else did she say?"

"When I was a little girl, I had a bleedin' nose and was chokin' and my stepdad just put on his coat and went to a party. And after the party he went to sleep in the park."

"Aren't you going to miss your stepdad, though?"

"No. But I'll miss my brother. My mom kicked my stepdad out for good, after last week."

"What happened last week?"

"My stepdad gave me a grown-up pill, and I started to cough. There was a pin stuck in it."

"Don't you ever want to see him again?"

"Just at Christmas, so's he can give me lots of presents. He told me he was goin' to spend lots of money on me."

Friday, June 10

There was a loud knock on the door. I opened it and was met by three women. The heaviest one, in a pink bathrobe with kitty fluff around the collar, carried a baseball bat.

"Where's Mr. Hartford's room?" the heavy one demanded in a raspy voice, adjusting her robe.

"Down the hall to your left," I replied. "Is there a problem?"

"One of my kids told me that Mr. Hartford roughed up my littlest one, Tony, at recess. And believe me, I'm gonna make him pay."

"I'll show you where his room is," I said nervously. "But I'm sure there must be some mistake."

We went down the hall together.

Hart was the staff heavy. He turned to face us, squaring his great shoulders. He was leaning against the wall, his massive arms folded over his Budweiser belt buckle.

"What's this about you slappin' Tony around at recess, Hartford?" the lady with the bat demanded.

"Are you his mother?"

"That's right! And I want an explanation."

"I suppose you were informed that Tony was in a fight at recess and kicking another boy in the face when he was down? I had to grab Tony and him off the kid. Is that a good enough explanation?"

"I didn't hear it that way," the lady responded, looking a bit puzzled.

"There was another teacher on yard duty who can back me up. Do you want me to call her?" Hart asked.

"Forget it," the lady said. "Come on, girl." she barked. "Let's go home. Somebody's been lyin' to me, and I'll be using this bat yet."

Monday, June 13

"Sir! I gots a rotten tooth! It wiggles and this gooey stuff leaks out!"

"It's just spit. Lemme knock it out for ya!"

"I think you should see the school dentist, Levon. You'd better hurry before he leaves for the day."

"No way. That dentist is a Paki!"

"Well, you're a nigger! Haaaaa!"

"Look! I've already spoken to you about using words like that!"

"A Paki is a Paki no matter what you say!"

"I gots this big pimple under my chin!"

"I'll punch that out too! I'll give you an uppercut!"

"Go jerk off, why don't you!"

"Hey, sir. Can I whisper you a secret?"

"What is it, Dan?"

"Only if you promise not to tell Duke."

"Okay. What is it?"

"Duke and I went to this movie on the weekend . . . right?"

"Right."

"So we sits down near the back to watch the show. Then this chick sits down a few seats away . . . right?"

"Right."

"Duke sits next to her and puts this popcorn box on his lap. The box is all empty . . . right?"

"Right."

"So he takes the bottom off the box—just rips it away. Then he puts the box over his thing . . . right?"

"Go on."

"Then he says to the chick, 'Want some popcorn?' The chick says, 'Sure,' so she reaches into the box. . . ."

"Sir! Duke's tryin to break my pimple!"

"Okay, class! Settle down! You've still got your stories to finish off before recess."

"I don't feel like doin' a story!"

"Hey . . . why don't you leave sir alone. His face is gray. Can't you tell he's constipated?"

Monday, June 20

On the weekend, snipers fired rifles from the roofs of nearby high-rises. I found a bullet hole in the front door of the school.

Wednesday, June 22

I was late getting my final report cards finished and went into a mild panic. I tried to work on them during class, but it was much too noisy. I even tried to work on them during yard duty, but that, of course, was doomed to failure.

During lunch, John noticed all my report cards spread out in front of me. He said I bore a strong resemblance to a newscaster who had just thrown an epileptic seizure. So I explained.

"When the noise in my room gets too much," he told me, "I simply throw the kids a test. That usually shuts them up for at least half an hour!"

Of course! I hurried into the office, grabbed a handful of stencils, drew up a math test, and quickly ran it off on the machine.

While I worked on my report cards, the class worked steadily on their test. Until, that is, Janice shouted, "Duke threw a magazine out the window!"

I let the incident go by in favor of peace and quiet. "No talking," I said. "Keep your mind on the test!"

Next, the door was kicked open and Karen somersaulted into the room. Her mother outside bellowed, "Get into that room! Don't you try and tell *me* you're sick!"

Shortly afterward, the recess bell sounded. I hurried over to the main building for a cigarette.

When I returned I noticed a crowd of tiny kindergarten kids gathered around a torn magazine outside my portable. I took a closer look.

On the cover was a nude and bloodied woman with mammoth breasts was bound by several studded leather straps, spread-eagle to a chair. Head over the picture was "Man Rapes Woman With Boyfriend's Bleeding Head."

"Wow," I heard one of the kids whisper.

Thursday, June 23

Now that the year was nearly over, I noticed that Duke had mellowed considerably, almost to the point where I wondered whether his toughness wasn't simply bravado all along.

It couldn't be disputed that he displayed a savagery, certainly a sadism, in several fights I witnessed. But the fighting seemed to be happening less frequently.

Last fall he had forced a kid named Lindsay to eat a piece of dog crap. Now he was acting more the benevolent despot. Since he no longer initiated fights, neither did his followers. He swore off smoking, so smoking became taboo. He took up gymnastics after school, and his gang dutifully practiced their somersaults on the gym mats.

One teacher told me she spotted Duke signing out a book from the library.

Wednesday, June 29

Rod had been asked by a Board trustee if the school could contribute some children's artwork to the Canada Day celebration at the nearby junior high school. Knowing more than a little Board politics, he agreed. Our school, he decided, would have the best display of the festival. I was to coordinate the exhibit, gathering together murals and paintings by the students which emphasized Canada as the land of opportunity, multiculturalism, solidarity, happiness, and wonderful community spirit.

Everybody showed up for the celebrations: parents, school trustees, social workers in denim overalls, red-nosed alkies, cops, glazed-eyed teenagers, senior citizens.

Buddy showed up, too. Within three minutes, my cassette tape recorder was missing. I called him over and asked if he'd like to play detective for me. He replied succinctly: "Go shovel shit, Mr. McLaren."

Then I politely asked if he'd like to reconsider playing Sherlock Holmes, this time offering a five-dollar reward. Buddy smiled. "Sure, Mr. McLaren gonna be a detective when I grows up. I'll get it back."

About five minutes later Buddy returned. The tape recorder was tucked under his arm, and there was a big grin on his face. "I caughts this son-of-a-bitch runnin' off with it to the plaza. So I runs after him, and tells him to give it back. When I caughts up to him, I says it belongs to Mr. McLaren, this real nice teacher friend of mine, so he'd better hand it over." Buddy could have easily surpassed Sherlock Holmes by simply solving only the crimes he himself committed.

I shouldn't have reinforced Buddy's theft by giving him a reward, but I needed my tape recorder for the celebrations.

Unfortunately, the festivities were canceled shortly after they began. Too many tires were being slashed in the parking lot (including the police cruisers), the lady that ran the dunking pool had her purse stolen, and one of the policemen on duty "lost" his hat!

"O Canada" blared out strangely through the cracked tape recorder speaker.

Epilogue

Congratulations were heaped on me by the administration—I had survived the year.

I threw a party for the kids, and they did a beautiful job of decorating the portable; it was a crepe-paper paradise. I felt it the best atmosphere to make my farewell.

The fun was cut short when Buddy floated by to check out the music. He wanted to be the disc jockey, but Muscle Lady was challenging him for the job. To avoid a confrontation, I decided to take the kids over to the gym, where a larger graduation dance was just beginning.

All the young calypsonians were there: Feet were tapping and hips were swaying to the beat of West Indian reggae. Scores of kids crammed into the gym, dancing as they came through the door. A mass of swirling bodies, arms upraised in celebration describing graceful arcs, heads thrown back in blissful abandonment, they slowly gravitated toward the stage. There they were met by a multitude of other revelers, knees buckling, feet shuffling, hips rolling.

Muscle Lady whirled onto the stage amid a pulsing strobe light, lip-synching her theme song, *Vibrations*, her thin legs revealed through her translucent pants.

Buddy stood in the middle of the floor, his shiny black hair reflected by the light as sharp crisscrossed wires. He danced wildly, with a covey of onlookers applauding.

"There's my man!"

"Watch him move, ladies!"

"Hang it all out!"

"Shake those feet!"

He smiled back, obviously enjoying the spotlight.

The next day there was a staff meeting. When I heard that a grade four class was being vacated by a teacher who was transferring, I asked if I could take the class; Fred agreed.

I suppose I expected a feeling of elation or accomplishment at the end of the year, some kind of emotional ovation. I had come through a long period of fragmentation, and now I was ready for a leap toward sanity. All year it had been as if I had been homesteading on the frontiers of despair. I had changed from a relatively even-tempered and reasonably patient person into a mass of raw nerve endings and brute instinct. I had formed a shell around my emotions in an attempt to keep myself from being drawn into the deeply wounded lives of the kids.

I had been too idealistic. I wanted the classroom to be a place where the whole would contribute to the health of its parts. I wanted to show the kids how to express their conflicts without tormenting each other. I suppose in a sense I had achieved some of my aims. After all, the kids did express their feelings. But with all the role-playing, psychodrama, and class discussions, I had expected greater harmony.

For most of their lives, school for these kids had been a kind of enforced lethargy, where violence became the natural culture of the classroom. I wanted to change their perception of school, to free them from everything about learning that seems so rote and mechanical: bells keeping kids in step and on time, curriculums plotting out each separate skill to be learned, and when.

I didn't want to be just a PR man probing the fractured psyches of the kids in the name of achievement and competition; I wanted to mend some of the tears in their emotional lives. But in attempting to do so, I was becoming an emotional wreck myself. It was almost impossible to teach kids who felt like rodents in a locked cage, fed crumbs by strangers, and from which there was no escape. I had seen sporadic, impulsive, and ultimately senseless violence with very few strands of hope.

The questions I asked myself over and over were: What kind of person had I really been to the kids? How much did I really help to empower them? A public school teacher has the responsibility of helping kids negotiate with all kinds of things: language, geography, art, drama, gym, reading, film, mathematics, social skills—and making them relevant to the world outside. At the very least I should be able to help them get along with each other, or so I thought.

I debated whether or not to attend a summer course at the university that might provide me with some theoretical grounding in inner-city teaching. Jenny insisted that what I really needed was a break from anything to do with teaching. So we took out a loan from the credit union and packed our bags for San Francisco. I hadn't been there since my visit in the sixties, and I looked forward to seeing that beautiful city again. The change of scenery and the chance to put my job out of my mind would be welcome.

But on the trip home I started thinking about the kids again: I couldn't put them out of my thoughts. My mind was filled with so many unanswered questions: Would the younger kids in grade four be more enthusiastic and less defiant of authority? Could I reach them before they were conditioned to be so defiant? Could school be more than just an expensive baby-sitting service? Could it alter the class structure?

My new class would be in the main building, actually the largest room in the school, the former library. When some kids had set fire to the building, the new wing was built, leaving the old library unoccupied.

A classroom would have many advantages over the portable. A delightful thought occurred: I wouldn't freeze in winter each time I had to go to the bathroom. Most of my boys, rather than trudge to the main building, preferred to urinate in the snow outside the portable. It was a fresh experience, having a gallery of yellow abstracts to gaze on. There must have been an art to it, since I definitely appreciated some more than others. Sometimes I'd walk by a row of "angels" that the kids had made by lying in the snow and flapping their arms and legs. All my angels had yellow eyes and yellow mouths. When I began to recognize individual artists by their style, I knew it was time to find an indoor classroom.

So now, I would have a new grade four class to teach. During our holiday I had sought spiritual refuge in books, to get ready for the following year. I also picked up some books on alternative schools and progressive teaching techniques from the local library.

At home, I searched for the grade four programs I had kept from my days at Teachers' College. I discovered I had used them to keep the refrigerator level.

2 The Invisible Epidemic

Friday, September 2

This morning I decided to get a head start on the term. I arrived at my "new" room to find chairs piled haphazardly on desks that had been pushed into a heap in the corner. The bulletin boards were still littered with debris left by the previous teacher, and old torn posters still hung on the walls.

Rather than put the desks into straight rows as I had done the previous year, I decided to arrange them in rectangular groups of six each. I dragged in a few tables from the stockroom and set up the art center near the sink. I also acquired a broken tape-recorder as an improvement for my "sound center." It complemented the record player and earphones.

My biggest challenge, I had learned, would not be in teaching the kids—my biggest challenge would not be in getting along with the other teachers—my biggest challenge would be in trying to please the caretakers!

They had insisted last year that I put my desks back into rows at the end of a day, because that way it was easier to sweep my room at night. And then, when I brought in some old furniture I had found down at the Sally Ann, they refused to help me carry it upstairs. They protested that my classroom was already a junkheap!

I found Rod in his office and asked him if I could borrow a TV for my room; there were three TV sets circulating. The one I asked for had a broken stand and was usually left idle in the stockroom. Teachers were unlikely to ask for it because it was large and heavy and a big pain to move. No one would get upset about me monopolizing *that* set! And maybe it would keep my class quiet after lunch when kids were usually at their rowdiest.

Rod helped me move the set to my room.

Tuesday, September 6

On the first day of class, I talked to the kids about the kind of program I wanted to run.

"Are we gonna to do any sports?" one student asked.

"Floor hockey?"

"I don't like floor hockey, sir," a tall kid offered, rising slightly out of his desk.

"What kind of sport do you like?" I asked, tensing.

He jerked his thumb at the lapel of his shirt. The button he wore read: "Breast Stroking Champion." "That's me!" he declared, grinning.

Friday, September 9

I had promised the kids we'd watch TV this morning. I settled on a program called "Cover to Cover" about children's books, with an artist illustrating the stories. The class sat and watched the show quietly.

As soon as the set was turned off, however, the kids became more hyperactive than ever.

I sadly reported to Rod that my TV experiment wasn't working out, and that I was going to return the set to the stockroom. One of the caretakers happened by and overheard us. "Hey McLaren! I'd be happy to lug that TV back to the stock room for you!" he volunteered, smiling.

Monday, September 12

My new location has a definite drawback—the washroom, conveniently situated just around the corner, has proven more popular than my classroom.

A steady stream of kids clutching their groins, hopping up and down, continually line up at the door waiting to be excused. Or three or four kids make a mad dash for the washroom without bothering to ask for permission. It got so bad I was forced to move my desk in front of the door to control the situation.

Then groups of kids complained about the continual noise in the classroom, and asked if they could do their seatwork in the hall. I reluctantly agreed, setting a limit of five kids at any time for my "hall group." Every five minutes or so I peeked out to check on them.

This afternoon I noticed whenever I checked that there were always some kids missing. When I asked where they were, the others simply shrugged their shoulders and exclaimed, "They're with the other freaks!"

"Other freaks?"

"Card freaks!" they shouted, and pointed to the end of the hall.

Down the hall a group of about twenty kids from different classrooms was huddled together in the stairwell tossing hockey cards against the wall. It was such a serious competition I felt a little guilty when I broke up the game and sent them all back to their classes.

Wednesday, September 14

It would drive anyone a little crazy. At least half the class wandered around the room at any given time, despite my attempts to keep them working quietly at their desks. The constant movement was threatening.

Relief happily appeared with Hartford, the gym teacher, who took my kids twice a week for half-hour sessions.

Usually I ended up chatting with a small group of kids who had forgotten their gym equipment and remained behind. It was the same group every week—a coincidence, I'm sure. I looked forward to my half-hour talks with these kids, nicknaming them "the rap pack." I dreamed of what it would be like to have a class with only six or seven students. There were kids in the group whom I could barely tolerate in a normal classroom with thirty-five students. But individually or in the small group, they were easy to talk to, sensitive, and communicative.

When the rest of the class returned from the gym, pleasant young people reverted to their former selves: distant, rowdy, agitated.

Friday, September 16

Behavioral modification was a term I was introduced to in Teachers' College. So when it came up as a topic at an "inner-city" professional development day conference, I wasn't a bit surprised.

"Behavioral mod is what you need to marshall these inner-city toughs," I was advised. One teacher described the "check system" to me, so I decided to try it out.

I stripped the bulletin boards on both sides of my room, and tacked up the names of all thirty-five of my pupils along the top. Under each name, I hammered in five nails forming a vertical straight line, spaced so that five pie plates could be punched and hung from the nails. Each pie plate stood for one day. One side of a pie plate was a happy face. The other side, a frown.

After explaining the rules to the class, I showed how I could turn over a pie plate to the frown if the child sinned. If one of my kids sinned twice, I could put a sticker on the plate. Five stickers meant the child had six checks against him or her. If a kid managed to go the entire week with only one check, he or she received a pack of gum and "free activity time." They cheered at that, of course. But if he or she managed to get zapped more than three times in any single day, then the culprit had to stay after school and do extra work from my "sad face" book.

But there was still more.

When I yelled "Carpet check!" the kids had to run over to the carpeted area and sit down. "Sound check!" meant that all the kids had to sit quietly and listen. "Desk check!" meant that all the kids should rush to their little desks. We all agreed to try it.

"Okay kids!" I began. "Carpet check!"

They all ran over each other rushing to the carpet, and knocking down a little girl in the process. Her lip started to bleed. While I made sure she was okay, I said "Sound check!" and everyone quieted down. Which was when Elvin stood up: "I don't like this game!"

"Check for Elvin!" I said at once.

Eddie, my newly chosen "check monitor," promptly took Monday's pie plate and turned it to the sad face.

"Class," I said, "the first check of the year goes to Elvin!"

I was suddenly overwhelmed with every kid demanding they get checks. Somehow, they had gotten things mixed up. I tried explaining the system all over again. Confident, I sent the kids back to their desks with a resounding "Desk check!"

After enough time had passed for the kids to finish their assignment, I called "Carpet check!" Thirty-five pairs of assorted sneakers pattered to the rug.

Wait a minute! It was only thirty-four pairs!

I heard fuming and muttering at the back of the room. T. J. was still at his desk, mumbling angrily. T. J. wasn't going to cooperate. Why should he? He was most at home in chaos, not order. The other kids would follow his lead if I didn't do something.

T. J. was staring at the ceiling, arms folded defiantly across his chest, red woolen beret pulled over one eye. Then he started to get up. I felt a surge of confidence. Then slowly he slunk back into his chair, glaring at me. Then, he stuck out his tongue. Everyone waited for me to make my move.

"Stay at your desk!" I told him, as if I had wanted him there all along. "Open your book!"

This caught him off guard. He started to open his speller, then suddenly slammed it shut, his eyes squinting. "You sucker! You ain't getting T. J. to the rug! Not that way! You gimme some gum like everybody else is gonna get! Eh, eh? Then I'll go! But you ain't keepin' me in! I got to get right home after school 'cause I gotta go for a blood test!"

"You'll get your gum just like everybody else if you follow the rules!"

"I want a promise!" he demanded.

"Uh . . . well . . . if you've got a good reason not to stay in, I'll look into it."

Suddenly there was a room full of excuses. "I can't stay in either, sir, 'cause my mom's takin' me to Towers to get me some socks!" Betsy had to take her younger cousin right home after school. Murray had "sore tonsils," and maybe the doctor would want to "cut 'em out" after school. And so on.

I was panic-stricken. I started checking everybody: "Check T. J.! Check Winston! Check Murray! Check Betsy! Double-check Betsy!"

But Eddie, my loyal check monitor, protested louder than the others. "I can't stay in either, sir, or my dad will beat me! I have to look after my little brother."

"Check yourself, Eddie!" I groaned in despair.

The next day, I told the class we were going back to our normal routine. T. J. told everyone it was because I was too cheap to buy gum.

Tuesday, September 20

Melissa wore a plastic charm with the signs of the zodiac around her neck. It was a good-luck token for her mother, who was dying of cancer. She clutched it tightly, and sometimes shoved it under her sweater so it rested next to her skin.

The day after her mother died, Melissa ripped the pendant from her neck and threw it out the window.

Wednesday, September 21

During the first few weeks in class, Sal had a gentle manner that lulled me into complacency. There was no way this kid would ever be a problem; it was simply out of the question. On the surface, he was all friendly gestures, eagerness, and ambition.

This afternoon Sal was sitting quietly at his desk, fingers laced behind his neck, leaning back in his seat. The kid beside him called him a name—some innocuous remark, like "goofball."

He reared back with a sideways look and threw his desk against the wall. He sprang growling, seizing the kid by the neck and screaming, "Fuck right off!" Then he violently brought his chin down onto the kid's head.

Flesh tore. Blood gushed like a tiny geyser into his eyes. The kid's face twisted into a cruel mask. In the few seconds before I pulled him away, Sal sent a flurry of kicks into the ribs.

I grabbed Sal under the arms and spun him around, forcing him back to his desk. He watched me guardedly, his head lowered. Then his wild, angry face suddenly melted into an ingratiating grin.

"Lost my cool, eh sir!"

The class, which had remained silent, now sputtered and giggled. Two boys took the wounded victim downstairs, while Sal pushed his hair back from his face, grinning.

Tuesday, September 27

Professional development days are traditionally set aside to allow teachers to attend lectures, conferences, and workshops to keep up with the latest developments in education. For us, it really meant a welcome day of relief from the kids.

Most inner-city teachers I talked with found the lectures irrelevant. It was hard to wait out the boredom of the lecture so we could go out together for lunch.

The "Halfway House" restaurant at Pioneer Village was the most popular eating spot. I think the staff enjoyed the walk through Pioneer Village, an exact replica of a Canadian town in the 1800s, as much as the meal itself. It was such a stark contrast to the bleak surroundings of the Corridor.

After listening to a particularly boring lecture, Hartford whispered in my ear: "Let's skip Pioneer Village and go to the Golden Star for a beer!"

After the lecture, Hart and I rounded up Big Arnie and Mrs. Rogers, piled into Hart's station wagon, and drove off to the Golden Star.

As Hart led us to a table at the front of the tavern, Mrs. Rogers pointed to the stripper on stage, remarking, "I hope my women's consciousness-raising group doesn't find out about this!"

The stripper, a lithe blonde in her teens, had almost finished her gyrations by the time we took our seats. Hart's eyes were glued on her final gyrations as the music on the juke box slowly faded. After a bit more scrutiny he thumped his fist on the table. "I knew it. That's Cathy Huston up there."

"Cathy who?"

"Cathy Huston!" Hart said emphatically. "I'm sure of it." A look of surprise and bewilderment covered his face. "I taught Cathy in grade six."

I watched his face turn red as the stripper, her act completed, now covered herself with a black lace negligee. She made her way across the room in the direction of our table. When she got to us, she stopped and looked down at Hart, puzzled, while he sat there stone-faced. Then she smiled.

"Hiya, Hartford!"

"Hiya, Cathy," Hart managed. She then went past our table and disappeared into a room behind the bar.

We quietly finished off our beers and left.

Wednesday, October 5

Jenny mentioned last night that I seemed to be losing much of my enthusiasm so early in the term. She'd noticed that I didn't spend as much time preparing lessons, and I avoided discussing school events. I couldn't give her a ready answer. After mulling it out, I finally decided to discuss it with Fred.

I told him that I felt helpless, ineffective. My enthusiasm seemed on the wane. No longer a neophyte, I felt I should be making much more progress with the students. The signs of physical and emotional abuse that the kids brought to class from their homes and the incidents of violence I had witnessed in class all seemed to be part of the normal state of affairs, rather than isolated incidents. Isolated pockets of classroom disturbances I could handle . . . react to . . . follow up on. But it was another matter to be confronted with a situation where every day, all thirty-five pupils seemed to be out of control. How could I possibly establish a close relationship with so many students?

I thought about the books and articles I had read on disadvantaged kids. In most of them, the authors wrote about problem children in special classes, with one teacher to every ten kids. Now that seemed reasonable. But life in my class was like being machine-gunned by events so quickly that it was impossible to keep track of everything. I was feeling numbed, insensitive, apathetic.

Fred's answer was so simple, I couldn't believe it, yet it had tremendous impact on me. He told me that although I should try to reach as many of them as possible, that if I only affected a single child in my entire class, my presence would have been worthwhile. He told me to relax, and not have such high expectations.

"This is the only way you can keep your spirits up," he said. "If you're going to worry about not reaching every one of them, you won't reach any. If you tell yourself that if something positive happens with a kid, no matter how small it seems, that it's worthwhile, well then, you'll do fine. You'll be in shape emotionally to help that next one who's standing in line."

Wednesday, October 12

Unless some miracle intervenes, I'll have T. J. in my class for the rest of the year. My fellow teachers admire me greatly for taking him on. Two years older than the others, by the time he'd hit grade four his records were thick with reports of classroom disruption.

T. J. is painfully thin, with the narrowest face imaginable and a shrill, bleating voice. His skin is stretched over his tiny head like a Halloween mask. He continually spews a steady stream of obscenities from thin lips that are covered with rose-colored herpes sores.

As soon as I saw him, gouging victims with pencil swipes, I feared the worst. When I asked him over to my desk for a friendly chat, he refused to move from his desk, held there by some unnatural gravity.

At ten, T. J. is the second youngest in a family of eleven. Everyone has police records, including his parents. The one exception is his six-year-old brother, Mickey.

This afternoon, while I was having lunch at T. J.'s, the police came in and arrested his second eldest brother for assault. Mickey ran after the police cruiser shouting: "You fuckin' pigs! Bastards! Bring my brother back!"

Lunch at T. J.'s is always eventful. Lining the windowsill above the sink are bowling trophies, plants in pink flamingo vases, the complete collection of Red Rose Tea china miniatures, and a toy model of an outhouse which features a plastic figurine urinating through a crescent-shaped hole in the door, a present from T. J.'s grandparents who live in a small farming community near London, Ontario.

T. J. loves to visit his grandfather. In class he tells me stories of visiting him in his stepdad's metallic green pickup truck, complete with whitewall tires. He'd show off the body work and pinstriping to Gramps, and let him feel the broadloomed dash. Gramps promised T. J. he'd buy him one of those toy dogs whose eyes burn red when the brake lights are on. T. J. wishes he could move in with his grandparents.

His mother seems interminably anxious. She directs the kitchen chaos in an orange negligee covered with black "happy face" designs, held together at the waist by a green tie belonging to her ex-husband, a security company monogram stitched on the front.

Mickey, the younger brother, shoved a pornographic wall calendar into my hands that he'd stolen from his sister's house. All of his sister's upcoming court dates had been penciled in, and they ran through to next year.

T. J.'s mother told me she had hopes that T. J. would be the black sheep of the family—the only offspring *not* to turn to crime. But her hopes were swiftly disappearing. T. J. has already been in court once for throwing gasoline at the mailboxes of a nearby high-rise and then setting them on fire. The blazes were fortunately quickly doused.

T. J.'s mother wanted me to drop by after school tomorrow to celebrate the release of her eldest son's best friend from the hospital. There was going to be lots of beer, chips, and Dolly Parton on the record player. The friend, who had been in a motorcycle accident, had been sitting behind the driver when they crashed suddenly into the rear end of a car. The driver's thigh bone popped out from its socket and shot backwards, puncturing the friend's left testicle.

T. J.'s mom commented: "In this life, you can still get by with one ball, as long as your pecker's all in one piece!"

Friday, October 14

When I went to public school, the worst you could be was the classroom informer. Squealing on somebody—anybody—was an outrage. Even among the very young, loyalty went unspoken. I was disturbed by the casual way Elvin betrayed the other kids in the class.

"Sir," Elvin began one morning, "Eddie's got two boxes of crayons in his desk instead of one. He stole one pack from your desk. I know 'cause I saw him do it."

Or, "Sir, I saw Betsy take an extra pencil from your filing cabinet. I saw her with my very own eyes."

"Hey, guess what?" one day he asked the class. "I saw sir put a box of thumb-tacks in his briefcase. I bet he stole 'em for his kid!"

I borrowed a slang term used in prisons for stool pigeons: "wearing the snitch jacket." The next day I brought in one of my more beat-up jackets. The idea was to make Elvin put it on each time he finked on somebody. The kids though it was a lark. Everybody started to snitch on their friends just to be able to put the jacket on and ham it up for the rest of the class!

I quietly took the snitch jacket home.

Monday, October 17

Big Arnie, formerly a kindergarten teacher, had been hired as the school's new compensatory teacher responsible for setting up a classroom to accommodate groups of students who found it difficult to function in regular classroom settings.

Arnie offered miniature hockey, table tennis, darts, macramé, lessons on how to use a yo-yo, and coloring Star Wars stencils. He also served as a sounding board for the kids' problems.

Teachers could choose up to five students from a class, and send them over to Arnie for half an hour at a time. Some teachers used the opportunity to go to Arnie's room as a bribe, so kids would finish their work. Other teachers admitted sending kids to Arnie that they didn't like, just to get them out of the room.

Friday, October 21

The local community center was offering soup-and-sandwich lunches for a dollar, so I went over. I met a beautiful West Indian woman named Saffron, who had a background in social work in Jamaica and was presently doing some volunteer work, counseling teenagers in our area. She started to talk about the fate of many West Indian youngsters coming into the country.

"The usual pattern is for West Indian immigrants to leave their children behind with relatives. When the parent finds a job, she—they're usually single mothers—sends for her kids. It's easy to leave kids back home temporarily, because there's always a big family, with aunts, cousins, and grandparents ready to take a child in.

"Many times, the mother marries again and starts a new family. When her children finally arrive from the Islands, they not only have to cope with a new culture, but with a new daddy."

Talking with her put the situation of one of my students into some perspective. Rhonda's brother, Leroy, had recently come from Jamaica to join her, their mom, and a new stepfather. Rhonda had joined her mother a year earlier. The transition had gone well, and Rhonda did well at school.

Her brother, on the other hand, took an instant dislike to his stepfather. Leroy was placed in Mrs. Rogers's class at school, and immediately was at odds with the other kids. During the first week, he pummeled one of his classmates after being called a "black bastard."

A few weeks later, he was caught shoplifting from the nearby plaza and charged by the police.

Monday, October 31

After we saw a slide show on West Indian culture, two of my West Indian girls asked if they could braid my hair.

Charleen, very hyperactive, and always in the throes of a high-strung dance, leaned a rickety shoulder into my back and started working on the crown of my head.

She put the comb through my hair, twisting it tightly, and winding it round and round. My hair became hopelessly entangled in the comb.

Rhonda had to get the scissors and cut the comb out.

T. J. lent me his Blue Jays cap until I got used to how ridiculous I looked.

Tuesday, November 1

When the kids asked me if they could play some music for the last half hour each day, I reluctantly agreed. They might get out of control, but it was worth the risk; music was an important part of their lives. In fact, if there was anything in the lives of the kids that could be termed "sacred," music was it. Radios, records, record players were ritual objects of worship, communication totems linking them with their gods.

More kids wanted to become rock heroes than firemen, policemen, scientists, or, perish the thought, teachers. I asked them what it felt like to listen to their favorite songs.

"Makes me feel free!"

"I feel like me!"

"I forget what's botherin' me!"

"I feel like a somebody!"

Because the kids took their music seriously and developed a tenacious loyalty to their individual favorites, fights often broke out over which records to play. Some kids were disco freaks, while others swore by rock 'n' roll. And some kids who liked radio asked for that. I agreed there could be one radio in the class, and told T. J. he could bring in one he claimed to have found in an abandoned car.

Sal argued that the class would be better off listening to his Elvis Presley collection, but T. J. plugged for his radio. I decided to let the class vote, and called a meeting to debate the issue.

Typically tough in a taut tee shirt and shades, T. J. opened the meeting by swaggering to the front of the room, hands in his pockets, clearing his throat. "Records are okay, but they got only one or two hit songs in an album. You gotta listen to all the others before you get to the hits. *Nobody* can argue about radio, 'cause radio plays *all* the hits."

"And another thing," he continued, warming up. "What happens when we go outside in the afternoon? Are we gonna plug a record player into a tree?" That brought a few laughs.

Sal hesitated before speaking, flashing an enraged look at T. J. "Okay smartass!" he said bitterly. "Bring in your dumb radio, but don't be surprised if it gets broke!"

"Here goes another fight," Charleen sighed.

T. J. grinned. "I got my radio right here, man!" Almost magically, he produced a tiny transistor radio, strapped to his wrist. "This is so I don't lose it!" he said to Sal, pointing to the strap.

Sal raised his fist angrily. "Who wants to listen to news? You don't get news on records!"

"News is only five minutes! And you get the hockey scores, too!"

"I hate that ole hockey!" Rhonda bellowed.

"And what about commercials?" Betsy cried.

T. J. jumped on top of his chair, waving his arm angrily. "If you don't want no radio then come and take it!" He stuck out his tongue at Sal.

I stepped in. "Class meetings are for talking things out, not fighting! I'm surprised nobody has suggested taking turns. One day bring in the radio; the next, the record player."

"Good idea!" Charleen exclaimed. "Why not let T. J. bring in his radio Mondays and Tuesdays. Sal and the other kids can bring records on Wednesdays and Thursdays!"

"What about Friday?" Betsy prompted.

"I'll bring my guitar!" Robert chimed in.

T. J. laughed, looked thoughtful, then said, "Deal!"

I rose to my feet. "Meeting adjourned!"

On the way back to my desk, T. J. suddenly turned up his radio full blast. Several kids started to dance. Soon the entire class was moving to the beat.

Friday, November 4

I joined a martial arts class to work off some frustration. I go twice a week and work out for several hours. Sometimes I even stay for an extra hour just to punch the bag.

Wednesday, November 9

Lynn was the bus driver who drove "slow learners" to the school from their homes in the outlying regions. The kids referred to her busload as "Lynn's Loonies."

Lynn was new at the job. Her first request was that the driver's area be enclosed in steel, with a shatterproof glass window directly behind her head.

When that suggestion was turned down, she asked if she could use, instead, a second-hand shark cage. She offered to install it herself if the Board would pay for it.

Lynn retired after two months.

Wednesday, November 16

John kept slipping nutrition books into my mailbox. I had resisted his attempts to sell me on the miracles of vitamins, bran, and other supplements as just food faddism. Impressed, however, by a number of scientific articles that seemed to back up John's claims, I decided to give it a chance.

I opened up a health store in the school, run solely by the students themselves. The office gave us a fifty-dollar loan, with the understanding that it would be paid back at the end of the year. I stocked up on oranges, apples, bananas, papaya juice, raisins, and peanuts. The kids advertised over the public address system.

In the beginning it caught fire. I had to make emergency trips for new supplies, and we were even thinking of opening up a new line of products.

After a few weeks, the sales dropped drastically.

The proprietor of the nearby variety store felt the pinch, and was offering specials on candy to win back customers.

Thursday, November 24

Winter has arrived, so I gave my class an assignment titled "What I Like to Do in the Winter."

Stash wrote that his favorite event was snuggling into bed at night, pulling the covers tightly over his head, and farting.

Wednesday, November 30

Franko appeared to be one of my better-adjusted students. He rarely got into trouble, was well-liked by the other kids, and showed a keen interest in his subjects. He seemed to be the model student.

Midway through the term, Franko was beaten up by some kids from another class, and shortly afterward he started to become involved in more fights, sometimes with kids from other classes, sometimes with his fellow classmates. It was puzzling, unsettling—why had a seemingly nonviolent kid turned into a bully, and in such a short time!

When I talked with Franko about it, he replied proudly, "My dad tells me to do it. He's teachin' me how to street fight."

I gave his dad a call, arranging an interview after school. He arrived about four o'clock. When he took his jacket off, I was dazzled: chinos, black boots, a black shirt open to the waist with sleeves rolled up, his powerful arms covered with tattoos—fearless tigers, hearts pierced with arrows, coiled serpents. His hair was slicked back like a James Dean character, a tiny dark curl resting on his forehead.

He greeted me unsmilingly, shaking my hand firmly. "I'm Franko Senior!"

"Glad you could make it," I replied, rubbing my hand.

"Well, I figure if my son's in trouble, then I should be here, eh?"

His voice was warm and friendly. I decided to get to the point right away.

"Franko Junior's been fighting a lot, sometimes without being provoked. I've talked to him, and he told me that you told him to fight. That you're teaching him how."

"I didn't know he went lookin' for fights," he said, frowning. "But if somebody's pickin' on him, that's different. I tell Franko Junior to beat the hell outta him, tell him to get the kind of reputation I had when I was a kid. Nobody wanted to tangle with me, and I'm goin' to teach Franko to do the same."

"Frankly," I said, "Franko's not simply protecting himself. He's turned into a bully."

He gritted his teeth: "Hell, if he's turned into a bully, I can fix that! I'll give him a lickin' he'll never forget!"

Tuesday, December 13

Betsy had more problems than a ten-year-old should have to cope with. An ugly red scar ran from her lips to her chin, the result of a freak accident on her bicycle. The kids called her "Flip-lip."

While Betsy was in the recovery room, the doctors had tied her into a strait-jacket to prevent her from picking at the scab. Her mother felt it was the experience of the straitjacket that was at the root of her hyperactivity—one explanation for the way Betsy whirled around my classroom.

She and her family lived in a tiny brown townhouse in the middle of the neighborhood. The family included two older brothers and a German shepherd named Wolf.

Both her parents had nearly identical back problems from a near-fatal car crash they had been in several years earlier. Now they spent most of their time stretched out on their sofa or bed.

A constant, gnawing tension ate at the household. The father, now on a meager disability pension, was unable to work. The mother found it equally as difficult to cope.

One afternoon Betsy's mother appeared at my classroom door. A tall woman with short, sandy hair, she needed crutches to help her walk. While I dismissed my class for the day, she waited.

I suspected that Betsy was being beaten at home. Her mother admitted it without much prompting. "She seems to be the easiest target, since she's so active, always jumping around and getting in the way all the time."

She told me that she had been beaten occasionally by her husband. Since the car accident, the family had changed. She agreed to try and control her anger.

"Doesn't it bother you that your husband beats you, though? Wouldn't it help to work on that end of things?" I asked gently.

"Of course he beats me!" she snapped. "Wouldn't you be upset if you couldn't find work and had to sit home all day doing nothing?"

Soon something came up that gave Betsy a chance to boost her confidence: the school's talent contest. Any student could put together an act. She eagerly took a spot in the show.

She found a dilapidated banjo. For weeks she practiced, but always one simple phrase. Over and over again, she played those same three notes to a perfected monotony.

The evening of the talent show, although I was busy marshaling the kids, I gave Betsy what support I could. She had arrived an hour early, dressed in a shocking-pink outfit, her hair in tiny ringlets, her lips smeared with lipstick to hide her scar. I tried to build up her confidence, but then the sound system blew, and Fred insisted I fix it. I didn't see her again until she came on stage.

She looked confident walking out to the center stage. I crossed my fingers. Using only a brittle finger, she began to play her single phrase, over and over: "Plunk-a-plunk . . . plunk-a-plunk . . . plunk-a-plunk . . ." After half a minute, the audience became fidgety. Some tried to smile to give her encouragement. Then I heard from the back what I had dreaded: shouts of "Freak!" and "Flip-lip go home!" Half-pleading, half-demanding that she make a fast exit, the audience called an end to Betsy's big night. More and more people began whistling, stomping, and complaining. She stood still, looking confused. At first she looked behind her, as if someone else on stage deserved the abuse. Finally a look of terror froze her face.

She strode off the stage dragging her banjo, fighting back tears. She stopped for a moment in the wings, looked out at the jeering audience, and stuck out a malevolent tongue.

She missed the next week of school.

Wednesday, December 14

"Mr. McLaren! T. J. punched me in the face!"

"Fuck you, Flip-lip! Quit lyin'!"

"Look at my nose, sir!"

"Did you hit her, T. J.?"

"She punched her own face—I didn't do nothin'! She's tryin' to get me!"

"Come and see my picture on the blackboard, sir!"

"Did you use paint on the blackboard?"

"It's okay. It washes off."

"I'm not tryin' to get him into trouble! He really did hit me!"

"Will you come up and look at it now, sir?"

"In a moment."

"Is this how you do today's number work?"

"No . . . you were borrowing here. It's an addition question. What do you do in an addition question?"

"Carry!"

"Right. You carry, not borrow."

"Sir, are you comin' up to see my picture?"

"T. J. just stole my comic books from my desk!"

"You said you'd help me with my printin', sir."

"Just a minute."

"I didn't take nothin' from Frankie's desk."

"I hate printin'! Can I just draw instead?"

"Tell Sal to watch his fuckin' welfare face. I'll punch it in for him!"

"You're welfare!"

"You're mom's a nigger!"

"Okay, outside boys! We're going to have a little talk!"

"My dad used to be welfare, sir, but he ain't now. He drives a pickup truck . . . he delivers these boxes of flowers."

"When are you going to tell T. J. to gimme back my comic books!"

"I said for you guys to wait outside!"

"Garth's dad don't drive a pickup truck, sir. I never seen him drive a pickup truck, and he lives right next door to me."

"He gets the truck at work, stupid!"

"When are you gonna do somethin' about T. J., sir?"

"Who cut the cheese and didn't put out no crackers?"

"Sal did! I heard him!"

"It's Betsy!"

"Come on kids, let's drop the fart questions, okay?"

"The person that smelled it first is the one who did it!"

"Then it was Betsy!"

"You stink, Flip-lip!"

"Fuck you!"

"How do you say this word, sir?"

"Restaurant."

"Restr . . . ant?"

"Restaurant. Res . . . taur . . . ant."

"Restrant."

"Close enough."

"We havin' gym this afternoon?"

"Yes—Monday afternoon as usual."

"Can I be captain!"

"I'm suppose to be captain!"

"It's my turn!"

"Sir, come over and look at my paintin'."

"I asked to be captain first!"

"We're not having teams today; we're doing gymnastics."

"Sir, Sal cut the cheese! This time, I'm sure!"

"The next time we have teams, can I be captain?"

"My picture's dry, sir! Will you hurry up or just forget it!"

"Who said it was me that cut the cheese? Was it you T. J.? If it was, I'll bash your fuckin' head in!"

"Garth's got a *Playboy* in his desk and he's feeling up the pictures inside his desk!"

"What?"

"Ya, he put his finger up the ass of one of the naked pictures. There was this picture of a woman bending over touching her toes."

"Garth, can I see you a moment?"

"Oh, oh."

"Sucker!"

"I got my comic books back, sir. They were in T. J.'s desk, just like I said."

"They're mine! I brought them from home! Honest. My brother give them to me yesterday!"

"You asshole! You just wait until I get you outside!"

"Shut up, welfare!"

"Okay, class, line up for recess."

Friday, December 16

Christmas reports are nearly due, and the only time I have to work on them is during lunch period. Since the staff room is filled with distractions, I took my folder down to the coffee shop in the local plaza and wrote while I ate.

I was about to leave when I noticed something familiar about a customer at the front counter.

Levon, hunched over a bowl, was slouching in his seat exactly as he slouched in his chair when he was in my class. His skin was grey and damp, an ugly cut hung on his forehead.

"How've you been doing?" I asked, sitting down next to him.

We shook hands. "Hi, McLaren . . . Good to see you. . . ." he said. Resting one hand on the counter, he wiped his forehead with the other. Beads of sweat reappeared at once. "Could you lend me some spare change for another bowl of soup, man?" His voice was weak. He paused frequently. I reached into my pocket. "Thanks man," he drawled. "I'll pay you back when I'm rich and famous."

Monday, December 19

Sal worked surprisingly hard, considering his well-known abhorrence of math. From time to time he glanced at me and whispered to himself. After ten minutes of concentration, his mouth tightened. "I can't do this work no more!" he howled. "I gotta get outta here! I hates my math! I won't do it no more! Nobody forces me to do nothin'!" he shrieked.

He disappeared out the door. Others followed suit.

By the end of the day, I had lost five of them.

Wednesday, December 21

Rocky is nine. He's a scruffy kid with a sincere farmlad face, big square shoulders, and extremely large hands. But his head is tiny, and he often grins.

He has the strangest habit of looking at you from an angle that should lead his sight in some other direction. All his movements seem oblique; when he approaches my desk, he never comes directly, but in zigzags. And he enters the room sideways, keeping close to the wall so that I can't make out which desk he's approaching. Then, at the last moment, he makes a dash for his own desk.

Rocky always looks perplexed. He'll raise his hand as if his life depended on it, and then withdraw it as soon as I call on him. A few moments later, he'll be standing in front of me to ask if it's time to go home. He'd sooner stare at the ceiling, scribble drawings in notebooks, anything, than read. He talks to himself out loud.

He once tricked a group of kindergarten kids into touching an icy metal fence post with their tongues. When they finally peeled themselves away, they had donated several layers of skin.

Rocky wants to join a motorcycle gang. He yearns to be an outlaw biker with full leathers, swastikas, and a club crest (his favorite was the Outlaw crest, a skull with two crossed piston rods). He likes the names bikers give themselves: Beast, Mad Dog, Chico, Pig. But the best thing about being an outlaw rider, Rocky told me, would be to have a biker funeral, to be ceremoniously carried past row of shining bikes and be buried in his leather jacket.

I arranged an interview with Rocky's mother. She looked in her early sixties, too old to have a nine-year-old son. Halfway through our interview she told me she was actually Rocky's grandmother. He was born nine years ago to her fifteen-year-old daughter. Rocky's natural father walked out of the relationship before he was born. The daughter later married and had given birth to two more children before she and her husband filed for a divorce. His grandmother had recently informed Rocky that his older sister was really his mother, and that his nephews were really his half brothers.

The man Rocky knew as his father (really his grandfather) became an alcoholic, and had left the family only months before.

The boy was thoroughly confused. He asked why his real mother had "divorced" him when he was only a baby. He was told how his mother was really too young at the time to look after a baby, so his grandmother and grandfather raised him as if they were his parents.

The grandmother's new boyfriend was waiting outside the classroom, holding a little baby in his arms. I asked Rocky who the baby was. He told me it was a present from Children's Aid.

Thursday, December 22

I have a full beard. At the class Christmas party, I received twelve bottles of after-shave.

Monday, January 9

I had always divided the morning and afternoon into forty-minute periods, each concentrating on a different subject area. First would come spelling, perhaps, then reading, then math, etc. But now, to give the kids more flexibility and responsibility, I modified this approach. After opening the day, I put the entire day's work on the board. Then I told the kids that they had the rest of the day to cover all the topics, in any order they decided.

They had a great time charting out their timetables. Once they completed the assigned work, they were given free time. Most of them finished about half an hour before the final bell, and spent the rest of the afternoon playing.

As time went on, I kept giving the kids more and more opportunities to generate their own ideas, to choose topics they were especially interested in. It was a slow process, but the kids certainly seemed to respond better when given a chance to make some decisions for themselves.

Tuesday, January 10

I asked Sal's mother to come in for an interview. I hadn't planned on the conversation centering on her older son, Jack. "How's he been doing?" I asked, after she had indicated she was worried about him.

She lowered her head. "Not too good," she said after a pause, mumbling, "he's been in trouble." She lit a cigarette, took a slow drag. "He broke into a house with three other boys. The owner was away for the weekend and the kids heard that he kept guns."

I asked what happened.

"It wasn't my kid's idea, but he went along with it. They really messed up this guy's house—they shit on the floors, and smeared it over the walls. Then they found a little budgie bird in a cage in the kitchen, and they tortured it and killed it. Just a little bird. First they cut its wings off with a pair of scissors, then poured boiling water over it, and finally killed it with a blow-torch.

"After nearly wrecking the house, the kids finally found the guns, and they brought them out of the house, wrapped in blankets. And they found bullets, too. They loaded the guns and took them over to the highway and shot them off over the cars."

A look of horror in her eyes and mine. I thought of all the people who use the highway, including myself.

"Did Jack get charged?" I asked.

"Yeah. He's got to see his parole officer, once a week."

Now I knew what Sal was referring to when he said his brother was a *big shot* in the neighborhood.

Friday, January 20

Every kid carried a comb. Combs were weapons. They were used in threatening gestures. Sometimes a wide swoop connected, leaving a light scar that became a status symbol, making me think of the sabre scars once proudly worn by Heidelberg duelists.

At first the black kids had the advantage with the five-pronged picks they used for their Afros. The white kids' standard-issue plastic combs were no match, so they all found long-handled combs to wear menacingly out of their back pockets. A long-handled comb could be used in forward lunges as well as side-swipes.

The most sophisticated comb available looked exactly like a switchblade. You pressed a button on the handle to release a jagged blade.

Wednesday, February 1

By the beginning of February the winter feels like it's dragging on forever. Both kids and teachers are despondent, lethargic. So I decided to boost my class's spirits by offering them an early Valentine's Day gift . . . I booked time at the local ice-skating rink.

A few kids nearly froze on the half-mile walk to the rink, lacking proper mitts and head-covering, and wearing worn sneakers instead of boots. But every kid managed to scrounge up a pair of skates!

While I was busy at one end of the arena, tightening some of the laces, T. J. and some friends sneaked outside to the parking lot. I saw him hacking away at a parked car with his skates, puncturing a tire and punching holes in the body.

I left my name and the school's phone number on a piece of paper and tucked it under the windshield wiper. Then I took the kids back to school. T. J. disappeared along the way.

I was shaking by the time we got back. Here I was trying to do the kids a favor, and I end up worrying about what would happen when the car's owner called!

I waited until four-thirty. There was still no call, so I decided to go home.

As I drove past the school, I glanced up at my classroom window. The kids had decorated the window with Valentine's Day messages.

I read the words "I love you, sir" on the cut-out hearts, driving down the icy road.

Thursday, February 2

John enjoyed eavesdropping at the office, and he picked up an interesting bit of information a few days ago which made me more than a bit apprehensive. One of the Board consultants would be coming in to visit my class.

"What's he like?" I asked, genuinely worried.

"Well . . ." John mumbled, scratching his chin, "he's a good man in many ways, but. . . ." I looked at him doubtfully, arching my back to loosen the tight muscles. "Look," he said, running his hand through his sparse hair, "let's say he lives a little in the past . . . on the other hand, make it the Stone Age. Know what I mean?"

"What exactly *do* you mean?" I wanted to be prepared for the worst.

"Listen . . . I'm getting on in years too . . . but I've managed to keep up with the times. Let's just say the consultant was arrested in time, oh, about ten thousand years ago.

"You started out here pretty square. But now you're more like a 'guide on the side,' less like a 'sage on the stage,'" John was fond of corny sayings. "You run a pretty flexible program. You let the kids sit where they feel the most comfortable—he wants to see them in straight rows. You make personal contracts with the kids, and assign work according to what they can handle—he wants to see the same material on everybody's desk. You're physical with your kids, you hug them and so forth—and he wants firm discipline."

I glanced at him uneasily. "I guess he'll destroy me," I said wearily.

He shrugged. "Look . . . let me give you a suggestion." He put a fatherly arm around my shoulder, and walked me down the corridor. "Go back into your class-room and do everything *just* as you've been doing it. The *kids* like what you're doing, and *that's* the important thing . . . not that you're not still a rookie and have lots more to learn." I detected a note of hope in John's voice. "You'll do all right. Tell your kids they'll be having a visitor sometime this month, and promise to give them a reward if they're good."

"Do you really think I ought to do that? Do you think it'll work? I mean, it's bribery, isn't it?"

"I hate to see a good teacher go down the tube," John grinned, waving away my questions like so many flies.

"Any suggestions about what I could give the kids?"

John paused, thinking. "Why not buy them a giant gingerbread house, like in the fairy tales?"

Wednesday, February 8

My class had settled down somewhat. There were still fights, and kids refusing to co-operate, but most of them were getting into better working routines, sometimes teaming up with a partner to investigate items that caught their interest.

In addition to the learning centers, I had set up a drama center, consisting of a makeshift stage and a box full of old clothes.

Our science center was a tub of water filled with metric beakers of different sizes and shapes. We also had a mini-library for science, a microscope, and some slides of insects the kids had collected down by the creek.

Despite the increased response of the kids, I often wondered how much differ-ence any of this would really make in empowering their lives.

Wednesday, February 15

This morning Rod offered to cover my class for the last half hour of the day. I wanted to get an early start downtown to hear a lecturer at the university speak on disadvan-taged kids.

I drove several blocks through a heavy snowfall before realizing I'd forgotten my briefcase. I made a quick stop at the variety store down the road to buy a pen and some paper for taking notes. When I was crossing the street, I turned to see T. J. and a friend right behind me.

"Where'd you guys come from? Shouldn't you be in school, T. J.?"

"We just came from there," he boasted, "and you gave us a lift." They had bumper-hitched the entire way.

I tried to explain the danger they were courting in hitching rides that way, but they walked away laughing. I felt cautious, respectable, and old.

Monday, February 20

Bob runs a drop-in center for adolescents. He's a good friend, and I see him fairly often.

When he began working at the center, one of his first projects was to get the kids to play floor hockey. They insisted that it was impossible because they had no equipment. Bob spent the next few days teaching them how to make hockey sticks out of broom handles, pucks out of wire and cloth, and goalposts out of sticks and Javex bottles filled with sand, with string for a netting.

Wednesday, February 22

My decision to try to provide my class with more opportunities for self-direction was unpopular with a few teachers, who regarded with skepticism my attempts to experiment. They pointed to the results of a meeting we had held with some of the neighborhood parents, who preferred a more authoritarian system. In fact, several parents had complained that I was not using standard readers. Instead, I preferred to create readers out of the kids' own stories.

But, to my surprise, the biggest obstacle to creating a freer attitude in class did not come from the parents. It came from the students themselves.

All their lives they had been ordered by teachers and parents to obey rules. They asserted themselves, logically enough, by going out and breaking as many rules as they could. Removing the rules made them uncomfortable; it left them with nothing to push against.

It took months before the kids were comfortable with planning their own timetables, choosing their own topics for discussion and reports, and exploring their own questions. It also took time and effort to free myself of the odd feeling that, because I wasn't following the standard list of teacher topics, I was somehow not actually teaching. . . .

Monday, February 27

Today I talked to an administrator who has done a lot of work with inner-city kids for the Toronto Board of Education. I asked him what his perceptions were about the plight of poor kids in the suburbs.

"I've criss-crossed the entire country and see situations like the one you teach in right across the map. What makes your area a little more frightening than, say, downtown Toronto is that it's so isolated. There are a half-dozen inner-city pockets in the suburbs that are pretty spread out, and there aren't enough social services to help. From the outside the problems are so invisible, they don't get the attention they deserve. At least downtown people know the situations exist, but in the suburbs people try to forget about the problem areas."

Tuesday, March 7

Renee says her mother doesn't want her bugging her in the house. Her mother tells her to get lost.

When she gets home from school, she disappears. From late afternoon until ten o'clock at night, she spends her time reading quietly in the bathtub.

Wednesday, March 8

From the moment Charlie came into Mrs. Rogers's class he made her life miserable. At times she had to resort to pinning him on the floor and calling for help. Once during recess, Charlie tried to settle a dispute with a classmate with a heavy lead pipe. Mrs. Rogers managed to wrestle it away from him. Several times he was caught rifling coats and purses in the teachers' staff room. He and his newly won followers would come into school late, lingering in the hallway to urinate in the rows of boots outside the kindergarten classes.

Mrs. Rogers didn't give up on Charlie easily. One weekend she invited Charlie to attend church with her, planning to take him afterward to a movie and a restaurant. He brought a friend, Tennessee. During the church service they excused themselves and went straight for the cloakroom, where they rifled the coats. They managed to steal enough money to take off for Funland, a popular arcade a few blocks away. Mrs. Rogers found them sitting in a tiny booth, watching a 25-cent strip film.

Without saying a word she drove them back to her apartment. When they arrived, she told them that she wanted to have a discussion, and asked them to wait in the living room while she went to the washroom. When she returned a few minutes later she found Charlie and Tennessee giggling together on the floor, a good portion of a bottle of her best Scotch gone.

She kept trying, but over the next few weeks she became completely fed up. After he stole eighty dollars from a secretary's purse, she had him placed on home study, which meant he had to go to court. The judge ordered him not to return to school. His education was to be provided by a home tutor. After several months of home study, Charlie's parents had him placed in Thistletown, a hospital for disturbed youths.

He'd occasionally show up in the school yard to announce to his former classmates that he was going to reform school.

"Hey Charlie!" the kids would say. "Far out!"

Friday, March 10

I constantly had to fight the conditioning I had received in my teacher training and in my first year of teaching. But more and more I was recognizing the incidental questions and conversations of the kids as a learning process. I saw that some of the most effective lessons took place spontaneously: What I often thought was disorder was, in fact, kids interacting in another form of learning.

For example, in the fall T. J. used to bring snakes in from the creek. The kids often crowded around his desk, excited, watching the snake writhe, touching its skin, exclaiming over its colors. It would take me a long time to get them back to their seats and settled down. I decided that what the kids were learning from T. J. was probably as real as any lesson I could have dreamed up.

Monday, March 13

She walked into the class with a noticeable limp, her eyes fixed on the floor. Her mouth was a black line; her eyes, which nervously scanned the class, were circled by purple streaks and red gashes; her cheeks were puffed and blue.

A student whispered to me that he had seen her running out of her high-rise building this morning pursued by her mother, who was waving a high-heeled shoe.

When I called her over to my desk, she looked up at me with an expression of guilt, as if she had done something wrong. She told me she had fallen off her bicycle.

Tuesday, March 14

One classroom activity that seemed to make the most impact on my group of grade fours involved printing out the phrase "LOVE IS . . ." in big, bold letters on a ten-foot-long sheet of paper. I tacked the paper to the inside of the classroom door. Students could volunteer their reflections on "Love is . . ."

Love Is . . .
When your brother goes to dad's place
A ham sandwich
Christmas presents
When my mom visits Gord in jail
McDonald's
The Ex
My parents don't fight
When I don't get it for being bad
Being allowed to smoke
Fingering your girlfriend
A honeymoon
Nobody to bug you at night
When your brother goes to dad's place
Fish and chips and vinegar
Going to see dad
Learning to drive
Seeing dad at the restaurant
Smoking grass

Looking after your little brother

Horseback riding at the Y camp

When dad comes over

Thursday, March 16

When Sal arrived in class half an hour late, I knew something was wrong. His eyes, usually clear and bright, were now red and glazed. His face looked blotchy, his hands were trembling.

"What's wrong, Sal?" I asked, giving him a hug, reassuring him I wasn't angry because he was late.

His mouth tightened. "It's . . . it's . . ." his voice quavered. "It's that dad came home last night, and . . ."

"What happened?"

Sal stared at the floor, breathing heavily, sniffling loudly. Then he blurted out, "He spent all his pay on lottery tickets, so my mom . . . she gots mad at him 'cause she needed the money to buy groceries, so I couldn't get no sleep last night 'cause they was shoutin' at each other." He raised his head and stared out the window, avoiding my eyes. "Dad was mad at me this morning, an' told me to keep out of his way or he'd bring out the extension cord."

Wednesday, March 29

T. J. arrived in class wearing a black bowling shirt with "Untouchables" stitched in gold thread on the back.

He gingerly walked to his desk and almost fell into his chair. His mouth was struggling to say something, but the words got stuck. When he managed to gain some composure, he moved from desk to desk, stammering "Hey you assholes! I'm floatin' on air!"

Most of the kids looked a little bewildered, but some of them found it uproariously funny.

"Hey T. J.!" one of the kids shouted. "Got any for me?"

"Come on over to my place after school," T. J. replied. "My mom's new boyfriend's gots lots."

It was hard to tell if T. J. was faking it. A few of the kids enjoyed acting drunk or stoned; they see it often in their environment. I tried to ignore him and continued with my work.

"What's the matter, McLaren? Don't you ever get stoned?" He began stomping around the room, hair flying, arms flailing. "Go ahead and call the principal, sucker!"

To T. J.'s surprise, I dismissed the class for recess ten minutes early. I asked if I could get him some coffee. "Sure, McLaren. Big trick, eh? Go get the principal when you go downstairs."

"T. J.," I said, "I'm going downstairs to get you a coffee. If you don't want it, I'll drink it!"

It took me only a few minutes to grab a coffee downstairs. But by the time I returned, T. J. was gone.

Friday, March 31

Betty had taught in our school for a number of years. Frustrated and bitter, she continually complained about her kids to other teachers.

During lunch, I asked Betty why she hadn't tried transferring from the school to a more middle-class setting. She assured me that the advantages, as far as she was concerned, were all with the inner city.

"In inner-city communities, parents don't really worry about what kind of program the teachers run, as long as the kid learns how to read and add. It's hard enough getting the parents to meet you for an interview!

"But when you think of it, less involvement means less pressure on you as a teacher. For one thing, you don't have to worry about too many busybody parents trying to run your class like they do in some middle-class schools. A friend of mine teaches in a pretty well-to-do neighborhood where the parents are always sticking their noses into the teachers' business: 'Why can't my Johnny do this? Why isn't my Johnny further ahead on that? Blah blah blah!'

"In this school, you don't get that kind of flack. So you put up with Johnny coming to school undernourished. You put up with his misbehaving in class. You put up with the fights at recess. For me, it's a lot better than having the community looking down your throat all the time!"

Few teachers, to be sure, felt the way Betty did. I spoke with many staff members who were proud to work in the inner city.

Monday, April 3

Today the consultant paid a visit. I had been nervous about it for weeks, and I took John's advice and promised the kids a giant gingerbread house if they behaved themselves.

A dyspeptic old crank who reminded me more of a hawk-faced prison guard, he was directed by the Board of Education to go into the classrooms of all new teachers in the area to make sure they knew how to keep the lid on.

One had to question the mentality that found succor in inspecting your cupboards, rating your blackboard script, how neatly you were dressed, how interesting your bulletin boards were and whether they had been changed recently, what kinds of seating arrangements you had and if the desks were veering off the lines marked on the floor by the edge of the tiles, and whether or not the dates in your daybook were underlined in red ink.

He sat down at the back of the room—a white-haired gentleman wearing a royal blue safari suit with a white belt, and matching white shoes. The desk was much too small for him, but he tried to squeeze in anyway. He appeared ridiculous. He tried to cross his legs, but his knees were too high. I noticed he wore diamond-patterned socks. The more foolish he appeared, the more anxious I became. This man could make or break me.

"I'll be observing you from the back of the room," he had said. "Don't be alarmed if you see me making notes." Butterflies in my stomach. "But carry on as usual," he stated matter-of-factly.

I felt like saying something to break the ice, like: "How do you feel about teaching life skills in the first grade?" But a wall of protocol stood between us. He would not break it. I didn't dare.

He stayed at the back of the room, chewing on the rims of his glasses, constantly attending to his little black book even though the lesson hadn't begun. His face alternately went blank and then animated—I had no idea what his expressions meant. I became terribly paranoid. Had something gone wrong already?

"Interesting bulletin boards," he said in a lugubrious tone, just as the kids came into the room.

What did that mean? Interesting?

I leaned back in my chair, planning ahead to myself, thinking that there shouldn't be any reason why today's lesson would be worse than any other day's. . . .

I decided that the reading lesson I had begun would have to be abandoned in favor of something where I could get away with more noise and movement. I sensed the kids were picking up on my uneasiness, and would not be able to contain themselves for long.

I decided to take the kids downstairs and play murderball—that way I wouldn't be faulted for having noisy kids. Luckily, there was a free gym period available.

He watched my control as I led the kids downstairs. I was certain he was observing how deftly I could get them into line. I imagined his breath on my neck all the way to the gym door. When I turned around at the bottom of the stairs to sneak a glance, I noticed with astonishment that he had disappeared!

All during gym period my nerves were on edge; I assumed he would pop in at any moment. The class must have wondered why I was still behaving like an armed forces sergeant with nobody there to watch. And the kids behaved beautifully. No fights, no swearing, no moaning and groaning.

When we returned to the classroom from an hour of jumping jacks, murderball, and relay racing, I was relieved to find he was gone. Apparently, he only intended to visit my room for twenty minutes.

I removed the large brown box from under my desk. Then I sat back and gleefully watched those happy kids devour the gingerbread house in less time than a school of piranha could finish off a roast beef sandwich!

Friday, April 7

Yesterday at lunch hour Fred and I played Ping-Pong. Fred prided himself on his athletic ability and, in fact, was a sensational player. I wasn't bad to begin with and, after playing so much, steadily improved.

I made a bet with Fred in front of the staff. Since I had been a bit late getting to school several times that week, I jokingly told him that if I won the game, I wouldn't have to show up till ten o'clock for a week. If he won, I'd have to arrive a half hour early for a week. Fred instantly took me on, grinning.

After a hard-fought battle, I won the game—and the bet. Of course, it was all a joke, but one teacher thought we had been serious. Today she complained to Fred privately that I was being given preferential treatment. If he didn't break the agreement between us, she'd report him to the Federation of Teachers!

Wednesday, April 12

When Laura and I stepped through the front door of her school's "Open House," I realized it was the first time I had been in any other school since I had begun working in the Jane-Finch Corridor; it was like another world. This was definitely not an "underprivileged" area.

The school was beautifully laid out—and no graffiti on the walls! The furniture looked new, and all the classrooms had wall-to-wall carpeting and tiny greenhouses off the balconies where the kids could grow plants.

I couldn't help but fantasize what my class would do to the place if they could switch schools for a day. All the fancy globe lights would be smashed, the greenhouses torn up, the carpets . . . !

I was surprised to see the sophisticated work Laura's teacher had put up on the bulletin boards. This third grade class was doing work that was more advanced academically than what my previous grade six class had been doing. I felt right out of it.

Laura's teacher told me that the only real "incident" in class had occurred when a kid took a pencil from someone's desk and broke it in half. The mother showed up after class with the kid who owned the pencil, complaining about the "permissiveness" of the teacher, since she had allowed such a "terrible" thing to happen!

I went home afterward and opened a beer, trying to numb the culture shock.

Monday, April 17

Rhonda spent all morning in the library making a cut-and-paste picture of her stepfather. She was going to give it to him as a Father's Day gift. When she proudly showed it to the class, however, the reaction was unexpected.

"Ha!" howled T. J. "It looks like a chocolate bar with a bow tie!"

"You know what?" Sal laughed. "If you wet a nigger's lips you can stick 'em to the wall!"

The class roared. Suddenly T. J. grabbed Rhonda and tried to drag her to the fountain at the back of the room.

"Wet her lips!" Sal cried.

"Stick her to the wall!" other kids screamed.

I rushed over and grabbed T. J., pulling him away from Rhonda, ordering him outside. He took off like a shot and disappeared out the door.

"I don't want to hear the word 'nigger' again!" I told the class sternly. "It's a foul word and hurts people's feelings!"

The class laughed nervously, but they did quiet down.

For a while Rhonda sat at her desk quietly, scribbling all over the picture of her stepfather. Then she finally tore it to shreds. She took out a new blank sheet of paper and began drawing a picture of Darth Vader from *Star Wars* instead.

Tuesday, April 25

For the first time since I came to this school, most of the parents showed up for interviews. Although I had scheduled parents for only fifteen minutes each, sometimes the interviews lasted over an hour.

When they had all left, I saw Fred in the hallway and we walked down to his office for a quiet talk. I told him how depressed I was to find that over half my class came from single-parent families who lived below the poverty line.

Fred cleared his throat, leaning forward. "What we have to do in this school is to accept the child for who he or she is. We can't cloud our minds with the fact that the child comes from a single-parent family, or that the father is an alcoholic, or that the mother is rarely home.

"As teachers, we can't ignore that, but we can't let it get in our way, either. We have to try to make these kids feel like people feel like they're worth something. We can't worry ourselves about what to do with a kid who says fuck off, because that's only a symptom of how the kid feels.

"You have to ask yourself if there is any way you can get children to feel good about themselves."

"But what about the racial problem?" I asked.

"Most of the kids from this area don't feel good about themselves," he replied. "Also, they don't want anybody to feel good as long as they're feeling bad. Misery loves company. So, they pick on the blacks; they pick on you; they pick on me; they pick on the whole damn community because they feel so trapped in their own situation.

"Listen. Teachers have to understand about the prejudices they bring to their job. Somehow, they have to respect the kids' own values, and where the kid is at. We can impose our values on them, but that implies their values aren't any good. That would be destructive. We've got to develop relationships with these kids, and relationships involve feelings, not simply content or information. With poor kids, it's even harder, because you almost have to say to them that they are worthwhile human beings, that you don't care how they dress or where they come from." Fred was getting very emotional. His jaw tensed, his arms waved as he spoke, his eyes burning right through me.

"The way you reach a poor kid who's doing badly at school is not by concentrating on arithmetic, but by getting something going with him or her that tells them that you care about them as people. Forget about the curriculum, at least for the time being. Reach your kids through feelings."

Friday, April 28

I told the kids they could choose any subject they wanted for composition. Here are two I've kept.

If I Could Change Things in the World

No hitting childs with brooms
Like no beeting childs
No punching childs
No kicking childs
No hitting childs
No burning childs
No hitting childs with brooms
No pulling childs hair
So nowne sould attak ther childs

When kids call other kids nigger or honkey. They are just looking for truble. And if someone calls you a nigger or a honkey it dose not mean have to start a fight. The right thing to do is to pretened that you don't hear what the person is saying. But the other day I had a fight with a girl who called me a nigger and a honkey. And I did the wrong thing. I went and started a fight. And I had a nother fight with a brown girl.

And I told her that me and her are both brown so, if I'm a honkey your a honkey too and if I'm brown your brown too.

Thursday, May 4

At the beginning of the term, Fred hired an American woman named Marsha, who had worked for a year in New York City's Bedford-Stuyvesant area, a rough urban ghetto populated mainly by blacks and Puerto Ricans. She was to replace our Special Education teacher who has resigned, on the verge of a nervous breakdown. Because she had two Master's degrees in education, the staff quickly looked to her for leadership.

"Listen," Marsha confided to me, after it was obvious that the other teacher wanted her to lead workshops in class management. "I came to Toronto to get away from the problems of teaching in New York! This was the only school that had a vacancy, and that's the only reason I'm here. And from what I've seen so far, you've got some pretty serious problems. Wait about five more years, until the unemployment situation gets worse, and then you'll really be in trouble!"

Marsha was soon making great headway with her kids. We were all pleased with the support and advice she offered us. Her contract, however, was not renewed for the following year because the Immigration Department felt that a Canadian should have the job.

Marsha went back to New York. Rather than return to teaching, she found a job as a legal secretary.

Friday, May 12

Jay had greasy hair as black as shoe polish, combed in the style of an early Elvis Presley. He carried his overweight avocado-shaped body clumsily into my room late in the school year.

"I'm the new kid," he said with a nervous smile on his lips. His foot tapped impatiently on the floor while his eyes darted back and forth, up and down . . . looking at everything but focusing on nothing. Even his clothes seemed to have a mind of their own. His shirt was half tucked into his pants, his fly unzipped and his shoes undone.

Jay was one of the most hyperactive kids I'd ever seen. For the first few days it took everything I had just to keep him at his desk. When I gave a lesson he'd just fidget around the room, constantly tapping everything and everybody with his ruler.

I decided to phone his mother. As soon as I introduced myself as Jay's teacher, she cut in. "I know . . . I know . . . he's blasting off again in class! Same thing happened in all his other schools!"

"How many other schools has he attended? I mean, he's only in grade four."

There was a brief silence at the other end of the line. "Six or seven," came the voice again. "Around six or seven other schools."

"Could you tell me why?"

"Well . . . these days you got to take each day as it comes, know what I mean? Last month I was all set to move into a house, but my boyfriend moves in with another woman. Before that I was living with a guy who started beating me up. And before that I was kicked out of my apartment because Jay started a fire in the building. Anyway, I'm not budging out of here . . . at least, not right now. My big problem now is Jay. I get so damn desperate with that kid.

"The little brat is always moving or squirming around. Try getting him into bed at night—it's like tucking in a beehive. And clumsy—like a bull in a china shop. I guess you noticed he can't even walk in a straight line. He's always stumbling into his little sister, knocking her down, and kicking her in the stomach when she tries to tell him to fu . . . to leave her alone. Every night he squirms in front of that TV and starts making all sorts of weird sounds; he thinks he's the soundtrack for the shows or something. I mean, he's always yelling and whining and screeching in the background. I get really desperate sometimes.

"He was on Ritalin 'cause the doctor said it would calm him down. But somebody told me it could screw up his sex drive when he grows up, so I stopped.

"The real problem was this neighbor I had in the building when he was first born. She's from Jamaica or one of those West Indian islands where they do all that voodoo and stuff like that. One of the tenants told me to watch out for her—she was a witch or something. I know she put a curse on him. I just know she did!"

Wednesday, May 17

Rocky's uncle, a former Black Diamond Rider in the early 1960s, and now a shoe salesman, made up a list for Rocky of all the active motorcycle gangs operating in the country.

All over the cover of his notebook he scribbled the names: Vagabonds—Satan's Choice—Para-Dice Riders—Last Chance—Outlaws Coffin Wheelers—The Wild Ones—Hell's Angels—The Henchmen—and Gatineau Popeyes.

For once, he spelled everything correctly.

Thursday, May 25

Jewel always seemed to be in a world of her own. She rarely spoke in class, but her creative writing never lacked excitement and richness of expression. Though often quiet and introspective, she always seemed to know what was going on in the outside world. Her stories dealt with adult problems: paying the rent, arguing with apartment superintendents, dealing with welfare officials, finding a decent job, making cheap but nutritious meals, picking up "hot" TVs or transistor radios, or finding ways to earn extra money.

There was a worldliness in Jewel's eyes, perhaps even a touch of smugness and a supercilious smile rarely left her lips.

Jewel asked me to accompany her home today because some boys who had threatened to beat her up were apparently waiting for her at her building. Asking for help was out of character for Jewel; she was usually so independent. I gave her a drive right to the front door of her building.

When we discovered no suspicious looking boys waiting outside, Jewel just shrugged her shoulders and invited me inside to meet her dad.

After a long ride in an elevator that seemed to stop at every floor, we finally reached her apartment. A sign on her door read: "Cheap Housing Is a Right—Not a Luxury." Jewel quietly opened the door and led me inside. I immediately tripped over a box of kitty litter in the middle of the living room floor.

Recovering my composure, I paused and looked around. A bird cage with three loudly chirping budgies hung in a corner of the room. Dominating one wall was a large mantelpiece over a false fireplace that held a plastic, plug-in log. Covering the mantelpiece was a glass vase with plastic roses, a tarnished golf trophy, a tiny porcelain zebra, a candle in the shape of a penis and testicles, and a brown earthenware jug that had the words "Brown Jug" painted under the rim. A tattered Mickey Spillaine paperback lay on the floor beside the television. The set was tuned to the "Little Rascals," but the sound was turned off. An orange vinyl couch covered in detective magazines and empty TV dinner trays stood only about a foot from the screen. On top of the set was a framed photograph of a young man in a purple tuxedo, purple shirt with black lace trim, and a peaked cap. The front of the cap bore the phrase "Do It" in big, block letters.

Jewel noticed me staring at the photograph. "That's my older brother," she said. "He just got married. He sure looks drunk, don't he?"

Beside the photograph stood a lamp with a picture of Niagara Falls painted on the plastic shade. The heat from the light bulb caused some kind of reaction in the shade which gave the appearance of moving water.

"Dad's probably out on the balcony," Jewel said, nudging my arm. "Come on."

She led me onto the balcony where a man was sitting on a lawn chair, buried in a book of detective stories. He looked to be in his mid-forties.

"Hi Dad!" Jewel exclaimed. "This is my teacher!"

I stepped across the balcony, ducking under a string of low-hanging patio lights. The man leaned back in his chair, arms dangling, his hair swept and matted up on top of his head like a greasy bird's nest. He looked up at me and extended his hand.

"Yeh. Glad to meet you. I saw you guys pull into the lot. I figured you was Jewel's teacher 'cause she said you looked like a hippie. Can I get you a brew?"

"No thanks. Beer hits me pretty hard when I'm tired, and I've had one of those days." I glanced over the balcony and saw the top of my van almost directly underneath. "Boy, you're high up here!"

He reached over, grabbed a plastic lawn chair, and dragged it beside him. "Have a seat here, but be careful. I nicknamed this chair 'The Toilet,' so don't fall through."

I noticed that the plastic braiding had been worn through at the center of the seat, so I sat perched over toward one side. Jewel's dad was grinning. He had a smile like broken glass; his front teeth were chipped and pointed, almost geometrical.

"I didn't know you was comin'," he said, removing his book from his lap and placing it gingerly on the floor. "Jewel always wanted me to meet you." He turned his head, blinking at me.

"Well, Jewel's a fine girl and doing well in my class. I brought her home today because she said there were some boys waiting around here to beat her up. I didn't see anyone when we came in."

"Damn kids around here!" he said. "Some of them are okay when you get to know them, but a lot of them are just punks." He spoke with a strange mixture of intensity and detachment, and kept patting his hand through his hair to smooth it back behind his ears, but the oily brown strands kept falling forward again. "There are always the rotten apples," he said, his mouth fixed in a stiff smile.

I glanced down from the balcony again. The sun was beginning to bathe the parking lot in an eerie, sulphur-colored light. A gang of kids got into a rust-splotched car. The car screeched away, leaving a cloud of blue smoke that lingered in the lot long after the car had disappeared.

"Damn kids!" Jewel's dad remarked bitterly. "Ain't they ever heard of noise pollution?" He took a pipe out of his vest pocket and clenched it, unlit, between his teeth. He sucked hard several times. "I feel sorry for all the riff raff you gotta teach in your class. If I were a teacher today, I'd carry a gun."

Jewel, who was sitting quietly in the corner, jumped up. "Daddy. Would you want Mr. McLaren to shoot me?"

Her father swung around in his chair. "Not you sweetheart. Just the punks." He turned around slowly and faced me again. There was a sad expression in his eyes. "I sometimes wonder what's happenin' in the world. I don't want Jewel mixed up with a lot of these kids. I was just readin' a story about two thirteen-year-old hit men charged with the killin' of a numbers racketeer in New York. It's a true story. Some crook gave the kids a loaded 20-gauge shotgun. And I just read that a coupla teenagers set a wino on fire for kicks. The mother of one of the kids is mad because her son is going to jail for killin' a bum. And here, in this country, this teenage girl threw herself off a balcony—only a mile or so from here. This guy finds the body, drags it behind the buildin', and rapes it like a piece of cold meat. I think the guy was from South America. They sent him back home." He paused. "Tell me Mr. McLaren, do you believe in castrating rapists? I do."

I stared at the floor. My head was swimming. I didn't know what to say. "Life is hard. Nobody has to tell you that. We live in troubled times. I don't know what's happening in the world. I'm just as confused being a teacher as you are as a parent. Somehow we've got to carry on—teachers and parents—and not give up and even work together." I was just mouthing the words, feeling an obligation to say something.

Jewel's dad sucked again on his unlit pipe. His jaw began to tighten and his aquiline nose gave his expression a certain regal quality. "Jewel likes you. At first I wanted her to have a woman teacher 'cause her mother walked out on us last year. Maybe now I should feel lucky she has you. You know, I just pray I can go through life without anythin' happening to Jewel. I mean . . . I mean I really worry about her. She's all I got and I'm all she's got. If anything ever happens to her I think I'll throw in the towel for keeps."

Monday, May 29

I told Marta that she couldn't go to the library before I dismissed the other kids; she had to wait her turn. She grabbed the stapler out of my desk, and before I could stop her, she had pumped three staples into her thumb.

Wednesday, May 31

It was a professional development day at Laura's school today, so I decided to bring her along with me to work. Even though she was a year younger than my students, she was looking forward to meeting them and seeing my classroom.

When I pulled into the parking lot, T. J. and Sal ran up to my van. "Who's that?" they asked.

"I'd like you to meet my daughter, Laura."

"I didn't know you had a kid," T. J. laughed. "Hiya, Laura. I'm the leader of the class, and I own all the kids in the room. They do what I tell them to."

Laura smiled as we made our way through the crowd of kids toward my room, Sal and T. J. following close behind.

"Hey, Laura," T. J. snickered. "You gotta nice ass."

"Easy does it, T. J.," I cautioned, "I want her to have a nice day."

Once inside, Laura took a seat next to my desk. The kids poured into the room, giggling and pointing at her. She just stared at the floor, feeling very embarrassed. Halfway through the morning art lesson, Betsy began shifting uneasily in her chair. Then she started to groan softly, smoothing her hands down her legs. "Oh, sir," she whispered, licking her lips slowly and sensuously, "you really turn me on." Her hands started to cup her underdeveloped breasts. "I wish I had x-ray glasses on so I could see your balls."

My face grew red. "Step outside the room, Betsy."

Laura continued staring at the floor. I picked up a yardstick, gripped it tightly, and started tapping the back of my chair.

Suddenly T. J. stood up. "Hey sir, can I go outside with Betsy?"

"Stay where you are!"

"But you got her mad!"

"She deserves to feel mad."

"Why're ya hasslin' her, just 'cause she's got the hots for you?"

"Okay, T. J. Change the subject. Everybody take out your math notebooks—we're going to have a little drill."

When the recess bell rang, I took Laura over to the main building, where the caretaker played Ping-Pong with her for the rest of the morning. During the afternoon she helped the librarian arrange books.

On our trip home she noticed something in her coat pocket—a crude drawing that depicted me having sex with a voluptuous woman.

After that, Laura never wanted to come back to the school.

Friday, June 2

T. J. enjoyed staying in the room at recess to fiddle with parts from a car engine that I had brought in for the class. When I wasn't on yard duty, I'd often join him. Despite the unpleasantness with Laura, I tried initiating conversations with him, with the idea that he needed somebody to talk to about his troubles, an adult who would actually listen.

When we talked, T. J. would doodle in his notebook. We started off slowly, so I wouldn't scare him off. At first, he doodled pictures of racing cars. He designed a special car that appeared in many of his drawings: the "Death Machine," as he called it. Later on, he drew other things . . . whatever came into his mind. Sometimes, when he was feeling burnt around the edges because of events at home, he'd illustrate some unpleasant episode centering around his family.

I showed his pictures to a friend of mine who was a trained art therapist. He told me that whoever drew those pictures was a very sick boy . . . possibly with alarming tendencies. But an art therapist can never know for sure until he interviews the child over a period of time.

Since it was almost impossible to talk to T. J.'s mother at her house, I tried to convince her to come to see me after school. I told her I wanted to try and improve their communication with each other.

"We're *communicating* just fine!" she told me over the phone. "He gets my message! When I tell him to do something, he does it, or else! And he knows what the 'or else' means!"

She also said that she didn't believe in all that "psychology bullshit." "If *I've* never had it, and *I've* made it this far, why can't T. J.?"

Thursday, June 8

Teresa hated going home after school. She asked me if she could stay after class not because she liked school; she wanted to avoid the gang of boys who waited outside for their "collection."

The gang demanded different things from different kids. Willy was told to bring coins; Tracy, comic books; and Teresa was to steal gum from the variety store at the plaza. Punishment for not coming through with the goods was a beating. No matter how carefully the teachers tried to prevent it, we simply couldn't be everywhere at once.

So Teresa's mother went to the store each week and bought bags full of gum for the gang members. She didn't want her daughter to be forced to steal.

Saturday, June 10

I decided to bring groups of kids home to my tiny bungalow in the Beaches district. We could walk down to the lake and explore the beach, stroll along the boardwalk, or skip stones in the water. Over four Saturdays, I planned to entertain the entire class.

Jenny spent hours dreaming up games and activities, and even more time overspending our budget, gathering an assortment of food that included oyster soup, lasagne, quiche lorraine, and shrimp.

This afternoon at the beach the kids ran around happily. They gathered odd bits of glass and stone, played games of tag and British bulldog, and sunbathed near the water. Some kids danced to blaring transistor radios, while others postured for my movie camera, much to the delight of the people strolling along the boardwalk.

The day went beautifully . . . until we decided to try having a campfire. Immediately, Sal and T. J. started fighting over who would light the fire. T. J. angrily threw a rock at Sal. I watched helplessly as the rock sped through the air and narrowly missed his head. He collapsed in a half-faint. First I made sure he was okay, then I calmed T. J. down. No one was physically hurt.

Later, I found the large rock T. J. had thrown. When I picked it up, I could barely manage to heave it any distance. His anger must have generated a great burst of strength. I could understand why he won so many fights.

Dinner was a big success.

At the end of the day, Jenny made her farewells to the kids.

"Did you kids have a good time?" she asked brightly, as they were getting into the van for the trip home.

One kid said, "Well, it was all right, I guess. . . ."

Another chimed in, "We shoulda gone to Ontario Place!"

"Na," T. J. jeered. "Who needs this, anyway? I have more fun at my place, just hangin' around."

Monday, June 12

Today I bumped into Brian, a boy I had taught in the middle-class school of my first year. I was sure he had been destined for good things—a textbook paradigm of a writer-to-be. At thirteen he was composing prolific verse which was incredibly sensitive and insightful for a boy his age.

He now loomed before me, over six feet tall, wearing a checked peaked cap, fatigue jacket over a goose-down vest, and worn Kodiak boots. His face, formerly soft and placid, had grown tight and severe. He looked as hard as a clenched fist.

"Hey McLaren, how you doin'?" he asked huskily, taking my hand in a vise grip and shaking it vigorously. "Are you still teachin'?"

"I sure am," I replied. "Tell me, how's that wonderful writing of yours coming along?"

A profound sigh. "I gave that shit up last year. I got a girlfriend now, though. She likes to dance so I'm into dancin' now."

I smiled. "How's your schoolwork coming along? Still at the top of the class?"

Brian's face twitched slightly and he nervously began playing with the peak of his cap. "I quit school last year," he said defiantly. "I'm over sixteen."

"Oh."

"Ya . . . well . . . I'm learning to lay foundations for cottages now. So if you ever want to build a cottage, you know who to call. But I've nearly decided to move down here. Damn mosquitoes up north this time of year are big enough to fuck hens!"

"Not exactly a poetic metaphor," I chuckled.

Brian smiled widely, revealing two missing front teeth, partly camouflaged by a flimsy moustache. "If I'm still up there this winter, why don't you gimme a holler and come up for a ride on my cat?"

"Your cat?"

"Ya—you know—Arctic Cat. I'm really heavy into snowmobiles."

He scribbled his address and phone number down on a piece of paper and pushed it into my hand. "See you later, sir. Don't do anythin' I wouldn't do and if ya do, name it after me."

Thursday, June 15

I was interrupted in class by a cry of "Sir! Sir! Your shoe!" Since it was raining heavily outside, my first thought was that my shoes were muddy, and I had trekked dirt into the classroom.

But when I looked down at my crossed legs, I was astonished to see one of my pupils, new to the school, vigorously licking the underside of my shoe.

I jerked my foot away. When I turned the shoe over, I saw a large patch on the sole had been licked clean.

Tuesday, June 20

At the end of the school year, I took the kids to the Metro Zoo. They seemed excited by the idea.

At first things went well, but problems arose almost as soon as the tour guide opened her mouth: "Now, boys and girls, let's find out as much as we can about these strange and wonderful creatures, shall we?" she minced, smiling sweetly.

"Do you mean T. J.?" Betsy quipped.

At once, the tour guide became angry. She tried to draw the kids' attention to the tapir and its snout, but the kids rapidly drowned her out with cries of: "What's a snout?" "Who cares?" and "I wanna see the gorillas!"

The tour guide's lines were well rehearsed, with a slogan-like rigidity my kids understandably couldn't handle: "This is a peacock, look at its pretty tail!" or "Look at all the wrinkles on the elephant . . . doesn't it remind you of your grandfather?" I didn't have the heart to tell her most of the kids probably weren't interested.

The kids soon found her an annoyance, and wanted her to get lost. I decided I'd better take them around on my own.

To placate the zoo's security staff, who were beginning to give us rueful looks, I marshaled the kids into a semblance of order, and started out for the hippos.

The Metro Zoo's plan for keeping the animals separated from the human visitors involves a series of dry moats instead of the usual pens and steel cages, though in some places there were fiberglass shields. It was possible to leap across the moats, if you were crazy enough to want to. Naturally, that's just what some of my kids wanted to do. It didn't seem to matter if the animals were hippos, rhinos, or giraffes. The kids wanted to shake hands—though I noticed they didn't try anything with the lions.

At the pink flamingo exhibit, T. J. thought it would be hilarious to see if he could throw a stone and snap the bird's spindly leg. "Its leg is so skinny I could break it with my little finger," he boasted.

At the gorilla exhibit, he pointed to one of the West Indian kids, remarking: "Hey, Winston! There's your mom and dad! Jump in, and let 'em wipe your ass!"

Next to the gorillas and Egyptian fruit bats (which, to the kids' delight, defecated upside down), the kids thought the best part of the trip was McDonald's restaurant.

Friday, June 30

I threw a class party, and it went very well. Afterward, Muscle Lady dropped by to wish me happy summer holidays. Her tee shirt read: "Four out of five dentists recommend oral sex." I asked her how my former students were doing. "Same as always," was the reply. "We ain't changed a bit."

On my way out I met a visiting teacher from the nearby junior high. "You taught Buddy in grade six, didn't you?" he asked.

"Not officially, but I spent a great deal of time with him. How did he make out this year?"

"He's a real behavior problem. But last week he ran into some problems outside the school, too."

"Problems?"

"Yeh," the teacher continued, "he was rushed to York-Finch Hospital on the weekend."

"No kidding. What for?"

"He got stuck to a dog—sexually, if you know what I mean. It took the intern in the emergency ward to get them apart."

Buddy had always been curious about the world.

Epilogue

During the last week of school, I asked Fred to reserve a position in the primary grades for me, just in case somebody decided to resign or transfer during the summer. He told me there was a vacancy in grades two–three; I could have it if I wanted it. Well, I told him I was still searching for my right grade level and was happy to take the offer.

Fred was glad to have a male teacher in the lower grades. He felt that kids should be exposed to male teachers as early as possible. Many of the children at the school, he felt, needed male teachers because they didn't have any permanent father figures at home.

Teachers make a ritual of getting together at the end of the year to discuss who would be getting this year's kids next year. Sometimes a big fuss was made when a teacher knew he was getting a student who was a real problem. Teachers trying to avoid having a certain child placed in their classroom might say their program "wasn't appropriate," or that their classroom wasn't designed to "accommodate excess motion." Staff members would even trade certain students for others; it was a marketplace, a slave auction.

T. J.'s little brother, Mickey, ended up on my list; Mickey's grade two teacher thought I was the right person for him. She had observed my program, liked what I was doing, and decided that a more tolerant atmosphere would be the best thing for him. At first, I didn't mind. But then I began to feel apprehensive. I remembered what I had just gone through with T. J., and every day Mickey was getting to be more like him.

I also remembered that first time I saw him—when I had gone to T. J.'s for lunch and saw Mickey running and swearing after a police cruiser carting one of his brothers to jail.

I was a little resentful about always being given the hard cases. Male teachers were usually given the wildest and most truculent students because males were better able to physically defend themselves. I didn't mind taking my share of hard cases, but I felt that some teachers sent me certain students to relieve other teachers who were their friends. It was a con game using the children as dice, and like any other con, it stank.

Still, in the end, I took Mickey.

"What kind of a plan do you have for him?" Rod asked when he'd heard that I'd finally agreed to take on a student no one else wanted.

"What Fred always prescribes. Tender loving care," I replied, somewhat sanctimoniously.

I had learned to be a better teacher and had made it through another year, doing my best to care for the kids. I knew I couldn't become one of the gang because kids have their own friends and certainly don't want their teacher to be one. I felt they were starting to respect me more because they knew I cared about them, and at the same time they knew I had reasonable expectations of them.

Now that I had a permanent teaching certificate, my future work seemed set. But could I remain happy as a teacher for the rest of my life? I was having misgivings about surviving emotionally for the next twenty or thirty years. I wasn't the type to become an administrator and had no intention of becoming a vice-principal, something many other teachers seem to long for and so many of them get trapped by. My mortgage payments looming every month tamped down my growing feelings of frustration. But I promised myself that once I felt that I wasn't offering a hundred percent to my class, I'd pack it in.

Jenny and I had been planning all spring to celebrate my new status with a trip to Cape Cod, and two days into the holidays we packed our van and left.

I saw T. J. toward the end of the summer vacation when I went back to the school to prepare my classroom for September. As I drove into the school parking lot, I noticed a wry-necked figure hunched over a skateboard. He was crouching on the curb, trying to fasten together the broken laces of his Kodiak boots. I smiled at him, but he didn't smile back.

"I came back to visit," he said dryly, balancing on the tip of his skateboard with admirable skill.

"Visit?"

"Didn't ya know? We got kicked out." He spoke quietly. "Ontario Housing kicked us out . . . we didn't have the bread."

"Where are you living now?"

"In the zoo, a couple of blocks over."

"How do you like it there?"

"It's the pits. The cops there are real turkeys. I got charged with assault, man. Can you believe it! This cop said I punched this kid out, but I didn't, so I clobbered the cop over the head with a stick. He tried to put the cuffs on me, but I didn't let him." He started riding his skateboard in little circles. "Can I still come and see you?"

"Of course, you're welcome any time."

"See you," he said, waving goodbye. "I gotta look up a few kids—got some unfinished business."

CHAPTER

3

"The Suburbs Was Supposed to Be a Nice Place . . ."

Tuesday, September 5

It was a great convenience keeping the same room. I was spared the job of moving all my paraphernalia; even the bulletin boards could remain the same. During the summer the caretaker had replaced all the desks and chairs with smaller versions to accommodate the younger students.

As they began hurrying through the door, I was amazed at how tiny they were. I felt like a giant shambling among a room full of elves.

"He's the first man teacher I ever had," I overheard one kid say. "If he's like my stepdad, I'm gettin' outta here."

Friday, September 8

"Does anybody know what the hardest part of the body is?" I asked the class during a science lesson.

"The head." "Feet." "My chin." "Knees." "Back." "A fist."

Finally a kid called out: "Teeth."

"Right you are," I exclaimed. "Now, does anybody know what teeth are made out of?"

"Stones." "Cement." "Bones." "Shells." "Plastic."

"It's called enamel," I told them, "and it's the hardest substance in the body."

At which Mickey shot up his hand at once, yelling, "If it's the hardest part of the body, then how come I broke a guy's front teeth with my fist?"

Monday, September 11

I decided to work on Fred's philosophy of improving the child's self-image—a difficult undertaking sometimes, trying to show concern for a child who is driving you crazy. But the method had worked fairly well for me with T. J., and I was confident that Fred's approach would be even more effective with the younger kids; they would be less hardened and would find it a little easier to accept a teacher as someone who actually cared about them.

I looked forward to giving students the support they needed, while not having to endure the resistance exhibited by the older students.

At first, I organized programs for the kids in role-playing and psychodrama, as well as other activities geared to improve their self-image. Later on, I abandoned the idea of working with the class as a whole.

Smaller groups proved more effective. Some of the students responded by calling me "daddy," and a few of them asked me if I'd marry their mothers. But, as usual, there just wasn't enough time in the day to give each child the care and attention he or she deserved.

Tuesday, September 19

Samantha and Priscilla were talking at my desk.

"I'm glad I'm black, aren't you?" Samantha asked her friend.

"Yah," Priscilla replied. "Black is beautiful. My mom keeps tellin' me that, over and over."

"We're brown now cause we're small. But when we gets older, we'll turn dark black."

"Yah. I wish sir was black, don't you? Mr. McLaren, will you be black?"

"How am I supposed to do that?" I asked.

"My mom says that if you're brown, you can go to the hospital and they make you white. If you're white, you can come out black. You gots to have an operation, though."

"If you're a girl and wanna be a boy," Samantha added, "you can get the doctor to make you a boy."

"I don't wanna be no boy," Priscilla protested.

"Me neither! My mother had a sister friend, you know, who don't want to be black. So she had a operation and came out white."

Thursday, September 21

Mickey worshipped his older brother, T. J. He acted as part sidekick, part slave, following T. J. wherever he went, scurrying down the halls ahead of T. J. just to open doors for him.

At the beginning of the term, T. J. dropped by my room to voice his approval of Mickey's being in my classroom. "Keep him outta trouble," he warned me, grinning.

"I'll do my best, T. J."

"If he gets outta hand, just call on me, man. I'll come down and smack him silly."

Friday, September 22

I went for a walk to the nearby variety store after school. It had been raining and the streets were glistening wet. I made my way past rows of identical bungalows with square hedges and bedraggled petunias. There were lots of dogs, including several fierce Dobermans on chain leashes sitting in the front yards.

The variety store was located in a tiny plaza, comprising a milk store, variety store, fish-and-chips shop, and a women's hairdressing salon. Scribbled over a long-faded sign was the warning: "Keep Out! Property of the Dukes!" Crowds of kids filled the streets and sidewalks, which were littered with refuse.

To prevent break-ins the variety store was covered by a protective wire mesh. One kid was trying to scale it like a human fly, but his feet were too big to gain a secure footing, and he soon gave up. Outside the store several boys stood spitting into rain puddles which filled the holes in the sidewalk. Two teenagers in overalls slumped against the wall, uncorked a bottle of cheap wine, and took several quick swallows. The empty bottle was tossed down a mud slope to the street below, where it smashed into pieces and woke up a toddler sleeping nearby, who started to cry. Children sat on the slope, watching the street and drawing figures in the dirt with their bare toes, while two laughing kids somersaulted down, somehow managing to stop themselves before they tumbled into the traffic.

I saw two girls from my class sitting on the curb across the street, smoking. One waved her hand while the other frowned and flicked her cigarette in my direction.

I bought some pipe tobacco in the store and watched the store manager threaten some kids with a sawed-off broom handle. Then I headed back to the school, wondering what I would teach the following day.

Monday, September 25

Victor had a problem. He was always pulling his pants down in front of other kids—and he was encouraging them to do the same. His mother would beat him for it, to no avail.

Once, in class, Victor swaggered up to Mickey, unzipped his fly, and stuck a glue bottle inside. Then while Mickey stood there startled, just staring at him, Victor wiggled the glue bottle up and down, chanting: "Mickey's got a sticky cock! Mickey's got a sticky cock!"

Mickey slugged him.

Victor did it again and, before I could intervene, Mickey hit him again.

This week Victor's mother enrolled him in a clinic.

Thursday, September 28

Anna and Suzanne asked if they could clean the classroom up during recess.

"We promise to make it look great, sir!"

"Wait till you see it, sir!"

When I returned after recess, I found that the desks were covered with fresh Magic Marker swipes and obscene graffiti. "Moosecock" was scribbled across the map. The ribbon on my typewriter was in shreds in the sink and inky blue water was spilled all over the floor.

Kids complained that their lunches were missing, and one girl couldn't find her glasses. I noticed the window facing the street was open and looked outside to see books, papers, lunch pails, and glasses scattered on the ground.

Thursday, October 5

Tracy now wears a brace.

Late one afternoon, she tried to imitate Evel Knievel's jump over the Snake Canyon, her version a make-shift wooden ramp in back of the local Miracle Mart. She had even less luck than Evel: She broke her back.

Her elaborate brace thrilled and inspired the other kids when she returned to class. They'd seen reruns of "The Bionic Woman" on TV, and decided to find out if Tracy was bionic too. They left tacks on her chair to see if she felt pain; they poked her in the legs with pencils to see if she would short-circuit. And not a few asked her to jump up to the school roof with her bionic legs to retrieve their lost balls.

Wednesday, October 11

Charlotte taught perceptually handicapped students. She wanted to integrate her kids occasionally into a regular class setting for part of the day, and asked if we could combine our two classes. I enthusiastically agreed.

She owned a giant Great Pyrenees dog, Pip, which she brought to school each day. Usually that's an impossibility, since there are always students who suffer allergies. But so far there hasn't been a single complaint. Everybody loves Pip.

One of Charlotte's kids—Bruce—took a special liking to Pip. He soon became obsessive about sitting next to the dog, developing a wild possessiveness that scared the rest of the class away. Bruce is a big kid. One day he attacked several of his classmates because they fed Pip some scraps from their lunch boxes.

Charlotte got in touch with Bruce's father. His parents were separated, and the father had custody of Bruce, while the mother kept his two brothers. Bruce had wanted to take his own dog with him when he left. But his father had moved into a building where dogs weren't allowed, so the dog remained at his mother's house.

Once Bruce left, his two brothers stoned the dog to death.

Friday, October 13

Today Mickey turned to me, smiling, and said, "Watch this, Mr. McLaren!"

Then he hit himself against his forehead with the steel edge of his ruler: three sharp blows. Deep red welts rose over his eyes. He continued to smile.

Tuesday, October 17

Samantha was staring at me, full of anger.

"Something wrong?" I asked her, walking up to her desk.

She put her hands on her hips, hissing: "Your face looks sickly pale today. You need a suntan!"

I frowned. "Do I look pale? I feel fine!"

"She means you're a whitey!" Sue snapped, also angry.

"Samantha's mad at you today!" Priscilla, sitting on the other side, barked.

"Is that true?" I asked. "Are you mad at me Samantha? If you are, let's talk about it."

Snorting at my suggestion, Samantha instead got up and walked slowly to the reading center, her face full of exasperation and suspicion, Sue and Priscilla following. The three girls had grown up together in Jamaica and were fast friends.

I followed them over. "Samantha, are you going to tell me what's bothering you?"

There was a profound hurt in her eyes. "Why do white people always fire black people from their jobs?" She used a tone of voice I'd never heard her use before.

Her question caught me by surprise. "What do you mean?"

"My dad got fired from his work yesterday. He told me whitey likes to fire black people. Is that true?"

"Well," I said, swallowing hard, "sometimes there is prejudice, but—"

"Last year we had a black teacher! Now she's gone!" Sue spat out. "We got lots of black kids in this school. How come we don't have more black teachers? How come Mrs. Jones was fired and not some white teacher?"

"Yah," Priscilla chimed in. "And how come the people who do all the firing's always white?"

I explained that the Board had fired all teachers who had the least experience, because of budget cutbacks. "Honest, Samantha, Mrs. Jones wasn't fired because she was black." But my voice lacked conviction.

A pause.

Samantha's brow raised in a curious puzzled expression. "I told my dad *you* don't lie, sir. So I guess I believes you. But you know what my dad said?" Her eyes softened and her mouth relaxed.

"What?"

"He said if you don't lie, you must be the only honkey that don't." She grinned.

I laughed and the girls laughed.

Friday, October 20

Mickey picked his nose and ate the snot. When I was a kid, one of my best friends was an avid snot-eater.

Sometimes several nose-pickers would have "snot wars," and often their assignments reflected the results of these battles in the form of little green boogies caked to the paper. Snot wars were not popular, but they did exist.

Snot competition was more commonplace, although it was not the sort of thing you would see every day. Kids would compete for the longest piece of snot, dangling their glistening finds on the ends of a raised fingertip.

Monday, October 23

A rummy lived in the park behind the school. The kids first spotted him picking through junk and putting choice items in a duffel bag he kept beneath the sewer pipe he called home. They were fascinated with his wizened old face festooned with coarse, scarlet patches. His lank, black hair was long and greasy.

Some kids claimed Rummy exposed himself to small kids who came across his hideaway. Then again, Rummy was accused of everything from mutilation to murder. I got a lot of mileage out of Rummy in the kids' creative writing assignments.

If a kid lost something on the way to school, Rummy had it. If there was a family fight, Rummy caused it. If a kid was mysteriously absent from class, Rummy had captured him on the way to school and was in the process of devouring him raw. The kids had found someone to blame for all the problems in their universe.

Now that Rummy has moved out, they continue to use him as a long-distance scapegoat.

Friday, October 27

"My dad's gettin' a new van," Jessie proudly told the class.

"Great," I prompted. "What kind?"

"I don't know, sir. But you know what, sir? It's gonna have a bar, and a bed, and lots of pictures of girls, naked girls, with big tits stickin' out and tips on them like bottle caps, Mr. McLaren! From magazines! Me and my brother gots a bunch we ripped out for the walls," he smirked wickedly, "and we gots to get some more for the ceilin'!"

I felt myself beginning to blush. Teachers aren't supposed to blush; we're always supposed to be in control. So I cleared my throat and tried to nip this in the bud. "What's your brother and a seven-year-old kid like you going to do with a van like that? And those naked girls. What do your mom and dad think?"

"Well, I can't drive yet. But my mom and dad says my brother can use it to screw his girlfriend in, but they has to have it for campin' in the summer."

Monday, October 30

Megan is a quiet, almost invisible child. She always stands alone at recess, almost motionless, except for fondling her lank hair. She hardly ever speaks, never gets into trouble, always completes her assignments, never interrupts a lesson or shows up late for class. I like her, but usually I hardly know she is there.

This afternoon the secretary left a message for me to call Mrs. Llewellyn. Who was Mrs. Llewellyn? When I returned the call, Mrs. Llewellyn turned out to be Megan's mother, and she was angry: "Now listen Mr. McLaren! I'm getting ready these psychiatrist papers on Megan! Tell me this! Does she daydream in class?"

"Megan? What's wrong?"

"How do I know! I just know I'm fed up with her! Fed up! I've got a nitwit for a daughter!"

I was able to calm Mrs. Llewellyn down and promised to have a closer look at Megan. Apparently she never talks at home, either, and spends most of her time alone in her room.

Thursday, November 2

When Gracie threw a heavy glue bottle at Pasquale, I called her mother in for an interview.

Gracie's dark-rimmed brown eyes, spiked lashes, and her long platinum-dyed hair presented a bizarre image. Only eight years old, she carried herself like a Vogue fashion model.

Gracie's mother wore an enormous cleavage and a blonde, lacquered bouffant hairdo with black roots. Her first question was: "Has Gracie been acting different lately?"

I mentioned the glue bottle incident.

This was her explanation: A while ago, Gracie and her mother returned home from Food City to find her dad in bed "shakin' the sheets" with a woman neighbor. He had been drinking steadily since his release from jail a month earlier, and was finding it extremely difficult to find a job.

When Gracie's mother cried out, he casually walked across the room and split her nose with an ashtray. Gracie ran out of the room. Her mother told me the scar from the incident was carefully hidden under a layer of makeup, and she pointed to her nose.

Gracie's dad moved out. He ended up living two floors below, with the other woman. Gracie would periodically bump into him in the elevator. To avoid him, she used the stairs—even though she lived on the twelfth floor.

What chagrined Gracie's mother the most was that all the neighbors told her that her husband was a fool, that she was so much better looking.

"Can you imagine how I feel? Like a bloody fool. This woman comes in and does a number with my man—right under my friggin' nose at that! He decides for hamburger when he could be getting a steak! Fine! Let him starve himself to death!"

Gracie had thrown the heavy glue pot at Pasquale because Pasquale's mother was the woman Gracie's dad had the affair with.

Friday, November 3

Faith was so hungry one day she brought a bottle of Kraft Thousand Island dressing to class and drank over half of it. Then somebody grabbed it away at recess.

Faith's mother showed up at the school today to ask me if I thought Faith had any acting potential. According to Faith's mother, there was money to be made in children's commercials.

Wednesday, November 8

Substitute teachers often claimed to be sick when asked to fill in at our school. And who could blame them? (One substitute lasted only fifteen minutes in my classroom.)

As everyone knows, a substitute teacher is fair game. And Mr. Cummings was new. He arrived early and eager.

Later that morning, I heard somebody screaming. I looked into a classroom and could hardly believe my eyes. Standing in the center of the room, dressed in bright green leotards and carrying a crossbow, was Mr. Cummings! A sheepskin vest and Alpine hat completed the outfit.

The costume was part of Mr. Cummings's innovative teaching. He was trying to tell the class the story of William Tell. He thought the kids would be bowled over by his colorful outfit. Instead, the kids were laughing and shrieking "Fairy boy," and "Fag," and mincing about in front of him.

I watched as he slipped his pants on over the leotards. Then he put math questions on the board.

He advised the office that he would not be available in the future.

Monday, November 13

Cecelia, a beautiful West Indian child in my class, has sickle-cell anemia. The disease keeps her absent for weeks at a time. Her eyes are yellowed by the daily destruction of her blood cells.

She bears her pain stoically. When she is pushed, shoved, or knocked over in gym, she never complains. I often find her alone at her desk, crying silently.

Thursday, November 16

A parent stormed into school. "Those kids!" he complained. "They live like pigs! They ain't got no respect for the human race!"

He warned me that I should be on guard at all times, explaining that seemingly loyal dogs sometimes turn on their masters for no apparent reason. "And blacks! They contaminate everything they touch! Don't let them breathe in your face!"

If the kids' families had problems he didn't want to hear about it. "Let those people booze away their lives with no jobs . . . just because they're too lazy to take the jobs you see advertised. Just look at the want ads! There are plenty of jobs! And besides, the wine they're soppin' up each day was paid for by me! That's right—by me!"

He barely stopped to take a breath.

"You should see all the money the government takes off my check each week so them winos can buy their bottles of brain rot! Their lives are paid for by the sweat of the workingman's brow! Damn foreigners come into this country and take away our jobs. Went into their garage and let the air out of their tires. That's so he'll learn not to park so close to the sidewalk.

"And I own a gun. Bought it last Saturday when somebody broke the latch on my gate and made off with the barbecue. Don't ever want to have to use it, mind you. But just let one of them jungle bunnies cross over onto my property, we'll see what happens!"

Friday, November 17

Although I was experiencing considerably more success with the kids, I was beginning to feel uncertain as to how effectively their needs were being met.

Most of the kids in my class faced hardships I'd never had to imagine coping with. Education should give every kid a chance to succeed. And I feared the prejudice and hostility of the society would make life rougher for them.

I was lucky; I was white and middle-class; I owned my home in the fashionable Beaches; I'd gone to university; I held a place in society.

The more I brooded about it, the more antisocial and withdrawn I became. I stopped eating in the lunch room, preferring instead to eat alone in the nearby Italian restaurant. I wondered what else I could do to earn a living besides teach.

Monday, November 20

Priscilla brought a picture of her newborn sister, Olivia, to school.

"How d'ya like her?" she asked Samantha.

"Looks like she's gonna turn out white, just like your mom!" Samantha exclaimed.

"But she might grow darker later, like my dad."

"If it turns out white, I'll give you my Barbie doll jumpsuit. If it gets dark by the end of the year, you gimme your Barbie halter top!"

"Deal!"

Tuesday, November 21

Dale had a mother whose wan face came alive when she remembered her life as a little girl on a farm: "Those were the best days of my life."

We were talking after class. Dale was aimlessly kicking a scrap of paper the care-taker had missed on his four o'clock round. I had asked his mother to come in because I wanted to know more about Dale's home life.

"I wish we were still living on a farm," she continued. "That's what I regret most—not raising Dale in the country." Suddenly she was brushing away tears from her cheeks. Dale looked embarrassed and left the room. "I want something out of life for Dale, but I just don't know how I can do it. He's still upset about his father leaving, and he just won't seem to settle down. I'm out working and I don't really have time for him when I get home. You don't know what factory work is like. It sucks all the energy out of you, so I don't have that much left over for him."

Dale reappeared and sat in a chair near the window. His mother started talking again, but soon broke down.

"Look," I said, doing my best to reassure her any way I could, "I'll try to keep Dale out of trouble in school. Don't worry."

When they left, Dale shot me his first smile of the term. Somebody's fist had punched out one of his teeth.

Wednesday, November 22

Mickey wasn't doing his assignment; he complained his arm was sore. When I asked him what was wrong with it, he replied, "It has bad germs in it."

"Okay, Mickey," I said. "Roll up your sleeve so I can see where the 'bad germs' are."

He could barely pull his sleeve past his elbow. With my help, we inched the sleeve up higher, revealing a running sore that looked like a face.

Mickey explained: "I asked T. J. to give me a tattoo like all the other kids. I wanted a 'screamin' skull.'" His brother had carved a skull into Mickey's arm, using a pin and some ink he had leaked out of a pen.

Mickey was too embarrassed to go to the school nurse. I had to insist.

Monday, December 4

A friend of mine introduced me to a teacher from British Columbia who was in Toronto for a speaking engagement. She worked with disadvantaged kids herself, and was starting up a new magazine to deal with teaching and capitalism. Before she left, we made arrangements to meet over a drink. She was a stunningly beautiful woman of about thirty, with something very compelling about the way she spoke.

At a nearby "working-class" tavern she told me over a beer that most curriculum materials presently used in classrooms condition working-class readers to have negative self-images, to believe in the inevitability of their lot in life, to perceive their predicament in an isolated way, and to regard the possibility of change in the class structure as futile, or at least merely wishful thinking. She maintained that as my kids grew up, they would become more and more aware of how much their social class places them outside of the "mainstream of society."

Over another round of beer she talked about class differences. "Your kids are too young for you to make them socially active. But already you can see what's happening to them as a result of their poverty. It must upset you, as a teacher, to feel so helpless."

Protesting that things weren't that hopeless, I outlined some of the units I was using in class to promote self-concept, understanding, and harmony. But I had to admit they weren't working very effectively.

"You're still working within the capitalist ideology!" she remarked, grabbing my arm in a friendly gesture, almost knocking over her draft in the process. "You're romanticizing the idea that people share a fundamental humanity that occurs through a common understanding. But, under the capitalist system, this basic humanity is perverted because the class structure of our society denies working-class kids equal opportunities. You're merely accommodating inequality."

I had to remind her that I was teaching seven- and eight-year-olds, and that nothing I could do in one year, even if I agreed with her philosophy, would dramatically change their lives.

"Kids who grow up feeling hopeless," she said, her voice rising, "become self-effacing and self-deprecating. If you can't reach your class because they're too young, then get your parents together! Organize them!"

I couldn't help but agree that there was a lot of truth in what she was saying. The real problem *was* the class system. In this kind of society, they had a right to be deviant.

Monday, December 11

I didn't notice Mickey leave. I sent some of the kids to find out where he had vanished to. They had one hell of a time finding him.

Finally, they noticed a pair of tiny brown shoes under the cubicle doors in the boy's washroom. When they opened the door, they found Mickey asleep on the toilet.

Wednesday, December 13

Charlotte's group of ten perceptually handicapped kids wanted to repay me for taking them on a field trip to the waterfront. She suggested to them that an interesting way to say thanks would be to make me up a nice hot lunch.

Mad Sid became the most excited. Mad Sid earned his name by jumping out of a second story window—and surviving without a scratch. Charlotte always had to keep one eye on him.

She took her kids down to the staff room kitchen. The idea was to surprise me with a spaghetti lunch, the recipe contributed by Mad Sid's mother.

Chester the Hypo (chondriac) was especially eager to help make the sauce. Like Mad Sid, he could be difficult in class. He complained daily that he had everything from an upset stomach to a brain tumor. He complained to Charlotte that Sid's mother probably put something poisonous in the recipe, warning her to watch out for suspicious-looking material.

There was a critical element in the recipe they didn't know about: I had a meeting with a parent during my lunch hour. I was, in fact, particularly eager to get that interview over with. Brad's mother always spieled out her woes for what felt like hours.

When I arrived, she was sitting on the staff room sofa looking as theatrical as ever. In her mid-forties, she was a platinum blonde (this time), and her eyebrows were plucked into thin half-circles.

"Sit over here, please, Mr. McLaren," she began at once. "I've a lot to talk about. Now, about Brad—"

Charlotte's kids had sneaked into the kitchen while I began my conversation with Brad's mother. On a signal from Charlotte, they formed a line, and with Sid in the lead holding the pot of steaming spaghetti, they marched into the staff room.

"All right!" Mad Sid ordered. "Right face!"

Everyone swung around.

"Ready, troops? Let's go!"

They marched up between us. Mad Sid was wearing army fatigues and a plastic German army helmet. Chester wore a pink 1950s sports jacket that came down to his knees and a pair of Charlotte's black leotards, which he claimed were giving him a rash. A kid named Sweeney was carrying the cutlery in a straw basket suspended from his mouth. He peered out at everybody through a pair of moss-green diving goggles. Candy, who was carrying up the rear, sported a black velvet opera cape and shook a noisy tambourine. I pretended to be embarrassed by this procession, but Charlotte knew I enjoyed every minute of it!

Brad's mother became upset. She rose to her feet, dramatically threw her coat around her shoulders, and paused at the door to tell me, "I'll be in touch with you when you aren't playing zookeeper!"

Monday, December 18

A few weeks ago, I decided to try a new strategy for stopping fights. Whenever two kids started to throw punches, I gathered the entire class around the combatants, and we all hummed the old "look sharp" Gillette Friday Night Fight theme. It was so silly, the fighters started to laugh. I broke up a lot of fights in class that way.

Rod told me that he was going to submit the idea to HAID (Humane Alternatives in Discipline), an organization of teachers and parents who opposed corporal punishment.

Wednesday, December 20

Yesterday, when Fred saw me wearing overalls stained with paint from the previous evening's art therapy course, and carrying some of the latest school journals under my arm, he laughed. "If you don't slow down and lay off a bit, you're going to steal my act!"

Some of the staff members, however, were raising more than merely curious eyebrows at my apparent headlong plunge into Fred's philosophy. As long as I confined my activities to my classroom, they didn't object, but when I let my class work in the hall or staff room, they felt threatened. The few teachers on staff who didn't really approve of Fred's approach felt he was filling the staff with "hippies"—me, for example—and at the staff meeting, with both Fred and Rod absent, they decided it was the opportune moment to nail me. They took me totally by surprise.

"I hear music coming from your class a lot, Peter. What kind of courses are you teaching?" one of them asked.

"Young kids need to be controlled. I'm going to get some of your hellions next year, and I don't want them running wild all over *my* class," another contributed.

"And why are you letting your kids work out in the halls?" one teacher demanded in a peremptory tone, rising out of her chair.

I was startled, unable to react to all this hostility.

John tried to come to my rescue. "Are they disturbing your kids?" he asked one of the irate teachers.

"Well . . . not exactly . . . but some of us have seen Peter's kids making his breakfast in the staff room! And they were unsupervised."

I found myself rising slowly out of my chair. "There were some grade six kids supervising the cooking," I said, trying to remain calm. "They weren't making my breakfast; they happened to be making their own breakfasts, because they didn't get a breakfast that morning or a dinner the previous night!" My voice was rising, but I couldn't hold back. "And if you're worried about the school budget, you can rest easy. The money for the eggs and oatmeal came out of my pocket!"

I called Fred later to tell him I'd had it.

"Peter, I want you at the school for as long as I'm here. And if you alter your program one iota, I'll fire you!" he reassured me.

Charlotte and Liz, buddies of mine, admitted they were too shocked at the staff meeting to say anything. To give me a lift, they treated me to a spaghetti lunch at the best Italian restaurant in the Corridor, and presented me with a gift. "It's to help you get over yesterday's staff meeting," Charlotte said.

It was a book on biofeedback.

Friday, December 22

I enjoyed celebrating Christmas with the kids. The class spent hours decorating the room with Christmas posters I was given or had bought. A plastic tree was donated by a previous staff member, and we decorated it with crepe paper, tinsel, popcorn, and cotton batting.

I played some Christmas carols on my guitar, not very well, I'm afraid, since I usually prefer to play Mississippi Delta blues.

The kids had shown up with presents for me: socks, wallets, bottles of wine, chocolates, beer mugs; well over half the class brought something for me. I had stressed that presents didn't matter, but I could see Mickey was upset because he didn't have anything for me. When he saw all the other kids giving me gifts, he ran out of the room.

About fifteen minutes later, he returned with a plastic bag. "This is a Christmas present for you" he said, handing me the bag, head lowered.

"Thanks, Mickey," I replied, cordially. He walked over to his desk and stood there, sort of squirming. "Why don't you come over here while I open it?" I suggested.

He took a few steps, then stopped.

I reached into the bag and pulled out a tattered copy of *National Geographic*. I immediately recognized it as one of the many I kept in the stockroom.

"Thanks, Mickey!" I exclaimed. "Just what I need for my collection."

"I . . . I," he stuttered. "I bought it at the store yesterday. Cost me five bucks."

"How did you know it was my favorite magazine?"

"'Cause it's got naked people inside."

The class laughed, and we all went on with the Christmas festivities.

Samantha, slouched despondently in her chair, refused to join in. All the kids were eating pizza and playing their favorite tunes on the record player, but she ignored them. Every so often she would look at someone with a sideways glance, but most of the time she stared glumly ahead.

"What's wrong, Samantha?" I asked, coming over when I had the chance. "Why aren't you joining the party?"

She looked up at me, her eyes dark and surly. "My head's playin' funny tricks again."

"Tricks?"

"It's that person in my head." Her voice was choked with anger. "Somebody's inside and won't leave!" She whirled around in her seat, contemptuously swept her hand through her dreadlocks, and rose out of the chair. Then she began trembling. "The voice keeps telling me about the end of the world, so there won't be no more Christmas, or summer, or winter, or nothin'!" Normally, she was not this disturbed.

"Look, Samantha, why on earth are you thinking of such awful things? This is Christmastime."

"My dad told me the world was gonna end soon, and Jesus was gonna come back." She fidgeted nervously.

"Try to think of something nice," I tried reassuringly. "I'm sure if Jesus did come back, he'd be okay. You wouldn't get hurt."

"On Saturday, this voice told me to gets rid of my sister friend, so I don't play with her no more. I like my best friend, but this voice inside me told me she's bad." Her tone was so bitter.

"What do you think the voice is?"

Her eyes dilated slightly. "It's the devil."

"Why do you think that?"

"My dad says the devil is strong and can go inside people's heads, and makes them think bad thoughts." Then she started to cry.

I put my arms around her. "Are you sure it's the devil and not just your imagination?" I was at a loss as to how to handle this.

"I . . . I don't know." She wiped away the tears. "I think so. Can you make the voices go away?"

"Well, I don't know, but I'll have a talk with your dad this evening. Anyway," I continued, "I'm sure that God is stronger than the devil. So don't you worry so much."

I called her dad tonight and told him the story. At my suggestion, he agreed to play down the devil and accent the more positive aspects of his beliefs.

Friday, December 29

An old friend of mine named Phil, who teaches in an inner-city school in Winnipeg, visited Jenny and me during the Christmas holidays. I brought out a bottle of Phil's favorite gin, and we talked late into the evening. Phil, as usual, was not at a loss for words, and he wasted no time in leading the discussion.

"So many kids in this country are emotionally starved," he told me. "Most of the kids I see pass through my door seem so wholly defeated and demoralized by life. They're filled with fear, suspicion, anger, hatred, you name it. Schools have to make these kids feel that they're human beings and worth something.

"I end up doing what you're doing, Peter; I end up functioning both as teacher and therapist. As a teacher, I try to inculcate a love of learning and impart knowledge and skills, and unfold some creative capacities. But as a therapist, I have to reduce so much excessive anxiety in these kids and try to dissolve so many emotional blocks that I'm becoming an emotional wreck myself!"

"Aren't we, as teachers, partially responsible for causing some of the problems?" I asked. "I mean . . . we support a system of education that's obviously failing the kids. What can we do when we're given thirty-five kids to teach in a crowded classroom who have already developed a mistrust and hatred for the world?"

Phil was always ready with an answer. "We've got to get the support of the community; we have to make them realize that their children aren't getting a fair shake. And listen, that includes all of them; they've got just as many problems as your immigrant kids. People are too ready to believe the poor are all welfare cheaters, or lazy, or that they keep having illegitimate children to get more mother's allowance checks. Somehow we've got to bridge that gap between the world of the ghetto and the middle-class pablum game of school."

We talked about the growing violence in the schools.

He shrugged his shoulders and breathed deeply. "Like jails and looney bins, schools isolate students from the real problems in society. I often wonder whether schools aren't just simply glorified baby-sitting institutions. . . . Look at it this way. We don't really need more manpower, and schools just delay the time the kids have to get out there and find jobs."

"Students are frustrated and feel like they don't belong. We expose them to aggressive models of success and then scream 'achieve! achieve!' until they turn off. And when they fail in school, they feel like failures in life. Look at what they're exposed to: TV, radio, newspapers, magazines, movies, ads. Then we drop these overstimulated kids into the slowest-moving institution in our society—our schools."

"Time for another drink. Am I pouring or are you?"

Monday, January 8

Dean, the school librarian, quit his job. He told me he simply couldn't take the kids any more—the noise level was unbearable. His new job is out in Moose Jaw, Saskatchewan, teaching at a private school.

A number of staff applied for Dean's job, and by secret ballot Helen, a special education teacher, was elected. I owe much of my sanity to her reorganization of the library.

Helen realized that, for inner-city kids, libraries were often boring places, and a library had to be a place for more than simply reading books. She set about changing the library from a place of passive silence to a center of creative activity.

Working late into the evenings, she set up over twenty activity areas where kids could work with sand, water, or blocks. They could also make their own newspapers, play with hockey cards, research just about any topic, make comics, tape stories, act out their own dramas on a makeshift stage, even play with the variety of puppets Helen had created. She arranged a schedule enabling a teacher to send a maximum of ten kids at a time each day. The kids loved the library more than anything else, with the possible exception of Big Arnie's room.

It was a relief to have ten fewer students for half an hour. But more important, the kids learned a lot there (whether they realized it or not); it was obvious from their projects and completed assignments.

Friday, January 12

Suzanne was dropped off at my door late this morning by her father. He wore a green snowmobile suit and a black cap with "Davey Boy" stitched in yellow across the brim, and he reeked of booze. "Suzanne hurt her leg this morning. Here," he grumbled, thrusting her toward me.

She hobbled up to my desk, eyes sunken into reddened sockets. Her father muttered goodbye through a half-smile of blackened teeth.

"That cocksucker!" Suzanne cried when he was gone. "He cracked me right across my leg with a stick just 'cause I wouldn't let him take my babysittin' money! Now he'll just go and buy another bottle!"

Tuesday, January 16

Mickey spent half the art period modeling his clay into a hot dog. When he finished, he walked to the front of the class and proudly showed it to me. Then he pretended to eat it, smacking his lips.

"That's too big for a hot dog!" Marta complained.

"My mom's got a plastic thing at home that looks like Mickey's hot dog," Diana chimed in. "Hers got bumps on it, and a battery inside to make it shake."

Wednesday, January 31

Well, all right. I do have a tendency to rattle on during a lesson. But this time, I had barely started when I noticed that Samantha looked bored. She was sitting at her desk, in deep thought. Her head moved from side to side as if she were struggling against an insistent voice inside her. I could see the muscles along her jaws tense as she seemed to forcibly stop herself from speaking.

As I went on with the lesson, I kept an eye on her.

She looked down, nervously tapping on her desk. Then her hands suddenly jerked back, and she shot to her feet, with both eyes bulging. When she had everyone's startled attention, she began to sing in a sweet, melodic voice:

"As I was walkin' down the lane, shh shh
I met a pretty girl in Spain, shh shh
When she leaned against the wall, shh shh
I gives her my balls and all, shh shh
Wouldn't momma be surprised, shh shh
To see her belly-button rise, shh shh
Won't momma be sad, shh shh
When she finds dad's mad, shh shh

Mommy on the bottom
Daddy on the top
Baby in the middle
Saying give it all you got!"

Tuesday, February 6

Angie's mother, looking very worried, came in this afternoon and told me that a child had been molested in the elevator of her apartment building. (Half my class lived in that building.) From tomorrow on, she would pick up Angie and her sisters from school every afternoon and escort them home to make sure nothing happened to them. "I'm going to do this every day, every week, every month of the year, for as long as my kids go to school," she told me, her voice filled with worry and anger. "If Angie has any work to finish after school, you'll just have to send it home with her."

She expected Angie to meet her in the school lobby at three-fifteen every afternoon.

Friday, February 9

Tasha, a grade six student from Mrs. Rogers's class, enjoyed staying after school to help me clean up my room. Mrs. Rogers was delighted that Tasha had taken a liking to me—she needed a male figure at this point in her life. Her father had recently walked out.

Always pale, with sad red eyes, Tasha shuffled listlessly around my room each afternoon, picking up scrap paper and depositing it in the wastepaper basket. Nearly every day she wore the same powder-blue denim dress, worn thin at the elbows.

Somewhere Tasha acquired a whisk broom, which she briskly used on the carpet. Down on her knees to brush chalk, she was very much the figure of Cinderella. After gathering all the debris into the wastepaper basket, she would carry it awkwardly down the stairs and empty it in the caretaker's office.

As soon as she finished, she would go to the art center I had set up at the back of the room. She always chose to play with modeling clay, shaping it into a figure resembling a man wearing a hat, carrying a suitcase. When I asked her who the figure was, she said only that it was "a traitor." After completing the figure, she would then viciously tear it apart.

She seemed to get a strange kind of comfort from the time she spent with me, but after a few weeks, Tasha no longer showed up to help with my room. Some of the other kids, I heard, had been teasing her about having a crush on me.

Monday, February 12

I met Priscilla's mother in the shopping mall at lunchtime. "Are you Mr. McLaren?" she said, her eyes wide and sparkling. "I'm Priscilla's mother."

"How are you?"

"I'm feelin' a lot better these days. The ladies in my buildin' finally got together this week and we had a meetin' in the basement." Her eyes roved over my face, a steaming hot dog clenched in her fist. "Well . . . a lot of us are getting fed up with nothin' happenin' around here. We decided to take things in own hands, so we're trying to set up some kind of day care for our kids. I mean, we have to do *something!*" She paused to watch a group of teenagers with large blaring transistors wander by, looking at clothing displays in the store windows.

"That sounds great. Do you think you'll be able to do it?" I asked.

"We can if we try. I was glad to see everybody really tryin' to help each other."

I wished her good luck and she shook my hand.

"Good luck to you, too," she said. "You know, you've got half the kids from my building in your class!"

Tuesday, February 20

A conversation I had with Marta's mother about her first night in the city, Jane-Finch area, sticks in my mind:

"We had just moved into the city from Tillsonburg," she began. "You know, a farming community. Well, it was our first real overnight in the new townhouse, and all of us were tickled to death, if you know what I mean.

"The furniture didn't arrive, and we had to sleep right on the floor, but I told the kids to pretend it was just like camping in a brick tent.

"In the morning my husband, George, heard this knock on the door. When he opened it, he saw this bottle on the porch with a piece of burning rag crackling and sticking out of the top . . . one of those Molotov cocktails you see in the war movies. George just gives it a big kick, and the bottle goes flying onto the sidewalk. The rag pops out and lands away from all that spilled gasoline, so nothing burned. Later, I found out that the next-door neighbor put it there."

"Did you talk to your neighbor about it?"

"Oh yes, we're good friends now. You see, the bomb was really for the former tenants. They had this child that kept the neighbor up all night. It had colic or something."

Monday, February 26

I had been getting depressed again. From the moment I woke up, I dreaded the thought of going to school. I found myself puttering around the house each morning: doing dishes, reading a book, finding any excuse not to leave until the very last minute. Usually I arrived at the school only moments before the bell.

Fred began to mention that I was "cutting my arrivals pretty close," so I decided to make a concerted effort to arrive early. Perhaps I could work out some material before the kids arrived: I could prepare the room, or have the work already on the blackboard. Maybe more advanced preparation would get me in a better frame of mind.

So I set my alarm for six-thirty, and if I rushed breakfast and traffic wasn't a problem, I could make it to the school before eight.

Every morning a depressed-looking kid, wearing a rumpled brown jacket and a Super Fly cap, would be standing in the same spot in the teachers' parking lot. Sometimes he whistled loudly, sometimes he hummed.

After the first few days, I decided he was trying to attract my attention. Usually I just gave him a wave or a smile. Now I began to invite him to come inside with me. He timidly introduced himself as Ralph.

He showed his appreciation by eagerly dashing around my room, tidying my cupboards, scrubbing graffiti off desktops, placing a freshly run-off mimeo sheet at each desk. After about half an hour of helping out, he'd curl up on my desk, tired and hungry.

He apologized for tiring out so fast. To combat hunger pangs he always carries a small brown envelope filled with jello powder, taking huge mouthfuls when he needs a lift.

Thursday, March 1

I was startled when Rod commented on the way I was dressing for work: bottle-green railroad overalls, Birkenstock sandals, lumberjack shirt. "You look just like the kids!" he explained, trying an engaging smile. "Maybe that's why they like you so much; they can't tell you apart from their classmates. When you first started teaching here, you were much straighter."

I was glad that the administration had a flexible dress code for the staff. I first began switching my dress pants and sports jackets to casual clothes for practical reasons: My good clothes always got covered in paint or torn when I tried to break up fights. One of my favorite jackets had to be thrown out when I found Magic Marker swipes all over the back.

I decided I could relate to the kids better if I didn't distance myself from them by wearing expensive clothes. I knew I was on the right track when a kid remarked, nodding at my attire: "You dress just like my dad does when he goes on shift."

Several teachers who are very fashion conscious objected to the "deterioration" in teacher image. They made a formal protest to Fred and Rod, requesting that teachers be forbidden to wear jeans, except for field trips or extracurricular sports. When the administration refused to make any such rule, the protesting teachers grew more upset. They're muttering about transferring to other schools, not wishing to be associated with a school full of "beatniks."

Tuesday, March 6

My gas tank was dry when I tried to start my van this afternoon. Empty container in hand, I headed off toward the nearest gas station.

My route took me through the housing project that some of my kids called "the zoo." Kids were everywhere. A few of them were climbing a TV antenna that ran up the side of a townhouse. Another group piled into a shopping cart that was pushed into the street. Passing cars swerved to a shrieking halt, narrowly missing running children. "Ya fuckin' kids! Get off the fuckin' streets!" a driver yelled.

A group of teenagers slumped on the sidewalk, waving a can in the air. One of them shouted: "Hey mister! You gonna get high on all that gas?" I grinned and kept walking.

A kid of about ten grabbed a screaming toddler by the hair and dragged him into a nearby townhouse. "Get in the goddam house before I fry your balls off on the stove!" The door slammed.

Monday, April 2

Ros handed me a shiny, cracked snapshot of her hometown in Nicaragua. The photo showed her grandmother standing outside of a cinderblock house, smiling.

Standing next to the house was a church that looked as if it were made from corrugated aluminium. Pointing to the church, Ros exclaimed: "God rests there on his trips 'round the world!"

Next to the church stood her father, wearing a moss-green military uniform and holding a submachine gun. "He shoots the people who robs the stores."

Standing next to him was a hollow-cheeked woman. "That's my mother. My sister just died—she was only three, and she made my mother cry and cry."

I looked at the photo for a long time.

"All the kids tease me 'cause I talk funny," Ros finally said. "I wanna go back home."

Thursday, April 12

Teachers can order special marking stamps from a supply catalogue or retailer. Usually the stamps bear standard captions: "Excellent," "Good work," "Do over," "Neater please," and so forth. A little cartoon figure accompanies each caption. Priscilla stole one of my stamps inscribed with an angel holding up a scroll which read "You can do better."

She was found in the girl's washroom, stamping sheet after sheet of toilet paper.

Tuesday, April 17

This morning there was a violent windstorm. Kids on their way to school were literally blown across the streets; cars were forced over to the curb; garbage littered the sidewalks. Naturally, few kids showed up for school, only ten in my class. Most of them wanted a free day in the library to work on projects of their own choice, and I gave them my permission. Only Colin wanted to stay in the classroom. Characteristically quiet and sullen, he was now unusually talkative. He began to tell me stories. He told me that on weekends he took a plane to either the White House or Elvis Presley's gravesite . . . depending on how he felt. He spoke very seriously.

With the wind howling outside, he talked about his sleepwalking. His mother would find him out in the hall in the middle of the night, pounding his fists against the wall. He told me about how he almost murdered a little girl.

"I get this funny feelin' inside of me," he said slowly. "It's like somebody else comes inside my body. When I get this feelin', I feel like I want to kill somebody. One night I saw this little girl down by the creek, and I almost killed her with my penknife. I would've killed her, too, if her brother hadn't come along. My mom and dad went to court with me, afterwards."

I didn't know what to think.

"Sometimes I dream of blood," Colin continued. "I love blood and guts and things like that. I dream sometimes about kissin' blood. That's why I like fightin'—all that blood! Once my dad cut his finger with a carving knife at dinner. He didn't want blood to drip all over the carpet, so I sucked his finger for him." The wind rattled the windows.

Thursday, April 19

Yesterday, I met with a group of about twenty teachers and principals from fourteen different schools in the city. We were trying to form a committee to investigate ways to help schools further meet the needs of working-class and immigrant children from poor families. Over hot pizza in a public school about a mile outside of the Corridor, we talked about some of our concerns.

We talked about the problems immigrant children have to cope with when adjusting to schools in the area: language or dialect barriers; conflicting traditions and customs; culture shock; parental expectations and personal goals; heavy workloads both in school and at home; academic upgrading; family conflicts. The children were often called names, misunderstood, made to feel inferior.

A grade five teacher told us that recently she was phoned late at night by a parent of one of her students. The parent was a single mother. Alone in her townhouse with her daughter at the time, she became panic-stricken as two adolescent boys tried to break down her door with a crowbar to get at her daughter. The parent demanded that the teacher "do something about it."

Another teacher spoke of two children in her class that were locked outside by their parents in the middle of winter, as punishment.

One teacher told the group in a husky voice, trembling with emotion, that she couldn't bear to see one child bring a lunch, day after day, consisting of only pieces of dried toast.

As the afternoon progressed, we all shared scores of classroom horror stories.

"There are lots more of us," one teacher told me, "who are afraid to speak out against the conditions in our schools because we're afraid of getting our knuckles rapped by the administration!"

Friday, April 20

Like so many other teachers, I joked about quitting after a hard day with the kids. Only now I was beginning to take the idea more seriously. I had been accepted as a graduate student in education, and two years of full-time study was compulsory. That would also mean two full years without earning a regular salary. But it would give me the chance to do some research, and perhaps work to make changes outside the system.

Wednesday, April 25

T. J. knocked on my door to give me a warning. "Sir!" he explained. "There's a fire engine parked out the front! A fire drill!" Unannounced fire drills occurred sporadically. Fire marshals and a truck would always show up just before a drill, so we could always prepare for them.

I turned to the kids and quickly reviewed fire-drill procedures: no talking, no shoving, no sliding down banisters. Also, the last person to leave shuts the door.

The fire bell began to ring. I swung open the door and came face-to-face with one of the fire marshals. Mickey suddenly broke out of line and shouted: "Lance called me a cocksucker! I'm gonna give him a punch!"

The fire marshal looked more embarrassed than I was.

"We'll settle it later, Mickey!" I yelled, urging the kids out the door and down the stairs.

"But sir!" Mickey insisted. He wasn't about to give up, especially in front of a fire marshal. "He called me a cocksucker!"

By now most of the kids had made their way downstairs on their own. A few hung around to watch the scene, as Mickey suddenly grabbed Lance and pounded his head on the floor screaming, "Goddam welfare prick!" I grabbed them both, one under each arm, and carried them down the stairs and out into the yard. The rest of the kids followed.

Once outside, Mickey kicked the wall angrily. "We didn't have to come outside. You tricked us! Look . . . there's no fire!"

The fire marshal gave me a rueful glance, tipped his hat to me, and murmured, "Nice place you got here," and walked quickly to his car.

Thursday, April 26

A senior administrator on the Board paid a visit to my classroom. Every few years he makes his rounds, visiting all the elementary schools in his jurisdiction to pay his respects. He walked into my room smiling. "Glad to see you!" he said heartily. "Fine group of kids you got here!" I smiled and shook hands.

"Like your set-up here," he continued. "Room sure is colorful." He was short and on the plump side, and he fingered a cufflink nervously. "Nice bunch of kids!"

The kids laughed and applauded themselves. "Who's the turkey?" one of them stage-whispered.

Mr. Brooks cleared his throat. "Hear you're doing a good job," he said. I nodded, and he smiled and walked out.

Mickey watched him go, then pulled urgently at my sleeve. "I've seen guys like that at my house. They come to see my brothers. He's your parole officer, ain't he!"

Friday, April 27

Georgette and Wendy picked up some dolls at the activity center. Georgette chose a G.I. Joe, and Wendy picked up a Farrah Fawcett doll.

"Let's pretend we're married," Georgette said.

"Okay," Wendy agreed, "let's start!"

Georgette took G.I. Joe's arm and promptly slapped the Farrah doll across the face with it, shouting: "That's what you get for talkin' to me like that!"

Monday, April 30

On the weekend I went to a neighborhood party held in a posh house near the lakefront. I'm not much of a party-goer, but I was feeling weary and depressed.

After downing a stiff martini, I heard a voice behind me say, "I hear you're a teacher."

I turned and discovered a woman who was staring at me rather intensely. "You *are* a teacher, aren't you?" she asked, ingenuously brightening up her smile.

I wasn't in the mood for niceties. I removed my plastic union card from my wallet and presented it to her. "I think I'm a teacher," I said sarcastically. "At least . . . I think that's what it says on my card."

"I've always wanted to be a teacher," she continued, with a pretentious, almost commercial civility. "I just love little kids. Youth is so much fun and so exciting . . . teaching must be so rewarding. Tell me, what are your pupils like?"

I paused for a long time. "Well," I said, "let me see. I have shy kids . . . aggressive kids . . . kids that need prodding . . . kids that balk if pushed . . . kids susceptible to colds . . . kids that never get sick . . . kids who aren't interested in playing music . . . kids who will bang out a tune on anything . . . black kids, white kids, mulatto kids, Spanish kids, Italian kids, West Indian kids, WASP kids, Catholic kids, kids from South America, kids from Nova Scotia . . . kids that had polio . . . kids that have sickle-cell anemia . . . kids that have cold sores and hangnails . . . one kid who had a nervous breakdown at seven . . . kids who have scars from beatings . . . kids whose parents never discipline them . . . kids who wear tattered clothes . . . kids who wear the latest fashions . . . kids who love me . . . kids who think I screw the teacher down the hall . . . kids that frown all the time . . . kids that never stop smiling. . . ."

I stopped. The woman stared at me as if I were crazy. I probably was crazy. After a few moments of silence the woman reached over and touched my arm and sensuously planted a fuchsia-colored kiss on the nape of my neck. "I'm curious," she said, stroking my arm. "Do you really screw the teacher down the hall?"

Tuesday, May 1

I was surprised when the mayor's secretary phoned me today and asked me to participate in a special session at City Hall involving a council that had been set up to help relieve the tension in the Jane-Finch Corridor.

Speaking through a stiff headcold, I told the council, using my experiences as ammunition, that schools must do more to meet the needs of poor children. I said it was a moral concern. Blank expressions nodded in unison.

Thursday, May 3

Upset with his son's progress report, Mr. Corelli called me at the school and requested an interview. Because he worked the late afternoon shift at a glass and paint factory, he was unable to come to the school during regular hours. I told him I'd be glad to drop by his place on Sunday afternoon.

I knocked on the door of the tiny brick townhouse shortly after twelve. A thin, wiry man in a sleeveless white tee shirt answered the door.

"I'm Frank's dad," he said, motioning me inside, offering me the lazy-boy armchair that dominated the tiny living room. I found myself facing about a dozen bowling trophies crowded together on top of a rusty filing cabinet. Portraits of John and Robert Kennedy, painted on black felt, hung above the window.

"As you can see, we're beer drinkers here!" and he pointed to the hall. I saw it was completely papered in Labatt's "50" beer bottle labels. "My wife did that," he proclaimed proudly. "Took her six months. If you can find even a speck of space between the labels, I'll give you a twelve-pack free!"

He brought me a beer, slumped down in the sofa, and groaned. "Frank ain't been doin' so good in school . . . has he?" he finally asked.

"No . . . not exactly," I replied, pushing back on the arms of the lazy-boy, trying to get comfortable.

"Do you think Frank's gonna pass?"

"I don't believe in failing pupils."

"But is he tryin'?" he snapped.

"I think it takes Frank a lot to get himself motivated," I hedged, uncertain of exactly what to say.

"Look," Mr. Corelli said matter-of-factly, as he smoothed back the black tufts of his thinning hair, "tomorrow I think I'll show up in your class and give him a few belts."

I was shocked. "You mean in front of the class?"

"I give him lickin's at home, but it doesn't do any good," he replied, shaking his head. "Maybe in front of his friends—"

"That's out of the question! You can't teach a kid anything through violence or humiliating punishment. I can't stop you from punishing your son at home, Mr. Corelli, but I would never allow him to be hit at school. Not under any circumstances." I was trying to control my anger.

"Well then," he said calmly, "*you* give it to him in front of the kids, if you don't want me to."

My face felt hot, and I laughed nervously. "No way, Mr. Corelli! Let's talk about the problem first, and maybe we can come up with some solution."

Head tilted, a somber expression on his face, Mr. Corelli then fired questions at me in swift progression, ranging from the "too lenient" disciplinary approach of most teachers to the high cost of school taxes. Eventually he got around to what was really bothering him.

"It's hard coping with Frank alone. Ever since his mother walked out on me it's been hell. She went out to the variety store one day and never came back. I know Frank blames me, 'cause we used to fight so much."

I placed Frank in an individualized program consisting mostly of arts and craft-oriented activities, and tried not to pressure him on his academic subjects, at the same time searching for a strategy.

I had previously put Frank in a special reading series, but he went through the readers perfunctorily. Then I remembered his dad mentioning Frank's comic book collection, and I asked him to bring some in. We went over the comic books together, and soon Frank's working vocabulary improved.

Monday, May 7

From a distance I could see Lambchops, a grade six student, standing at the end of the hall. He hitched up his pants, lifted his shoulders, and snapped his fingers. Responding to his signal, three kids suddenly ran out of the washroom and pounced on a kid whom Lambchops had seen walking by. "Kick his fuckin' head in," one of them cried.

The kids took off like a shot when they saw me coming. The victim was left to nurse a split lip and a few bruises.

"It was only a joke," the kid whined when I questioned him. His eyes searched mine, sad and pleading. "Don't do anything, please! They'll get me on the way home."

Friday, May 11

Orantes, nine, swaggered over to my desk. "You got any hair on your chest?" It wasn't the kind of question I expected to be asked. "Sir," Orantes continued, "you ain't got no hair on your chest. My daddy gots lots of hair on his."

"You're wrong, Orantes. I do happen to have some hair on my chest, I replied, with a mixture of embarrassment and pride. "Most men do. But I'm sure your dad has more than anybody else."

"Lemme see then!" was the immediate shouted response. I had been trapped, outfoxed. "Lemme see! Undo your shirt and lemme have a look!"

I tried to gracefully ease myself out by saying, "Take my word for it, Orantes. Your dad has lots of hair on his chest. I don't have very much. Your dad wins!"

"You gots more hair on your head," he continued, undaunted, "but my dad gots more on his chest. He looks like a hairy monster."

"I'm sure your dad looks much more like a monster than I do, Orantes. And I really don't have any hair on my chest, either. I was just kidding."

"Show me then," he demanded at once. I had been suckered right in. "Show me right now! Prove you ain't got no hair!"

I gave up. I opened my shirt a little and pulled down the neckline of my tee shirt, revealing a few blond tufts. "See! I've just got a few—not like your dad. Okay?"

But Orantes had more up his sleeve. "My dad's gots a cock this big!" he went on, holding his hand a good two feet apart.

Monday, May 14

Fred warned me he wouldn't be around next September. He was taking a year's sabbatical to study in England. He thought he'd probably be placed in a new school on his return. It was Board policy to move a principal to a new school every five years. He offered me a job on his new staff if I ever wanted to join him.

"Would you like to be principal of a nice middle-class school?" I asked.

"Not really. And even if I did, the Board would stick me in another inner-city school anyway. Once you've been successful as an inner-city school principal, they always place you in another one. That's their idea of a reward."

Wednesday, May 16

It was one of the first warm days after the long winter. After class I decided to soak up some sun on a park bench near the school. The air smelled fresh and the sun felt good on my face. I lit my pipe and started marking a batch of exercise books I had brought along.

Shortly afterward I was approached by three black kids—two boys and a girl—about ten years old. They wore identical shiny nylon jackets, tight-fitting jeans, and orange fluorescent sneakers. I didn't recognize them as students from the school.

As soon as the girl caught my eyes she flashed a wide smile and started snapping her fingers. The two boys also joined in, finger-snapping and slowly rocking back and forth. Weaving gracefully in my direction, they stopped only a few feet from where I was sitting and began a rhythmic cooing. Then the girl began to strut and sashay, moving faster, her companions following. I put down my book and drew heavily on my pipe, swaddled by the soft beauty of their voices, and mesmerized by the fluid movements of their bodies that shifted effortlessly from one intricate pattern to another.

Suddenly the girl's arms shot up and the voices and dancing stopped. They stood there motionless, hands on their hips. After a few seconds, blissful smiles drooped into frowns. I reached into my pocket, pulled out some change, and handed it to the girl—a small price for the pleasure they had given to me. Wide smiles blossomed once again. Then they turned and headed back toward the street.

Thursday, May 17

I stayed at the school late last night, setting up a reading clinic in my class. At one end of the room I equipped a large rectangular table with a record player and a dozen headphones. In the other corner I set up a language master and two filmstrip projectors so the kids could watch cartoon strips of classic fairy tales.

My pièce de résistance was an eight-track cassette machine complete with tapes of children's stories. I recorded the stories myself, and my voice was still hoarse from reading aloud into the microphone.

Whenever I stayed late at the school, I usually spent the night at my parents' house, just a couple of miles outside the Corridor.

That night I woke up about four o'clock in the morning, and couldn't get back to sleep. Rather than toss and turn, I decided to go for a drive. Almost instinctively, I headed back to the Corridor. I parked my van in the school lot and sat on the street curb across from the school.

For a long time, I just sat staring at the school in the predawn light, thinking of all the events that had gone on behind those drab, brown walls. From the outside, the building looked just like any other school; it was hard to imagine all the lost and troubled souls that passed through those doors each day.

One by one, people emerged bleary-eyed from the nearby buildings, clutching lunch pails or brown bags, heading toward the bus stops. A drizzle of rain began to fall.

I sat in the rain watching the Italian laborers in heavy shirts and trousers of thick fabric, West Indian workers in woolen caps, some carrying transistor radios the size of small suitcases. One black woman lifted her skirt and whirled in a little dance. Another woman in a colorful print shawl looked up into the sky, inviting the rain to cool her face.

The whole area looked so bleak, so sterile, yet strangely at peace. The gray high-rises seemed aloof, almost stoic in the soft mist that was forming. I listened to the steady rumble of trucks down the nearby industrial streets, birds chirping on the telephone wires, the screech of the garbage trucks pulling up to the backs of the buildings. Everything seemed so integral, even purposeful. But I knew that behind the faceless concrete facades, families were awakening to a new day of troubles . . . hustling to survive . . . or just giving in to despair.

I needed a wake-up coffee before the school day began. I headed over to the local plaza.

Friday, May 18

This morning John decided I should purify my blood. He sent a strange drink up to my class, which he claimed would do the trick. Made of vinegar, water, and honey, and perhaps several other unidentified ingredients, it emitted a putrid stench.

Phil watched me taste it, and then remarked: "Jeez, sir, you're just like my dad. He needs his shot in the mornin', too!"

Sunday, May 20

On Sunday, I went down to the boardwalk for a stroll along the lake. As I strolled along, hands in my pockets, head down, the planks in the boardwalk seemed like measured steps in an uphill climb to sanity. I was mentally calculating my fitness for another year in the classroom. Was I up to it? The thought of teaching for another year made me feel that I was trapped in a dungeon, losing all count of time. The warden might be a nice guy and the food palatable, but I was suffocating. I had to get out. I'd put in my time.

I decided to quit. I took a deep breath and started for home.

Jenny was sitting in the living room. When I told her she looked at me intently. "I know. I sensed it."

"Well? How do you feel about it?"

"I feel you'll be an old man by the time you're thirty-five if you keep on the way you're going. You know I'm behind you . . . and the kids will still be there."

Tuesday, May 22

I couldn't sleep last night; my mind was flooded with doubts. Did it really make any difference, my being there? Am I copping out, running away? And so on and so on. . . .

I loathed to tell Fred; I felt I was betraying him. When I finally got up the nerve, he took it well, understanding my position.

"Sure, Peter, I'll sign your leave of absence papers, only because I know you'll change your mind."

Wednesday, May 23

After lunch, Mickey told me he had tried to take a bite out of his townhouse. He showed me a chipped tooth and bleeding gums to prove it.

Friday, May 25

Duke, my wild and unruly former student, liked to return periodically for a talk. He had quit school after junior high. When he was in my class, he often wore a button: "Sure I raise hell. So what?"

Out in the parking lot, he showed me the new paint job on his motorcycle. Like always, he wore faded jeans, a wrinkled tee shirt, and a leather jacket. A fat friend was kneeling beside Duke's bike, checking the engine. Painted on the deep-blue gas tank was a picture of the earth and a distant star, with a bright beam of white light shooting from the star toward the earth. The words "The King Is Coming" were stenciled in gold letters over the picture. Running down the back fender were the fluorescent-green words "Bikers for the Lord."

"Remember when I got Lindsay to eat that dog shit, after shoving a Kleenex full o' snot in his mouth?"

"Do I!"

"Well," he said, leaning against his bike, "I didn't really mean it. I don't do things like that no more. I've changed."

Wednesday, May 30

I visited the group home where Barry lives. It had been two years since he left my class, and I decided to see how he was doing.

A teenage girl, both of whose arms were wrapped in gauze from fingertips to armpits, opened the door for me. She was bandaged to prevent her from hurting herself: She bit spoon-sized chunks from her arms with her own teeth. One side of her head was a mass of black scabs, with a few remaining tufts of hair sticking out. Barry, she told me, was out on a camping trip.

Friday, June 1

One of Mickey's older brothers had just been released from jail, and Mickey was excited about it. All day long, he drew pictures of the event. One picture showed his brother being led away from jail by a giant creature.

"What's that thing with your brother?" I asked.

"Don't you know who *that* is?" Jessie asked, a puzzled grin breaking across his face as he leaned across to Mickey's desk.

"Not really. Who is it, Mickey?"

"It's the Amazing Hulk! *He saved my brother!* Didn't you know that? He sprang Tommy from jail!"

Monday, June 4

Last March, Fred invited several art therapists to speak to the staff on the benefits of spontaneous art for inner-city children. A recently published research paper, demonstrating that kids who had difficulty talking about their anxieties often had remarkable success drawing pictures of what was troubling them, caught his interest.

After listening to the art therapists describe their program, the staff agreed to hire one for a probationary period, with an option for extending the program if it were successful.

We were each asked to submit the name of one student who might benefit. Although I felt I had many kids who could be helped by the program, I decided to put Mickey's name on the list.

Each week Anthony, his therapist, would withdraw Mickey from class and take him down to a corner of the student lunch room. Under his expert guidance, Mickey was encouraged to express himself with crayons, paint, and clay. He responded by painting pictures of army tanks in battle and, later, of his house and family.

Anthony also encouraged him to talk about his paintings. After the first month, Mickey was able to open up to him and talk freely, and soon a good relationship grew between them.

While following Mickey's progress through weekly meetings with Anthony, I began to know the therapist as a person, and was impressed. He explained that art therapy had its theoretical roots in the psychoanalytic work of Sigmund Freud, utilizing his theories of the anal, oral, and genital personalities. As he analyzed Mickey's drawings within this framework, I became fascinated.

"Mickey didn't even have to draw a thing before I knew he was a combination of oral and anal personality development," Anthony told me the first time we spoke about Mickey.

"Really?"

"Because the first thing he said to me was 'Eat shit!'"

But the staff eventually decided that not enough kids were receiving help; teachers could send only one student per class. And although we all agreed the therapy was beneficial, some teachers wondered whether more kids would be helped if the money was spent instead on school supplies. So the art therapy program died. The option was not picked up; there was simply not enough support for it.

When Mickey had to say goodbye to Anthony, he became extremely upset. Anthony was one person he'd become attached to. Now his behavior began to revert, and it was as if nothing had happened at all.

Wednesday, June 6

Suzanne stormed into the staff room while I was eating lunch—"I just went home for lunch and the super in my buildin' kicked us out! He changed the lock on our door so's we can't get back in! I couldn't even get my sweater!"

I offered her some of my lunch and she sat down beside me. "Why did your super kick you out?" I asked.

"He says my mom's a welfare bum and can't pay the rent. But mom's already paid! She just got a new job! And he threw out my baby sister and her babysitter and says we're good-for-nothin' niggers! My mom's gonna go to court 'cause she's real mad, and she don't even know where we're gonna stay tonight."

I thought only for a moment. "Tell your mom you can stay with me." She smiled and threw her arms around my neck.

After speaking to her mom, Suzanne told me they would be staying with a neighbor on another floor in their building, but she thanked me for the offer.

For the next two days her mother went to court, trying to settle the problem. She got her apartment back, but because of the days she took off to appear in court, she lost her new job.

Thursday, June 7

At nine o'clock, I assembled the kids on the carpet. "Well, boys and girls, does anybody have any news?" I asked, as I did first thing every morning.

Two kids immediately leaped up, as if the law of gravity had been temporarily suspended. Esther Anne was one of them. I was surprised she volunteered; she seldom spoke, even when asked. For her to volunteer news was quite an event.

"Me first! Me first!" Georgette howled suddenly. She jumped up, waving her arms wildly. "Me first! I'm before Esther Anne! You promised!"

She was right. "I'll be right with you, Esther Anne, but I already promised Georgette that she could be the first today to give the news."

I was impatient as Georgette described her sister's birthday party. Esther Anne was on my mind, and I was eager to hear what news she had to report.

When Georgette finished, I turned to Esther Anne. She stared at me for a moment, her burning eyes darting from my face to the floor. "I changed my mind," she said at last. "I ain't got no news today."

I was disappointed, but tried to be positive. "Okay, Esther Anne. Maybe you'll have some news tomorrow. . . ."

At the end of the day, she came up to me as I was packing up. "Sir, do you want to know what my news was?"

"Why, I sure do," I answered, eager to draw her out of her shell.

"Well . . ." she began, slowly, "my mom, she burned me with a cigarette yesterday."

"Where?"

"Right here . . . and here . . . and here," she replied, pointing to her neck, hand, and forearm.

Friday, June 8

Carmen and Sasha were delightful. In other schools they might have been labeled "slow learners" or "behavior problems," but I thought they were great. At the end of a long day, it was always a joy when they volunteered to stay after class and help me tidy up.

This afternoon, while they were helping me clean out the cupboard, I casually remarked that kids today don't seem to really try to get along with each other.

"How you expect them to get along with other folks," replied Sasha, "when they don't even like the person that they are?"

Monday, June 11

During the last weeks of school, I took the kids to the park almost daily. I brought a cassette machine along with some vintage tapes of blues artists. Listening to the blues has always had a peaceful effect on me, and I hoped they could relax to some of the songs.

I put the machine under a tree and turned it on. A half dozen kids started tapping their feet almost immediately as Bessie Smith, Charlie Patton, Blind Lemon Jefferson, and Billie Holiday sang haunting parables about the tragicomic underbelly of urban life.

Kids who weren't interested in the music ran across the park to the baseball diamond or else made for the swings. I lay down on the park bench and watched a sky full of dark clouds move slowly overhead, as if they were slowed in passing by the beauty of the music. A brisk gust of wind scattered paper and debris; the leaves flicked and eddied about the bench.

Mickey inched up to me and nudged my arm. "The music sounds real good," he said. "But it's sad."

Birds fluttered in the tops of nearby trees. A group of kids, groaning, puffing, and wet with sweat, tried to grab onto a large overhanging branch on one of the large trees. Finally, after many failed attempts, Lance dragged over a trash can and tipped it upside down. The kids propped the can against the tree and used it to boost themselves up.

Samantha sat down in the dirt in front of me. She stared for a few minutes across the field, her eyes scanning the rows of high-rise apartments that loomed on the outer edges of the park. They resembled giant gravestones under the low, menacing sky.

"You wanna know somethin', sir," she said wistfully, still staring into the distance. "We used to live right downtown in this rotten place called Regent's Park. Then my mom said, 'We're gonna move to the suburbs.' Now that we're here we gots more people callin' us names and beatin' us up more than before. I thought the suburbs was supposed to be a nice place. Now I wanna go back downtown."

I put my arm around her shoulder and watched a tiny figure making its way from the school yard across the field to the park. As the figure grew closer I realized it was Priscilla, who had been absent during the morning. She ran the last few yards up to my bench, a sweet smile wrinkling her face.

"I'm the best kid in the class now, sir!" she announced triumphantly.

"No you're not!" Samantha snapped and impulsively kissed me on the cheek.

"I am!"

Priscilla placed her hands on her hips and looked up at the sky. "I gots baptized last night—so there! Hallelujah and praise the Lord!"

"Congratulations, Priscilla," I said.

"I went to a healin' meetin, too," she continued, a tumult of emotions. "This man touched people on the head and the Holy Spirit knocked them out. There was this fat lady there, and the man with the Spirit touched her and turned her skinny. I saw it! Her shoes was so big they didn't fit her no more! Then the man cured my brother's sickle-cell blood. Praise the Lord!"

"I don't believe you!" Mickey broke in viciously. "You're a liar!"

"Shut your face!" Priscilla snapped back.

Vinnie came running up to the bench, arms pumping and face sweat-streaked. He sat down heavily beside Priscilla, trying clumsily to fasten his sneakers.

"God praise you Vinnie!" cried Priscilla.

Vinnie looked stunned. "What?"

"I gots the spirit, Vinnie!" she cried, grinning widely.

Vinnie stopped struggling with his shoelaces and sat still. "There's no such thing as spirits!" he declared. "The guy in our buildin' everybody says is a boogey man, he's jus' an ole drunk."

Priscilla was annoyed. "I'm not talkin' about boogey men. I mean God's spirit. I gots religion!"

Mickey scowled and muttered, "You're crazy!" and ran across to the tree where kids were starting to climb down. Then he pulled away the trash can just as Pasquale was about to descend. Pasquale dropped from the tree onto the ground, landing with a loud thud—and a curse. Priscilla watched the event with growing disdain. "You needs the spirit!" she shouted. Mickey raised his fist in a mock salute. "Up yours!"

Tuesday, June 12

Usually, if you have to hide out, the bathroom is the place to do it. At least you're assured privacy in the toilet, if nowhere else. And that was why I began hiding out in the staff washroom during recess, trying to get the peace and quiet I needed to finish off some paperwork.

During recess this afternoon I was sitting on the throne marking papers, when I heard the door to the washroom open. I froze.

A pair of red sneakers appeared suddenly under the door of my hideaway cubicle. Just as suddenly the sneakers disappeared, only to be replaced by a pair of knees, then two hands, and then Mickey's head thrust under the door, grinning up at me.

"Havin' a nice shit, sir?"

Wednesday, June 13

Mickey's teenage sister showed up at my door, Mickey standing behind her, crying. He had been beaten on the way to school, she explained, and had returned home in tears. So she decided to walk him to school.

As soon as Mickey entered the room, he started screaming. "T. J.'s going to kill fuckin' Leroy," he shouted. "He's gonna punch him out for beatin' me up!" He wailed, blinking away tears, and flailing his arms as if at an invisible adversary.

I drew him close to me, and it was the only time he didn't push me away. While I wiped the tears from his eyes, I began rubbing his back slowly, rhythmically. His tight little face began to relax as I stroked his damp forehead soothingly and told him to take a deep breath. He sighed, and slowly the frenzy melted away. His shoulders loosened, then he crawled up on my lap and fell asleep.

Oddly enough, my kids just went on quietly with their work, and no one disturbed us.

Thursday, June 14

I took the class to Ontario Place as an end-of-the-year outing. Most of the kids had never been there, although they had heard stories about the excellent playground and the giant water slide. Because of the budget cuts I wasn't able to reserve a school bus, so we had to travel by public transportation. Several parent volunteers came along to help me with the kids.

Except for a scuffle between Mickey and Vinnie over who was going to sit at the very back of the bus, the kids were reasonably well-behaved. The bus let us off at Exhibition Stadium, and we walked the rest of the way to Ontario Place, a short stroll.

Once inside, the children ran off everywhere, and it took about half an hour to round them up.

We saw a short film about Ontario that was playing at Cinesphere, a theater with a giant, curved screen. At the beginning of the film the Premier of Ontario, William Davis, also known as "Smiling Bill," appeared on the screen, mouthing homilies about the greatness of the province.

"Hey . . . lookit him!" Mickey blurted. "It's Al Capone!"

"Yahoo," Vinnie exclaimed, "a real gangster!"

"He ain't no hood!" Samantha cried. "He's a millionaire. Lookit his clothes!"

"So what if he's rich!" Priscilla bellowed, "who wants to get dressed up like that all the time!"

I hushed the kids, explaining to them that other people were trying to watch the film, and that they had to behave if they wanted to go to the playground.

"He's bribin' us again," Mickey laughed. But they did settle down for the remainder of the film.

After the film the kids complained that they were hungry, so we ate lunch by the water, outside the entrance to the theater. Vinnie started throwing rocks at the swans and was joined by several other kids. I moved the class to the middle of an open area.

After lunch we marched over to the adventure playground, full of activities designed for children: rope forts, climbers of every shape and description, teeter-totters, pulley rides, tunnels, and slides. Most of the kids wanted to go on the water slide, but couldn't afford the two dollar charge.

"Everywhere kids go they gotta pay money for the most fun thing!" Priscilla complained. She kicked the fence outside the water slide, and watched the kids who could afford it laugh deliriously as they sailed down the giant curving slide, landing in various positions in the pool below. Most of the other kids forgot about the slide and amused themselves with other things. But Priscilla stood staring at the water slide for a long time.

After several hours of horsing around, we left. Samantha threw up all over my lap on the bus ride home, much to my wife's disgust when I arrived at my front door.

Friday, June 15

When I found out the local junior high was putting on a year-end variety show, I decided to go. Maybe I'd see some of my old kids.

Sure enough, several showed up. The first performer, in fact, was none other than Buddy. Even though he hadn't officially been one of my students, he was still one of the family—sort of.

Buddy was part of a dancing troupe, which did a beautifully choreographed disco set to the background of a Thelma Huston song. He was dressed in patch-work quilt knickers, striped suspenders, and platinum-colored satin shirt, his former mountain of Afro hair now neatly dreadlocked. The name of his group was "Fight the Power!"

The performance ended with some teenage girls reading an essay called "The Black Manifesto," aimed at getting the black community organized in fighting racism.

After the show, Buddy and I had a friendly chat. It's funny how much affection I had for this character who gave me so many rough moments. He told me he didn't hang out anymore with his old friends; most of his buddies were older. He was seriously taking up boxing. "And if I ever get to be Champ, I'll mention your name to the TV guys."

Tuesday, June 19

"This world is dumb! A man on the TV said a piece of a spaceship is gonna fall on our heads!"

"Hey, gimme back my pencil!"

"Yes, Vinnie, I agree. The world really does seem dumb sometimes."

"It's my pencil! I found it on the floor!"

"Sir! Wasn't Elvis the best?"

"He was pretty good. I liked him."

"See! I told you! White people are the best singers!"

"Hey, I didn't say white people were the best singers."

"There are good black singers as well as white singers."

"Liar! You just said Elvis was the best!"

"Brown people can sing good, too!"

"My aunt put my little cousin in the dryer last night. He lost five dollars at the store so my aunt put him in the dryer and he went 'round and 'round."

"Is that true, Mickey?"

"Wipe your nose Georgette! It's full of snot!"

"Welfare face!"

"It's true! I saw it!"

"Don't eat it! Mr. McLaren! Georgette's licking off her snot!"

"You looks just like my dad, sir. Exceptin' my dad's black."

"My friend said I look like Elvis."

"I look like Debbie Boone then!"

"Yuck! I hates Debbie Boone! She's gots pimples."

"You . . . you light up my life . . ."

"Shut up your stupid singin'!"

"You gots an awful voice, Samantha."

"My mom threw a wooden spoon at me this mornin'."

"What happened?"

"It missed. That's all."

"I was at the creek last night, Mr. McLaren. I saw these teenagers with their pants down."

"Wait a minute. Mickey wants to tell me about his cousin and Vinnie wants to tell me about his mother."

"I don't wanna talk no more about my mother."

"Take your finger out of your zipper!"

"Awww! I thought it was his cock stickin' out!"

"Mr. McLaren! Georgette's nose is all green again from snot. There's a little green worm comin' out of her nose!"

"You . . . you light up my life . . . light up my life. . . ."

"Shaddup! You sound welfare!"

"My mom told me I look just like Harry Belafonte."

"He's an old man, stupid. I seen him on a record. My mom says he's an Oreo cookie—black on the outside and white in the middle."

"What does that mean?"

"I dunno. He tastes good."

"I gots a new mom. She's deaf."

"She's a mental!"

"No she ain't! She just can't hear."

"You ain't nothin' but a hound dog. . . ."

"Shaddup! You ain't no good either!"

"Is the sky really gonna fall, Mr. McLaren?"

"Probably the bits from the space station will land in the ocean."

"I hope it lands on Vinnie's balls."

Wednesday, June 20

On our daily walk to the park, everything was going smoothly until little Carlos, a moment before happy and cheerful, suddenly fell to the ground, weeping uncontrollably.

"I miss my mom! My *real* mom!" he cried out to me.

"Your real mom? Where is she?" I asked, as I picked him up in my arms to comfort him.

"She's in New Brunswick," he whimpered. "My dad's sendin' me on the train to see her in July, and they're gettin' a divorce!"

I tried to cheer him up by saying, "Why, that's only a few weeks away; all you have to do is wait awhile."

But he continued to sob. "But my dad's getting divorced now from my other mom so that means I'm gonna have three moms!"

I had no idea what to say, trying to sort out which mom he meant when, as suddenly as he began to cry, he jumped up, wiped away his tears, and headed over to a bunch of kids playing soccer.

Thursday, June 21

Guy taught English to new Canadians who could barely understand a word of what was being said to them. He was a valuable resource. Every day he withdrew three or four kids from each class, and in unique ways taught them to speak English: He took them to supermarkets and had them read the food labels; he showed them places like the Kensington Market and other ethnic communities that radiated different atmospheres.

I didn't really get to know Guy until recently, when we had a chat in the staff room. He had just finished a frustrating interview with the father of one of his students and looked exhausted.

"I finally met the father of one of my kids . . . finally," he began. "For the last two months, Wally has been telling me, 'My daddy's gone away! My daddy's gone away again!' I didn't know if he was a traveling salesman, or what.

"Well, his dad just showed up, and we had a long talk. It turns out he's a mercenary, he hires himself out to fight in wars all over the world. He just came back from a campaign in Arabia, where he said it had been 'particularly gory'—that's all he'd tell me, just that it was a 'private war.' Now he's decided to take an interest in his kid. I told him that Wally missed him when he was away, and he just looked at me and said, 'What can I do? It's my job.'"

Guy and I compared notes and found we had much in common; our teaching philosophies were very similar. He was a bit worried that Fred hadn't come around to see what he was doing—he didn't know whether that meant Fred thought he was doing a good job, or whether he simply wasn't interested. "The only time he's ever come into my room," Guy remarked, "was to get a light for his cigar."

I explained that it was Fred's philosophy not to go into a teacher's room until the end of the semester, unless he was invited.

Guy had been hired on a short-term basis in January, so he was on the teachers' surplus list. Although he had ten years' experience teaching with the Toronto Board, he had been with North York only for a short while, and the Board does not consider work done for other Boards to count when compiling the seniority list.

He received his pink slip and has decided to go into the travel agent business.

Last night I ran into an old acquaintance at a shopping mall, who told me that Zeke had killed himself in a Paris rooming house. Over the years, I had realized just how important his friendship had been to me. Zeke symbolized an era; he had always thought that somehow life's rules didn't apply to him. Now he was permanently exempt from playing the game. I can still see him dancing on a hilltop, shaking his fists at the sky. The least I can do is remember him at his best.

Friday, June 22

As I was walking through the parking lot at lunch I met Duke on his "Bikers for the Lord" motorcycle. His tee shirt read, "A message to all you virgins: Thanks for nothin'!" Straddling the back of the seat was a young girl about twelve, on the back of her windbreaker a fluorescent slogan: "Save a Mouse—Eat a Pussy."

"This is Mary Lynn," Duke announced. "I'm workin' on savin' her soul."

I smiled and shook her hand.

Duke cleared his throat and reached into his pocket: "This note's from my mom. She heard you was leavin' the school. Whatever she says goes for me, too."

Then Duke and his girlfriend put on their helmets and raised their fists in a salute. "You're one of the decent ones!" Duke yelled, revving up the engine. "So long, sir!" he cried, pulling one last dramatic "wheelie" and waving goodbye. It reminded me of a scene from the old Lone Ranger television series when the Lone Ranger reared on his white horse and waved into the camera.

I opened the note.

> When Duke told me you were leaving teaching to go back to school, I felt I had to write you a note. I hope you will always work with children in some way. I would like every child to have at least one teacher like you. You make learning fun, but still learning. Thanks for all you've done for Duke.

It was rare for a parent to say thank you. Not that they weren't often grateful, but many found it difficult to communicate their feelings openly.

I put the note in my wallet and headed off toward the restaurant, the smoke from Duke's bike still lingering in the parking lot.

Monday, June 25

There was only one day of school left before the summer holidays. I earlier had sent home a note with each kid, reminding the parents not to forget to send some cookies or cakes or other treats for our party.

Kim arrived this morning looking depressed. "My mom won't give me nothin' to bring," she said, wiping away tears. "She says she's savin' all our money to move out of this crappy neighborhood."

Liz invited my class to her room to share some of the fun of the final party of the year. She put a disco album on, and started dancing with the kids. "Let's *really* give them something to talk about," she said to me, grinning. She stuck out her hip my way, and for the next few songs we did "the bump." Our hips bounced and we twirled around and around, much to the delight of the kids.

To our surprise, there were no lewd remarks or obscene gestures. Some of the kids had tears in their eyes; others couldn't wait to get out the door.

Tuesday, June 26

On the last day of school, Samantha left a note on my desk.

> Dear Sir. I have something to tell you. I want to tell you that I love you I not only love you because you are my teacher. I love you and I'm respecte. I love you like a father not just because you teacher. But I wich that I had the hart to tell you I love you other than write this letter.
>
> Yours truly
>
> From Samantha

Summer Vacation

Priscilla's mother phoned me during the summer to tell me about the growing number of mothers in the community who were organizing themselves to create some kind of recreational program and get a daycare center going. "We're really pickin' up steam. We've felt hopeless for so long it feels good to be gettin' somewhere. Maybe we can hang in here for a while longer, and thanks for taking such an interest in Priscilla."

Driving down Yonge Street one hot August day, I heard a familiar voice shouting at me from the curb.

"Sir! Sir!" T. J. was standing on the street corner waving his arms. "Hey, sir! Gimme a lift!"

I pulled my van over, and he hopped in. He asked me to take him to the nearest subway station, pulling a package of cigarettes from his shirt pocket and offering me one.

"Export A's the strongest you can get," he grinned. "It's a real man's brand."

I sighed. "No thanks, T. J. I'm smoking a pipe these days."

"Well, if you need some hash, I can get you the best stuff on the street."

I gave him a friendly scowl, and he winked, taking a drag.

"You're such a square, man," he laughed.

When I asked him how his mother was, his face suddenly became serious. "I'm not livin' at home," he said. "I'm in a group home now. There's me, four other guys, and two girls. Me and one other guy fuck one of the girls. The other girl is a hose bag—nobody'd ever fuck her. The counselors there give us spendin' money, and I usually buy cigarettes and skin mags."

"Still the same T. J.," I said. "How're your parents?"

"Still separated," he said. "Last time I was at my mother's my dad called up and told her she was a fuckin' whore, so I went over to my dad's place, and he was so drunk he could hardly stand up. So I beat the shit out of him. I took off my boots and hammered him good. The first shot hit him in the throat with the steel toe—he went right down and didn't get up. I gave him a few more shots in the head and left."

I stopped the van outside the subway.

"Anyway, sir," T. J. concluded, "you don't want to hear all that shit." He squeezed my arm and jumped out of the van. I called out to him, but he disappeared down the subway entrance.

At the end of August, I took a last walk through the Corridor.

Boisterous, ragged kids ran pell-mell through the dark warrens of the tenements. A fat, ruddy-nosed man leaned over a balcony and cried, "Get your butts outta here!" Women wearing black shawls and carrying shopping bags waited anxiously at the bus stop.

I walked past "St. Welfare" and recalled a conversation I once had with one of the Catholic teachers. She quoted a few lines from the Trappist monk and writer Thomas Merton: "We refuse to love our neighbors, and excuse ourselves on the premise that society's laws will take care of everything, or that a revolution will solve all our problems."

I finally reached the school and looked in through a front window. The room was clean, waiting for the new year. I glanced up at the window. Bits of tape were still stuck to the glass, tape that had held the February Valentines. For a moment I thought I saw a student's face pressed against the glass, but it must have been my imagination. . . .

During quiet walks along the beach on the long, summer nights I remembered good times and bad, and silently made my farewell to my kids.

Afterword

> . . . *When You Wish Upon a Star*
> *It Makes a Difference*
> *Who You Are* . . .

In too many instances where the politics of education is played, it's the children who lose out—especially the children of the poor. Economically disadvantaged children are being groomed by society at an early age to fail, doomed to perpetuate a vicious and endless cycle of poverty created by a culture obsessed with success and wealth.

When I first began teaching, I ascribed to certain myths and assumptions about education. I believe many educators and parents today still cling tenaciously to these myths. We have learned to believe the formal goal of our education system, that it is the "great equalizer" of our society, that it will assist disadvantaged students to bridge the chasm of opportunity that divides them from children from more affluent backgrounds. Unfortunately, this type of platitude hides more than it reveals. I believe this notion of equality to be false. In fact, I would reverse the argument by saying that it's the latent function of the educational system to maintain the status quo, including existing social inequalities.

We claim to live in a meritocracy where social salvation is supposedly achieved through scholastic merit: Every student will, more or less, reap the academic rewards of his or her own initiative, regardless of sex, religion, or family background. That all sounds fine on the surface, but in reality it's simply hollow rhetoric. Research has shown that one of the greatest predictors of academic success is socioeconomic status. In other words, although we profess to believe in equal opportunity for rich and poor alike, the fact remains that an individual's social class and race at birth have a greater influence on social class later in life than do any other factors—including intelligence and merit. Put simply, each child appears to get as many chances for success in school as his or her family has dollars and privileged social status.

The race of each generation through our classrooms usually enhances the success of those with the most "favored" environment. I liken this race to one in which the disadvantaged students line up and "get set" at the starting line, while the more affluent students wait for the whistle at the other end of the track a few feet from the finish line.

As someone raised to believe in the virtues of equality, I find this fact of life particularly disturbing. The root cause of this inequality can be traced directly to the disproportional access to wealth in a society where, despite lip service, the poor are often ostracized to states of unworthiness and inferiority. I found this time and again in my teaching experiences. I could have written a "safer" book by emphasizing the more positive aspects of my teaching career. But that would have ignored the real issue.

Democracies like ours exhort equal opportunity but often ignore ways in which our schools operate unconsciously and unknowingly to guarantee that there will be no real equality. Despite intentions to the contrary, schools reproduce and perpetuate the inequalities and injustices of society-at-large. Children from affluent backgrounds generally get ahead. Yet the chances that disadvantaged students will finish high school—let alone attend university—are staggering. There are, of course, exceptions to the rule, and by focusing on the exceptions we are able to take some of the sting from our guilt.

It would be a mistake to think of the reproduction of social inequality in the schools as an educational conspiracy: In my angrier moments, I styled education officials as belligerent despots huddled in smoky back rooms, sporting diamond derrick stickpins in their "old boy" ties; they munched on Davidoff cigars, poured through their Tory blue file folders, and plotted ways to keep poor students out of the universities. Although I don't deny that these officials sometimes exhibit spectacularly cramped forms of imagination—if not, at times, a facile ambivalence toward their vocations (especially when it comes to addressing the needs of disadvantaged students)—I don't believe that they're *consciously* trying to reduce the competition for their sons at Harvard.

My perspective now is not to point an inquisitorial finger at any specific group of persons, but is directed toward the ideologies, structures, and myths that help reproduce our present culture. At the foundation of such a culture is the exploitation of living labor by means of the material conditions of capitalist social relations of production.

While it is probably true that schools cannot *remake* society, they must find better ways of making themselves vital places for all students—places where students can be empowered to gain a sense of control over their destinies rather than feel trapped by their class position.

Though many poor parents continue to struggle with dignity to better their lives and their children's lives, they themselves are victims of society's myths about them: that the poor deserve their lot in life because they're lazy . . . because they don't care if their children succeed . . . because their children carry a scanty pack of intellectual baggage with them when they enter school. These myths are absurd. Yet we continue to perpetuate them and to blame the victims for *society's* collective irresponsibility.

The incidents of violence and brutality in this book are undeniably part of the working-class experience. (I suspect there are subtler, but equally as debilitating, forms of violence in middle-class communities.) But before we judge too quickly the casualties of societal oppression, we would do well to examine the inhumane conditions in which the poor are permitted to become entrapped. We need only to witness the growth of "instant cities" springing up in the suburbs—high-density apartment living with few, if any, social or recreational services—to realize the extent of our "benign" neglect. Family violence cannot be considered solely as individual action outside the context of social forces and social relations of production that position the poor within asymmetrical relations of power as toilers for the ruling class (which is not to say that violence does not occur among the ruling class).

The school system is mostly geared to the interests, skills, and attitudes of the middle-class child. Though I also argue that the system is failing to educate middle-class students, it is the children of poverty who really suffer, being streamed into courses that prepare them for a life of temporary, dead-end, underpaid, undignified, and menial jobs. And it isn't only the minimum-wage employers, greedy developers, and other sharks who benefit from this poverty. We *all*, to some degree, are dependent on poverty for our own security. It is part of the inexorable logic of capital.

A prevalent educational preoccupation of ours is to concentrate on the failure of society to socialize the "deviant" or "underachiever" to be homogeneous, amorphous, passive, docile, compliant—willing to embrace the time-clock world and mind- and body-deadening norms of the assembly line: the ethos of the shop floor; or the boring routines of fast food restaurants—the new factories for youth.

Educators especially must resist the misperception that regards immigrant students and students from low-income backgrounds as "deficient," "pathological," or "undersocialized dopes."

Such a condescending and patronizing attitude can only reinforce a vicious myth that too often becomes a self-fulfilling prophecy in the classroom. We must begin to acknowledge the fact that underachievement in disadvantaged students is not individual or personalized failure as much as a product of economic and social life as we know it.

The present failure of inner-city education is not in the genes or the attitudes of the poor, but in the failure of society to change the economic and social structures that regulate their lives and to produce an alternative social universe to the charnel house of capitalism. Rather than blaming the victims—the students and their parents—for problems in our inner-city schools, it is important that we take into account our tolerance of the existence of grinding poverty, frightened and condescending teachers, self-serving politicians, irrelevant curricula, the spirit-breaking quality of many current administrative and teaching practices, lack of community participation in the educational process, and the reluctance of educational officials to meet the special needs of inner-city students.

The Corridor kids I worked with had enormous potential to learn and enjoy learning. But in order to build a more positive view of the abilities of my students, I had to struggle to unlearn a great many of my bourgeois prejudices. During my teaching career, I began to realize I couldn't talk about culturally deprived students, but rather *culturally depriving schools*. Certainly these kids didn't have easy lives. But the majority of them possessed the intelligence and will to adapt—and learn—despite their often forbidding surroundings.

As soon as I became less outraged by what my students said and did, as soon as I stopped expecting T. J. and Duke and the rest of them to become upright, middle-class, productive, consuming citizens, then I had a chance to understand them. Actually, I had rejected the validity of some of these values myself. Yet, I found myself asking my students to mirror back to me images of the world I had been reluctant to embrace.

I finally accepted the fact that my students needed to be taught on their own terms first, and then taught to critically transcend those terms in the interest of empowering themselves and others. The traditional middle-class pathways to success were not open to them, pathways that they, in turn, were able to resist. In the classroom, they had become, understandably, street-wise cynical about the social candy of academic rewards such as good grades on term papers or tests. I began to be effective with these students when I dignified their own experiences as worthy of inquiry.

What teachers and parents are summoned to do—and this is part of the purpose of this book—is to confront the structures of oppression, and the myths legitimating injustices toward disadvantaged students in the name of equality and democracy. Immediate actions are obvious: Improved social planning, smaller classes, breakfast programs for those who need them, respect by teachers for the values and abilities of the disadvantaged student, striving to eliminate poverty rather than altering the attitudes of the impoverished working class, adequate daycare facilities for working parents, more specialized teachers, more teachers from a wide variety of ethnic backgrounds, more preschool programs, improvements in the welfare system as well as tax reforms that will truly benefit the needy as opposed to *appear* to benefit the needy.

But governments—national, state, or local—rarely have ears for the "cries from the corridor."

The battle to save our children will never be won as long as we sit back comfortably and let history take its course instead of actively taking part in creating history.

In Memoriam—Jim Montgomerie ("Fred") 1930–1985

He was an ethical rebel, an educational outlaw. He was visionary, a seeker, driven by a desire to remake schools. No one involved with the fate of our children fought with such determination against the fettering of the human spirit and imagination than this man.

His name was Montgomerie. Many Canadians prefer to remember him as "the hugging principal."

I shall attempt in a short space to sketch out the measure of Jim's spirit and vision, knowing that no words can do justice to the history of his personal accomplishments.

Jim's death from cancer in April came suddenly and stunned those of us who knew him as tenacious and unstoppable. His vibrant personality, his unmatched and unbounded wit, and his keen and discerning intellect provided a combination so formidable that it earned Jim a national reputation as one of education's finest leaders. Although his humanitarian efforts as vice-president of the Canadian Association for the Mentally Retarded, immediate past president of the Ontario Association for the Mentally Retarded, and fund-faising chairperson of the Cash for Life lottery have been well documented and duly acclaimed, it was Jim's pioneering style as an inner-city school principal that made him a legend in his own time. Jim's philosophy of "loving each and every child" and his self-concept approach to teaching stirred considerable controversy in the days before the Hall-Dennis Report. And, in these days of conservative assaults on social equality and public schooling, Jim's symbol of the rocking chair (which he used to replace the standard executive chair used by most principals) becomes all the more significant.

The road to winning acceptance for his humanistic approach to teaching was often rough, but invariably rewarding.

"I was lucky," Jim once told me, "I landed in a school (Flemington) where the staff was willing to take risks along with me. It was an incredible experience. For many of us, it was the most rewarding time of our lives."

As a teacher who served under Jim at Driftwood School in North York's Jane-Finch Corridor, I remember the way he was able to instill in the staff a respect for all students. They were tumultuous times back in the seventies, but the caring and trust that developed among us as a staff will never be forgotten.

Jim would be sent to a different school and in his remarkable way would turn things around; then he would be sent to another school that was experiencing problems, and he would turn things around again. Though other, less gifted, individuals may wish to take credit for North York's attempts at inner-city reform, it was undeniably Jim's pioneering efforts that laid the groundwork and made it easier for others to do their jobs. Regrettably, nobody could ever quite fill Jim's shoes.

A gifted teacher, Jim was unwilling to disengage love from the teaching of practical skills or abstract ideas. For Jim, teaching was fundamentally a moral craft. Jim's way of doing things became a powerful metaphor for the consummate teaching act. Jim's entire life embodied and gave substance to the meaning of the word *love*. Many of us stood in awe of Jim's extraordinary capacity to love and care for others. Undoubtedly, this had to do with the love and strength Jim gathered from his family.

Had Jim been more compromising in his beliefs, had he been more willing to go against what his conscience told him was in the best interest of students, his career would no doubt have been less turbulent politically. But for Jim the interest and well-being of his staff and students always came before personal gain.

Jim's enigmatic and often unpredictable methods of reaching out to students sometimes threatened more conservative-minded educators. Yet even those who found Jim's values a challenge to their own could not deny the positive impact Jim made on teachers, students, and administrators alike.

Jim understood how, through the mediations of class, capital, and relations of power and privilege, schools served to disempower the children of the dispossessed and disenfranchised. Much of his time was spent in finding ways to encourage fellow administrators and teachers to give up their antiquated pedagogy in the face of a changing society so that school sites could be remade into laboratories of freedom. Jim was very knowledgeable in the realm of theorizing, but his mission could hardly be defined in the abstract; Jim was fundamentally a "hands-on" administrator—a "doer."

Although Jim's methods were humanistic, he rarely hid his disdain for educational leaders who were committed only to the reproduction of the moribund and for a system that, if left unchecked, could easily become burdened by a philistinism and unimaginative pedagogy. Jim understood better than most that schooling was not a value-free enterprise and that could often become antagonistic to the true meaning and purpose of democracy.

For many of us involved with schooling and social change, Jim's philosophy of education was—and remains—a catalyst for much of our work. Had Jim been able to write with the same verve and creative lucidity that he brought to the articulating of his ideas through conversation, he would have become an international figure. And I make bold to say that his name would appear alongside better-known educators.

Since some critics and colleagues questioned the accuracy of my book [*Cries from the Corridor*], I was particularly grateful to Jim when he was quoted in the *Toronto Star* as saying: "Everything in that book is true." He told reporter David Vienneau: "I'll vouch for all the things that happened. . . . It has to be seen as a cry from disadvantaged kids by a person who had the insight to put down what he saw." Naturally the North York Board was not pleased that he defended a book that generally condemned its policies and practices in inner-city schools. Jim knew he would take flak for this and he did.

Several months before his death, Jim visited Brock University in St. Catharines, where a student committee had arranged for him to address the College of Education's student teachers. I was in the audience as a new professor of education and recall vividly the impact he made on the student body. His address was not just a call to humanize the classroom; it was a challenge to fight against racism and discrimination, and was a challenge to meet the needs of those who are less fortunate.

After his speech, it became evident to me that Jim was in considerable physical discomfort. Although he never once mentioned being sick, I could tell by the look in his eyes and his shortness of breath that something was wrong. Others would probably have canceled the engagement. But that wasn't Jim's style. In the following weeks, a number of students made a point of telling me that they felt Jim's talk was beyond a doubt the single most important event of the college year. I could not agree with them more.

During our last conversation together, Jim told me not to forget about his retirement party later in the year. When I told him that I could never imagine him as retired, he proceeded to tell me how he planned to study to become a lawyer so that he could represent the mentally handi-capped. Jim was accepted by Osgoode Hall law school.

Jim died beloved and revered by many. Some will remember him as a maverick administrator who was able to work within the system while attempting to reform it. Others will remember him best as a gifted com-municator and humanist who spent his life trying to educate others to be-come more active in living out their moral and democratic ideals of creating a just society where the needs of the disadvantaged and disaf-fected would be met. Still others will remember Jim as a dedicated hus-band, father, son, and brother.

Jim exemplified, in his own life, the possibilities that exist for us to realize our humanitarian goals. Although Jim did not exemplify the prac-tice of critical pedagogy (to be discussed throughout the remainder of the book), he still was able to weave new meanings into the tapestry of con-temporary schooling without losing sight of the overall pattern of social justice. Jim has bequeathed to us, through his own example, a new model for teaching and leadership. Jim's life provides an incentive for us all.[1]

ENDNOTE

1. Reprinted with minor alterations from the Ontario Public School Men's Teachers Federation, *News*, June 1, 1985, now defunct.

PART THREE

Critical Pedagogy
An Overview

Critical Pedagogy and the Egalitarian Dream

In the following section, you will be introduced to the tradition of critical educational theory, or *critical pedagogy*. My purpose in culling perspectives from a variety of critical theorists extends beyond providing an explanation for the harmful effects schooling has had on minority students and the poor. Rather, I urge you to connect these theoretical perspectives to the journal entries in Part Two, and more importantly, to your own experiences in the schools. I am asking *you* to mediate among the theory presented in the following sections, my journalistic documentation of my experiences as an inner-city teacher, and your own personal history that, if it is not already rich in teaching experiences, is most certainly rich in the experiences of being a student. This book can then provide a dialectical tension among theory, practice, and experience—a tension necessary for critical learning. I want to emphasize that I am distressed by the way I was produced as a public school educator, and that this book was written as a way of helping to unscroll the means whereby I have been able to re-form my pedagogy and politics through an engagement with critical theory and transformative praxis.

I want to make clear from the outset that my own elementary school teaching experiences are not offered as evidence that in some way "proves" the theories that follow. This book is not meant to be read either as an empirical study or as a devout acolyte's conversion journal to the critical tradition. A concern with the validity and verifiability of theory is beyond the scope of this book; those wishing for empirical studies are encouraged to consult my book, *Schooling as a Ritual Performance*,[1] or the numerous other books within the critical educational tradition listed at the end of Part Three. I do hope that my journal accounts add some flesh and blood to what are essentially abstract theoretical formulations. But my decision to include the journal is more than a cry for texture. Rather, I hope to illustrate the contradictions embodied in the teaching process itself and to chart out the tension between the perspectives held by the beginning teacher, who is trying to find a larger purpose in the day-to-day *practice* of teaching, and the social theorist, who presumably has a better *theoretical* grasp of what should be done and who is calling for practitioners to appropriate critical theory into their own work.

Why should you embrace the theories presented throughout these pages if they are not all clearly illustrated by my own teaching experiences? Conservative critics could easily offer my journal accounts as evidence that schools are in need of stricter discipline, more rules, regulations, and enforcement procedures, tougher standards for evaluating students and teachers, and a return to the basics. Liberal critics might argue for more funds and specialized programs. But all this is just the point. The literature on schooling abounds with both conservative and liberal perspectives.

In this book, you are given access to a *different kind* of analysis. Here I am using the term *difference* to refer to *a difference* that makes a difference. The challenge of critical pedagogy does not reside solely in the logical consistency, rhetorical persuasiveness, or the empirical verification of its theories; rather, it resides in the moral choice put before us as teachers and citizens, a choice that American philosopher John Dewey suggested is the distinction between education as a function of society and society as a function of education. We need to examine that choice: Do we want our schools to create a passive, risk-free citizenry, or a politicized citizenry capable of fighting for various forms of public life and informed by a concern for equality and social justice? Do we want to accommodate students to the existing capitalist division of labor by making them merely functional within it or do we want to make students uncomfortable in a society that exploits workers, that demonizes people of color, that abuses women, that privileges the rich, that commits acts of imperialist aggression against other countries, that colonizes the spirit and that wrings the national soul clean of a collective social consciousness? Or do we want to create spaces of freedom in our classrooms and invite students to become agents of transformation and hope? I trust that we do.

ENDNOTE

1. Peter McLaren, *Schooling as a Ritual Performance: Towards a Political Economy of Educational Symbols and Gestures* (London and New York: Routledge and Kegan Paul, 1986).

CHAPTER

4

The Emergence of Critical Pedagogy

In the context of that choice, a radical theory of education has emerged in the last twenty years. Broadly defined as "the new sociology of education" or a "critical theory of education," critical pedagogy examines schools both in their historical context and as part of the existing social and political fabric that characterizes the class-driven dominant society. Critical pedagogy poses a variety of important counterlogics to the positivistic, ahistorical, and depoliticized analysis employed by both liberal and conservative critics of schooling—an analysis all too readily visible in the training programs in our colleges of education. Fundamentally concerned with the centrality of politics and power in our understanding of how schools work, critical theorists have produced work centering on a critique of the political economy of schooling, the state and education, the representation of texts, and the construction of student subjectivity.

Critical educational theory owes a profound debt to its European progenitors. A number of critical educational theorists continue to draw inspiration from the work of the Frankfurt School of critical theory, which had its beginnings before World War II in Germany's Institut für Sozialforschung (Institute for Social Research). The membership of this group, who wrote brilliant and ethically illuminating works of Freudo-Marxist analysis, included such figures as Max Horkheimer, Theodor W. Adorno, Walter Benjamin, Leo Lowenthal, Erich Fromm, and Herbert Marcuse. During the war, a number of Institute members fled to the United States as a result of persecution by Nazis because they were Leftist and Jewish. After the war they reestablished the Institute in Frankfurt. Members of the second generation of critical theorists, such as Jürgen Habermas, have since moved from the Institute to carry on elsewhere the work initiated by the founding members. In the United States, the Frankfurt School of critical theory is currently making new inroads into social research and influencing numerous disciplines such as literary criticism, anthropology, sociology, and educational theory. Critical pedagogy also has distinctly U.S. roots, as well: such as the work of John Dewey and the social reconstructionists, all the way to educators such as Myles Horton of the Highlander School and the teachings of civil-rights activists including Martin Luther King, Jr. and Malcolm X.

Critical pedagogy has begun to provide a radical theory and analysis of schooling, while annexing new advances in social theory and developing new categories of inquiry and new methodologies. Critical pedagogy does not, however, constitute a homogeneous set of ideas. It is more accurate to say that critical theorists are united in their *objectives:* to empower the powerless and transform existing social inequalities and injustices. The movement constitutes only a small minority within the academic community and public school teaching as a whole, but it presents a growing and challenging presence in both arenas.[1]

Foundational Principles

Critical pedagogy resonates with the sensibility of the Hebrew symbol of *tikkun,* which means "to heal, repair, and transform the world, all the rest is commentary." It provides historical, cultural, political, and ethical direction for those in education who still dare to hope. Irrevocably committed to the side of the oppressed, critical pedagogy is as revolutionary as the earlier views of the authors of the Declaration of Independence: Since history is fundamentally open to change, liberation is an authentic goal, and a radically different world can be brought into being.

Politics

A major task of critical pedagogy has been to disclose and challenge the role that schools play in our political and cultural life. Especially within the last decade, critical educational theorists have come to view schooling as a resolutely political and cultural enterprise. Recent advances in the sociology of knowledge, cultural and symbolic anthropology, cultural Marxism, and semiotics have led these theorists to see schools not only as instructional sites, but also as cultural arenas where a heterogeneity of ideological and social forms often collide in an unremitting struggle for dominance. Within this context, critical theorists generally analyze schools in a twofold way: as sorting mechanisms in which select groups of students are favored on the basis of race, class, and gender; and as agencies for self and social empowerment.

Critical educational theorists argue that teachers must understand the role that schooling plays in joining knowledge and power to the value form of labor in capitalist society in order to use that role for the development of critical and active citizens with the courage to struggle for a new society outside the division of labor found within capital's social universe. The traditional view of classroom instruction and learning as a neutral process antiseptically removed from the concepts of power, politics, history, and context can no longer be credibly endorsed. In fact, critical researchers have given primacy to the social, the cultural, the political, and the economic, in order to better understand the workings of contemporary schooling.

Culture

Critical theorists see schooling as a form of *cultural politics;* schooling always represents an introduction to, preparation for, and legitimation of particular forms of social life. It is always implicated in relations of power, social practices, and the favoring of forms of knowledge that support a specific vision of past, present, and future. In general, critical theorists maintain that schools have always functioned in ways that rationalize the knowledge industry into class-divided tiers; that reproduce inequality, racism, sexism, and homophobia; and that fragment democratic social relations through an emphasis on competitiveness and cultural ethnocentrism.

Although critical pedagogy is indebted to a wide variety of European intellectual traditions, it also draws upon a uniquely American tradition extending from the mainstream progressive movement of John Dewey, William H. Kilpatrick, and others, through the more radical efforts of the social reconstructionists of the 1920s such as George Counts and the work of Dwayne Huebner, Theodore Brameld, and James McDonald. In Roger Simon's terms, *pedagogy* must be distinguished from *teaching*.

> "Pedagogy" [refers] to the integration in practice of particular curriculum content and design, classroom strategies and techniques, and evaluation, purpose, and methods. All of these aspects of educational practice come together in the realities of what happens in classrooms. Together they organize a view of how a teacher's work within an institutional context specifies a particular version of what knowledge is of most worth, what it means to know something, and how we might construct representations of ourselves, others, and our physical and social environment. In other words, talk about pedagogy is simultaneously talk about the details of what students and others might do together and the cultural politics such practices support. In this perspective, we cannot talk about teaching practices without talking about politics.[2]

Economics

Unfortunately, in their discussion of "critical thinking" the neoconservatives and liberals have neutralized the term *critical* by repeated and imprecise usage, removing its political and cultural dimensions and laundering its analytic potency to mean "thinking skills." In their terms, teaching is reduced to helping students acquire higher levels of cognitive skills. Little attention is paid to the purpose to which these skills are to be put. The moral vision that grounds such a view encourages students to succeed in the tough competitive world of existing social forms.

By defining academic success almost exclusively in terms of creating compliant, productive, and patriotic workers, the new conservative agenda for a "resurgent America" dodges any concern for nurturing critical and committed citizens. Instead, students are viewed as the prospective vanguard of America's economic revival. Critical educational theorists have responded to the New Right by arguing that the increasing adoption of management-type pedagogies and accountability schemes to meet the logic of market demands has resulted in policy proposals that actively promote the deskilling of teachers. This is most evident in the proliferation of state-mandated curricula claiming to be "teacher-proofed," which effectively reduce the role of the teacher to that of a semiskilled, low-paid clerk. The neoconservative agenda has, in effect, brought the advancement of democracy in our schools to a state of arrest. Neoconservatives reject the view that schools should be sites for social transformation and emancipation, places where students are educated not only to be critical thinkers, but also to view the world as a place where their actions might make a difference.

Critical pedagogy is founded on the conviction that schooling for self and social empowerment is *ethically prior* to a mastery of technical skills, which are primarily tied to the logic of the marketplace (although it should be stressed that skill development certainly plays an important role). Concern over education's moral dimension has provoked critical scholars to undertake a socially critical reconstruction of what it means to "be schooled." They stress that any genuine pedagogical practice demands a commitment to social transformation in solidarity with subordinated and marginalized groups. This necessarily entails a preferential option for the poor and the elimination of those conditions that promote human suffering. Such theorists are critical of the emphasis that liberal democracy places on individualism and autonomy from the needs of others.

According to critical educational theorists, analyses of schooling undertaken by liberal and conservative critics necessarily favor the interests of the ruling class. The liberal perspective especially has been reappropriated by the very logic it purports to criticize. By contrast, the *critical* perspective allows us to scrutinize schooling more insistently in terms of race, class, power, and gender.

Americans traditionally have assumed that schools function as a mechanism for the development of democratic and egalitarian social order. Critical educational theorists argue otherwise; they suggest that schools do *not* provide opportunities in the broad Western humanist tradition for self and social empowerment and in fact often work against those opportunities. Critical pedagogy also challenges the assumption that schools function as major sites of social and economic mobility. Theorists like Paula Allman, Henry Giroux, Donaldo Macedo, Glenn Rikowski, Dave Hill, Mike Cole, and Richard Brosio argue that American schooling has defaulted on its promise of egalitarian reform and does not, in fact, provide opportunities for large numbers of students to become empowered as critical, active citizens. Rather, they argue, the economic returns from schooling are far greater for the capitalist class than for the working class.

In their attempts to explode the popular belief that schools are fundamentally democratic institutions, critical scholars have begun to unravel the ways in which school curricula, knowledge, and policy depend on the corporate marketplace and the fortunes of the economy. Their goal is to unmask the inequality of competing self-interests within the social order that prohibits equal opportunity from being realized. They warn against being deluded as educators into thinking that either conservatives or liberals occupy a truly progressive platform. In their view, no decisions can be made on the basis of transparent and disinterested standards of value, and no educational practices—whether they center on the issue of excellence, evaluation, or accountability—are ever innocent of the social, economic, and institutional contexts in which schooling takes place. Rather, they suggest that schooling must always be analyzed as a cultural and historical process, in which select groups are positioned within asymmetrical relations of power on the basis of specific race, class, and gender antagonisms. In other words, critical scholars refuse the task capitalism assigns them as intellectuals, teachers, and social theorists, to passively service the existing ideological and institutional arrangements of the public schools. These scholars believe that the schools serve the interests of the wealthy and powerful, while simultaneously disconfirming the values and abilities of those students who are most disempowered in our society already: minorities, the poor, and the female. In short, educators within the critical tradition argue that mainstream schooling supports an inherently unjust bias, resulting not only in the transmission and reproduction of the dominant status quo culture, but more fundamentally in the reproduction of the division of labor and the interests of the ruling class.

Central to their attempt to reform public education is a rejection of the emphasis on scientific predictability and measurement that has been tacitly lodged in models of curriculum planning and in other theoretical approaches to educational practice. Critical theorists challenge the often uncontested relationship between school and society, unmasking mainstream pedagogy's claim that it purveys equal opportunity and provides access to egalitarian democracy and critical thinking. Critical scholars reject the claim that schooling constitutes an apolitical and value-neutral process. In fact, to argue that schools are meritocratic institutions is a conceptual tautology: Successful learners are those whom schools reward. If you happen to be successful, it must be because of your individual merit. Missing from this logic is a recognition that students from white, affluent backgrounds are privileged over other groups, not on the basis of merit but because of the advantage that comes with having money and increased social status. Critical pedagogy attempts to provide teachers and researchers with a better means of understanding the role that schools actually play within a race-, class-, and gender-divided society, and in this effort, theorists have generated categories or concepts for questioning student experiences, texts, teacher ideologies, and aspects of school policy that conservative and liberal analyses too often leave unexplored. In effect, critical pedagogy has sharply defined the political dimensions of schooling, arguing that schools operate mainly to reproduce the values and privileges of existing elites. Critical pedagogy commits itself to forms of learning and action undertaken in solidarity with subordinated and marginalized groups. In addition to questioning what is taken for granted about schooling, critical theorists are dedicated to the emancipatory imperatives of *self-empowerment* and *social transformation*.

Critical pedagogists would like to pry theory away from the academics and incorporate it in educational practice. They throw down the gauntlet to those conservative and corporate multiculturalists, who wish schools simply to teach students about America's great cultural heritage.[3] They aim at providing teachers with critical categories, or concepts, that will enable them to analyze schools as places that produce and transmit those social practices that reflect the ideological and material imperatives of the ruling class.

Critical educators argue that we have responsibility not only for how we act individually in society, but also for the system in which we participate. Critical theorists put forward what might be labeled pedagogical surrealism: They attempt to make the strange familiar and the familiar strange. They set out to "relativize" schools as normalizing agencies—i.e., as agencies that essentially legitimate existing social relations and practices, rendering them normal and natural—by dismantling and rearranging the artificial rules and codes that make up classroom reality. Unlike the liberal humanist who begins with the different and renders it comprehensible, the critical education theorist attacks the familiar, perturbing commonplace perspectives.[4] Critical theorists attempt to go beyond the conventional question of *what* schooling means by raising instead the more important question of *how* schooling has come to mean what it has. The result is that schools—often seen as socializing agencies that help society produce intelligent, responsible, committed, and skilled citizens—turn out to be strange and disturbing institutions that not only *teach* subjects but also *produce* unreflective human subjects who, in their day-to-day activities, play out through the ideologies of the dominant culture and in so doing give ballast to the underlying set of socioeconomic relations bound to the rule of capital.

Critical educational theorists argue that Marxism has not been taken seriously in this country as a means of social-historical analysis; Marxist theorists and those who work within traditions of radical social thought indebted to Marxism often are subject to knee-jerk "marxophobia." Though many if not most critical educational theorists work outside the orthodox Marxian tradition and do not consider capitalism an irrevocable evil, they do insist that its pattern of exploitation has produced an economic rationality that infuses current thinking on social and educational issues and continues to contribute to massive social problems such as racism, sexism, and classism. In order to ensure that all individuals have a voice in the surplus value their labor generates, critical educators argue that those responsible for our current brand of capitalism must be held morally accountable. A new class struggle is needed that will help guide and eventually reshape existing social relations of exploitation in the interests of *everyone*, one with the vision and power to counter the dehumanizing effects of modern supply-side capitalism. This can only be achieved with the overthrow of capitalist society itself in favor of a society in which the full development of the individual is the basis for the full development of society.

Critical educators question the very basis of school funding. Why, they ask, are schools funded on the basis of property taxes, which ensures that the children of the wealthy and privileged will inherit better schools in terms of resources, teacher salaries, clean buildings, etc.? Why don't state governments and the federal government assume responsibility for full educational funding? After all, the federal government assumes responsibility for operations such as Desert Storm. Critical educators oppose deregulation and opening school success to the logic of the marketplace, supposedly through the new "choice" schemes and voucher plans. Letting the market "equalize" education through vouchers will only exacerbate the disparity of chances between rich and poor students—inner-city schools will collapse. "Choice" means that the poor are "free" to become poorer while the rich are given the "choice" of becoming richer. Choice means Jim Crow education for the 1990s. Choice schemes need to improve the conditions of low-performing schools or else state funding will shrink due to declining enrollments, and students and teachers will transfer to other schools. In fact, some critical educators (and I include myself among them) challenge the very foundations of the global capitalist social order.

Theories of Interest and Experience

Critical educational theorists such as Henry Giroux argue that curriculum must be understood in terms of a *theory of interest* and a *theory of experience*. By theory of interest, Giroux means that curriculum reflects the interests that surround it: the particular visions of past and present that they represent, the social relations they affirm or discard. By theory of experience, Giroux means that curriculum is an historically constructed narrative that produces and organizes student experiences in the context of social forms, such as language usage, organization of knowledge into high- and low-status categories, and the affirmation of particular kinds of teaching strategies. Curriculum represents not only a configuration of particular interests and experiences, however; it also forms a battleground where different versions of authority, history, the present, and the future struggle to prevail. Critical theorists want to provide for educational theorists in general a public language that not only confirms the voices of teachers and of subordinate groups in the student population, but also links the purpose of schooling to a transformative vision of the future.

Beyond agreeing that schools reproduce inequality and injustice, contemporary critical theorists differ in many points of analysis. Recent work in the critical tradition can generally be divided into two categories: those that believe capitalism can be reformed in the interests of the working-class (most exponents of critical pedagogy) and those Marxist educators who believe that social justice can only be authentically achieved with the abolition of class society and the realization of a socialist alternative, such as Paula Allman, Glenn Rikowski, Dave Hill, Richard Brosio, Ramin Farahmandpur, myself, and others.

Critical pedagogy deals with numerous themes, many of which are situated in distinct fields of research and criticism. Some of these relatively new fields include feminist pedagogy, critical constructivism, and multicultural education. In addition, postmodern social theory has been taken up by some educational critics. Cultural studies is another area that in recent years has also generated a burgeoning interest among some critical educators. Transdisciplinary scholarship is growing among educational theorists and is likely to continue. The work of Lankshear and McLaren has drawn on interdisciplinary critical social theory to advance the analysis of literacy.[5] Patti Lather's work combines postmodernist and feminist theory, but regrettably does little to contest capitalist social relations of exploitation.[6] Critical literacy and media literacy are important new directions that are making serious inroads in school reform efforts, especially in urban areas. Disciplinary boundaries are beginning to blur, and in my estimation this makes for more innovative and important research within the critical tradition. More will be said about these fields throughout the volume.

There are many different strands to critical pedagogy: the libertarian, the radical, and the liberationist, all with points of difference and fusion. In addition to discussing the recent shifts toward a Marxist analysis in my own theoretical work, this book draws primarily on radical perspectives exemplified in the works of such theorists as Paulo Freire and Henry Giroux, who make an important distinction between *schooling* and *education*. The former is primarily a mode of social control; the latter has the potential to transform society, with the learner functioning as an active subject committed to self and social transformation.

ENDNOTES

1. Stanley Aronowitz and Henry A. Giroux, *Education Under Siege: The Conservative Liberal, and Radical Debate Over Schooling* (South Hadley, MA: Bergin and Garvey Publishers, Inc., 1985), 69–114. See for a review and critical analysis of this literature.

2. Roger Simon, "Empowerment as a Pedagogy of Possibility," *Language Arts* 64, 4 (1987, April): 370.

3. William J. Bennett, *What Works: Research about Teaching and Learning.* (Washington, DC: The United States Department of Education, 1986). Also, Henry Giroux and Peter McLaren, "Teacher Education and the Politics of Democratic Life: Beyond the Reagan Agenda in the Era of 'Good Times'," in C. C. Yeakey and G. S. Johnston (Eds.), *Schools as Conduits: Educational Policymaking during the Reagan Years* (New York: Praeger Press, in press).

4. James Clifford, "On Ethnographic Surrealism," *Comparative Studies in Society and History* 23, 4 (1981): 539–564.

5. Colin Lankshear and Peter McLaren (Eds.), *Critical Literacy* (Albany, NY: SUNY Press, 1993).

6. Patti Lather, *Getting Smart: Feminist Research and Pedagogy with/in the Postmodern* (New York and London: Routledge, 1991).

5

Critical Pedagogy
A Look at the Major Concepts

In practice, critical pedagogy is as diverse as its many adherents, yet common themes and constructs run through many of their writings. I have talked about the general characteristics of critical pedagogy in the previous chapters. In the chapters that follow, I will outline in more detail the major categories within this tradition. A category is simply a concept, question, issue, hypothesis, or idea that is central to critical theory. These categories are intended to provide a theoretical framework within which you may reread my journal entries and perhaps better understand the theories generated by critical educational research. The categories are useful for the purposes of clarification and illustration, although some critical theorists will undoubtedly argue that additional concepts should have been included, or that some concepts have not been given the emphasis they deserve.

The Importance of Theory

Before we discuss individual categories, we need to examine how those categories are explored. Critical theorists begin with the premise that *men and women are essentially unfree and inhabit a world rife with contradictions and asymmetries of power and privilege.* The critical educator endorses theories that are, first and foremost, *dialectical;* that is, theories which recognize the problems of society as more than simply isolated events of individuals or deficiencies in the social structure. Rather, these problems are part of the *interactive context* between individual and society. The individual, a social actor, both creates and is created by the social universe of which he/she is a part. Neither the individual nor society is given priority in analysis; the two are inextricably interwoven, so that reference to one must by implication mean reference to the other. Dialectical theory attempts to tease out the histories and relations of accepted meanings and appearances, tracing interactions from the context to the part, from the system inward to the event. In this way, critical theory helps us focus *simultaneously on both sides of a social contradiction.*[1]

Wilfred Carr and Stephen Kemmis describe dialectical thinking as follows:

> Dialectical thinking involves searching out . . . contradictions (like the contradiction of the inadvertent oppression of less able students by a system which aspires to help all

students to attain their "full potential"), but it is not really as wooden or mechanical as the formula of thesis-antithesis-synthesis. On the contrary, it is an open and questioning form of thinking which demands reflection back and forth between elements like *part* and *whole, knowledge* and *action, process* and *product, subject* and *object, being* and *becoming, rhetoric* and *reality,* or *structure* and *function.* In the process, *contradictions* may be discovered (as, for example, in a political *structure* which aspires to give decision-making power to all, but actually *functions* to deprive some access to the information with which they could influence crucial decisions about their lives). As contradictions are revealed, new constructive thinking and new constructive action are required to transcend the contradictory state of affairs. The complementarity of the elements is dynamic: it is a kind of a tension, not a static confrontation between the two poles. In the dialectical approach, the elements are regarded as mutually constitutive, not separate and distinct. Contradiction can thus be distinguished from paradox: to speak of a contradiction is to imply that a new resolution can be achieved, while to speak of a paradox is to suggest that two incompatible ideas remain inertly opposed to one another.[2] [Italics original]

The dialectical nature of critical theory enables the educational researcher to see the school not simply as an arena of indoctrination or socialization or a site of instruction, but also as a cultural terrain that promotes student empowerment and self-transformation. My own research into parochial education, for instance, showed that the school functions *simultaneously* as a means of potentially empowering students around issues of social justice and as a means of sustaining, legitimizing, and reproducing dominant class interests directed at creating obedient, docile, and low-paid future workers.[3]

A dialectical understanding of schooling permits us to see schools as sites of *both* domination and liberation; this runs counter to the view of schooling which claims that schools simply reproduce class relations and passively indoctrinate students into becoming greedy young capitalists. They do reproduce class relationships but also can serve as a site where these class relationships can be contested. This dialectical understanding of schooling also brushes against the grain of mainstream educational theory, which conceives of schools as mainly providing students with the skills and attitudes necessary for becoming patriotic, industrious, and responsible citizens. It argues that schools do create patriotic, responsible citizens and that this is precisely the problem. As recent events have revealed, educated U.S. citizens have difficulty distinguishing among leaders who are bent on imperialist wars to secure "resources" for accumulating capital and those who are truly committed to peace and social justice.

Critical educators argue that any worthwhile theory of schooling *must be partisan.* That is, it must be fundamentally tied to a struggle for a qualitatively better life for all through the construction of a society based on nonexploitative relations and social justice. The critical educator doesn't believe that there are two sides to every question, with both sides needing equal attention. For the critical educator, there are *many* sides to a problem, and often these sides are linked to certain class, race, and gender interests.

Let's turn for a moment to an example of critical theorizing as it is brought to bear on a fundamental teaching practice: writing classroom objectives. In this example, I will draw on Henry Giroux's important distinction between *micro* and *macro* objectives.[4]

The common use of behavioral objectives by teachers reflects a search for certainty and technical control of knowledge and behavior. Teachers often emphasize classroom management procedures, efficiency, and "how-to-do" techniques that ultimately ignore an important question: "Why is this knowledge being taught in the first place?" Giroux recasts classroom objectives into the categories of macro and micro.

Macro objectives are designed to enable students to make connections between the methods, content, and structure of a course and its significance within the larger social reality. This dialectical approach to classroom objectives allows students to acquire a broad frame of reference or worldview; in other words, it helps them acquire a political perspective. Students can then make the hidden curriculum explicit and develop a critical political consciousness.

Micro objectives represent the course content and are characterized by their narrowness of purpose and their content-bound path of inquiry. Giroux tells us that the importance of the relationship between macro and micro objectives arises out of *having students uncover the connections between course objectives and the norms, values, and structural relationships of the wider society.* For instance, the micro objectives of teaching about the Vietnam war might be to learn the dates of specific battles, the details of specific Congressional debates surrounding the war, and the reasons given by the White House for fighting the war. The micro objectives are concerned with the organization, classification, mastery, and manipulation of data. This is what Giroux calls *productive knowledge.* Macro objectives, on the other hand, center on the relationship between means and ends, between specific events and their wider social and political implications. A lesson on the Vietnam war or more recently the invasion of Grenada, the Desert Storm assault on Iraq, or the war in Afghanistan, for instance, might raise the following macro questions: What is the relationship between these invasions as rescue missions in the interests of U.S. citizens and the larger logic of imperialism? During the Vietnam era, what was the relationship between the American economy and the arms industry? Whose interests did the war serve best? Who benefited most from the war? What were the class relationships between those who fought and those who stayed home in the university? Other than replacing the corrupt Taliban regime and destroying terrorist compounds and networks in the war in Afghanistan, did the United States hope to secure vital resources such as oil?

Developing macro objectives fosters a dialectical mode of inquiry; the process constitutes a sociopolitical application of knowledge, what Giroux calls *directive knowledge.* Critical theorists seek a kind of knowledge that will help students recognize the *social function of particular forms of knowledge.* The purpose of dialectical educational theory, then, is to provide students with a model that permits them to examine the underlying political, social, and economic foundations of the larger white supremacist capitalist society.

Critical Pedagogy and the Social Construction of Knowledge

Critical educational theorists view school knowledge as historically and socially rooted and interest bound. Knowledge acquired in school—or anywhere, for that matter—is never neutral or objective but is ordered and structured in particular ways; its emphases and exclusions partake of a silent logic. Knowledge is a *social construction* deeply rooted in a nexus of power relations. When critical theorists claim that knowledge is socially constructed, they mean that it is the product of agreement or consent between individuals who live out particular social relations (e.g., of class, race, and gender) and who live in particular junctures in time. To claim that knowledge is socially constructed usually means that the world we live in is constructed symbolically by the mind through social interaction with others and is heavily dependent on culture, context, custom, and historical specificity. There is no ideal, autonomous, pristine, or aboriginal world to which our social constructions necessarily correspond; there is always a referential field in which symbols are situated. And this particular referential field (e.g., language, culture, place, time) will influence how symbols generate meaning. There is no pure subjective insight. We do not stand *before* the social world; we live *in the midst* of it. As we seek the meaning of events we seek the meaning of the social. We can now raise certain questions with respect to the social construction of knowledge, such as: Why do women and minorities often view social issues differently than white males? Why are teachers more likely to value the opinions of a middle-class white male student, for instance, than those of a middle-class black female?

Critical pedagogy asks how and why knowledge gets constructed the way it does, and how and why some constructions of reality are legitimated and celebrated by the dominant culture while others clearly are not. Critical pedagogy asks how our everyday commonsense understandings—our social constructions or "subjectivities"—get produced and lived out. In other words, what are the *social functions* of knowledge? The crucial factor here is that some forms of knowledge have more power and legitimacy than others. For instance, in many schools in the United States, science and math curricula are favored over the liberal arts. This can be explained by the link between the needs of big business to compete in world markets and the imperatives of the new reform movement to bring "excellence" back to the schools. Certain types of knowledge legitimate certain gender, class, and racial interests. Whose interests does this knowledge serve? Who gets excluded as a result? Who is marginalized?

Let's put this in the form of further questions: What is the relationship between social class and knowledge taught in school? Why do we value scientific knowledge over informal knowledge? Why do we have teachers using "standard English"? Why is the public still unlikely to vote for a woman or an African-American or a Latinola for president? How does school knowledge reinforce stereotypes about women, minorities, and disadvantaged peoples? What accounts for some knowledge having high status (as in the great works of philosophers or scientists) while the practical knowledge of ordinary people or marginalized or subjugated groups is often discredited and devalued? Why do we learn about the "great men" in history and spend less time learning about the contributions of women and minorities and the struggles of people in lower economic classes? Why don't we learn more about the American labor movement? How and why are certain types of knowledge used to reinforce dominant ideologies, which in turn serve to mask unjust power relations among certain groups in society?

Forms of Knowledge

Critical pedagogy follows a distinction regarding forms of knowledge posited by the German social theorist Jürgen Habermas.[5] Let's examine this concept in the context of classroom teaching. Mainstream educators who work primarily within liberal and conservative educational ideologies emphasize *technical knowledge* (similar to Giroux's *productive knowledge*): Knowledge is that which can be measured and quantified. Technical knowledge is based on the natural sciences, uses hypothetico-deductive or empirical analytical methods, and is evaluated by, among other things, intelligence quotients, reading scores, and SAT results, all of which are used by educators to sort, regulate, and control students.

A second type, *practical knowledge*, aims to enlighten individuals so they can shape their daily actions in the world. Practical knowledge is generally acquired through *describing and analyzing social situations historically or developmentally*, and is geared toward helping individuals understand social events that are ongoing and situational. The liberal educational researcher who undertakes field-work in a school in order to evaluate student behavior and interaction acquires practical knowledge, for instance. This type of knowledge is not usually generated numerically or by submitting data to some kind of statistical instrument.

The critical educator, however, will be interested in what Habermas calls *emancipatory knowledge* (similar to Giroux's *directive knowledge*), which attempts to reconcile and transcend the opposition between technical and practical knowledge. Emancipatory knowledge helps us understand how social relationships are distorted and manipulated by relations of power and privilege. It also aims at creating the conditions under which irrationality, domination, and oppression can be overcome and transformed through deliberative, collective action. It has the potential to contribute to social justice, equality, and empowerment. Only in the name of the general rights of society can any knowledge claim to be emancipatory. Only if such knowledge abolishes bourgeois civil society can it lay claim to serve the working class. Knowledge that does not go beyond contemplating the world and observing it objectively without transcending given social conditions merely affirms what already exists. Revolutionary critical knowledge combines theory and practice and contributes to the transformation of existing social relations in the interest of emancipation from the rule of capital.

Class

Class refers to the *economic, social, and political relationships that govern life in a given social order*. Class relationships reflect the constraints and limitations individuals and groups experience in the areas of income level, occupation, place of residence, and other indicators of status and social rank. Relations of class are those associated with surplus labor, who produces it, and who is a recipient of it. Surplus labor is that labor undertaken by workers beyond that which is necessary. Class relations also deal with the social distribution of power and its structural allocation. Today there are greater distinctions within the working classes and it is now possible to talk about the new *underclasses* within the American social structure consisting of black, Hispanic, and Asian class fractions, together with the white aged, the unemployed and underemployed, large sections of women, the handicapped, and other marginalized economic groups. However, it is perhaps more illuminating to identify two main groupings both within the U.S. economy and the global economy: the transnational capitalist class and the working class. Marx argued that the means by which people determine their material world essentially determines how they, themselves, will be produced. Marx also revealed how in capitalist societies, the ruling class extracts a "surplus value" from wage laborers that they employ. On a larger scale, this leads to the exploitation of one class (the working class or class of producers) by the ruling class (the class of appropriators) who extract from the producers a surplus value beyond what is necessary for the productive class to survive. It is precisely this "surplus value" that enables the ruling class to exist. Under capitalist relations of production, capitalists purchase the labor power of the worker in exchange for a wage in order to create value that accrues to capital on behalf of the capitalist. In other words, the capitalist purchases from the worker a commodity that has "use value": the labor power of the worker. Labor power (the capacity to labor) is always of greater value than its own exchange value because it produces profits from capitalists. The wage appears on the surface to be equivalent to the use value (labor power) it purchases from the workers. Surplus labor is unpaid labor and serves as the basis of capitalist profit. The greater the unpaid labor of the workers, the more profit for the capitalists. The law of value states that the value of a commodity can be found in the labor time socially necessary for its production. According to Marx, class struggle leads to the dictatorship of the proletariat. The revolution to come will occur under the banner of class struggle.

To approach the concept of class from a dialectical Marxist conception stipulates a grasp of Marx's philosophy of internal relations. As adumbrated in the work of Paula Allman, Glenn Rikowski, and other Marxist educationalists, the philosophy of internal relations underscores the importance of relational thinking. Relational thinking is distinct from categorical thinking. Whereas the former examines entities in interaction with each other, the latter looks at phenomena in isolation from each other. Relational thinking can refer both to external relations or internal relations. Marx was interested in internal relations. External relations are those that produce a synthesis of various phenomena or entities that can exist outside of or independent of this relation. Internal relations are those in which opposite entities are historically mediated such that they do not obtain independent results. In fact, once the internal relationship ceases to exist, the results of their interaction also cease to exist.

A dialectical concept of class examines the internal relations between labor and capital in terms of their dialectical contradictions. A dialectical contradiction is an internal relation consisting of opposites in interaction that would not be able to exist in the absence of their internal relationship to each other. When this internal relationship is abolished, so are the entities. All dialectical contradictions are internal relations. However, not all internal relations are dialectical contradictions. Dialectical contradictions, or the "unity of opposites," are those phenomena that could not exist, continue to exist, or have come into existence in the absence of their internal relation to one another. The very nature (external and internal) of each of the opposites is shaped within its relation to the other opposite. The antagonistic relation between labor and capital or the relation between production and circulation and exchange, constitute the essence of capitalism. Workers' labor is utilized within the capital-labor relation. Workers then constitute the dialectical opposite of capital and enter into a value creation process. The basis of the rift or split within capitalist labor is the relation internal to labor: labor as a value producer and labor as a labor-power developer. One of the oppositions always benefits from the antagonistic internal relationship between capital and labor. Capital (the positive relation) structurally benefits from its relation to labor (the negative relation). To free itself from its subordinate position, labor must abolish this internal relation through the negation of the negation.

To understand class society in this way offers a more profound analytical lens than operationalizing notions of class that reduce it to skill, occupational status, social inequality, or stratification. This is because what is at stake in understanding class as a dynamic and dialectical social relation is undressing the forces that generate social inequality. This can only be accomplished by analyzing the value form of labor within the entire social universe of capital, including the way that capital has commodified our very subjectivities. This mandates that we grasp the complex dialectics of the generation of the capital-labor relation that produces all value.

The capital-labor contradiction constitutes the key dialectical contradiction that produces the historically specific form of capitalist wealth or the value form of capitalist wealth. It is important to remember that the worker does not sell to the capitalist the living active labor which she performs during the hours of her work, but rather sells her labor-power or her capacity to work for a certain number of hours per week. In exchanging her labor-power for wages, the worker receives in return not wages but what Marx called *wage goods*. That is, the worker gets what is determined in amount by what is required for her maintenance and her reproduction as a worker. Thus, she gets no general or abstract form of power over commodities in exchanging her labor-power for a wage. She only gets power over those particular commodities which are needed for her maintenance and for the reproduction of other workers. It is the capitalist who has the power to consume the labor-power which he has bought. Labor-power purchases for the worker only exchanges with values. Labor, as distinct from labor-power, is the exercise of labor-power and it is labor that produces value. The worker is paid for the availability of her labor-power even before commodities have been produced. A certain proportion of the values produced by the worker by means of her labor are over and above the value that she has received as equivalent to the availability of her labor power. When the capitalist consumes what he has paid for, he therefore receives a higher value than that which is represented in the wages paid out to the worker. The capitalist receives a surplus value created by the worker's labor. The wages the worker receives are therefore not the equivalent of her labor or of her value-producing activity.

It is important to realize that the money equivalent of labor-power is not the same as the money equivalent of labor. The surplus value extracted by the capitalist is actually the unpaid labor of the worker. Labor-power *exchanges with* value whereas labor *produces* value. The capitalist exchanges wages for the worker's labor-power (her power and skills) for a certain number of hours per week. Because the capitalist owns the worker's labor-power, he can sell that labor-power as a commodity for a money-equivalent of the value of that labor-power. The worker's labor-power does not create value but the worker's labor does. Labor-power (the potential to labor), when it is exercised concretely by the worker in the very concrete act of laboring, is what creates capital or value—a relation of exploitation. Concrete labor exercised by the worker constitutes value produced over and above what she gets paid for her labor-power. The worker thus creates the very relation that exploits her. What appears to be an equal exchange—the social transaction of wages for work done as equivalents—is actually a relation of exploitation. It is a relation between persons reduced to a relation between things. The labor/wage relationship as one of equal exchange is only equal from the perspective of its relationship to the market. But what appears to be the exchange of equivalents is actually an exploitative extraction of surplus value by the capitalist. What we are dealing with here, in other words, is the fetishized appearance of a relation of equality. The value produced by labor is "fetishistically" represented equivalently by wages. The dialectical contradiction or internal relation inheres in the fact that the capitalist mode of production of wealth premised on an exchange of equivalents is, in essence, a relation of exploitation through the extraction of surplus value on the part of the capitalist. There is no way to approach the analysis of class within the social universe of capital without addressing the central relation of class struggle that permeates all of social life within capitalist societies.

Culture

The concept of *culture*, varied though it may be, is essential to any understanding of critical pedagogy. I use the term *culture* here to signify *the particular ways in which a social group lives out and makes sense of its "given" circumstances and conditions of life*. In addition to defining culture as *a set of practices, ideologies, and values from which different groups draw to make sense of the world*, we need to recognize how cultural questions help us understand who has power and how it is reproduced and manifested in the social relations that link schooling to the wider social order. The ability of individuals to express their culture is related to the power which certain groups are able to wield in the social order. The expression of values and beliefs by individuals who share certain historical experiences is determined by their collective power in society.[6]

The link between culture and power has been extensively analyzed in critical social theory over the past fifteen years. It is therefore possible to offer three insights from that literature which particularly illuminate the political logic that underlies various cultural/power relations. First, culture is intimately connected with the structure of social relations within class, gender, and age formations that produce forms of oppression and dependency. Second, culture is analyzed not simply as a way of life, but as a form of production through which different groups in either their dominant or subordinate social relations define and realize their aspirations through unequal relations of power. Third, culture is viewed as a field of struggle in which the production, legitimation, and circulation of particular forms of knowledge and experience are central areas of conflict linked to class struggle. What is important here is that each of these insights raises fundamental questions about the ways in which inequalities are maintained and challenged in the spheres of school culture and the wider capitalist society.[7]

Dominant Culture, Subordinate Culture, and Subculture

Three central categories related to the concept of culture—dominant culture, subordinate culture, subculture—have been much discussed in recent critical scholarship. Culture can be readily broken down into "dominant" and "subordinate" parent cultures. *Dominant culture* refers to social practices and representations that *affirm the central values, interests, and concerns of the social class in control of the material and symbolic wealth of society.* Groups who live out social relations in subordination to the dominant culture of the ruling class are part of the *subordinate culture.* Group *subcultures* may be described as subsets of the two parent cultures (dominant and subordinate). Individuals who form subcultures often use distinct symbols and social practices to help foster an identity outside that of the dominant culture. As an example, we need only refer to punk subculture, with its distinct musical tastes, fetishistic costumery, spiked hair, and its attempt to disconfirm the dominant rules of propriety fostered by the mainstream media, schools, religions, and culture industry. For the most part, working-class subcultures exist in a subordinate structural position in society, and many of their members engage in oppositional acts against dominant ruling-class interests and social practices. It is important to remember, however, that people don't inhabit cultures or social classes but *live out class or cultural relations*, some of which may be dominant and some of which may be subordinate.[8]

Subcultures are involved in contesting the cultural "space" or openings in the dominant culture. The dominant culture is never able to secure total control over subordinate cultural groups. Whether we choose to examine British subcultural groups (i.e., working-class youth, teddy boys, skinheads, punks, rude boys, Rastafarians) or American groups (i.e., motorcycle clubs such as Hell's Angels, ethnic street gangs, or middle-class suburban gangs), subcultures are more often *negotiated* than truly *oppositional.* As John Muncie points out, this is because they operate primarily in the arena of leisure that is exceedingly vulnerable to commercial and ideological incorporation.[9] Subcultures do offer a symbolic critique of the social order and are frequently organized around relations of class, gender, style, and race. Despite the often ferocious exploitation of the subcultural resistance of various youth subcultures by bourgeois institutions (school, workplace, justice system, consumer industries), subcultures are usually able to keep alive the struggle over how meanings are produced, defined, and legitimated; consequently, they do represent various degrees of struggle against lived subjugation. Many subcultural movements reflect a crisis within dominant society, rather than a unified mobilization against it. They defang the symbolic potency of the ruling class catechism found in the dominant corporate media apparatuses and the cultural institutions controlled by conglomerate ownership and economies of grand scale. For instance, the hippie movement in the 1960s represented, in part, an exercise of petit bourgeois socialism by middle-class radicals who were nurtured both by idealist principles and by a search for spiritual and lifestyle comfort. This often served to draw critical attention away from the structural inequalities of capitalist society. As Muncie argues, subcultures constitute "a crisis within dominant culture rather than a conspiracy against dominant culture."[10] The youth counterculture of the sixties served as the ideological loam that fertilized my pedagogy in Part Two. I had learned the rudiments of a middle-class radicalism and coffee shop outlawry that was preoccupied with the politics of expressive life and avoided examining in a minded and a critical manner the structural inequalities within the integuments of global capitalist society.

Cultural Forms

Cultural forms are those symbols and social practices that express culture, such as those found in music, dress, food, religion, dance, and education, which have developed from the efforts of groups to shape their lives out of their surrounding material and political environment. Television, video, and films are regarded as cultural forms. Schooling is also a cultural form. Baseball is a cultural form. Cultural forms don't exist apart from sets of structural underpinnings which are related to the means of economic production, the mobilization of desire, the construction of social values, asymmetries of power/knowledge, configurations of ideologies, and relations of class, race, and gender.

Hegemony

The dominant culture is able to exercise domination over subordinate classes or groups through a process known as hegemony.[11] Hegemony refers to the maintenance of domination not by the sheer exercise of force *but primarily through consensual social practices, social forms, and social structures produced in specific sites such as the church, the state, the school, the mass media, the political system, and the family.* By *social practices*, I refer to what people say and do. Of course, social practices may be accomplished through words, gestures, personally appropriated signs and rituals, or a combination of these. *Social forms* refer to the principles that provide and give legitimacy to specific social practices. For example, the state legislature is one social form that gives legitimacy to the social practice of teaching. The term *social structures* can be defined as those constraints that limit individual life and appear to be beyond the individual's control, having their sources in the power relations that govern society. We can, therefore, talk about the "class structure" or the "economic structure" of our society. Social structures are themselves shaped by the social forces and social relations of production and the dialectical contradiction between labor and capital.

Hegemony is a struggle in which the powerful win the consent of those who are oppressed, with the oppressed unknowingly participating in their own oppression. Hegemony was at work in my own practices as an elementary school teacher. Because I did not teach my students to question the prevailing values, attitudes, and social practices of the dominant society in a sustained critical manner, my classroom preserved the hegemony of the dominant culture. Such hegemony was contested when the students began to question my authority by resisting and disrupting my lessons. The dominant class secures hegemony—the consent of the dominated—by supplying the symbols, representations, and practices of social life in such a way that the basis of social authority and the unequal relations of power and privilege remain hidden. By perpetrating the myth of individual achievement and entrepreneurship in the media, the schools, the church, and the family, for instance, dominant culture ensures that subordinated groups who fail at school or who don't make it into the world of the "rich and famous" will view such failure in terms of personal inadequacy or the "luck of the draw." The oppressed blame themselves for school failure—a failure that can certainly be additionally attributed to the structuring effects of the economy and the class-based division of labor.[12]

Hegemony is a cultural encasement of meanings, a prison-house of language and ideas, that is "freely" entered into by both dominators and dominated. As Todd Gitlin puts it,

> Both rulers and ruled derive psychological and material rewards in the course of confirming and reconfirming their inequality. The hegemonic sense of the world seeps into popular "common sense" and gets reproduced there; it may even appear to be generated *by* that common sense.[13]

Hegemony refers to the moral and intellectual leadership of a dominant class over a subordinate class achieved not through coercion (i.e., threat of imprisonment or torture) or the willful construction of rules and regulations (as in a dictatorship or fascist regime), but rather through the general winning of consent of the subordinate class to the authority of the dominant class. The dominant class need not impose force for the manufacture of hegemony since the subordinate class actively subscribes to many of the values and objectives of the dominant class without being aware of the source of those values or the interests which inform them.

Hegemony is not a process of active domination as much as an ethical, political, and economic active structuring of the culture and experiences of the subordinate class by the dominant class. The dominant culture is able to "frame" the ways in which subordinate groups live and respond to their own cultural system and lived experiences; in other words, the dominant culture is able to manufacture dreams and desires for both dominant and subordinate groups by supplying "terms of reference" (i.e., images, visions, stories, ideals) against which all individuals are expected to live their lives. The dominant culture tries to "fix" the meaning of signs, symbols, and representations to provide a "common" worldview, disguising relations of power and privilege through the organs of mass media and state apparatus such as schools, government institutions, and state bureaucracies. Individuals are provided with "subject positions," which condition them to react to ideas and opinions in prescribed ways. For instance, most individuals in the United States, when addressed as "Americans," are generally positioned as subjects by the dominant discourse. To be an "American" carries a certain set of ideological baggage. Americans generally think of themselves as lovers of freedom, defenders of individual rights, guardians of world peace, etc.; rarely do Americans see themselves as contradictory social agents. They rarely view their country as lagging behind other industrial economies in the world in providing security for its citizens in such areas as health care, family allowance, and housing subsidy programs. As citizens of the wealthiest country in the world, Americans generally do not question why their government cannot afford to be more generous to its citizens. Most Americans would be aghast at hearing a description of their country as a "terrorist regime" exercising covert acts of war against Middle Eastern countries such as Iraq. The prevailing image of America that the schools, the entertainment industry, and government agencies have promulgated is a benevolent one in which the interests of the dominant classes supposedly represent the interests of all groups. It is an image in which the values and beliefs of the dominant class appear so correct that to reject them would be unnatural, a violation of common sense.

Within the hegemonic process, established meanings are often laundered of contradiction, contestation, and ambiguity. Resistance does occur, however, most often in the domain of popular culture. In this case, popular culture becomes an arena of negotiation in which dominant, subordinate, and oppositional groups affirm and struggle over cultural representations and meanings. The dominant culture is rarely successful on all counts. People *do* resist. Alternative groups do manage to find different values and meanings to regulate their lives. Oppositional groups do attempt to challenge the prevailing culture's mode of structuring and codifying representations and meanings. Prevailing social practices are, in fact, resisted. Schools and other social and cultural sites are rarely in the thrall of the hegemonic process since there we will also find struggle and confrontation. This is why schools can be characterized as terrains of transactions, exchange, and struggle between subordinate groups and the dominant ideology. There is a relative autonomy within school sites that allows for forms of resistance to emerge and to break the cohesiveness of hegemony. Teachers battle over what books to use, over what disciplinary practices to use, and over the aims and objectives of particular courses and programs.

One current example of the battle for hegemony can be seen in the challenge by Christian fundamentalists to public schooling. Fundamentalist critics have instigated a debate over dominant pedagogical practices that ranges all the way from textbooks to how, in science classes, teachers may account for the origins of humankind. The important point to remember, however, is that hegemony is always in operation; certain ideas, values, and social practices generally prevail over others.

Not all prevailing values are oppressive. Critical educators, too, would like to secure hegemony for their own ideas. The challenge for teachers is to recognize and attempt to transform those undemocratic and oppressive features of hegemonic control that often structure everyday classroom existence in ways not readily apparent. These oppressive features are rarely challenged since the dominant ideology is so all inclusive that individuals are taught to view it as natural, commonsensical, and inviolable. For instance, subordinate groups who subscribe to an ideology that could be described as right wing are often the very groups hurt most by the twelve years of Republican government they elected. Yet the Republican party has been able to market itself as no-nonsense, get-tough, anti-Communist, and hyper-patriotic—features that have always appealed to subordinate groups whose cultural practices may include watching Fox-TV news, following the televangelist programs and crusades, or cheering the pugilistic exploits of the Terminator. Those who seek to chart out the ways in which the wealthy supporters of the capitalist class and transnational capitalist elite are favored over subordinate working-class groups are dismissed as wimpish liberals. Who needs to use force when ideational hegemony works this well? As Gore Vidal has observed about the United States: "The genius of our system is that ordinary people go out and vote against their interests. The way our ruling class keeps out of sight is one of the greatest stunts in the political history of any country."[14]

Ideology

Hegemony could not do its work without the support of ideology. Ideology permeates all of social life and does not simply refer to the political ideologies of communism, socialism, anarchism, rationalism, or existentialism. Ideology refers to *the production and representation of ideas, values, and beliefs and the manner in which they are expressed and lived out by both individuals and groups.*[15] Simply put, ideology refers to the production of sense and meaning. It can be described as a way of viewing the world, a complex of ideas, various types of social practices, rituals, and representations *that we tend to accept as natural and as common sense.* It is the result of the intersection of meaning and power in the social world. Customs, rituals, beliefs, and values often produce within individuals distorted conceptions of their place in the sociocultural order and thereby serve to reconcile them to that place and to disguise the inequitable relations of power and privilege; this is sometimes referred to as "ideological hegemony."

Stuart Hall and James Donald define ideology as "the frameworks of thought which are used in society to explain, figure out, make sense of or give meaning to the social and political world. . . . Without these frameworks, we could not make sense of the world at all. But with them, our perceptions are inevitably structured in a particular direction by the very concepts we are using."[16] Ideology includes both positive and negative functions at any given moment: The *positive function* of ideology is to "provide the concepts, categories, images, and ideas by means of which people make sense of their social and political world, form projects, come to a certain consciousness of their place in the world, and act in it"; the *negative function* of ideology "refers to the fact that all such perspectives are inevitably selective. Thus a perspective positively organizes the 'facts of the case' in *this* and makes sense because it inevitably excludes *that* way of putting things."[17]

In order to fully understand the negative function of ideology, the concept must be linked to a theory of domination. *Domination* occurs when relations of power established at the institutional level are systematically asymmetrical; that is, when they are unequal, therefore privileging some groups over others. According to John Thompson, ideology as a negative function works through four different modes: legitimation, dissimulation, fragmentation, and reification. *Legitimation* occurs when a system of domination is sustained by being represented as legitimate or as eminently just and worthy of respect. For instance, by legitimizing the school system as just and meritocratic, as giving everyone the same opportunity for success, the dominant culture hides the truth of the hidden curriculum—the fact that those whom schooling helps most are those who come from the most affluent families. *Dissimulation* results when relations of domination are concealed, denied, or obscured in various ways. For instance, the practice of institutionalized tracking in schools purports to help better meet the needs of groups of students with varying academic ability. However, describing tracking in this way helps to cloak its socially reproductive function: that of sorting students according to their social class location. *Fragmentation* occurs when relations of domination are sustained by the production of meanings in a way which fragments groups so that they are placed in opposition to one another. For instance, when conservative educational critics explain the declining standards in American education as a result of trying to accommodate low-income minority students, this sometimes results in a backlash against immigrant students by other subordinate groups. This "divide and rule" tactic prevents oppressed groups from working together to secure collectively their rights. *Reification* occurs when transitory historical states of affairs are presented as permanent, natural, and commonsensical—as if they exist outside of time.[18] This has occurred to a certain extent with the current call for a national curriculum based on acquiring information about the "great books" so as to have a greater access to the dominant culture. These works are revered as high-status knowledge since purportedly the force of history has heralded them as such and placed them on book lists in respected cultural institutions such as universities. Here literacy becomes a weapon that can be used against those groups who are "culturally illiterate," whose social class, race, or gender renders their own experiences and stories as too unimportant to be worthy of investigation. That is, as a pedagogical tool, a stress on the great books often deflects attention away from the personal experiences of students and the political nature of everyday life. Teaching the great books is also a way of inculcating certain values and sets of behaviors in social groups, thereby solidifying the existing social hierarchy. The most difficult task in analyzing these negative functions of ideology is to unmask those ideological properties which insinuate themselves within reality as their fundamental components. Ideological functions which barricade themselves within the realm of common sense often manage to disguise the grounds of their operations. What is crucially important here is that domination not be left as a free-floating concept linked to the diffuse nature of power. Domination needs to be linked to the process of capitalist exploitation and the extraction of surplus-value and the reproduction of capitalist social relations of production.

At this point it should be clear that ideology represents a vocabulary of standardization and a grammar of design sanctioned and sustained by particular social practices. All ideas and systems of thought organize a rendition of reality according to their own metaphors, narratives, and rhetoric. There is no "deep structure," totalizing logic, or grand theory pristine in form and innocent in effects which is altogether uncontaminated by the production of value through the dialectical contradiction between capital and labor, by the mediative effects of ideas, or by the way culture is shaped by social relations of production—in short, by *ideology*. There is no privileged sanctuary separate from culture and politics where we can be free to distinguish truth from opinion, fact from value, or image from interpretation. There is no "objective" environment that is not stamped with social presence or troubled by the insinuation of the forces of production.

If we all can agree that as individuals, we inherit a preexisting sign community, and acknowledge that all ideas, values, and meanings have social roots and perform social functions, then understanding ideology becomes a matter of investigating *which* concepts, values, and meanings *obscure* our understanding of the social world and our place within the networks of power/knowledge relations, and which concepts, values, and meanings *clarify* such an understanding. In other words, why do certain ideological formations cause us to misrecognize our complicity in establishing or maintaining the dialectical contradiction between capital and labor that constitutively privileges capital over labor, and provides ballast to the value form of labor.

The *dominant ideology* refers to patterns of beliefs and values shared by the majority of individuals who have been persuaded not to remove the mystical veil draped over everyday life processes within capitalism. The majority of Americans—rich and poor alike—share the belief that capitalism is a better system than democratic socialism, for instance, or that men are generally more capable of holding positions of authority than women, or that women should be more passive and housebound. Here, we must recognize that the economic system requires the ideology of consumer capitalism to naturalize it, rendering it commonsensical. The ideology of patriarchy also is necessary to keep the nature of the economy safe and secured within the prevailing hegemony. We have been "fed" these dominant ideologies for decades through the mass media, the schools, and family socialization.

Oppositional ideologies do exist, however, which attempt to challenge the dominant ideologies and shatter existing stereotypes. On some occasions, the dominant culture is able to manipulate alternative and oppositional ideologies in such a way that hegemony can be more effectively secured. For instance, "The Cosby Show" on commercial television carries a message that a social avenue now exists in America for blacks to be successful doctors and lawyers. This positive view of blacks, however, masks the fact that most blacks in the United States exist in a subordinate position to the dominant white culture with respect to power and privilege. The dominant culture secures hegemony by transmitting and legitimating ideologies like that in "The Cosby Show," which reflect and shape popular resistance to stereotypes, but which in reality do little to challenge the real basis of power of the ruling dominant groups.

The dominant ideology often encourages oppositional ideologies and tolerates those that challenge their own rationale, since by absorbing these contradictory values, they are more often than not able to domesticate the conflicting and contradictory values. This is because the hegemonic hold of the social system is so strong, it can generally withstand dissension and actually come to neutralize it by permitting token opposition. During my teaching days in the suburban ghetto, school dances in the gym often celebrated the values, meanings, and pleasure of life on the street—some of which could be considered oppositional—but were tolerated by the administration because they helped defuse tension in the school. They afforded the students some symbolic space for a limited amount of time; yet they redressed nothing concrete in terms of the lived subordination of the students and their families on a day-to-day basis.

The main question for teachers attempting to become aware of the ideologies that inform their own teaching is: How have certain pedagogical practices become so habitual or natural in school settings that teachers accept them as normal, unproblematic, and expected? How often, for instance, do teachers question school practices such as tracking, ability grouping, competitive grading, teacher-centered pedagogical approaches, and the use of rewards and punishments as control devices? The point here is to understand that these practices are not carved in stone, but are, in reality, socially constructed within material conditions that function to serve capital's drive to augment value and to reproduce abstract labor and the unjust distribution of use-values. How, then, is the distilled wisdom of traditional educational theorizing ideologically structured? What constitutes the origins and legitimacy of the pedagogical practices within this tradition? To what extent do such pedagogical practices serve to empower the student, and to what extent do they work as forms of social control that support, stabilize, and legitimate the role of the teacher as a moral gatekeeper of the state? What are the functions and effects of the systematic imposition of ideological perspectives on classroom teaching practices?

In my classroom journal, what characterized the ideological basis of my own teaching practices? How did "being schooled" both enable and contain the subjectivities of the students? I am using the word *subjectivity* here to mean forms of knowledge that are both conscious and unconscious and which express our identity as human agents. Subjectivity relates to everyday knowledge in its socially constructed and historically produced forms. Following this, we can ask: How do the dominant ideological practices of teachers help to structure the subjectivities of students? What are the possible consequences of this, for good and for ill? Can education be more than the social production of labor-power in ways that reproduce the capitalist form of class society? Is education an aerosol term that hides class exploitation in the mist of its ideological rhetoric?

Prejudice

Prejudice is the negative prejudgment of individuals and groups on the basis of unrecognized, unsound, and inadequate evidence. Because these negative attitudes occur so frequently, they take on a commonsense or ideological character that is often used to justify acts of discrimination.

Critical Pedagogy and the Power/Knowledge Relation

Critical pedagogy is fundamentally concerned with understanding the relationship between power and knowledge. The dominant curriculum separates knowledge from the issue of power and treats it in an unabashedly technical manner; knowledge is seen in overwhelmingly instrumental terms as something to be mastered. That knowledge is always an ideological construction linked to particular interests and social relations generally receives little consideration in education programs.

The work of the French philosopher Michel Foucault is crucial in understanding the socially constructed nature of truth and its inscription in knowledge/power relations. Foucault's concept of "power/knowledge" extends the notion of power beyond its conventional use by philosophers and social theorists who, like American John Dewey, have understood power as "the sum of conditions available for bringing the desirable end into existence."[19] For Foucault, power comes from everywhere, from above and from below; it is "always already there" and is inextricably implicated in the micro-relations of domination and resistance. Foucault's work on power is limited in that he does not link power sufficiently to the production of value within global capitalist social relations.

Discourse

Power relations are inscribed in what Foucault refers to as *discourse* or a family of concepts. Discourses are made up of discursive practices that Foucault describes as

> a body of anonymous, historical rules, always determined in the time and space that have defined a given period, and for a given social, economic, geographical, or linguistic area, the conditions of operation of the enunciative function.[20]

Discursive practices, then, *refer to the rules by which discourses are formed, rules that govern what can be said and what must remain unsaid, and who can speak with authority and who must listen.* Social and political institutions, such as schools and penal institutions, are governed by discursive practices.

> Discursive practices are not purely and simply ways of producing discourse. They are embodied in technical processes, in institutions, in patterns for general behavior, in forms of transmission and diffusion, and pedagogical forms which, at once, impose and maintain them.[21]

For education, discourse can be defined as a "regulated system of statements" that establish differences between fields and theories of teacher education; it is "not simply words but is embodied in the practice of institutions, patterns of behavior, and in forms of pedagogy."[22]

From this perspective, we can consider *dominant* discourses (those produced by the dominant culture) as "regimes of truth," as general economies of power/knowledge, or as multiple forms of constraint. In a classroom setting, dominant educational discourses determine what books we may use, what classroom approaches we should employ (mastery learning, Socratic method, etc.), and what values and beliefs we should transmit to our students.

For instance, neoconservative discourses on language in the classroom would view working-class speech as undersocialized or deprived. Liberal discourse would view such speech as merely different. Similarly, to be culturally literate within a conservative discourse is to acquire basic information on American culture (dates of battles, passages of the Constitution, etc.). Conservative discourse focuses mostly on the works of "great men." A liberal discourse on cultural literacy includes knowledge generated from the perspective of women and minorities. A *critical* discourse focuses on the interests and assumptions that inform the generation of knowledge itself. A critical discourse is also self-critical and deconstructs dominant discourses the moment they are ready to achieve hegemony. A critical discourse can, for instance, explain how high-status knowledge (the great works of the Western world) can be used to teach concepts that reinforce the status quo. Discourses and discursive practices influence how we live our lives as conscious thinking subjects. They shape our subjectivities (our ways of understanding in relation to the world) because it is only in language and through discourse that social reality can be given meaning. Not all discourses are given the same weight, as some will account for and justify the appropriateness of the status quo and others will provide a context for resisting social and institutional practices.[23]

This follows our earlier discussion that knowledge (truth) is socially constructed, culturally mediated, and historically situated. Cleo Cherryholmes asserts that dominant discourses determine what counts as true, important, and relevant. Discourses are what gets spoken and are generated and governed by rules and power.[24] Truth cannot be spoken in the absence of power relations, and each relation necessarily speaks its own truth. Foucault removes truth from the realm of the absolute; truth is understood only as changes in the determination of what can count as true.

> Truth is a thing of this world: it is produced only by virtue of multiple forms of constraint. And it induces regular effects of power. Each society has its regime of truth, its "general politics" of truth: that is, the types of discourse which it accepts and makes function as true; the mechanisms and instances which enable one to distinguish true and false statements, the means by which each is sanctioned; the techniques and procedures accorded value in the acquisition of truth; the status of those who are charged with saying what counts as true.[25]

In Foucault's view, truth (educational truth, scientific truth, religious truth, legal truth, or whatever) must not be understood as a set of "discovered laws" that exist outside power/knowledge relations and which somehow correspond with the "real." We cannot "know" truth except through its "effects." Truth is not *relative* (in the sense of "truths" proclaimed by various individuals and societies are all equal in their effects) but is *relational* (statements considered "true" are dependent upon history, cultural context, and relations of power operative in a given society, discipline, institution, etc.). The crucial question here is that if truth is *relational* and not *absolute*, what criteria can we use to guide our actions in the world? Critical educators argue that *praxis* (informed actions) must be guided by *phronesis* (the disposition to act truly and rightly). This means, in critical terms, that actions and knowledge must be directed at eliminating pain, oppression, and inequality, and at promoting justice and freedom.

Lawrence Grossberg speaks to the critical perspective on truth and theory when he argues:

> The truth of a theory can only be defined by its ability to intervene into, to give us a different and perhaps better ability to come to grips with, the relations that constitute its context. If neither history nor texts speak its own truth, truth has to be won; and it is, consequently, inseparable from relations of power.[26]

An understanding of the power/knowledge relationship raises important issues regarding what kinds of theories educators should work with and what knowledge they can provide in order to empower students. *Empowerment* means not only helping students to understand and engage the world around them, but also enabling them to exercise the kind of courage needed to change the social order where necessary. Teachers need to recognize that *power relations correspond to forms of school knowledge that distort understanding and produce what is commonly accepted as "truth."* Critical educators argue that knowledge should be analyzed on the basis of whether it is oppressive and exploitative, and not on the basis of whether it is "true." For example, what kind of knowledge do we construct about women and minority groups in school texts? Do the texts we use in class promote stereotypical views that reinforce racist, sexist, and patriarchal attitudes? How do we treat the knowledge that working-class students bring to class discussions and schoolwork? Do we unwittingly devalue such knowledge and thereby disconfirm the voices of these students?

Knowledge should be examined not only for the ways in which it might misrepresent or mediate social reality, but also for the ways in which it actually reflects the daily struggle of people's lives with a capitalist society riven by class antagonism. We must understand that knowledge not only distorts reality, but also provides grounds for understanding the actual conditions that inform everyday life. Teachers, then, should examine knowledge both for the way it misrepresents or marginalizes particular views of the world and for the way it provides a deeper understanding of how the student's world is actually constructed within existing capitalist relations of production. Knowledge acquired in classrooms should help students participate in vital issues that affect their experience on a daily level rather than simply enshrine the values of business pragmatism and the rule of capital. School knowledge should have a more emancipatory goal than churning out workers (human capital) and helping schools become the citadel of corporate ideology.[27] School knowledge should help create the conditions productive for student self-determination in the larger society that can only be achieved when class society is abolished and a community of freely associated procedures is created.

Critical Pedagogy and the Curriculum

From the perspective of critical educational theorists, the curriculum represents much more than a program of study, a classroom text, or a course syllabus. Rather, it represents the *introduction to a particular form of life; it serves in part to prepare students for dominant or subordinate positions in the existing capitalist society.*[28] The curriculum favors certain forms of knowledge over others and affirms the dreams, desires, and values of select groups of students over other groups, often discriminatorily on the basis of race, class, and gender. In general, critical educational theorists are concerned with how descriptions, discussions, and representations in textbooks, curriculum materials, course content, and social relations embodied in classroom practices benefit dominant groups and exclude subordinate ones. In this regard, they often refer to the *hidden curriculum.*

The Hidden Curriculum

The *hidden curriculum* refers to *the unintended outcomes of the schooling process.* Critical educators recognize that schools shape students both through standardized learning situations, and through other agendas, including rules of conduct, classroom organization, and the informal pedagogical procedures used by teachers with specific groups of students.[29] The hidden curriculum also includes teaching and learning styles that are emphasized in the classroom, the messages that get transmitted to the student by the total physical and instructional environment, governance structures, teacher expectations, and grading procedures.

The hidden curriculum deals with the tacit ways in which knowledge and behavior get constructed, outside the usual course materials and formally scheduled lessons. It is a part of the bureaucratic and managerial "press" of the school—the combined forces by which students are induced to comply with dominant ideologies and social practices related to authority, behavior, and morality. Does the principal expel school offenders or just verbally upbraid them? Is the ethos of the office inviting or hostile? Do the administration and teachers show respect for each other and for the students on a regular basis? Answers to these questions help define the hidden curriculum, which refers, then, to the *non-subject-related* sets of behaviors produced in students.

Often, the hidden curriculum displaces the professed educational ideals and goals of the classroom teacher or school. We know, for example, that teachers unconsciously give more intellectual attention, praise, and academic help to boys than to girls. A study reported in *Psychology Today* suggests that stereotypes of garrulous and gossipy women are so strong that when groups of administrators and teachers are shown films of classroom discussion and asked who is talking more, the teachers overwhelmingly choose the girls. In reality, however, the boys in the film outtalk the girls at a ratio of three to one. The same study also suggests that teachers behave differently depending on whether boys or girls respond during classroom discussions. When boys call out comments without raising their hands, for instance, teachers generally accept their answers; girls, however, are reprimanded for the same behavior. The hidden message is "Boys should be academically aggressive while girls should remain composed and passive." In addition, teachers are twice as likely to give male students detailed instructions on how to do things for themselves; with female students, however, teachers are more likely to do the task for them instead. Not surprisingly, the boys are being taught independence and the girls dependency.[30]

Classroom sexism as a function of the hidden curriculum results in the unwitting and unintended granting of power and privilege to men over women and accounts for many of the following outcomes:

- Although girls start school ahead of boys in reading and basic computation, by the time they graduate from high school, boys have higher SAT scores in both areas.
- By high school, some girls are less committed to careers, although their grades and achievement-test scores may be as good as boys. Many girls' interests turn to marriage or stereotypically female jobs. Some women may feel that men disapprove of women using their intelligence.
- Girls are less likely to take math and science courses and to participate in special or gifted programs in these subjects, even if they have a talent for them. They are also more likely to believe that they are incapable of pursuing math and science in college and to avoid the subjects.
- Girls are more likely to attribute failure to internal factors, such as ability, rather than to external factors, such as luck.

The sexist communication game is played at work, as well as at school. As reported in numerous studies, it goes like this:

- Men speak more often and frequently interrupt women.
- Listeners recall more from male speakers than from female speakers, even when both use a similar speaking style and cover identical content.
- Women participate less actively in conversation. They do more smiling and gazing; they're more often the passive bystanders in professional and social conversations among peers.
- Women often transform declarative statements into tentative comments. This is accomplished by using qualifiers ("kind of" or "I guess") and by adding tag questions ("This is a good movie, isn't it?"). These tentative patterns weaken impact and signal a lack of power and influence.[31]

Of course, most teachers try hard not to be sexist. The hidden curriculum continues to operate, however, despite what the overt curriculum prescribes. The hidden curriculum can be effectively compared to what Australian educator Doug White calls the *multinational curriculum*. For White,

> The multinational curriculum is the curriculum of disembodied universals, of the mind as an information-processing machine, of concepts and skills without moral and social judgment but with enormous manipulative power. That curriculum proposed the elevation of abstract skills over particular content, of universal cognitive principles over the actual conditions of life.[32]

White reminds us that no curriculum, policy, or program is ideologically or politically innocent, and that the concept of the curriculum is inextricably related to issues of social class, culture, gender, and power. This is, of course, not the way curriculum is traditionally understood and discussed in teacher education. The hidden curriculum, then, refers to learning outcomes not openly acknowledged to learners, because to do so would undermine the social universe in which capitalist schooling thrives in its reproduction of labor-power for the transnational capitalist class. But we must remember that not all values, attitudes, or patterns of behavior that are by-products of the hidden curriculum in educational settings are necessarily bad. The point is to identify the structural and political assumptions upon which the hidden curriculum rests and to attempt to change the institutional arrangements of the classroom so as to offset the most undemocratic and oppressive outcomes and therefore begin to de-capitalize our individual and collective social existences and the value form of labor that supports them and gives them their potency.

Curriculum as a Form of Cultural Politics

Critical educational theorists view curriculum as a form of *cultural politics*, that is, as a part of the sociocultural dimension of the schooling process. The term cultural politics permits the educational theorist to highlight the political consequences of interaction between teachers and students who come from dominant and subordinate cultures. To view the curriculum as a form of cultural politics *assumes that the social, cultural political and economic dimensions are the primary categories for understanding contemporary schooling.*[33]

School life is understood not as a unitary, monolithic, and ironclad system of rules and regulations, but as a cultural terrain characterized by varying degrees of accommodation, contestation, and resistance. Furthermore, school life is understood as a plurality of conflicting languages and struggles, a place where classroom and street-corner cultures collide and where teachers, students, and school administrators often differ as to how school experiences and practices are to be defined and understood.

This curriculum perspective creates conditions for the student's self-empowerment as an active political and moral subject. I am using the term *empowerment* to refer to the process through which students learn to critically appropriate knowledge existing outside their immediate experience in order to broaden their understanding of themselves, the world, and the possibilities for transforming the taken-for-granted assumptions about the way we live. Stanley Aronowitz has described one aspect of empowerment as "the process of appreciating and loving oneself";[34] empowerment is gained from knowledge and social relations that dignify one's own history, language, and cultural traditions. But empowerment means more than self-confirmation. It also refers to the process by which students learn to question and selectively appropriate those aspects of the dominant culture that will provide them with the basis for defining and transforming, rather than merely serving, the wider social order.

Basing a curriculum on cultural politics consists of linking critical social theory to a set of stipulated practices through which teachers can dismantle and critically examine dominant educational and cultural traditions in the context of wider social relations of production within the larger capitalist social order. Many of these traditions have fallen prey to both a technocratic and *instrumental rationality* (a way of looking at the world in which "ends" are subordinated to questions of "means" and in which "facts" are separated from questions of "value") that either limits or ignores democratic ideals and principles. Critical theorists want particularly to develop a language of critique and demystification that can be used to analyze those latent interests and ideologies that work to socialize students in a manner compatible with the dominant culture. Of equal concern, however, is the creation of alternative teaching practices capable of empowering students both inside and outside of schools.

Social Reproduction: A Critical Perspective

Over the decades, critical educational theorists have tried to fathom how schools are implicated in the process of *social reproduction*. In other words, they have attempted to explore how schools *perpetuate or reproduce the social relationships and attitudes needed to sustain the existing dominant economic and class relations of the larger society.*[35] Social reproduction refers to the intergenerational reproduction of social class (i.e., working-class students become working-class adults; middle-class students become middle-class adults). Schools reproduce the structures of social life through the colonization (socialization) of student subjectivities and by establishing social practices characteristic of the wider capitalist society.

Critical educators ask: How do schools help transmit the status and class positions of the wider society? The answers, of course, vary enormously. Some of the major mechanisms of social reproduction include the allocation of students into private versus public schools, the socioeconomic composition of school communities, and the placement of students into curriculum tracks within schools.[36] A group of social reproduction theorists, known as *correspondence theorists* have attempted to show how schools reflect wider social inequalities. In a famous study by Bowles and Gintis,[37] the authors argue in deterministic terms that there is a *relatively simple correspondence between schooling, class, family, and social inequalities.* Bowles and Gintis maintain that children of parents with upper-socioeconomic standing most often achieve upper-socioeconomic status while children of lower-socioeconomic parents acquire a correspondingly lower-socioeconomic standing. However, schooling structures are not always successful in ensuring privilege for the students' advantaged class positions. The correspondence theorists *could not explain why some children cross over from the status of their parents.* Social reproduction, as it turns out, is more than simply a case of economic and class position; it also involves social, cultural, and linguistic factors.

This brings into the debate the *conflict* or *resistance theorists*, such as Henry Giroux and Paul Willis, who pay significantly more attention to the *partial autonomy* of the school culture and to the role of conflict and contradiction within the reproductive process itself.[38] *Theories of resistance* generally draw upon an understanding of the complexities of culture to define the relationship between schools and the dominant society. Resistance theorists challenge the school's ostensible role as a democratic institution that functions to improve the social position of all students—including, if not especially, those groups that are subordinated to the system. Resistance theorists question the processes by which the school system reflects and sustains the logic of capital as well as dominant social practices and structures that are found in a class-, race-, and gender-divided society.

One of the major contributions to resistance theory has been the discovery by British researcher Paul Willis that working-class students who engage in classroom episodes of resistance often implicate themselves even further in their own domination.[39] Willis's group of working-class schoolboys, known as "the lads," resisted the class-based oppression of the school by rejecting mental labor in favor of more "masculine" manual labor (which reflected the shop floor culture of their family members). In so doing, they ironically displaced the school's potential to help them escape the shop floor once they graduated. Willis's work presents a considerable advance in understanding social and cultural reproduction in the context of student resistance. Social reproduction certainly exceeds mobility for each class, and we know that a substantial amount of class mobility is unlikely in most school settings. The work of the resistance theorists has helped us understand how domination works, even though students continually reject the ideology that is helping to oppress them. Sometimes this resistance only helps secure to an even greater degree the eventual fate of these students.

How, then, can we characterize student resistance? Students resist instruction for many reasons. As Giroux reminds us, not all acts of student misbehavior are acts of resistance. In fact, such "resistance" may simply be repressive moments (sexist, racist) inscribed by the dominant culture.[40] I have argued that the major drama of resistance in schools is an effort on the part of students to bring their street-corner culture into the classroom. Students reject the culture of classroom learning because, for the most part, it is delibidinalized (eros-denying) and is infused with a cultural capital to which subordinate groups have little legitimate access. Resistance to school instruction represents a resolve on the part of students not to be dissimulated in the face of oppression; it is a fight against the erasure of their street-corner identities. To resist means to fight against the monitoring of passion and desire. It is, furthermore, a struggle against the capitalist symbolization of the flesh. By this I mean that students resist turning themselves into worker commodities in which their potential is evaluated only as future members of the labor force. At the same time, however, the images of success manufactured by the dominant culture seem out of reach for most of them.

Students resist the "dead time" of school, where interpersonal relationships are reduced to the imperatives of market ideology. Resistance, in other words, is a rejection of their reformulation as docile objects where spontaneity is replaced by efficiency and productivity, in compliance with the needs of the corporate marketplace. Accordingly, students' very bodies become sites of struggle, and resistance a way of gaining power, celebrating pleasure, and fighting oppression in the lived historicity of the moment.

What, then, are the "regimes of truth" that organize school time, subject matter, pedagogical practice, school values, and personal truth? How does the culture of the school organize the body and monitor passion through its elaborate system of surveillance? How are forms of social control inscribed into the flesh? How are students' subjectivities and social identities produced discursively by institutionalized power, and how is this institutional power at the same time produced by the legitimization of discourses that treat students as if they were merely repositories of lust and passion (the degenerative animal instincts)? How is reason privileged over passion so that it can be used to quell the "crude mob mentality" of students? What is the range of identities available within a system of education designed to produce, regulate, and distribute character, govern gesture, dictate values, and police desire? To what extent does an adherence to the norms of the school mean that students will have to give up the dignity and status maintained through psychosocial adaptations to life on the street? To what extent does compliance with the rituals and norms of school mean that students have to forfeit their identity as members of an ethnic group? How have identities been formed as reservoirs of labor-power within the crucible of capitalism, within the social universe of capitalism? How can a critical education help implode these identities in a struggle against capitalist life formations and the internal relations that link being human to capitalist social relations? These are all questions that theorists within the critical tradition have attempted to answer. And the answers are as various as they are important.

Some versions of student resistance are undoubtedly romantic: The teachers are villains, and the students are antiheroes. I am not interested in teacher-bashing, nor in resurrecting the resistant student as the new James Dean or Marlon Brando. I much prefer the image of Giroux's resisting intellectual, someone who questions prevailing norms and established regimes of truth in the manner of a Rosa Luxemburg or a Jean-Paul Sartre.[41]

I would like to stress an important point. Our culture in general (and that includes schools, the media, and our social institutions) has helped educate students to acquire a veritable passion for ignorance. We have effectively debarred knowledge from critique. The French psychoanalyst Jacques Lacan suggests that ignorance is not a passive state but rather an active excluding from consciousness. The passion for ignorance that has infected our culture demands a complex explanation, but part of it can be attributed, as Lacan suggests, to a *refusal to acknowledge that our subjectivities have been constructed out of the information and social practices that surround us.*[42] Ignorance, as part of the very structure of knowledge, can teach us something. But we lack the critical constructs with which to recover that knowledge *which we choose not to know*. Unable to find meaningful knowledge "out there" in the world of prepackaged commodities, students resort to random violence or an intellectual purple haze where anything more challenging than the late night news is met with retreat or despair; and of course, it is the dominant culture that benefits most from this epidemic of conceptual anesthesia. The fewer critical intellectuals around to challenge its ideals, the better.

What do all these theories of resistance mean for the classroom teacher? Do we disregard resistance? Do we try to ignore it? Do we always take the student's side?

The answers to these questions are not easy. But let me sketch out the bare bones of a possible answer. First of all, schooling should be a process of understanding how subjectivities are produced. It should be a process of examining how we have been constructed out of the prevailing ideas, values, and worldviews of the dominant culture. The point to remember is that if we have been made, then we can be "unmade" and "made over." What are some alternative models with which we can begin to repattern ourselves and our social order? Teachers need to encourage students to be self-reflexive about these questions and to provide students with a conceptual framework to begin to answer them. Teaching and learning should be a process of *inquiry*, of critique; it should also be a process of *constructing*, of building a social imagination that works within a language of hope. If teaching is cast in the form of what Henry Giroux refers to as a "language of possibility," then a greater potential exists for making learning relevant, critical, and transformative. Knowledge is relevant only when it begins with the experiences students bring with them from the surrounding culture; it is critical only when these experiences are shown to sometimes be problematic (i.e., racist, sexist); and it is transformative only when students begin to use the knowledge to help empower others, including individuals in the surrounding community. Knowledge then becomes linked to social reform. An understanding of the language of the self can help us better negotiate with the world. It can also help us begin to forge the basis of *social transformation:* the building of a better world, the altering of the very ground upon which we live and work. Understanding our lived experiences is important but must be accompanied by class struggles that can reshape the social relations in which experiences are produced. This means overcoming alienated labor by challenging the very nature of capitalist social relations: in short, through a struggle for a socialist alternative to capitalism.

Teachers can do no better than to create agendas of possibility in their classrooms. Not every student will want to take part, but many will. Teachers may have personal problems—and so may students—that will limit the range of classroom discourses. Some teachers may simply be unwilling to function as critical educators. Critical pedagogy does not guarantee that resistance will not take place. But it does provide teachers with the foundations for understanding resistance, so that whatever pedagogy is developed can be sensitive to sociocultural conditions that construct resistance, lessening the chance that students will be blamed as the sole, originating source of resistance. No emancipatory pedagogy will ever be built out of theories of behavior which view students as lazy, defiant, lacking in ambition, or genetically inferior. A much more penetrating solution is to try to understand the structures of mediation in the sociocultural world that form student resistance. In other words, what is the larger picture? We must remove the concept of student resistance from the preserve of the behaviorist or the depth psychologist and insert it instead into the terrain of social theory.

Cultural Capital

Resistance theorists focus on *cultural reproduction* as a function of class-based differences in *cultural capital*. The concept of *cultural capital*, made popular by French sociologist Pierre Bourdieu, refers to the general cultural background, knowledge, disposition, and skills that are passed on from one generation to another. Cultural capital represents *ways of talking, acting, and socializing, as well as language practices, values, and styles of dress and behavior.* Cultural capital can exist in the embodied state, as long-lasting dispositions of the mind and body; in the objectified state, as cultural artifacts such as pictures, books, diplomas, and other material objects; and in the institutionalized state, which confers original properties on the cultural capital that it guarantees. For instance, to many teachers, the cultural traits exhibited by students— e.g., tardiness, sincerity, honesty, thrift, industriousness, politeness, or a certain way of dressing, speaking, and gesturing—appear as natural qualities emerging from an individual's "inner essence." However, such traits are to a great extent culturally inscribed and are often linked to the social class standing of individuals who exhibit them. Social capital refers to the collectively owned economic and cultural capital of a group.[43] Taking linguistic competency as just one example of cultural capital, theorists such as Basil Bernstein contend that class membership and family socialization generate distinctive speech patterns. Working-class students learn "restricted" linguistic codes while middle-class children use "elaborated" codes. This means that the speech of working-class and middle-class children is generated by underlying regulative principles that govern their choice and combination of words and sentence structures. These, according to Bernstein, have been learned primarily in the course of family socialization.[44] Critical theorists argue that schools generally affirm and reward students who exhibit the elaborately coded "middle-class" speech while disconfirming and devaluing students who use restricted "working-class" coded speech.

Students from the dominant culture inherit substantially different cultural capital than do economically disadvantaged students, and schools generally value and reward those who exhibit that dominant cultural capital (which is also usually exhibited by the teacher). Schools systematically *devalue* the cultural capital of students who occupy subordinate class positions. Cultural capital is reflective of material capital and replaces it as a form of symbolic currency that enters into the exchange system of the school. Cultural capital is therefore symbolic of the social structure's economic force and becomes in itself a productive force in the reproduction of social relations under capitalism. Academic performance represents, therefore, not individual competence or the lack of ability on the part of disadvantaged students but *the school's depreciation of their cultural capital.* The end result is that the school's academic credentials remain indissolubly linked to an unjust system of trading in cultural capital that is eventually transformed into *economic* capital, as working-class students become less likely to get high-paying jobs.

When I worked with students in my suburban inner-city classroom, those whose cultural capital most closely resembled my own were the students with whom I initially felt most comfortable, spent the most instructional time, and most often encouraged to work in an independent manner. I could relate more readily and positively—at least at the beginning—to those students whose manners, values, and competencies resembled my own. Teachers—including myself—easily spotted Buddy, T. J., and Duke as members of the economically disadvantaged under class, and this often worked against them, especially with teachers who registered such students as intellectually or socially deficient. Intellectual and social deficiencies had little, if anything, to do with their behavior. Class-specific character traits and social practices did.

QUESTIONS FOR DISCUSSION

1. If teachers unwittingly participate in what critical educational theorists call social reproduction, what would you as a teacher do to overcome the worst dimensions of this process?

2. As teachers or prospective teachers, what can we do to make the hidden curriculum less hidden and less harmful? Is this really possible in a capitalist society grounded in class antagonisms?

3. If teaching and learning are forms of cultural politics, what are the ways in which we unconsciously silence or exclude different student voices in our classrooms, such as the voices of minority and economically disadvantaged students? How do we speak in the name of emancipation without showing scorn for those who are caught in the grip of domination or ignorance, regardless of their class positions? Discuss using examples from Part Two's classroom journal.

4. How does our approach to curriculum help shape student attitudes and perceptions about the nature of the world? Is the world made problematic? Is it open to questioning and analysis? Do you see the social structure as unchanging and inviolable or as open to new possibilities for emancipatory change? How can we develop an education discourse that integrates the language of power and purpose with the language of intimacy, friendship, and caring?

5. Should teachers attempt to change a student's cultural capital to be more like the teacher's? How can teachers give legitimacy to the cultural capital of disadvantaged or minority students? Should they still provide them with an opportunity to "act middle class" for the purposes of strengthening their chances for job placement? Can you relate these issues to your own teaching experiences or experiences as a student?

6. Should teachers be answerable for the larger social consequences of their collective individual acts? Should a consistent failure of teachers to act on the obligations incurred at the social level—i.e., to redress social injustice, racism, and sexism—be legitimate ground for challenging their personal actions in the classroom? What are the moral variants against which we shall construct ourselves as social agents of change?

7. If educational hegemony means the incorporation of students and teachers into relations of consumption and consumerist ethics, what kind of pedagogy can we develop to challenge the ability of the dominant ideas of the capitalist class to win our consent in these matters?

8. How would you evaluate my role as a beginning teacher? What would you have done differently if you were in my place, and why?

This last question raises the sensitive issue of how well-intentioned teachers willingly or unwillingly create classroom environments that mirror the social division of labor in the capitalist workplace. The implicit messages transmitted by teachers about work, authority, and social rules are essential to the functioning of society and the reproduction of the social division of labor and economic privileges enjoyed by dominant social groups. For instance, can you see how teachers in my school exercised forms of symbolic violence (cultural domination) through their imposition of white, Anglo-Saxon perspectives, thereby devaluing the experiences of minority and disadvantaged students? In what ways did my colleagues and I inculcate the cultural capital (i.e., the linguistic and cultural competencies that one inherits by virtue of the social class into which one is born) of the dominant class and thereby (unconsciously or otherwise) disconfirm and delegitimate the voices of students who did not happen to share our cultural capital? All of this raises yet another issue: that is, in what ways does the moral leadership of teachers and administrators help the dominant class secure hegemony over subordinate groups?

Some readers may be offended at the suggestion that teachers frequently function as unwitting pawns in class and cultural domination and exploitation. Schools, of course, are much more than instruments of the dominant culture in its ideological struggle, its "war of positions," so to speak, against the proletariat. I certainly do not view my role as an elementary school teacher as entirely oppressive. In fact, I believe much good came out of my classroom teaching.

Just as teachers are not total oppressors, it is equally true that students don't sit passively and absorb the culture of the classroom without some resistance. We need to relate such resistance to the symbolic domination characteristic of dominant pedagogical practices and to see student resistance not as a measure of wanton destructiveness (although some resistance is undeniably of this nature) or learned helplessness but as a form of moral and political indignation. Many students resist what the school has to offer, including the subtextual contours of instruction—what we have termed the "hidden curriculum"—in order to survive with a measure of dignity the vagaries of class and cultural servitude. In what ways, then, do schools serve as contradictory sites which both empower students and oppress them? Is this contradiction inevitable, or is it a process that needs to be seriously examined?

There are many more issues to be raised. I have provided the above questions simply as a starting point to help you unravel some of the implications that the critical perspective has to offer for rethinking schooling in the light of transforming society. To raise more questions here would be to undercut the purpose of this book. It remains for *you* to raise other issues, for it is with you, as living agents of history, that the real struggle for human freedom begins. After all, it is your labor-power that is currently being commodified by capital and thus it is in your power to challenge value production through class struggle and to bring about new forms of non-alienated labor.

ENDNOTES

1. The sources for this section are as follows: Bertell Ollman, "The Meaning of Dialectics," *Monthly Review* (1986, November): 42–55; Wilfrid Carr and Stephen Kemmis, *Becoming Critical: Knowing Through Action Research* (Victoria: Deakin University, 1983); Stephen Kemmis and Lindsay Fitzclarence, *Curriculum Theorizing: Beyond Reproduction Theory* (Victoria: Deakin University, 1986); Henry A. Giroux, *Ideology, Culture, and the Process of Schooling* (Philadelphia: Temple University Press and London: Falmer Press, Ltd., 1981); Ernst Bloch, "The Dialectical Method," *Man and World* 16 (1983): 281–313.

2. Carr and Kemmis, *Becoming Critical*, 36–37.

3. McLaren, *Schooling as a Ritual Performance.*

4. This discussion of micro and macro objectives is taken from Henry A. Giroux, "Over-coming Behavioral and Humanistic Objectives," *The Education Forum* (1979, May): 409–419. Also, Henry A. Giroux, *Teachers as Intellectuals: Towards a Critical Pedagogy of Practical Learning* (South Hadley, MA: Bergin and Garvey, 1988).

5. See Jürgen Habermas, *Knowledge and Human Interests*, trans. J. J. Shapiro (London: Heinemann, 1972); see also Jürgen Habermas, *Theory and Practice*, trans. J. Viertel. (London: Heinemann, 1974). As cited in Kemmis and Fitzclarence, *Curriculum Theorizing*, 70–72.

6. For a fuller discussion of culture, see Enid Lee, *Letters to Marcia: A Teacher's Guide to Anti-Racist Teaching.* (Toronto: Cross Cultural Communication Centre, 1985).

7. Henry A. Giroux and Peter McLaren, "Teacher Education and the Politics of Engagement: The Case for Democratic Schooling," *Harvard Educational Review* 56 (1986): 3, 232–233. Developed from Giroux's previous work.

8. For this discussion of culture, I am indebted to Raymond A. Calluori, "The Kids are Alright: New Wave Subcultural Theory," *Social Text* 4, 3 (1985): 43–53; Mike Brake, *The Sociology of Youth Culture and Youth Subculture* (London: Routledge and Kegan Paul, 1980); Graham Murdock, "Mass Communication and the Construction of Meaning," in N. Armstead (Ed.), *Reconstructing Social Psychology* (Harmondsworth: Penguin, 1974); Dick Hebidge, *Subculture: The Meaning of Style* (London and New York: Methuen, 1979); Ian Connell, D. J. Ashenden, S. Kessler, and G. W. Dowsett, *Making the Difference: Schooling, Families, and Social Division* (Sydney, Australia: George Allen and Unwin, 1982). Also, Stuart Hall and Tony Jefferson, *Resistance Through Rituals: Youth Subcultures in Post-War Britain* (London: Hutchinson and the Centre for Contemporary Cultural Studies, University of Birmingham, 1980).

9. John Muncie, "Pop Culture, Pop Music, and Post-War Youth Subcultures," *Popular Culture*, Block 5, Units 18 and 19/20, The Open University Press (1981): 31–62.

10. Muncie, "Pop Culture," 76.

11. The section on hegemony draws on the following sources: Giroux, *Ideology, Culture, and the Process of Schooling*, 22–26; *Popular Culture* (1981), a second level course at The Open University, Milton Keynes, England, published by The Open University Press and distributed in the United States by Taylor and Francis (Philadelphia, PA). Several booklets in this series were instrumental in developing the sections on ideology and hegemony: Geoffrey Bourne, "Meaning, Image, and Ideology," *Form and Meaning* 1, The Open University Press, Block 4, Units 13 and 15, 37–65; see also Tony Bennett, "Popular Culture: Defining Our Terms," *Popular Culture: Themes and Issues I*, Block 1, Units 1 and 2, 77–87; Tony Bennett, "Popular Culture: History and Theory," *Popular Culture: Themes and Issues II*, Block 1, Unit 3, 29–32. Another important source is a booklet for a third level course at The Open University: *The Politics of Cultural Production*, The Open University Press, 1981. Relevant sections include: Geoff Whitty, "Ideology, Politics, and Curriculum," 7–52; David Davies, "Popular Culture, Class, and Schooling," 53–108. See also P. J. Hills, *A Dictionary of Education* (London: Routledge and Kegan Paul, 1982), 166–167; and Raymond Williams, *Keywords: A Vocabulary of Culture and Society* (London: Fontana, 1983), 144–146.

12. William Ryan, *Blaming the Victim* (New York: Vintage Books, 1976).

13. Todd Gitlin, *The Whole World Is Watching: Mass Media in the Making and Unmaking of the New Left* (Berkeley and London: University of California Press, 1980), 253–254.

14. Gore Vidal, *Monthly Review* 19 (1986, October), as cited in Allen Fenichel "Alternative Economic Policies," *The Ecumenist* 25, 4 (1987, May–June): 49.

15. For this section on ideology, I am indebted to Henry A. Giroux, *Theory and Resistance in Education: Pedagogy for the Opposition* (South Hadley, MA: Bergin and Garvey, 1983), 143. See also Stanley Aronowitz and Henry A. Giroux, *Education Under Siege* (South Hadley, MA: Bergin and Garvey, 1985); Douglas Kellner, "Ideology, Marxism, and Advanced Capitalism," *Socialist Review* 8, 6 (1978): 38; Gibson Winter, *Liberating Creation: Foundations of Religious Social Ethics* (New York: Crossroad, 1981), 97. See also: Geoff Whitty, "Ideology, Politics, and Curriculum," 7–52, and David Davies, "Popular Culture, Class, and Schooling," 53–108; Williams, *Keywords*, 153–157; Tony Bennett, "Popular Culture: Defining Our Terms," 77–87; and Geoffrey Bourne, "Meaning, Image, and Ideology," 37–53.

16. James Donald and Stuart Hall, "Introduction," in S. Donald and S. Hall (Eds.), *Politics and Ideology* (Milton Keynes: Philadelphia, The Open University Press, 1986), ix–x.

17. Donald and Hall, *Politics and Ideology*, x.

18. John Thompson, "Language and Ideology," *The Sociological Review* 35, 3 (1987, August): 516–536.

19. John Dewey, in J. Ratner (Ed.), *Intelligence in the Modern World: John Dewey's Philosophy* (New York: The Modern Library, 1939), 784. See also Michel Foucault, *Power/Knowledge*, in C. Gordon (Ed.) (L. Marshall, J. Mepham, and K. Spoer, Trans.), *Selected Interviews and Other Writings 1972–77* (New York: Pantheon, 1980), 187.

20. Michel Foucault, *The Archaeology of Knowledge* (New York: Harper Colophon Books, 1972), 117.

21. Foucault, *Power/Knowledge*, 200.

22. Richard Smith and Anna Zantiotis, "Teacher Education, Cultural Politics, and the Avant-Garde," in H. Giroux and P. McLaren (Eds.), *Critical Pedagogy, the State, and Cultural Struggle* (Albany, NY: SUNY Press, 1989), 123.

23. See Chris Weedon, *Feminist Practice and Post-Structuralist Theory* (Oxford: Basil-Blackwell, 1987).

24. Cleo Cherryholmes, *Power and Criticism: Post-Structural Investigations in Education* (New York: Teachers College Press, 1988).

25. Foucault, *Power/Knowledge*, 131.

26. Lawrence Grossberg, "History, Politics, and Postmodernism: Stuart Hall and Cultural Studies," *Journal of Communication Inquiry* 10, 2 (1987): 73.

27. For more about the relationship of power and knowledge, see Kathy Borman and Joel Spring, *Schools in Central Cities* (New York: Longman, 1984); Henry Giroux, "Public Education and the Discourse of Possibility: Rethinking the New Conservative and Left Educational Theory," *News for Teachers of Political Science* 44 (1985, Winter): 13–15.

28. See Doug White, "After the Divided Curriculum," *The Victorian Teacher* 7 (1983, March); Giroux and McLaren, "Teacher Education and the Politics of Engagement," 228.

29. See the wide range of articles in H. Giroux and D. Purple (Eds.), *The Hidden Curriculum and Moral Education: Deception or Discovery?* (Berkeley, CA: McCutchen Publishing Corp., 1983).

30. Myra Sadkev and David Sadkev, "Sexism in the Schoolroom of the 80's," *Psychology Today* (1985, March): 55–57.

31. Sadkev and Sadkev, "Sexism in the Schoolroom," 56–57. Also, the 1980 *Nova* television program, *The Pinks and the Blues* (WGBH, Boston), summarized by Anthony Wilden. "In the Penal Colony: The Body as the Discourse of the Other," *Semiotica*, 54, 1/2 (1985): 73–76.

32. White, "After the Divided Curriculum," 6–9.

33. Giroux and McLaren, "Teacher Education and the Politics of Engagement," 228–229.

34. Stanley Aronowitz, "Schooling, Popular Culture, and Post-Industrial Society: Peter McLaren Interviews Stanley Aronowitz," *Orbit* (1986): 17, 18.

35. See Kemmis and Fitzclarence, *Curriculum Theorizing*, 88–89. Also, H. A. Giroux, *Ideology, Culture, and the Process of Schooling*.

36. Glenna Colclough and E. M. Beck, "The American Educational Structure and the Reproduction of Social Class," *Social Inquiry* 56, 4 (1986, Fall): 456–476.

37. Samuel Bowles and Herbert Gintis, *Schooling in Capitalist America* (New York: Basic Books, 1976); see also Kemmis and Fitzclarence, *Curriculum Theorizing*, 90; and Colclough and Beck, "The American Educational Structure," 456–476.

38. See, for instance, Peter McLaren, "The Ritual Dimensions of Resistance: Clowning and Symbolic Inversion," *Boston University Journal of Education* 167, 2 (1985): 84–97, and Giroux, *Theory and Resistance*.

39. Paul Willis, *Learning to Labour: How Working Class Kids Get Working Class Jobs* (Westmead, England: Gower, 1977).

40. Giroux, *Theory and Resistance*, 103.

41. Aronowitz and Giroux, *Education under Siege*.

42. Jacques Lacan, "Seminar XX," *Encore* (Paris: Editions du Seuil, 1975): 100. As cited in Constance Penley, "Teaching in Your Sleep: Feminism and Psychoanalysis," in C. Nelson (Ed.), *Theory in the Classroom* (Chicago: University of Illinois Press, 1986), 135.

43. Pierre Bourdieu, "Forms of Capital," in John G. Richardson (Ed.), *Handbook of Theory and Research for the Sociology of Education* (New York: Greenwood Press, 1986), 241–258. See also Henry A. Giroux, "Rethinking the Language of Schooling," *Language Arts* 61, 1 (1984, January): 36, and Henry A. Giroux, *Ideology, Culture, and the Process of Schooling*, 77.

44. Paul Atkinson, *Language, Structure, and Reproduction: An Introduction to the Sociology of Basil Bernstein* (London: Methuen, 1986).

PART FOUR

Analysis

I want now to explore in more detail the process of schooling. You are familiar now with the social problems that beset both schools and society (Part One), have some sense of the day-to-day challenges and demands of inner-city teaching (Part Two), and have been introduced to some basic theoretical concepts with which to analyze the process of schooling (Part Three). Again, I ask you to draw upon your own experiences and the journal transcription in Part Two to understand this new material. Some of you may have begun to formulate an analysis of schooling in the inner city. Here, then, are some further critical perspectives on why disadvantaged students often don't "make it" in school.

6

Race, Class, and Gender

Why Students Fail

The Black Underclass: Racial Stratification and the Politics of Culture

The development of an underclass in American society can be linked not only to economic stratification due to capitalist relations of exploitation but also to racial stratification. Economically disadvantaged whites and many ethnic minority groups undeniably make up such an underclass, but I limit myself here to a discussion of subordinated and marginalized blacks. A number of theorists within the critical tradition argue that it is virtually impossible to understand the classroom behavior and performance of economically disadvantaged and minority students without understanding their history as oppressed groups, their cultural frames of reference, and their everyday social practices. Despite his tendencies toward functionalism, John Ogbu argues convincingly that dominant and subordinate groups occupy caste-like strata in our society. Ogbu maintains that the subordinate positioning of black students in the larger society constitutes a *folk system* that embodies

> the attitudes, knowledge, and competencies transmitted to and acquired by black children as they grow up and form a part of what the children bring to school pertaining to schools, schooling, and white people who control the schools.[1]

Ogbu maintains that in the face of past and present job ceilings and technocratic barriers, blacks have evolved folk theories of "making it" which do not necessarily emphasize strong academic pursuit. Personal survival strategies undertaken by black students foster a particular *cultural capital* that is seldom congruent with mainstream or dominant practices associated with success. The disillusionment among black youth about "making it" through education results, in part, from observing both their parents' situation and that of other adults in their communities. It is not hard to imagine the deep distrust between blacks and public schools and blacks and white authorities, which Ogbu claims is communicated to children from a very early age by parents, relatives, and neighbors.

As a result of their subordinate position, blacks have formed an identity system that is perceived and experienced not merely as different from but *in opposition* to the social identity of their white dominators. Of course this is true to some degree for all members of the underclass, and not just blacks. Ogbu claims that within the black community itself, there are informal and formal sanctions against blacks who step into what their peers and the black community in general regard as the "white cultural frame of reference." School learning in white-controlled institutions often is equated with abandoning the imperatives, values, and collective solidarity of black culture.

> Specifically, blacks and similar minorities (e.g., American Indians) believe that in order for a minority person to succeed in school academically, he or she must learn to think and act white. Furthermore, in order to think and act white enough to be rewarded by whites or white institutions like the schools, a minority person must give up his or her own minority-group attitudes, ways of thinking, and behaving, and, of course, must give up or lose his or her own minority identity. That is, striving for academic success is a subtractive process: the individual black student following school standard practices that lead to academic success is perceived as adopting a white cultural frame of reference . . . as "acting white" with the inevitable outcome of losing his or her black identity, abandoning black people and black causes, and joining the enemy, namely, white people.[2]

Ogbu draws attention to no less than seventeen behavioral categories that constitute for black students what it means to "act white." These include speaking standard English, working hard in school to get good grades, being on time, and so on. *Resistance* among black students cannot, therefore, be attributed solely to their subordinate socioeconomic status; it also stems from *racial stratification*, which cuts directly across class boundaries. Ogbu points out that problems of school "dropouts" and "suicide" plague not only high school students but also college students and blacks who have "made it" in traditionally white positions within the corporate economy. Certainly Ogbu's analysis can be applied to many of the black students I worked with in my inner-city classroom.

Despite my own attempts at establishing a strong relationship with the students, I nevertheless remained at some level one of "them"—the "other." As a white, middle-class teacher, I was always confronting my own position in the dominant culture which, in relation to my minority and disadvantaged students, constituted a fundamental part of the problem. To what extent did I, due to my inability to name racism and link it to its originating source in the social structure, become for them a symbol of the age-old history of domination and legacy of exploitation that had planted seeds of bitter resentment in generations of black families? To what extent did I unconsciously collude with formations—both discursive and institutional—that reproduced white, patriarchal, Anglo supremacy?

What about other minorities and disenfranchised white students? I would argue that each group needs to be understood separately, within its own cultural, class, race, and gendered frames of reference. A study I did on Azorean students who had immigrated to Toronto and were attending an inner-city high school there explored the contradictory notion that many of these students held toward doing schoolwork. Portuguese parents frequently encouraged their children to drop out of school at sixteen to help out their families economically, often in the family business. Consequently, doing homework and being successful in school constituted for many of them an attempt to escape the social conditions of the family and an insult to those relatives who accepted the conditions. As members of the working class, Portuguese parents had come to realize that a diploma from high school would not necessarily give their children a chance for more than a blue-collar job. Though many Portuguese parents held high aspirations for their children to succeed and pushed them to do well in school, their own struggles as semiskilled laborers and unemployed workers served as a tacit message to their children not to depend on school as a way out of their poverty.[3] Success in school for working-class students usually means making it through the vocational level tracks, and this success does not necessarily guarantee that they will secure a good job, or that adult life will be any less harsh or conflictual.

Resistance and the Reproduction of Class Relations

We were introduced to the topic of resistance in Part Three under the category of "social reproduction." Let's take a closer look now at Paul Willis's work and the concept of resistance.

Paul Willis's *Learning to Labor*, a classic analysis of a group of twelve nonacademic working-class English boys through their last two years of school and their first six months of work, considerably alters the view held by many orthodox Marxist educators that schools function mechanically to reproduce social class divisions in the larger society.[4] Willis's study explains why many working-class students reject the possibility of high-status careers, apparently committing themselves willfully to a life of boring, drudging, generalized labor jobs. According to Willis, the "lived sense of difference" of these students in their everyday class-based culture expresses a *realistic* understanding of their future options in the labor force, an understanding acquired from their families, peers, and the values encoded into working-class life in general.

Moreover, the lads see the career counseling offered by the school as a hostile act of class imposition. Through such an imposition, the school creates an oppositional culture, and the lads actually appropriate working-class values for the purpose of actively *resisting* the bourgeois values of the school. In their resistance and in their often brash yet innovative flouting of conventional classroom maxims, the lads consider the "mental labor" of schoolwork an essentially "weak" and passive ploy to control their free time. Manual work, on the other hand, is masculine, independent, and active. Yet by rejecting mental labor so vehemently—especially at a time when their life chances are at stake—the lads freely implicate themselves in their own domination by foreclosing alternative career options. They unwittingly secure their own subservient positions in the division of labor. Resistance, then, is a process in which the working-class student further solidifies his or her position in the lowest tier of the class system, helping to confirm the view established by critical theorists that a nation's educational system is subservient to its economic system.[5]

In general terms, resistance is part of the process of hegemony, which works through the ideology-shaping characteristics of the school. Schools help structure the ideological field in which students participate by establishing and certifying the limits placed on competing definitions of reality. In light of Willis's observations, we can now see that *social reproduction* occurs with both the willing compliance and the active refusal of its own victims—a striking example of how *hegemony* is maintained by the capitalist class at the *cultural level* through the very resistance of students to the oppressive logic and practices of schooling.

In summary, Willis's study illustrates how schools serve as more than simple sorting stations that unproblematically reproduce the labor stratification and occupational differentiation that exists in the wider society. Students are not merely passive victims. They actively contest the hegemony of the dominant culture through *resistance*. They act in opposition to the process of social reproduction but, as a result of these very acts of opposition, they sadly foreclose the few options available to them to break out of their lived class subordination. In other words, they fail to take advantage of the school's potential to give them at least a slight edge in the job market over their peers who choose to drop out.

I would argue that Buddy, T. J., Duke, and the others in my own experience are actively participating in securing their domination by resisting what school has to offer them. But we cannot unqualifiedly condemn such resistance in view of the students' subordinate social position. Their "failure" in school cannot be interpreted as resulting simply from individual deficiencies; it must be understood as part of a play of differences between radically disparate *cultural fields*. For example, the students were actively contesting the unconscious efforts of teachers—including me—who valued their own middle-class *cultural capital* over that of the students. The teaching encounter in this instance served to disconfirm, delegitimate, and at times erase the cultural meanings and social relations valued by the students. My students were experiencing the material constraints of economic and racial stratification and were living the painful contradictions between *street-corner culture* and *student culture*. Knowledge acquired by T. J., Buddy, Duke, and others in their street-corner world was qualitatively different from knowledge acquired in the school. In the streets, knowledge was "felt," whereas classroom knowledge was objectified and often sullied by an inflated rationalism, including a stress on deductive reasoning. In the street, students made more use of bodily engagement, organic symbols, and intuition. Students struggled daily to reconcile the disjunction between the lived meaning of the streets and the subject-centered approach to learning in the classroom. School placed an inordinate emphasis on knowledge *about* (a stress on precision, procedure, and logic); on the street, emphasis was on knowledge *of* (the stress on description, ambiguity, and equivocation). Robert Everhart has commented that during classroom resistance students acquire a *regenerative knowledge* by which they are able to assert at least some creative control over the process of knowledge production.[6] It is a knowledge formed out of *interpretive* (open to question) rather than *assumed* (taken for granted) experiences and within a shared sense of community. This may be contrasted with the *reified* (presenting concepts and facts as concrete *things*) knowledge of the classroom which is often treated by teachers as unproblematic and which places students in the role of passive recipients.

For many economically disadvantaged students, success in school means a type of forced cultural suicide, and in the case of minority youth, racial suicide. During her study of a group of South Bronx students, Michelle Fine discovered that those who remained in school, when compared to dropouts, *were significantly more depressed, less politically aware, less likely to be more assertive in the classroom if they were undergraded, and more conformist.* According to Fine, "A moderate level of depression, an absence of political awareness, the presence of self blame, low assertiveness, and high conformity may tragically have constituted evidence of the 'good' urban student."[7]

At what price do we ask our students to conform to our version of "the good student"? For some, the price we exact is obviously too much to bear. That's when dropping out becomes not so much an option as an urgent and necessary act of survival. On the other hand, we have to recognize that students rarely "drop out" by reflective choice. More realistically, they are "pushed" out. In other words, they are placed in a double-bind situation. If they remain in school and desire to be successful, they are forced to forfeit their own cultural capital, street-corner knowledge, and dignity. They are made to compete at a decided disadvantage. Without a critical pedagogy, they lack the analytical skills both to analyze their location within the social order and to alter the conditions of their oppression. Yet if they leave school, they face a future in which they can carve out some self-esteem in the streets, but come up against a social order decidedly antagonistic to their aspirations for material success. Mainstream schooling offers working-class students little choice but to negotiate a life for themselves somewhere among the psychologist's office, the compensatory program set up to remediate their deficiencies, and the streets where they will eventually be dumped. If the economic climate is good, perhaps they will end up in low-skilled, low-paying jobs. If they are lucky, they will get jobs in the service sector, perhaps in retail, selling hip-hop clothes on Melrose Avenue.

Bein' Tough: Bein' Female

The disadvantaged female population represents one of the largest segments of any stratified capitalist society.[8] It remains the unfortunate case, however, that educational researchers have generally been shortsighted about female culture, as if only males inhabit subordinate groups. The female in contemporary school culture is often overlooked—fenced off from the mainstream of sociological writing on youth—which may be explained in part by the predominance of males in the field of classroom study. However, promising work has recently emerged on disaffected female youth.

The diary entries presented in Part Two tend to overturn the stereotypes of the thrifty, industrious, docile, and well-mannered schoolgirl. For the purposes of analysis, however, we must situate the behavior of these girls within the context of class, race, and gender and the way in which these distinctions are treated in the public school. The female underclass does not exist in a social vacuum; it is not independent of the multiplicity of relations that constitute the larger society. Disadvantaged females not only constitute an economically subordinate group; they are also oppressed by the very fact that they are females.

The West Indian female students in my class had a particularly difficult time. Not only did they suffer the sting of racism on a day-to-day basis, they often had to adjust to stepparents and a separation from supportive kin that had existed in their homeland. Common-law marriages were frequent, and grew out of a history of poverty in their homelands (which necessitated the father working away from home) and the social relations of slavery (which prized maternity). Great stress at home was placed on domestic labor. Parents usually had high aspirations for their children, and many joined grass roots organizations that offered support in the struggle against racism and exploitation.

The rituals and slang of Muscle Lady, Ruth, Jabeka, and others are largely symbolic responses to basic societal constraints and structural inequalities; they are reactions on the part of an oppressed group. The social lives of these girls have been developed as a distinctive subcultural style—a "lived sense of difference" from their middle-class teachers and peers, as "us" against "them."

Schooling transmits and reinforces those ideologies that reflect the prevailing values and ethos of a male-dominated, hierarchical, middle-class social structure. Conflict broke out in my classroom when the girls deliberately resisted the role expectations and concomitant patriarchal codes that the schools tried to impose on them. Much of their abrasive behavior was a direct rejection of middle-class propriety. Although a number of teachers in my school attempted to provide more flexible classroom procedures, most of the girls remained in passionate opposition to the intentions of the school as a vehicle for upward mobility—for eventually attaining monetary benefits and improved social status through the Protestant ethic of hard work and good deportment. Sympathetic teachers could not dissolve their ingrained hostility to institutionalized forms of domination and authority. *To Sir with Love* is, after all, a Hollywood fantasy. According to many of the girls, school failed to make a difference in the lives of their parents. Who could say that the educational system would be any kinder to them? The girls fatalistically accepted their position in society as members of a subordinate class and gender grouping.

Many incidents of violence, sexism, and racism in the classroom are in reality reactions to economic exploitation and cultural dislocation and to what is perceived as the oppressive experience of schooling. As Paul Willis points out in *Learning to Labor*, the resistance of British working-class boys to the dominant ideology of the school ultimately supports the modes of oppression it attacks. Physical labor and masculinity are celebrated; mental labor is defined and rejected as effeminate and therefore socially inferior. Such adulation of masculinity is fueled by a deep-rooted sexism. Subordinate roles are adopted more easily when they are enhanced by the appeal of regressive machismo. Patriarchy serves less as a relic of the social past, as some historians maintain, than as an Archimedian fulcrum for capitalism.[9]

The girls in my class were primarily concerned with popularity and physical attractiveness—areas of interest that far superseded academic aspirations. Girls were constantly experimenting with makeup and improvising clothing styles. Subcultural dress codes (tight-fitting denims, taut tee shirts covered with sexual slogans, bright red nail polish, Afros, dreadlocks, Kodiak boots) established by the disaffected denizens were not only symbolic challenges to the conservative sartorial codes of teachers and more affluent peers, but a way of fostering group identity and solidarity.

One way in which girls combat class-bound and oppressive patriarchal features of school is to assert their "femaleness," to replace the officially sanctioned code of neatness, diligence, application, femininity, passivity, and so on, with one that is more womanly, even sexual, in nature.[10] It is significant that dress and makeup for the girls in my classrooms constituted a direct rebellion against the authorized ideological codes of the school that situated them as passive subjects in which they were not permitted to exercise critique of existing social arrangements that favored the cultural capital and social power of the rich. It was fundamentally a reaction against the policing of the body and the moral regulation experienced in school; the girls' dress constituted a struggle for social power within a male-dominated culture and an oppressive economic system. The manifestly masculine, but tight-fitting "sexy" look was a refusal by the girls to be positioned as feminine subjects, as agents of patriarchal hegemony. The girls were rejecting the patriarchy inscribed in stereotypical feminine clothes: the neat blouses, the print skirts, the "wholesome girl" look. The girls then became "resisting subjects," exerting control in the cultural process of constructing meaning and social identity. They were transgressing the codes governing "good girlishness." Such acts of sartorial resistance inverted consensually validated norms of appearance, symbolically violating the magazine-stand iconographies of women's publications—especially the back-to-school issues of *Seventeen*.

Just as male resistance in the schools often serves to more firmly cement the boys in their low-caste status, female resistance often means rejecting the culture of the classroom only to be positioned in a culture in which girls are viewed as sex objects. The Corridor girls started to "go" with boys as early as age twelve. If in the process of "making out" they responded to the boys' advances too readily or indiscriminately, however, they were labeled as "sluts." Such names, employed viciously and randomly, were also bestowed on girls who were physically unappealing. Girls often found themselves in the double bind of losing their group status if they engaged in "too much" sexual activity, or of being rejected as "cold" if they engaged in too little. The boys' status, however, was fundamentally enhanced by similar incidents of increased sexual engagement. This double standard has existed historically, of course, and feminists have consistently and rightly attacked it.

The girls in the Corridor often rejected marriage as a desirable option for the future. At the same time, however, some felt that marriage would be preferable to working in a meaningless job. Marriage at least provided the status of "wife"— undoubtedly worth more than having no status at all. For many, however, marriage appeared as a trap from which they saw few avenues of escape.

I witnessed numerous daily incidents in which girls clashed physically and violently with boys or with other girls. In fact, some of the girls were among the school's most menacing and gifted pugilists.

It was important for the girls to assert very early their capacity to defend themselves physically. For girls, as well as for boys, "bein' tough" was a way to win respect and a coterie of followers.

Many of the girls had home lives that were turbulent and difficult. A large percentage lived in single-parent families with a number of brothers and sisters. Some parents were frequently out of work or on the dole. Even if they were fortunate enough to be working, many held menial, dead-end jobs in which their pride was constantly perforated. Girls with younger siblings took on parental roles very early, especially when mothers or fathers were working. Consequently, a number of girls would routinely miss part of the school day in order to look after brothers and sisters. Others were latchkey children who went home after school to an empty apartment. Parents who held menial jobs could rarely afford a babysitter, and day-care facilities were either inadequate or nonexistent. For both boys and girls, the most stinging insult was to be stamped as "welfare," a symbolic defilement.

Family violence frequently erupted as a result of the pressures of daily life. The theme of violence in the home often came up in discussions with girls and their parents. You may recall in Part Two an interview with the mother of one of my students:

> "Doesn't it bother you that your husband beats you, though? Wouldn't it help to work on that end of things?" I asked gently.
> "Of course he beats me!" she snapped. "Wouldn't you be upset if you couldn't find work and had to sit at home all day doing nothing?"

Although the girls found life full of antagonistic relationships and domestic dilemmas, home represented, at the very least, a place where commonsense knowledge and practice were appreciated and where a lack of mastery over middle-class discourse and rhetoric did not make the girls feel "deficient" or "deprived." My work with female students in inner-city classrooms confirmed many of the findings of critical educational theorists who describe the latent function or "hidden curriculum" of schooling as an attempt to reproduce the values, attitudes, and behaviors necessary to maintain our society's present class-based division of labor and male-dominated gender relations.

Although many of the Jane-Finch girls suffered the indignities of poverty, racism, sexism, physical abuse, and, in some cases, the culture shock of recent immigration, they managed to create and maintain a distinct subcultural resistance to the consensually validated norms of the school—norms which attempted to make girls into passive, pliable, docile, tidy, neat, and diligent workers. In order to resist this conventional version of femininity, designed to nurture their "domestic instincts," the girls developed attributes that were drawn from working-class culture in general: toughness, aggressive sexuality, distrust of authority, rebelliousness. The girls then resisted the contradictory myth that schools function as agencies of equality, that educational institutions possess the power to help disadvantaged students bridge the chasm of opportunity that separates them from their more affluent peers.

Because the school system is structured tacitly to reinforce and reward middle-class values, attitudes, and behavior (and thereby penalize the "deprived" by omission), educators and the public alike often assume that the failure of the schools to educate disadvantaged girls is really the failure of the girls themselves. The girls fail because they are perceived to be mindless, shiftless, worthless, pathological, burdened by dubious hereditary traits, or the products of deviant home backgrounds. We blame the victim rather than looking for ways in which the class and educational systems militate against the success of those who are economically powerless and who are disadvantaged by gender and race.

So pervading and intransigent is this myth of equal educational opportunity that many working-class girls come to believe that their school failure is their own fault, that they must be "stupid or something." In their day-to-day behavior, the Jane-Finch girls resisted what they unconsciously felt to be an oppressive situation; yet paradoxically, because school did not provide the rhetoric with which to articulate the experience of this oppression, they blamed themselves.

The liberal ideology that promises success to anyone who is prepared to work and sacrifice prevented the girls from understanding how they were being fed into a preordained future by the patriarchal, economic, and cultural forces of consumer capitalism. Paralyzed by the belief that they lacked the intelligence of the more affluent girls, many of the working-class girls gave up. (Naturally, there were some exceptions. But since bookish intelligence was equated with middle-class status, most girls soon abandoned any attempts to please teachers or achieve academic excellence. Instead their attention was soon diverted to the enhancement of their subcultural status.) For the most part, their class/cultural identity became defined for them by dirt-stained high-rises, unemployment, sexism, the strip-plaza splendor, and the general failure of educators and politicians to redress their plight. This led to strong emotional bonding, as networks of "girlfriends" were created collectively to resist the world of the dominant class. Many of the girls had a sense that the cards were stacked against them from the very beginning. After all, did not the legacy left by our ancestors emphasize the superiority of one class of people over another? And one sex over another? And what more natural reaction to this predicament than to jettison the official ideology of the school through rituals of resistance?

When we embrace the derisory ideology that conceives of disadvantaged girls as undersocialized, as "unfinished products" on the conveyor belt of social success, we place a veneer on the basic class structure and gender bias of society and obscure the ways in which the structure of the system within white supremacist patriarchal capitalism determines to a great extent which class and gender will be successful and which will fail. In this way, the educational system ensures the hereditary transmission of the status quo—by appearing neutral, by concealing its social function of reproducing class relations by constructing technologies of gender, by perpetuating the myth of equality of opportunity based on scholastic merit.

Until the educational system from kindergarten to high school reevaluates the working-class culture of femininity, schools will continue to underwrite the restricted and inferior role of women and function as sorting and processing stations through which girls are prepared for a lifetime of routine labor or dependency on men: the spirit-breaking and mind-deadening norms of the factory floor or the oppressive limbo of domestic labor, either paid or for husbands for whom they also function as baby machines. Until schools are recognized as sites of class and gender conflict, they will remain boot camps for bureaucracy; they will continue to emphasize the need for passive rule compliance, cooperation, and meager skill development in order to prepare disadvantaged students to accept unquestioningly the sexist and exploitative aspects of the world of domestic and manual labor. Educators must begin to question the class and value assumptions informing our dominant forms of pedagogy and the gender discrimination inherent in present-day schooling and social life.

In reading through my elementary school diary, it is painfully evident that at that time I was not able to confront my own sexism or sufficiently contest my own inscription in the discourses and practices of white supremacist patriarchy. Critical educators need to confront their own limitations in order to surpass them and eventually transform their pedagogies into a praxis of liberation. This is a lifelong struggle that has to be waged.

Psychologizing Student Failure

If we understand that the active refusal of African-Americans and Latinolas, other minorities, and working-class whites, male and female, to adopt or appropriate the *cultural capital* of the dominant culture (often translated by teachers as doing homework, being punctual, speaking politely, working quietly, not distracting your neighbor, showing deference to authority, etc.) is in fact a class-, culture-, or race-specific form of resistance, then we can understand that school failure is more than just *individual deficiencies* on the part of students.

The *deficit model of student failure* rests on the propensity of teachers to "psychologize" that failure. "Psychologizing" student failure amounts to blaming it on an individual trait or series of traits (e.g., lack of motivation or low self-concept). This is what William Ryan refers to in his famous phrase "blaming the victim."[11] This attitude is particularly frightening because teachers often are unaware of their complicity in its debilitating effects. Psychologizing school failure is a part of the hidden curriculum that relieves teachers from the need to engage in pedagogical self-scrutiny or in any serious critique of their personal roles within the school, and the school's role within the wider society. In effect, psychologizing school failure indicts the student while simultaneously protecting the social environment from sustained criticism.

Teachers must be aware of how *school failure is structurally located and culturally mediated*, so they can work both inside and outside of schools in the struggle for social and economic justice. Teachers must engage unyieldingly in their attempt to empower students both as individuals and as potential agents of social change by establishing a critical pedagogy that students can use in the classroom and in the streets.

When middle-class students and working-class students are matched for intelligence and ability, the differences in academic achievement are the result of what Boudon calls *secondary effects*.[12] These secondary effects are related to the differences in students' cultural capital and the social practices lived out within various cultural fields of experience. Working-class students operate within different "decision-fields" (i.e., family, workplace, peer culture) that involve specific class, gender, and race relations.[13]

Understanding school failure as the secondary effect of cultural capital and class- and gender-specific social practices runs directly counter to the prevailing neoconservative social logic, which attributes school failure to individual deficiencies on the part of a lazy, apathetic, and intellectually inferior underclass of students or to uncaring or selfish parents. This kind of logic works as a form of purity rite, a social mechanism that protects the educational system by projecting the myth of minority inferiority onto those who in some way are perceived to threaten or jeopardize the system. Within the capitalist class, many doyens of the establishment believe that in order to accommodate "inferior races" the schools must lower standards, an act which is disastrous for society as a whole. Eventually the myth of the inferiority of minorities and working-class groups becomes part of the social heredity of the transnational capitalist elite. Such a perspective, which carries with it the shame of racism, prevails in many mainstream theories of schooling.

ENDNOTES

1. John Ogbu, "Class Stratification, Racial Stratification, and Schooling," in L. Weis (Ed.), *Race, Class, and Schooling* 17 (1986), 22. Special Studies in Comparative Education, Comparative Education Center, Faculty of Educational Studies, State University of New York at Buffalo.

2. Ibid., 25–26.

3. Peter McLaren, *Schooling as a Ritual Performance: Towards a Political Economy of Educational Symbols and Gestures* (London and New York: Routledge and Kegan Paul, 1986).

4. Paul Willis, *Learning to Labor* (Lexington: D.C. Heath, 1977).

5. For further discussion, see The Open University (1981): *The Politics of Cultural Production;* Whitty, "Ideology, Politics, and Curriculum," 9–49; and Davies, "Popular Culture, Class, and Schooling," 53–108.

6. Robert Everhart, *Reading, Writing, and Resistance: Adolescence and Labor in a Junior High School* (New York: Routledge and Kegan Paul, 1983).

7. Michelle Fine, "Silencing and Nurturing Voice in an Improbable Context: Urban Adolescents in Public School," in H. A. Giroux and P. McLaren (Eds.), *Critical Pedagogy, the State, and Cultural Struggle* (New York: State University of New York Press, 1989).

8. See Peter McLaren, "'Bein' Tough': Rituals of Resistance in the Culture of Working-Class Schoolgirls," *Canadian Woman Studies* 4, 1 (1982, Fall): 20–24.

9. See Paul Willis, *Learning to Labor.*

10. See Angela McRobbie and Jenny Garber, "Girls and Subcultures," in S. Hall and T. Jefferson (Eds.), *Resistance through Rituals* (London: Hutchinson, 1980), 209–222. I am indebted throughout this section to the work of Angela McRobbie for her insights on working-class girls. See especially A. McRobbie, "Working Class Girls and the Culture of Femininity," in Centre for Contemporary Cultural Studies Women's Group, *Women Take Issue* (London: Hutchinson, 1978).

11. William Ryan, *Blaming the Victim* (New York: Vintage Books, 1976).

12. R. Boudon, *Education—Opportunity and Social Inequality: Changing Prospects in Western Society* (New York and London: Wiley Interscience, 1974). As cited in Davies, "Popular Culture, Class, and Schooling," 91–92.

13. See Davies, "Popular Culture, Class, and Schooling," 91–92.

CHAPTER

7 New and Old Myths in Education

Technologizing Learning

Many mainstream approaches to curriculum development and implementation currently offered to classroom teachers are politically laundered and culturally sterile programs of learning in which students are taught to think componentially—in fragments isolated from the flow of everyday experience.[1] Students develop a mechanistic cognitive style within classrooms that appears at times to conform to Henry Ford's rust-proofed assembly lines. The file keepers, accountability-mongers, and "knowledge specialists" at both state and local levels have instructed teachers to segment behavior, measure fluid social activity in terms of "inputs" and "outputs," and reduce human beings to computer printouts. They inscribe the terrain of our crisis-ridden classrooms with the logic of domination through an insistence that teachers take the experiences, values, and cultural capital of working-class and minority students *less seriously than they do those of the dominant culture*. This situation often unknowingly helps to perpetuate the reproduction of social and cultural inequality. As teachers, we are encouraged to be good "systems people," to create synthetic environments for our students. We dish out knowledge like fast food; burger specials arrive limp and overcooked from the Insight Kitchens of IBM, Xerox, and Enron.

Today, technocratic consciousness is looked upon as the new educational mechanism for generating classroom health. Teachers often give technocratic theories the benefit of the doubt and exhibit at times an incredulous penchant for following instructions and deferring to the "experts." Some of the new curriculum technologies have even been "teacher-proofed," which only contributes further to the devaluing and deskilling of teachers by removing them from the decision-making process. As teachers, we need collectively to demythologize the infallibility of educational programmers and so-called experts, who often do nothing more than zealously impose their epistemological assumptions on unassuming teachers under the guise of efficiency and procedural smoothness. What we are left with is an emphasis on *practical* and *technical* forms of knowledge as opposed to *productive* or *transformative* knowledge.

A particularly serious problem with the technocratic mentality is its appearance of objectivity and value-neutrality. What its adherents don't tell you is that a hidden political agenda oftentimes informs new policy and program directives.

Our classrooms need theory, but not the life-obstructing theories that are embedded in a technocratic worldview. We need theories that provoke teachers to question the value assumptions that underlie their technocratic cultural terrain and throw open to scrutiny the classroom practices and social relations linked to the capitalist law of value that future teachers are forced to acquire during the course of their teacher education.

Neoconservatism and the
Myth of Democratic Schooling

Rarely discussed—or even considered—in proposed solutions to the plight of students in our nation's schools are the many invidious myths that underlie current approaches to urban education. By myths, I refer to the resurgent "truths" of conservative educational thinking that were temporarily buried in the sixties but began stirring their bones again in the educational compost during the seventies and continue to be embraced in the nineties.[2] One of the most dangerous of these is the myth of *equal opportunity*, which maintains that the educational system is the glorious equalizer of our free society. Success can be achieved by intelligence, hard work, and creativity. Like many myths, this one forms part of our everyday perception, even though it has been continually proven untrue.

Believers in this myth suggest that inequality results from our established form of "meritocracy," which provides students who are more capable—who try harder and have more innate intelligence—with their rightful rewards and excludes those who are less able. Some neoconservatives even claim that biology is at the root of class division, and that minority and working-class students are at the greatest disadvantage due to their unfortunately deficient gene pool. In other words, culturally and economically disadvantaged students have *inherited* a lower intellectual aptitude. It is only natural and desirable, then, that our society rewards the brightest and most able students differentially. This "intellectual impediments model" stresses that different racial and class groups are endowed with different intellectual capacities, which regrettably inhibit the success in school of minority and economically disadvantaged students.

Neoconservatives choose to ignore or misinterpret recent research which indicates that one of the greatest determinants of academic success is parental income. Referring to this cruel reality as the "Frankenstein and Einstein" syndrome, Paul Olson, a critical educational theorist, points out that parental background makes a greater difference to school achievement than measured IQ.[3] The myth of equal opportunity therefore masks an ugly truth: The educational system is really a loaded social lottery, in which each student gets as many chances as his or her parents have dollars.

Neoconservatives argue that the desire for parity is in reality a "cult of envy." They equate the liberal vision of equality for all with their perception of Chinese society: zombie-like, conformist, and emotionally malleable. What a dull world equality would bring. But no one argues that individual differences don't exist. The real issue is that *the education system gives those who begin with certain advantages* (the right economic status and thus the right values, the right speech patterns, the right mannerisms, the right behavior) *a better chance to retain those advantages all through school, and ensures that minority and economically disaavantaged students will remain at the bottom rung of the meritocratic ladder.*

Neoconservatives will tell you that not everybody can be president of General Motors or a CEO for Microsoft. What you can read between the lines translates somewhat differently: Why waste good taxpayers' money on the lesser breeds? They're hardly going to lead this country, except maybe at the head of the welfare rolls. This view completely ignores Noam Chomsky's argument that "success is also correlated with traits much less sanguine than intelligence: manipulativeness, greed, dishonesty, a disregard for others, and so on."[4]

Neoconservatives predict a resurgence of the individual. Horatio Alger, we are told, will be resurrected from the cultural woodwork where he has lurked for decades. In this atmosphere, the perennial failure of the ghetto student can often be blamed on a lack of motivation and will to succeed. Though most mainstream educational pundits fortunately don't ascribe to the myth of genetic inferiority or lack of natural ability, they do continue to rationalize the failure of lower-class, minority, and immigrant students by blaming their home environments.

This is the myth of *cultural deprivation*, which interprets social and educational problems in terms of student failure to "fit" into the social milieu. As a result, economically disadvantaged and minority students are labeled "deviant," "pathological," or "impulse-ridden" when they don't behave in the ways expected by middle-class teachers. Of course, this theory cannot account for why "deficiencies" are consistently grouped along class lines. Schools foster programs to correct these problems, to build up the skills and attitudes of ghetto children, to make up for their so-called cultural deficits and motivate their lazy, apathetic souls—rather than consider structural changes in the wider society, changes in school policy, negative teacher feeling, or curriculum implementation that might be exacerbating the problems in the first place. This again amounts to blaming students for their own miseducation.

Please don't let me be misunderstood: A student's self-image and a teacher's attitude in school do play important roles to be certain, but they are not as likely to alter the ghetto student's class position as they are to affect where he or she ultimately resides within a particular class grouping. Those within the critical tradition know that the majority of parents among the working poor do hold reasonably high expectations for their children. Nevertheless these parents have a *realistic expectation* of how schools work for their own children, as distinct from how they work for more privileged children.

As Feinberg and Soltis point out, some advocates of the "cultural impediments model" claim that since achievement is largely the function of class culture, and since it is believed that little can be done to alter behavior that is rooted in class culture, compensatory school programs will have a negligible effect on school achievement.[5] These same advocates claim that schools may even make matters appreciably worse in trying to change the social standing of the working poor, since by catering to the poor, educators water down the entire curriculum and relax academic standards for everyone. These theorists argue that inequality is the natural outgrowth of urban development, an attitude that effectively undercuts the imperatives for equality of opportunity and equality of outcome.

Once educational programs have been shrouded in these myths, they need not be abandoned when they fail. Failed programs can be—and are—used by the dominant culture as evidence to support the myth-based definitions of academic failure: that failure lies in the genes, character traits, or home lives of the students themselves. Even good programs can fail because the clientele is unreachable, hence unteachable. Failure, therefore, simply proves the assumptions on which the policy was based.

Life chances are *socially conditioned* by capitalist social relations of production, exchange, and circulation to a greater extent than they are determined by individual effort. Yet we live in a culture that stresses the merits of possessive individualism, the autonomous ego, and individual entrepreneurship. In this prevailing view, social conflicts are reduced to individual, subjective concerns rather than problems having to do with social and material inequality and collective greed and privilege.

ENDNOTES

1. For a fuller discussion of this point, see Peter McLaren, "The Technocratic Classroom," *Ontario Public School Teachers' Federation News* (1982, April 1): 11.

2. See Peter McLaren, "Education as Myth," *Ontario Public School Teachers' Federation News* (1981, October 15): 17.

3. Paul Olson, "Methods, Interpretations, and Different Views of Aspirations," *Interchange* 17, 1 (1986): 78.

4. Noam Chomsky, "I.Q. Tests: Building Blocks for the New Class System," in B. Casin et al. (Eds.), *School and Society* (London: Routledge and Kegan Paul, 1971), 244–299, as cited in Olson, "Methods, Interpretations," 78.

5. Walter Feinberg and Jonas F. Soltis, *School and Society* (New York: Teachers College Press, 1985), 34–35.

8 Teachers and Students

The Primacy of Student Experience

The pedagogy that I propose *takes the problems and needs of the students themselves as its starting point.*[1] On the one hand, a pedagogy based on student experience encourages us to analyze the dominant forms of knowledge that shape student experiences; on the other hand, it attempts to provide students with the means to examine their own particular experiences and subordinate knowledge forms. We must help students analyze their own experiences so as to illuminate the processes by which those experiences were produced, legitimated, or disconfirmed. R. W. Connell and his associates in Australia provide a cogent direction for this curricular approach in their formulation of the kinds of knowledge that should be taught to empower working-class students.

> Working-class kids get access to formal knowledge via learning which begins with their own experience and the circumstances which shape it, but does not stop there. This approach neither accepts the existing organization of academic knowledge nor simply inverts it. It draws on existing school knowledge and on what working-class people already know, and organizes this selection of information around problems such as economic survival and collective action, handling the disruption of households by unemployment, responding to the impact of new technology, managing problems of personal identity and association, understanding how schools work and why.[2]

Any emancipatory curriculum must emphasize student experience, which is intimately related to identity formation. Critical educators need to learn how to understand, affirm, and analyze such experience. This means not only understanding the cultural and social forms through which students learn to define themselves, but also understanding how to use that student experience in ways that neither unqualifiedly endorse nor delegitimate it. As Giroux has often pointed out, knowledge must be made meaningful to students before it can be made critical. School knowledge never speaks for itself; it is constantly filtered through the ideological and cultural experiences that students bring to the classroom. To ignore the ideological dimensions of student experience is to deny the ground upon which students learn, speak, and imagine.

Students cannot learn "usefully" unless teachers develop an understanding of the various ways in which student perceptions and identities are constituted. Teachers need to understand how experiences produced in the various domains of everyday life produce in turn the different voices students employ to give meaning to their worlds and, consequently, to their existence in the larger society. Of course, not all student experiences should be unqualifiedly affirmed, since some of them undoubtedly will draw from an uncritical categorization and social construction of the world (racist and sexist stereotyping, for example). Teachers must understand that student experience arises from multiple discourses and subjectivities, some of which must be questioned more critically than others. It is crucial, therefore, that educators address the question of how the social world is experienced, mediated, and produced by students. Failure in this will not only prevent teachers from tapping into the drives, emotions, and interests that give students their own unique voice, but will also make it difficult to provide the momentum for learning itself.

Unfortunately, most approaches to teaching and learning treat knowledge as an isolated product of meaning and abjectly deny the knowledge and social forms out of which students give relevance to their lives and experiences. Lusted is worth repeating on this issue:

> Knowledge is produced in the process of interaction, between writer and reader at the moment of reading, and between teacher and learner at the moment of classroom engagement. . . . To think of fields or bodies of knowledge as if they are the property of academics and teachers is wrong. It denies an equality in the relations at moments of interaction and falsely privileges one side of the exchange, and what that side "knows" over the other. Moreover, for critical cultural producers to hold this view of knowledge carries its own pedagogy, an autocratic and elite pedagogy. It's not just that it denies the value of what the learners know, which it does, but that it misrecognizes the conditions necessary for the kind of learning—critical, engaged, personal, social— called for by the knowledge itself.[3]

Teachers often fall into the trap of defining success solely through the *ideological correctness* of what they teach. Giroux offers the example of a middle-class female teacher who is horrified by the blatant sexism exhibited by her male students. Predictably, the teacher presents her students with a variety of feminist tracts, films, and other curricular materials. Instead of responding with interest and gratitude for this political enlightenment, however, the students demonstrate only scorn and resistance. The teacher is baffled; the students' sexism appears only further entrenched. As Giroux points out, the teacher "falsely assumes the self-evident nature" of the correctness of her position; she has refused to allow the students to "tell their own stories, to present and then question the experience they bring into play." She has also denied her students an opportunity to question sexism as a problematic experience; she is, in other words, simply telling them once again what to think—as middle-class/ institutional authority so often does.[4]

Sharon Welch argues that the most important concern in teaching is *to support the process of theorizing and not the mere exposure to correct ideas.* Yet she points out the inherent trap in teaching theory: that theory can function as a form of social control. Teachers often, for instance, greet student ideas with the smug reminder that those ideas are not new, that they have been formulated many times previously, often with greater sophistication. Teachers also often teach theory only in its final form, rather than moving through the complex process of engendering ideas. Welch encourages teachers to use the elementary-level technique of "reinventing the wheel"—students are given the problems that encourage them to create the formula for solving the area of a rectangle, the volume of a box, etc. By creating the formulas themselves, students are able to understand the mathematical theory more thoroughly, and gain confidence as thinkers.[5]

In my own situation as an inner-city teacher, I was unequipped to examine many of the ideological assumptions that informed my own pedagogy. My "authoritative discourse" was immune to its own hidden biases and prejudices. When I was too caught up with my role as teacher, I failed to learn more from my students. There is often a defensiveness surrounding the practice of letting students tell their own stories. Teachers must be careful not to silence students unwittingly through hidden biases lodged in their own pedagogical practices.

Certainly students should on occasion be encouraged to listen rather than speak, especially if their voices tend to dominate and control others. But teachers *should never tell students that their stories don't count.* Michelle Fine provides an excellent example of one teacher who unwittingly silences a student during an attempt to establish a lively debate on an issue relevant to the lives of her students:

> In early Spring, a social studies teacher structured an in-class debate on Bernard Goetz—New York City's "subway vigilante." She invited "those students who agree with Goetz to sit on one side of the room, and those who think he was wrong to sit on the other side." To the large residual group who remained mid-room the teacher remarked, "Don't be lazy. You have to make a decision. Like at work, you can't be passive." A few wandered over to the "pro-Goetz" side. About six remained in the center. Somewhat angry, the teacher continued: "OK, first we'll hear the pro-Goetz side and then the anti-Goetz side. Those of you who have no opinions, who haven't even thought about the issue, you won't get to talk unless we have time." Deirdre, a black senior, bright and always quick to raise contradictions otherwise obscured, advocated the legitimacy of the middle group. "It's not that I have no opinions. I don't like Goetz shootin' up people who look like my brother, but I don't like feelin' unsafe in the projects or in my neighborhood either. I got lots of opinions. I ain't bein' quiet cause I can't decide if he's right or wrong. I'm talking." Deirdre's comment legitimized for herself and others the right to hold complex, perhaps even contradictory positions on a complex situation. Such legitimacy was rarely granted by faculty—with clear and important exceptions including activist faculty and para-professionals who lived in central Harlem with the kids, and understood and respected much about their lives.[6]

The social studies teacher in Fine's anecdote has unreflectively favored her own ideological position and consequently undermined Deidre's refusal to simplify what she considers a complex issue. Teachers frequently unintentionally devalue student experience despite the best political and ethical intentions. As a consequence, any sense of equality in the exchange between teacher and students is lost. In other words, a teacher's own pedagogy can be unintentionally elitist and autocratic.

The Primacy of Voice

In the welter of accountability schemes, management pedagogies, and rationalized curricula now flooding the schools, there is an ominous silence regarding how teachers and students produce and reconstruct meaning in everyday life. In the attempts to rationalize and streamline classroom pedagogy, the New Right is promoting curriculum approaches that remove both the teacher and the student from the center of action. The categories that students themselves use to make sense of the world, to understand why they act in a particular way, or why they resist in the face of dominating practices, appear superfluous to the champions of the new high-tech accountability schemes.

I would argue along with Henry Giroux that a critical and affirming pedagogy has to be constructed around the stories that people tell, the ways in which students and teachers author meaning, and the possibilities that underlie the experiences that shape their voices. It is around the concept of *voice* that a theory of both teaching and learning can take place, one that points to new forms of social relations and to new and challenging ways of confronting everyday life.[7]

Giroux's concept of *voice* refers to the multifaceted and interlocking set of meanings through which students and teachers actively engage in dialogue with one another. *Voice* is an important pedagogical concept because it alerts teachers to the fact that all discourse is situated historically and mediated culturally and derives part of its meaning from interaction with others. Although the term *voice* may refer to an internalized, private discourse, such a discourse cannot be understood without situating it in a universe of shared meanings, that is, in the symbols, narratives, and social practices of the community or culture in which the dialogue is taking place. The term *voice* refers to the cultural grammar and background knowledge that individuals use to interpret and articulate experience.

Individual voice must be understood within its cultural and historical specificity. How students, teachers, and others define themselves and name experience is a central pedagogical concern because it helps educators understand how classroom meaning is produced, legitimated, or delegitimated. This is not merely a technical concern but more importantly a moral and political consideration that must provide the basis for any critical pedagogy, especially a pedagogy that is attentive to the dialectic of power and meaning as it is shaped within capitalist social relations of production. In many cases, schools do not allow students from disadvantaged or subordinate groups to affirm their own individual and collective voices, yet teachers rarely understand how this happens.

A *student's voice* is not a reflection of the world as much as it is a *constitutive force that both mediates and shapes reality within historically constructed practices and relationships shaped by the rule of capital*. Each individual voice is shaped by its owner's particular cultural history and prior experience but exercised within capitalist social relations of production that help to populate student voice with meanings not of the student's own making. Voice, then, suggests the means that students have at their disposal to make themselves "heard" and to define themselves as active participants in the world. Exhibiting an individual "voice" means, to cite Bakhtin, "retelling a text in one's own words."[8] With words produced in contexts undetermined by the students and embedded in social relations outside of students' immediate control.

The dominant school culture generally represents the privileged voices of the white middle and upper classes. In order for teachers to demystify and make the dominant school culture an object of political analysis, they need to question those voices that emerge from *different* ideological spheres or settings, such as the school voice and the teacher voice.

Each of these voices works simultaneously to produce specific pedagogical experiences within different configurations of power. Teachers must analyze the interests that these different voices represent less as oppositional in the sense that they work to counter and disable each other than as an interplay of dominant and subordinate practices that shape each other in an ongoing struggle over power, meaning, and authorship.

To "learn the discourse of *school voice*," teachers must analyze the directives, imperatives, and rules that shape particular configurations of time, space, and curricula within the institutional and political settings of schools. The concept of school voice, for example, helps to illuminate particular ideologies that structure how classrooms are arranged, what content is taught, and what general social practices teachers are required to follow. More often than not, school voice represents what Bakhtin refers to as "authoritative discourse"—that which permits little or no flexibility within the context that frames it.

Teacher voice reflects the values, ideologies, and structuring principles that teachers use to understand and mediate the histories, cultures, and subjectivities of their students. For instance, teachers often use the voice of "common sense" to frame their classroom instruction and daily pedagogical activities. As in the case of school voice, teacher voice partakes of an authoritative discourse that frequently silences the voices of the students. On the one hand, the *oppressive power* of a teacher's authoritative voice can be seen in instances of what Bourdieu refers to as *symbolic violence*.[9] Symbolic violence is exercised when, for instance, a teacher draws his or her values narrowly in order to challenge and disconfirm the experiences and beliefs of students from subordinate groups. On the other hand, the *emancipatory power* of a teacher's authoritative voice is exercised when a student's voice is allowed to assert itself so as to be both confirmed and analyzed, in terms of the particular values and ideologies that it represents. In the latter instance, the teacher's voice can provide a critical context within which students can understand the various social forces and configurations of power that have helped give shape to their own voices. Students who exhibit the values and everyday practices of subordinate groups can learn to free themselves from the authoritative hold of middle-class discourse as a means to self-empowerment, without rejecting either their own working-class discourse or, for that matter, middle-class discourse.

It is often through the mediation of teacher voice that the very nature of the schooling process is either sustained or challenged. The power of teacher voice to shape schooling according to the logic of emancipatory interests is inextricably related not only to a high degree of self understanding, but also to the possibility for teachers to join together in a collective voice as part of a social movement dedicated to restructuring the ideological and material conditions both within and outside of schooling. Thus, we must understand the concept of teacher voice in terms of its own values, as well as in relation to the ways it functions to shape and mediate school and student voices.

The concept of voice acknowledges the political and pedagogical processes at work in the construction of forms of authorship within different institutional and social spheres. Moreover, it represents an attack on the unjust practices that are actively at work in the wider capitalist society. But most important, such a pedagogy begins with the assumption that the stories that schools, teachers, and students construct can form the basis for a variety of approaches to teaching and learning in which hope and power and class struggle play integral roles. I am referring to "voice" as the development of a consciousness of the necessity of class struggle against the rule of capital and not the formation of individual agency or bourgeois assertiveness encouraged by existing capitalist social relations. The concept of voice as a "critique" of existing social relations of production must not be subsumed by the idea of voice as a rhetorical trope. Voice must always imply the notion of collective agency as political praxis. It is both a testimony about the hidden and not-so-hidden injuries of class exploitation, racism, sexism, and homophobia and a proactive struggle against these and other forms of oppression and dehumanization.

Beyond Conversations with the "Other"

The journal entries presented in Part Two, which I wrote during my first four and a half years as an elementary teacher, illustrate the debilitating way in which poverty entraps groups of individuals as a result of the social relations of capitalist exploitation. My preoccupation at that time with the more disturbing characteristics of resistance among disadvantaged and minority students illustrates my own entrapment in bourgeois culture. I both admired and loathed the students' visceral rebellion.

Unfortunately, at the time I wrote my journal I had little access to theoretical constructs that would help me make sense of what was occurring in my classroom. My inability to criticize my own ideological shortcomings undoubtedly foreclosed opportunities for empowering my students and raised the danger of demoting their experiences to a lesser status than my own.

My views toward my students sometimes lapsed into a form of liberal pity that is incompatible with the critical frame of reference I now use to examine schooling. Throughout my days in the classroom, I had unknowingly ascribed to the pedagogical mainstay of many liberal teachers: I felt sympathy and compassion for my students while employing a pedagogy geared to "compensate" for the deficiencies of society's young victims. Because mine was the "stronger and superior culture," I felt I could penetrate and give shape, meaning, and hope to the mystery of the deprived. My pedagogy was bourgeois populism spiced with a liberal dose of humanism; it rendered me ineffective in educating community members about how power relations in society work under a dominant regime of truth that protected the interests of the capitalist class. This was an index of how far I had succumbed to the power and pervasiveness of the ruling elite. I had not yet committed class suicide.

We need to ask what injustices may be perpetrated in the name of liberal pedagogy. The ability to articulate and change the real relationships of power and privilege and class exploitation were not part of my pedagogical repertoire; consequently, such relationships remained camouflaged in my language of moral outrage.

As I tried to help my students succeed in their schooling by teaching them relevant social and educational skills, I was culpable at another level: I was a teacher employed by an oppressive system bent on turning students into laboring subjects, conditioning them to sell their labor-power in the capitalist marketplace in ways that inexorably lead to the commodification and alienation of their labor. I failed to minimize my individual complicity in institutional oppression, and liberal humanism in no way exonerated me. I failed to recognize that my pedagogy was rooted in the very reality I was attempting to challenge. The liability remains, and with it the imperative to do more than lessen the harshness of the world for our students. We must try to provide them with the ability to overcome oppression and transform the world. The interests of the dominant class were implicit in the very teaching practices I used—practices readily handed to teachers and student teachers which are steeped in the ideology of domination. I refer here to the institution of tracking, the stress on individualism, the employment of the "cultural deficit" model of pedagogy, and the prevalence of teacher-centered learning, to name just a few. I was unable to see that my liberal theories of education were in fact ideologically loaded. The fateful irony of combating the oppressors with their own weapons instituted for me a crisis of legitimation and accountability with respect to my own teaching.

Were I to do it all over again, I would construct my curriculum around the celebration, validation, and critical questioning of the symbolic and expressive forms within the specific cultural practices of the students' street-corner milieu. I would follow with concerted attempts to understand and appreciate the meanings invested in students' opposition to the dominant culture. I would make a conscientious effort to introduce students to key concepts of Marxist analysis, making the appropriate adjustments for their intellectual development. I would employ a Freirean approach, utilizing cultural circles and beginning with themes generated within the lived experiences of the students. In addition, I would attempt to make active alliances with popular constituencies outside the classroom—the workers', women's, and peace movements, and especially the anti-globalization movement.

A critical pedagogy situates itself in the intersection of language, culture, and history—the nexus in which the students' subjectivities are formed, contested, and played out. The struggle is one that involves *their history*, *their language*, and *their culture* and the pedagogical implications are such that students are given access to a critical discourse or are conditioned to accept the familiar as the inevitable. Worse still, they are too often denied a voice with which to be present in the world; they are made invisible to history and rendered powerless to shape it.

Philip Corrigan has developed a three-part form of analysis and action that I appropriate here to suggest an approach to critical pedagogy.[10] First, encourage students to develop a *pedagogical negativism*—to doubt everything, and to try to identify those forms of power and control that operate in their own social lives. Second, assist students in *making a judgment* about these forms of power and control. What can be used to promote empowerment, and what must be discarded? Finally, help students *affirm* their judgments. Return to history to help them find a language that registers or *names* the dominant forms of power and control that deny the knowledge of subjugated groups.

To achieve these steps, I suggest a special kind of classroom approach that Michelle Fine calls *naming*.[11] Naming is simply identifying and defining those social and economic relationships that most clearly affect students' lives, particularly the inequitable distribution of power and resources. During my own teaching days, naming those social inequities that contribute to insidious social class, racial, ethnic, and gender divisions in the wider society might have provided an initial step in permitting students to analyze their own situations. Macro objectives for my classroom that linked knowledge to wider social arrangements might have provided directive knowledge useful in students' daily lives. Such objectives would have encouraged students to draw on their own cultural histories and neighborhood experiences to discuss *how they saw and experienced oppression and social injustice.* I could have asked Duke, Buddy, and T. J., for instance, to interview members of the community, beginning with their parents, and to develop an oral history of the area. We could have documented grievances, discussed reasons why people in the area were suffering, and analyzed their oppression. We might then have raised these issues with local agencies, providing at least a beginning step in linking self-empowerment and social change.

I might also have invited students to understand youth protest in its various forms through music and culture. We might have compared the cultures of various local gangs with those of more publicized gangs, like the Bloods and Crips of Los Angeles. A comparison of well-studied British groups—skinheads, punks, Rastas, rude boys, mods, rockers, teddy boys—with the local manifestations of protest in the Jane-Finch youth subculture might have taught students to be more critical about their own culture and the dominant culture that subordinates them. I might then have given my students the opportunity to move beyond self-criticism to an analysis of monopoly capitalism, to strategies of self and social transformation: I might have asked how we can struggle to become active agents of social change through anti-capitalist struggle.

Unfortunately, in most schools the act of *naming*—of identifying and defining the oppressive social and cultural facts of life—is deemed "dangerous conversation." It runs counter to the politically laundered beliefs about equality and meritocracy that dominate public schooling. *Not naming*, however, constitutes an active refusal to create reflective citizens; it is quite simply a means of silencing students.

Michelle Fine argues that not naming leads to exceptionally damaging outcomes, particularly for low-income and minority students. "To not name is to systematically alienate, cut off from home, from heritage and from lived experience and ultimately severs these students from their educational process."[12] Fine goes on to describe how an administrative policy of not naming can, for instance, restrict information provided to potential dropouts concerning the severe economic and social consequences of dropping out of high school. When students are discharged from school in New York State, crucial conditions are *not named*, thereby denying students what amounts to informed consent.

> [Discharged students] are guaranteed an exit interview, which, in most cases, involved an attendance officer who asked students what they planned to do, and then requested a meeting with parent/guardian to sign official documents. The officer handed the students a list of GED/outreach programs. The student left, often eager to find work, get a GED, go to a private business school, or join the military. Informed conversations about the consequences of the students' decision are not legally mandated. As they left, these adolescents *did not learn:*
>
> - that over 50% of black high school dropouts suffer unemployment in cities like New York City (U.S. Commission on Civil Rights, 1982);
> - that 48% of New Yorkers who sit for the Graduate Equivalency Diploma test fail (New York State Department of Education, 1985);
> - that private trade schools, including cosmetology, beautician and business schools have been charged with unethical recruitment practices, exploitation of students, earning more from students who drop out than those who stay, not providing promised jobs, and having, on average, a 70% dropout rate;
> - that the military, during "peacetime" refuses to accept females with no high school degree, and only reluctantly accepts males, who suffer an extreme less than honorable discharge rate within 6 months of enlistment.[13]

My own teaching experiences were rife with the politics of not naming. Although I did encourage students to tell their own stories, the most that I could accomplish was a liberal version of moral outrage at the injustices of the system, followed by a sympathetic embrace or reassuring pat on the shoulder that told the students I identified with their plight. Let me stress that the pedagogical position I am advocating does not prohibit students or teachers from acquiring a sense of outrage, or students and teachers from developing a sympathetic, affectionate, confidence-building relationship with each other; rather, it emphasizes that *such sentiments and relationships need to be pursued within a pedagogical context in which the issue of self and social transformation is taken seriously within a wider orbit of anti-capitalist, anti-sexist, and anti-racist practices.*

My teaching would have been more effective if I had been able to engage in a critical analysis of those aspects of everyday life that resonated with and affirmed the dreams, desires, and histories of the students. I suggest, with Henry Giroux and Paulo Freire, that we must take the *experiences* and *voices* of students themselves as a starting point. We must *confirm and legitimate the knowledges and experiences through which students give meaning to their everyday lives.* Such experiences, however, must not be unqualifiedly endorsed. We must be attentive to their *contradictory nature* and establish grounds whereby these experiences can be questioned and analyzed in both their strengths and their weaknesses. For instance, some of Duke's expressive values might have been confirmed by celebrating his love of music, his sense of humor, his personal style, and his street wisdom. Duke is undeniably wise (as opposed to academically "smart"), in that he recognizes the subtle ways in which the system works to disempower himself, his peers, and his family. But he lacks a language in which to further ground his insights into the dominant capitalist ideology. Duke's way of resisting the "authoritative discourse" of the school is steeped in racist and sexist behavior that needs to be named, understood, and eventually transformed through the process of understanding that Freire calls *conscientization*. (See Part Three discussion on Paulo Freire.)

Although Freire's approach empowers students through language, language *is not a tool to express an already made self. Rather, as Giroux notes, language is one of the means whereby we give form and shape to the development of a more critical self.* Freire's approach to learning is based on genuine dialogue between students and teachers, who work as partners in a united quest for "critical consciousness" leading to a humane transformation of, rather than a passive accommodation to one's world.

This partnership approach is directly opposed to most mainstream learning, which Freire refers to as "banking education." In the banking approach, the teacher "deposits" information into an "empty account" (the student) who "receives, memorizes, and repeats." Students are passive objects of the teacher's knowledge. Freire's "problem-solving" approach turns students into active and critical subjects who work collaboratively to construct historically—and politically—sensitive analyses of existing social practices in order to transform them.

Giroux adds that critical pedagogy must develop out of *a politics of difference* and a sense of community not rooted simply in a celebration of plurality. In other words, tolerance of differences is not enough. *Students, despite their differences, must become unified in a common struggle to overcome the conditions that perpetuate their own suffering and the suffering of others. Critical pedagogy must be undertaken within a language of public life, emancipatory community, and individual and social commitment.*[14] In other words, this critical approach to teaching is based on a social imagination rooted in history and intent on a resurrection of the "dangerous memory" and "subjugated knowledges" of oppressed groups such as women and minorities. The task of such an imagination is to build a world in which power relations grounded in the capitalist law of value are contested actively and suffering is finally overcome through efforts at building a socialist alternative to capitalism.

Giroux's work involves assisting students in analyzing their own theoretical and political positions. This means teachers must attempt to understand the often contradictory nature of subjectivity, and the reasons why students adopt some ideological positions over others both within and outside schools.

To do this, teachers must uncover the hidden ideological interests that underlie their own pedagogical practices and their ability to both teach and learn with others. Teachers and students must engage each other as agents of different/similar cultures. For Giroux, this suggests being critically attentive not only to the teacher's relationship to the established apparatus of power, but also to the fears, resistance, and skepticism that students from subordinate groups bring with them to the classroom.

The critical pedagogy suggested here is one in which students are continually asked to examine the various codes—that is, the beliefs, the values, and the assumptions—that they use to make sense out of their world. They are also encouraged to examine how they "codify" events themselves, not only in the classroom but outside the school as well. One way to implement this is to ask students to write a number of short papers in which they not only consider various ways of making sense of an issue or event, but also reflect upon their own previous writings in order to re-think past perspectives and to modify or reshape positions. For instance, I ask my un-dergraduate students to examine what traits and characteristics in the opposite sex they consider appealing and attractive. This leads to a discussion of how ideals of masculinity and femininity are constructed and then to an examination of sexual stereotyping and how gender distinctions are manufactured through various cultural forms (i.e., magazine advertisements, television commercials, soap operas, music vid-eos). We then view a video, Tony Wilden and Rhonda Hammer's "Chorus Line: Women in Production," which graphically illustrates the militarism, sexism, racism, and symbolic violence so prevalent in Hollywood depictions of female chorus lines from the 1930s to the present.[15] Finally, I ask students to reconsider their initial ideals of masculinity and femininity and account for any changes in their personal views. Students are thus encouraged to sort through the dialectical contradictions of their own experiences; they are given the chance to raise a fundamental question put for-ward by Giroux: "What is it this society has made of me that I no longer want to be?" In short, students are asked to look at their everyday, taken-for-granted experiences (the ideologies of everyday life), as possible sources of learning.

In his masterful work, *The Grain of the Voice*, Roland Barthes warns teachers against assuming a voice of power—a voice that can smother student talk by assigning the teacher's meanings (his or her "authoritative text") to the texts students have read or the ideas in which they are presently engaging.[16] Barthes suggests that teachers should employ the strategy of *disappropriation;* that is, they should deliberately cast off authority as speaker so that students can claim some authority of their own. In this way, the teacher is no longer a hegemonic overlord, a representative of the dominant culture who tells students whether their interpretations of events are valid—in short, who tells them *who they are.* Instead the teacher actively assumes a *counterhegemonic* role; the teacher actively contests existing relations of power and privilege. One has to be careful here. As Freire notes, teachers should not reduce themselves to mere facili-tators and relinquish their roles as teachers. Any relinquishing of authority must be strategic and never compromise the ability of the teacher to direct the dialogue in ways that both deepen and extend self and social analysis. The overall purpose of the critical educator is to reveal to students the forces behind their own interpretations, to call into question the ideological nature of their experiences, and to help students dis-cover the interconnections between the community, culture, and larger capitalist so-cial relations of exploitation: in short, to engage in the dialectic of self and society.

ENDNOTES

1. This category was first developed by Giroux and expanded in his *Schooling and the Struggle for Public Life* (Minneapolis, MN: University of Minnesota Press, 1988). This section is based on Henry A. Giroux and Peter McLaren, "Teacher Education and the Politics of Engagement: The Case for Democratic Schooling," *Harvard Educational Review* 56, 3 (1986): 234–235.

2. Robert W. Connell, Dean J. Ashenden, Sandra Kessler, and Gary W. Dowsett, *Making the Difference: Schools, Families, and Social Division* (Winchester, MA: Allen and Unwin, 1982), 199.

3. David Lusted, "Why Pedagogy?" *Screen* 27, 5 (1986, September/October): 4–5.

4. Henry A. Giroux, *Schooling and the Struggle for Public Life: Critical Pedagogy in the Modern Age* (Minneapolis, MN: University of Minnesota Press, 1988), 164.

5. Sharon Welch, *A Feminist Ethic of Risk* (New York: Fortress Press; and South Hadley, MA: Bergin and Garvey Publishers, 1989).

6. Michelle Fine, "Silencing and Nurturing Voice," 26.

7. See Henry A. Giroux, "Radical Pedagogy and the Politics of Student Voice," *Interchange* 17, 1 (1986, Spring): 48–69. The three categories used in this section are taken directly from Giroux's work.

8. As quoted in Harold Rosen, "The Importance of Story," *Language Arts* 63 (1986): 234.

9. Pierre Bourdieu, "Symbolic Power," *Critique of Anthropology* 13/14 (1977, Summer): 77–85.

10. Philip Corrigan, "State Formation and Classroom Practice." Paper delivered at the Ivor Goodson Seminar, University of Western Ontario, Canada.

11. Fine, "Silencing and Nurturing Voice," 16.

12. Ibid., 18.

13. Ibid., 17.

14. See Giroux, *Schooling and the Struggle for Public Life*, 21.

15. See the discussion of "Chorus Line: Women in Production," in Tony Wilden, *The Rules Are No Game* (New York: Routledge and Kegan Paul, 1987).

16. Roland Barthes, *The Grain of the Voice: Interviews*, Trans. Richard Miller (New York: Hill, 1977), 149. As cited in Joseph Harris, "The Plural Text/The Plural Self: Roland Barthes and William Coles," *College English* 49, 2 (1987, February): 158–170.

CHAPTER

9 Conclusions to Parts Three and Four

I have tried to provide educators and prospective educators with a theoretical framework that defines schools as sites of possibility, in which classrooms provide conditions for student empowerment. I've tried to suggest that particular forms of knowledge, social relations, and values can be taught in order to educate students to take their places in society from a position of empowerment, rather than from a position of ideological and economic subordination. I have tried to construct a language of analysis and to liberate the concept of education from the realities of present-day schooling.

For critical pedagogy to become viable within our schools, teachers must learn to employ critical analysis and utopian thinking. Henry Giroux refers to this as combining the language of critique with the language of possibility. Educators must develop forms of analyses that acknowledge the spaces, tensions, and opportunities for democratic struggles and transformations within the day-to-day activities and events of the classroom. Similarly, educators must develop a language that allows teachers and others to view schooling in a critical and potentially revolutionary way. Two important directions for reforming contemporary school practices put forward by Aronowitz and Giroux involve viewing schools as democratic public spheres and teachers as transformative intellectuals.

Viewing schools as democratic public spheres means regarding schools as sites dedicated to forms of self- and social empowerment, where students have the opportunity to learn the knowledge and skills necessary to live in an authentic democracy. Instead of defining schools as extensions of the workplace or as frontline institutions in the battle for international markets and foreign competition, schools as democratic public spheres function to dignify meaningful dialogue and action and to give students the opportunity to learn the language of social responsibility. Such a language seeks to recapture the idea of democracy as a *social movement* grounded in a fundamental respect for *individual freedom* and *social justice*. As Giroux argues, viewing schools as democratic public spheres provides a rationale for defending them, along with progressive forms of pedagogy and teacher work, as institutions that perform public service essential to the best aspects of the democratic state.

By politicizing the notion of schooling, we also illuminate the role that educators may play as transformative intellectuals performing a particular social and political function. The term *transformative intellectual* is important here for analyzing the particular social practices in which teachers routinely engage. I follow Aronowitz and Giroux in using it to describe one who attempts to insert teaching and learning directly into the political sphere by arguing that schooling represents both a struggle for meaning and a struggle over power relations.[1] I also refer to one whose intellectual practices exhibit concern for the suffering and struggles of the disadvantaged and oppressed. Here the traditional view of the intellectual as someone who is able to analyze various interests and contradictions within society is extended *to refer to someone capable of articulating emancipatory possibilities and working toward their realization.* Teachers who assume the role of transformative intellectuals treat students as critical agents, question how knowledge is produced and distributed, utilize dialogue, and make knowledge meaningful, critical, and ultimately emancipatory.

If schools are to be linked to the imperatives of radical democracy and civic courage, educators must examine how the schools themselves reproduce those aspects of the wider society that contribute to gender, class, and racial injustices. Democracy in this case begins in the school itself, and this suggests the need for educators to question both the formal and the hidden curricula of public schooling so as to identify those ideologies and social practices that operate both for and against the imperatives of democracy. Teachers must be willing to develop and use a critical language in order to structure school experiences around a public vision of self- and social empowerment, both in and outside of schools. Giroux argues that this struggle not only dignifies teachers in their capacity as intellectuals and social critics; it also links their work to those practical pedagogical concerns that make the preconditions for critical learning, social empowerment, and democracy possible. I take a position that pushes the democratic equation even further, by arguing that democracy is only possible in a society that has abolished class relations, that is, in a socialist society.

An excellent example of liberating education can be seen in the efforts of students and teachers at Dr. Pedro Albizu Campos Puerto Rican High School in West Town, Chicago. Here, the staff use critical pedagogy in their collective work with the Puerto Rican community. They try to help students acquire a sense of humanity and purpose in their lives after an often brutal and dehumanizing colonization within the United States, where the material conditions of their labor are controlled in the interests of the capitalist class and their dreams, desires, hopes, and visions are often ideologically subjugated. Teachers at Pedro Albizu Campos are committed to equality and social justice and demonstrate an unyielding dedication to the empowerment of the Puerto Rican people. The accomplishments of the school are profound; students (many of whom are former street gang members) have not only gained access to university programs, but have also acquired a resistance to the socially manufactured dreams of consumer wealth and a desire to become social and moral agents dedicated to transforming the structural injustices that threaten their community. The pedagogy of the teachers, which has evolved from the historical plight of a colonized people, is linked to wider social problems outside the school and is grounded in the ongoing struggle of community members to secure jobs, to reform repressive legislation, and to redefine the concept of education.

Of course, liberating education runs its risks. Dr. Pedro Albizu Campos Puerto Rican High School has been invaded by FBI agents wielding shotguns and searching for evidence of FALN (Armed Forces for National Liberation) terrorist activity; an award from the U.S. Department of Education citing it as an exemplary private school was rescinded because of allegations that the school teaches revolution and sedition. What the school does, in fact, teach is a revolution in consciousness and in understanding; students and teachers learn to see schooling as a transformative agency of social change. More recently, members of the school who were working in developing a project in the neighboring high school, Roberto Clemente High School, were falsely accused by the FBI of diverting funds to the FALN. Around the same time, a professor of education, José Solís Jordán, was arrested and sentenced to prison time for alleged acts of sedition. All of these charges were trumped up. Resistance to the forces of colonization within and outside of the U.S. mainland carries a price. Immigrant communities have paid dearly for their insights, their courage, and their liberating pedagogies.

Liberating education hopes to develop a new kind of critical discourse, one that will inspire us to play a more active role in school, community, and classroom life. In my view, such a discourse is vital in order for educators and others to understand the specifics of oppression and the possibilities for democratic struggle and renewal in our schools. Of course, such a discourse always presents a risk to those who use it, but one that is worth taking if we believe that democracy itself is worth fighting for.

The development of an incipient critical consciousness on the part of students must be followed by its transformation to social action through public engagement and participation. Guiding this transformation must be a commitment to authentic democracy and social justice, a commitment that is undertaken in solidarity with the subordinated and the disenfranchised. The commitment here is to move beyond liberal bourgeois reform to creating conditions for a socialist society no longer subordinated to the rule of capital.

The Teacher as Social and Moral Agent

Nowhere does the challenge of shaping social history, fashioning new social relations outside of the social universe of capitalism, new cultural narratives, and rethinking the nature and purpose of schooling become more urgent than in the struggle to define the civic responsibility of the teacher.[2] The dialectics of hope expounded by early twentieth century writers such as Walter Benjamin and Ernst Bloch now appear silenced and forgotten. New forms of social theory and educational practice that are profoundly anti-utopian in character have, in their propensity to retreat from both history and a politics of commitment and struggle, helped to forge a new generation of intellectuals who have failed to take seriously Benjamin's maxim that freedom requires that we brush history against the grain.

Abandoning the project of political engagement and human possibility, educators and professional critics alike have promoted despair at the expense of analyzing the fundamental relationships of capitalist relations of exploitation that characterize existing forms of cultural and political hegemony. They have jettisoned a consideration for the realities of suffering, pain, and torture, not to mention the barrenness of everyday life, in favor of mastery learning techniques and the "teacher-proof" curriculum. Current reform efforts demonstrate an unwillingness to construct and sustain a clearly articulated political project, in which pedagogy can be linked to the creation of social practices and moral referents necessary for the construction of a democratic public sphere.

Teaching always takes place in relation to a particular regime of truth or dominating logic linked to capitalist social relations and the social division of labor. Acquiring knowledge does not provide students with a reflection of the world; it creates a specific rendering of the world that is only intelligible within particular ideological configurations, social formations, or systems of mediation. Knowledge, therefore, *refracts* the word. Teaching itself functions to produce students and teachers as social and cultural subjects. How we, as subjects, are positioned by various pedagogical discourses and classroom practices constitutes an ideological process that often provides us with an illusion of autonomy and self-determination and helps us to misrecognize ourselves as free agents. Although it may be true that we can never escape ideology, the teacher must both *reveal how subjectivity gets constructed and legitimated through dominant pedagogical discourses and eventually challenge the imaginary relations that students live relative to the symbolic and material conditions of their existence.*

The teacher's task must take the form of a critical pedagogy. That is, the teacher must do more than simply further legitimate shared assumptions, agreed upon proprieties, or established conventions. He or she must make classrooms into critical spaces that truly endanger the obviousness of culture—i.e., the way reality is usually constructed—as a collection of unalterable truths and unchangeable social relations. Within such critical spaces, he or she must excavate the "subjugated knowledges" of those who have been marginalized and disaffected, whose histories of suffering and hope have rarely been made public. Thus, we must point to the histories of women, people of color, economically disadvantaged groups, and others whose banished legacies challenge the moral legitimacy of the state. The stories and struggles of the oppressed are often lodged as "dangerous memories" in the social system's repressed unconscious.[3] As teachers of "dangerous memory," we are called to rub these narratives against the more normative frames of reference which give dominant knowledge its meaning and legitimacy. In addition, teachers need to challenge the very law of motion of capital and the social relations of production within which the dominant culture solidifies its rule.

The teacher performs a social function that is never innocent. There is no neutral, nonpartisan sphere into which the teacher can retreat to engage student experience. Giroux maintains that, as one who takes seriously the link among language, knowledge, and power, the teacher must first dignify his or her position by recognizing that the foundation for all human agency as well as teaching is steeped in a commitment to the possibilities for human life and freedom.

Finally, I would argue that teachers must function as more than agents of social critique. They must attempt to fashion a language of hope that points to new forms of social and material relations attentive to the principles of freedom and justice. And they must actively intervene in the conduct of human affairs. Critical discourse must be more than simply a form of cultural dissonance, more than a siphoning away of the

PART FOUR / Analysis

potency of dominant meanings and social relations. It must function instead to create a democratic community built upon a language of public association and a commitment to social transformation. Critical discourse must call for a new narrative through which a qualitatively better world can be both imagined and struggled for. We must be united in the face of overwhelming odds, and the pedagogy we use must be capable of inflating the human capacity to vie with the forces of domination at a scale that makes us reject despair and refuse capitulation to the rule of capital. Teaching is anticipatory, rooted in a dialectical logic that makes critique and socialist transformation its central challenge. The perilous and immense task ahead of us is to engage the real needs of the oppressed and to foster an unending commitment to their empowerment. We must work hard to reverse the current decline of moral passion and the socially induced depletion of the human spirit. The anger and sullen outrage that fills the gap between need and fulfillment for many of our youth must be met in the classroom, in the courts, in the legislature, and in the streets with a redemptive pedagogy of commitment and compassion and class struggle. Only in this engagement can we, as agents of transformation and hope, begin to both feel and understand the suffering and alienation of the world and also be provided with the will, the purpose, and the understanding to overcome it. Overcoming it cannot be achieved by trying to make capitalism adjust itself to human needs, but by abolishing the capitalist system itself.

ENDNOTES

1. The term "transformative intellectual" comes from Stanley Aronowitz and Henry A. Giroux, *Education Under Siege: The Conservative and Radical Debate Over Schooling* (South Hadley, MA: Bergin and Garvey Publishers, 1985), 40–43. See Giroux and McLaren, "Teacher Education and the Politics of Engagement," 215.
2. This section is adapted from Peter McLaren, "The Writer as Social Agent," *University of Toronto Review* 11 (1987): 24.
3. For a discussion of "dangerous memory" see Sharon D. Welch, *Communities of Resistance and Solidarity: A Feminist Theology of Liberation* (New York: Maryknoll, 1985).

PART FIVE

Looking Back, Looking Forward

The most important reason for including Part Five in the new edition is that it provides me with a context for exploring new ideas that were only tangentially addressed in the initial volume. Since the initial publication of *Life in Schools*, I have focused to a much greater extent on the themes of multiculturalism and postmodernism. These are themes that are currently at the center of the debate over educational reform and democratic citizenship and in my estimation will be themes that will occupy educators for the foreseeable future, especially given the worsening economic and social conditions in our urban centers. Since the first publication of *Life in Schools*, I have been fortunate to have worked with progressive educators in Mexico, Argentina, Costa Rica, Brazil, Cuba, Eastern Europe, Japan, Taiwan, and other parts of the world. As a result, I have a better sense of situating the struggle over conditions in our schools and in the larger society in a geopolitical perspective—one that I have tried to share in the pages that follow.

My present and persistent concern with the relationship among capitalism, racism, and patriarchy has been heightened by the Dickensianizing of postmodern megalopolises such as Los Angeles (where I currently reside) and has provoked me politically to develop a critique of mainstream multiculturalism and to advance a theory of what I refer to as critical multiculturalism. In so doing, I argue that an analysis of the social construction of whiteness is needed in any formulation of multiculturalism. Whiteness is rarely discussed in contemporary discussions of multiculturalism and because of this it often serves as the invisible marker against which "otherness" is defined. Consequently, in Part Five, I shall attempt a provisional geneaology of whiteness. The triumph of neo-liberal economic and social policies, of the globalization of capitalist social relations, and a reconfiguration of racialized social relations in cities such as Los Angeles mandates for me a reexamination of contemporary perspectives on multicultural education in the United States.

I would caution against employing the construct of "race" as an analytic category without qualification because race has no biological basis or philosophical legitimacy (and here I agree that race should not be seen as a determinant of specific phenomena associated with levels of intelligence or personality characteristics). We should not give credibility or legitimacy to the notion that humanity exists as genetically distinct racial groups marked by a specific combination of biologically defined or imagined phenotypical characteristics and discrete cultural practices. In other words, we must always problematize the term "race" and see it as an ideological or social construction produced within the historical and geopolitical specificity of its explanatory deployment and as an artifact of the social science literature itself.[1] For similar reasons, I would caution against the use of the term "race relations." Instead, I believe that educational researchers should understand racism as a plurality of racialized social and cultural practices. There are numerous historically specific racisms. In this sense, race relations are really racialized ethnic relations. The idea of "race" or "race relations" should not be upheld as a causal factor. Rather than focus on phenotypical features, educational researchers should focus on the historical, social, and discursive production of processes of racialization.

While I caution against using the terms "race" and "race relations" unproblematically, I need to stress that racialized identities have political, economic, and sociological consequences for groups of people in our so-called "race-neutral" society. Jobs and careers, access to heath care and human resources, and the way one is treated in the legal system and by law enforcement are proof of this. Racialized social practices correlate with wage levels, poverty levels, and the likelihood of incarceration.[2] In this sense I agree that race approximates an ontological category, that is, it operates as if it were real. While the concept of race is a social construct and while it is also culturally variegated and historically contextual, racialized discourses and practices are nonetheless determinant over the experiences and choices of some groups over and against others. Race is lived and inscribed in the body and, in our society, people are conditioned to perceive and think within racialized categories.

The invisibility of whiteness as a racialized set of social and cultural practices of power and privilege is another important reason why I have included this section. I want to make whiteness more visible in order to unveil its discourses, its hidden transcripts, its social practices, and the historical and material conditions that conceal its incessant and compulsive practices of domination. The white mask must be removed so that whiteness as a discursive configuration, a narrative space, a social position, a semiotic density, and a set of lived social and economic relations can be deconstructed, challenged, and, quite simply put—destroyed. Whiteness must be abolished because it is the major enabling condition for white supremacy and racialized prejudice. Of course, to say that whiteness must be abolished is not the same thing as saying that people who are considered white must be destroyed.

This section attempts to rethink pedagogy as a narrative space that interrupts the patterns of everyday life, that brushes against the grain of daily social practices, that seeks to liberate spaces occupied by the commodifying forces of capital's law of value. A pedagogy of liberation must create a new place for narrative voices to emerge. It must attempt to "unforget" the regime of whiteness in order to re-map its processes, to challenge its hegemony and to re-open, re-member, and re-tell the story of emancipation and freedom. A pedagogy of liberation is the telling of the story of the "something more" that can be dreamt only when domination and exploitation are named and challenged. To challenge exploitation is no easy task. It requires the courage to live dangerously, to examine the social, gender, and racial character of human labor. It stipulates that we stand alongside those who have nothing but their labor power (the nonowners of the means of production) to sell. We need to stand in solidarity with the working-class so that they are no longer exploited by capitalist owners and capitalist modes of production. To achieve this requires an end to the rule of capital itself.

ENDNOTES

1. Peter Mclaren and Rodolfo Torres (in press), "Racism and Multicultural Education: Rethinking 'Race' and 'Whiteness' in Late Capitalism." In Stephen May (ed.) *Rethinking Multiculturalism and Antiracist Education: Towards Critical Multiculturalism.* London: Falmer Press. See also, Peter McLaren, *Revolutionary Multiculturalism: Pedegogies of Dissent for the New Millennium.* Boulder, CO: Westview Press, 1997.

2. Linda Alcoff, "Philosophy and Racial Identity." *Radical Philosophy.* No. 75 (1996): 5–14.

10 Unthinking Whiteness, Rethinking Democracy

Toward a Revolutionary Multiculturalism*

> *Now, this is the road that White Men tread*
> *When they go to clean a land—*
> *Iron underfoot and the vine overhead*
> *And the deep on either hand.*
> *We have trod that road—and a wet and windy road—*
> *Our chosen star for guide.*
> *Oh, well for the world when the White Men tread*
> *Their highway side by side!*
>> —Rudyard Kipling, (Cited in Edward Said, Orientalism, p. 226).

> *The price of freedom is death.*
>> —Malcolm X (El Hajj Malik El Shabazz)

> *We don't want to be around that ol' pale thing.*
>> —Malcolm X (El Hajj Malik El Shabazz)

> *El deber de cada revolucionario es hacer la revolución.*
>> —Che Guevara

As the millennium draws closer and my time on this earth stretches beyond half a century, I look back at my twenty-five years as an educator and social activist with few regrets. Yet I must confess a world-weariness has overtaken much of what I thought was my inviolate resolve, a feeling of anger and despair about living and dying in these

---

*Approximately 30 pages from *Revolutionary Multiculturalism: Pedagogies of Dissent for the New Millennium* by Peter McLaren. Copyright © by WestviewPress. Reprinted by permission of WestviewPress. This article also appears in *Educational Foundations*, Spring, 1997.

new times, at this current and painful juncture in world history. I try to hide my despair and rage toward the system from my students, many of whom yearn to find in my writings and those of my colleagues some hard and fast ways to permanently dismantle structures of oppression that imprison the spirit and harden the hearts of so many of our brothers and sisters in struggle.

Despite the present social conditions that beset us, I am not in a perpetual state of dismay, forced to camouflage a secret despair. In my darkest hours I have on more than one occasion been graced by what could be described as a momentous shimmering of the human spirit, a slight breaking free from the deep inertia of this planetary soul. Occasionally light splinters the darkness in various shapes: a nascent social movement attempting to unite the barrios; a hip hop message that becomes a rallying cry for social justice in a community under siege; a million black men marching to Washington; a hundred thousand marchers striding down César Chavez Avenue to protest Proposition 187 with a resolve so formidable that you could feel the sting of electricity in the air; hundreds of high school students in East Los Angeles defying their teachers and walking out of their classrooms to show their solidarity with the anti-Proposition 187 activists. Even a single pedagogical act, such as a group of students trying to undo the image of the Mexicano as the demon poster-boy by confronting white racists in a seminar, is enough to drive a tiny wedge between despair and cynical resignation.

Spaces of hope do appear. But rarely by historical accident. Sometimes they occur in the momentary indecision of the marketplace; sometimes in a rare paralysis of hate in the menacing machine of capital; but whatever the reason, these spaces need to be strategically seized. Spaces of hope offer encouragement to the forces of justice but they are not sufficient in themselves. Spaces—often private—must be made public. They must be expanded from spaces into spheres—from personal, individual spaces and private epistemologies into public spheres of hope and struggle and collective identities.

The specific struggle that I wish to address is that of choosing against whiteness. Yet is it possible for us to choose against whiteness given that, historically, the practice of whiteness has brought about such a devastating denial, disassembly, and destruction of other races? One would think that such a choice against whiteness would be morally self-evident. However, precisely because whiteness is so pervasive it remains difficult to identify, to challenge, and to separate from our daily lives. My message is that we must create a new public sphere where the practice of whiteness is not only identified and analyzed but also contested and destroyed. For choosing against whiteness is the hope and promise of the future.

Where do those of us, living in this vaunted western democracy, stand as a nation? Look around you; look inside as well as outside for the outside is really a mirror of who we are as a people. The Dickensianizing of postmodern megalopolises like Los Angeles (the enhancing of the personal wealth of the few who live in places like Beverly Hills at the expense of the many who live in places like Compton or East L.A.) is not a natural historical event (there is nothing natural about history). It is a politically contrived dismemberment of the national conscience. And it is comfortably linked to global economic restructuring.

Sustaining a meager existence is becoming frighteningly more difficult with the passage of time for millions of Third World peoples as well as First World urban dwellers, including millions of inhabitants of the United States. Global capitalism is excluding large numbers from formal employment while the poor, trapped within post-Fordist arenas of global restructuring and systems of flexible specialization, appear to be less able to organize themselves into stable and homogeneous social movements. Standardized forms of mass production, in which companies retool and keep production costs down in order to keep competitive in the international marketplace, are now disappearing. Economies of global efficiency are sidestepping the ability of nation states to mediate the control of money and information.

Labor markets are growing more segmented as full-time workers are replaced with part-time workers who are unable to secure even meager health or dental benefits. The days of high-wage, high-benefit mass production manufacturing are receding into the horizon as the First World bids farewell to industrialized regimes. Yet manufacturing has not completely disappeared from the United States. In Los Angeles, where I live, you can witness the Latinization of the Southland's working-class, as Latinos now make up 36 percent of Los Angeles County's labor force in manufacturing (the nation's largest manufacturing base). And the exploitation of these workers continues to increase.

Stock options go up in companies that downsize and lay off thousands of employees. It used to be a sign that a company was in trouble when it laid off large numbers of workers. Now it's an indication of strength, making stockholders proud. Cutting costs is everything, as business moves farther away from even a peripheral engagement with the world of ethics. In fact, capitalism has made ethics obsolete. The buying and selling of labor power is all about aesthetics, which does share a hinge with ethics, true, but the latter is subsumed by reification's terrible beauty.

The war on poverty has given way to the war on the poverty-stricken—a war that is about as mean-spirited as wars can get. The average worker has to do without the luxury of decent living standards because to improve conditions for the majority of the population would cut too deeply into the corporate profitability of the ruling elite. Rarely has such contempt for the poor and for disenfranchised people of color been so evident as in the hate-filled politics of the last several decades.

The greed and avarice of the United States ruling class is seemingly unparalleled in history. Yet its goals remain decidedly the same. Michael Parenti writes:

> Throughout history there has been only one thing that ruling interests have ever wanted—and that is *everything:* all the choice lands, forest, game, herds, harvests, mineral deposits, and precious metals of the earth; all the wealth, riches, and profitable returns; all the productive facilities, gainful inventiveness, and technologies; all the control positions of the state and other major institutions; all public supports and subsidies, privileges and immunities; all the protections of the law with none of its constraints; all the services, comforts, luxuries, and advantages of civil society with none of the taxes and costs. Every ruling class has wanted only this: all the rewards and none of the burdens. The operational code is: we have a lot; we can get more; we want it all. (1996, p. 46)

As long as the small business lobby and other interests tied to capital successfully derail health care reform whenever the issue raises it's disease-ravaged face, as long as the bond market continues to destroy public investment, and as long as business continues to enjoy record-high profits, acquisitions, and mergers (with the aid of corporate welfare) at the expense of wages and labor, then prosperity in the United States, like its administration of social justice, will remain highly selective. And all of us know who benefits from such selectivity. To remain in a state of political paralysis or inertia is to aid and abet the sickening suburbanization of the country—a suburbanization driven by a neo-liberal agenda designed to serve mainly whites. Working under existing rules established by the National Labor Relations Act and the procedures carried out by the National Labor Relations Board, unions are being deprived of their right to organize, and this is contributing in no small way to wage decline. The situation reflects only too well what Parenti calls his "iron law of bourgeois politics": When change threatens to rule, then rules are changed (1996, p. 248).

Residents of the United States do not have a natural disposition to swindle the gullible, to target the poor more forcefully than a F-16 fighter locks onto an enemy "hunkered down" in the sands of Iraq, to scapegoat immigrants and to fashion them into *los olvidados* (the forgotten ones). The current evisceration of public protection programs, shamefully absent enforcement of environmental standards, rising health insurance premiums, drastic declines in salaries for working people, erosion of the primary sector proletariat, and steady increase of the chronically unemployed have catapulted the United States onto a tragic course toward social decay and human misery—a course that is far from inevitable.

It is possible that a half century from now whites might be a minority in the United States. As they continue to feel that their civil society is being despoiled and to blame immigrants for their increasing downward mobility and the disappearance of "traditional" American values, whites fall prey to the appeal of a reactionary and fascist politics of authoritarian repression. This is especially true at a time when whites continue to feel removed from their ethnic roots and undergo what Howard Winant (1994, p. 284) has called "a racializing panethnicity as 'Euro-Americans.'"

The kindling of fascism lies in the furnace of United States democracy waiting for a spark to ignite a firestorm of state repression. Previous firestorms have occurred in the Watts rebellion of August 1965, the civil rights movement, and the antiwar movement of the 1960s, but also in more current forms such as the Los Angeles uprising of April 29, 1992, and the East L.A. high school walkouts of 1994 over Proposition 187. We don't get many firestorms because, as Parenti (1996) has so presciently noted, fascism is already here on low flame, which burns just fine with the occasional stoking from reactionary governors such as Pete Wilson.

The citizenry of the United States has been sold a damaged bill of goods in the Republican Contract with America. Parenti captures its ideology perfectly:

> The GOP socio-economic agenda is not much different from the kind pushed by Mussolini and Hitler: break the labor unions, depress wages, impose a rightist ideological monopoly over the media, abolish taxes for the big corporations and the rich, eliminate government regulations designed for worker and consumer safety and

environmental protection, plunder public lands, privatize public enterprises, wipe out most human services, and liberal-bait and race-bait all those opposed to such measures. (1996, p. 42)

In the United States we are living at a time of undeclared war. Each day we negotiate our way through mine-sown terrains of confrontation and uncertainty surrounding the meaning and purpose of identity. American democracy faces Janus-like in two simultaneous directions: into a horizon of hope and co-existence and into the burning eyes of Klansmen in sheets soiled with blood. While on the one hand this current historical juncture is witnessing an unprecedented growth of white supremacist organizations living on the fringes of social life, on the other hand establishment conservatives are stridently asserting nativistic and populist sentiments that barely distinguish them ideologically from their counterparts in racialist far right groups and citizen militias: The Ku Klux Klan, Posse Comitatus, The Order, White Aryan Resistance, Christian Identity, National Alliance, Aryan Nations, American Front, Gun Owners of America, United Citizens of Justice and militia groups have organizations in most, if not all, of the fifty states.

Young white males and females who may find these racist groups unappealing can still find solace in politicians such as Pete Wilson and Bob Dole whose antiimmigrant and Latinophobic policies and practices deflect their racializing sentiments through flag waving, jingoism, and triumphalist acts of self-aggrandizement—such as the disguising of Proposition 209 as a civil rights initiative—designed to appeal to frightened white voters who feel that growing numbers of Spanish-speaking immigrants will soon outnumber them. Politicians have become white warriors in blue suits and red ties dedicated to taking back the country from the infidel. Recently, amid headlines of African American churches in the south being razed by arson, a Los Angeles newspaper ran a photograph of Bob Dole at a Southland political rally. The magnetic allure of Dole's head, its skin a translucent blue, tensile; its shiny yellow tongue as if dipped in kerosene, seemingly wagging, appeared in metonymic relationship to his message: Anglos feel under siege from the most alien of alien nations—Mexico—and it is time that civilized white folks wrestle back the land from the barbarians.

Guillermo Gómez-Peña writes:

This identity crisis translates into an immense nostalgia for an (imaginary) era in which people of color didn't exist, or at least when we were invisible and silent. The political expression of this nostalgia is chilling: "Let's take our country back." The far right, like Pete Wilson, Newt Gingrich, Jesse Helms, and Pat Buchanan, along with many Democrats, are in agreement on the following: This country must be saved from chaos and collapse into Third-Worldization; "illegal" immigrants must be deported; the poor should be put in jail (three strikes, you're out); welfare, affirmative action, and bilingual education programs must be dismantled; and the cultural funding infrastructure that has been infiltrated by "liberals with leftist tendencies" (the National Endowment for the Arts and the Humanities and the Corporation for Public Broadcasting) must be decimated. In the euphemistic Contract with America, ethnic "minorities," independent artists and intellectuals, the homeless, the elderly, children, and especially immigrants from the South, are all under close watch. (1996, p. 173)

On the day of General Colin L. Powell's address to the 1996 Republican Convention in San Diego, former Education Secretary and current director of Empower America, William J. Bennett, published a commentary in the *Los Angeles Times* entitled "Civil Rights is the GOP's mission" (Monday, August 12, 1996, B5). Evoking the figure of Dr. Martin Luther King, Jr., Bennett called for the end of racial discrimination through the abolition of affirmative action. Bewailing the civil rights leaders of the past 30 years (with the exception of Dr. King, of course, whose symbolic power he seeks to conscript into his own agenda) whom he argued are a group of malcontents who have wielded a "racial branding iron," have "diminished the moral authority of the civil rights movement," have "fanned the flames of racial resentment," and have "helped Balkanize America," Bennett calls for the government to eliminate "race-based preferences" for people of color. He putatively wants African Americans, Latinos, and other ethnic minority groups to be judged by the "content of their character." He cites African Americans such as Ward Connerly, chairman of the Civil Rights Initiative and General Powell as continuing "the great civil rights tradition of Dr. King."

However, Bennett's vision is perniciously shortsighted and malificent and effectively domesticates King's place in the civil rights struggle. And his logic is disturbingly flawed. It is similar to the conservative school board that abolishes school breakfast programs for hungry children because such programs are "antifamily." Since the children eat at school and not with their parents and siblings at home, they are apparently offending the values that made this country great. Supposedly, it is better to go hungry with your family than to be fed at school. Bennett's arguments are similarly confused. First, he appears to work under the mistaken assumption that U.S. society has reached a point of relative economic justice and affirmative action is no longer necessary. Second, he appears either to be unable or unwilling to fathom the nearly intractable reality of white privilege and uncontested hegemony in the arena of the economy. Third, he fails to realize that racist white people are going to be suspicious of African Americans and Latinos whether they are assisted by affirmative action initiatives or not. And fourthly, his vision is propelled by a nostalgic view of a United States as a middle-class suburban neighborhood in which people of color don't have so much "attitude" and where whites are the uncontested caretakers of this prelapsarian nation of consensus and harmony. To be colorblind in Bennett's restricted use of the term is to be naive at best and ignorant at worst. Because not to see color in Bennett's view really amounts in ideological terms to be blind to the disproportionate advantage enjoyed by white people in nearly all sectors of society. Winant has argued:

> In many ways no African American, however affluent, can feel as secure as even the average White: for example, in an encounter with the police. . . . Yet the malevolent attentions of floor walkers in Bloomingdales cannot be compared with those of the Los Angeles Police Department. (1994, p. 283)

Bennett's view is akin to conservative politicians who bemoan critics of tax breaks for the rich (welfare for the rich) for engaging in "class warfare." You don't have to be an economist to realize that since the Reagan administration, money has been transferred from the ranks of the poor into the coffers of the rich in record proportions. Yet conservative politicians resent people who label these practices as "unjust." After all, if rich (mainly white) people can work the system to their advantage, then all the more power to them. Bennett has turned the logic of Martin Luther King, Jr. upside down. He has replaced social analysis with homilies about "character." That a former Secretary of Education would take a position like this is especially telling, given the state of critical self-reflection among politicians in this country.

Politicians of Bennett's ilk want to increase the role of charitable institutions in this country. If economically disenfranchised people of color are to be helped, then it should be done by private individuals or organizations and not the government—or so the conservatives maintain. But wealthy private organizations have benefited from the hegemony of white privilege in the government and the marketplace for centuries. Unbridled capitalism in our present post-Fordist service economy is ruthlessly uncharitable to the poverty-stricken. Nevertheless, transferring the challenge of economic justice from the government into the hands of philanthropists who feel "pity" for the poor is not the solution. Bennett misses the crucial point: that not to have affirmative action for people of color in the present social structure amounts to a hidden affirmative action for white people. Bennett's position tacitly seeks the incorporation of racialized groups into the corporate ethics of consumption where white privilege increasingly holds sway. His ethics of racial tolerance can therefore work as a means of social control of populations of color. His motivated amnesia with respect to the history of capitalism causes him to ignore the macrostructures of inequality and injustice and the class-bound hierarchies and institutionalized racism of United States' society and to act as if United States' society has already achieved economic equality across diverse ethnic populations. There is a false assumption at work in Bennett's logic that views culture as essentially self-equilibrating, as providing similar sets of shared experiences to all social groups. The culture of diversity heralded by Bennett is a decidedly homogenized one, cut off from the contingencies of state power and economic practices. He fails to recognize the ideology of colonialism as a founding discourse of United States democracy and refuses to acknowledge that the skull and crossbones logic of imperial piracy that stole the land from its indigenous inhabitants is still largely with us both in domestic and foreign policy.

If Bennett is so intent on character building and fears that African Americans are now being viewed by white people as bearing the "stigma of questionable competence" because of affirmative action, why doesn't he, rather than dismantle affirmative action, place greater emphasis on improving the social practices of white people, by encouraging them not to stigmatize, demonize, and peripheralize people of color and women not only in the boardrooms but also in all walks of life.

It is precisely Bennett's stubborn unwillingness to recognize the asymmetrical allocation of resources and power that overwhelmingly favor white people as much now as during King's era, that effectively truncates Bennett's vision, fashioning it into a form of sound-byte histrionics.

In her article, "Whiteness as Property" (1993), Cheryl I. Harris makes the compelling case that within the legal system and within popular reasoning there exists an assumption that whiteness is a property interest entitled to legal protection. Whiteness as property is essentially the reification in law of expectations of white privilege. Not only has this assumption been supported by systematic white supremacy through the laws of slavery and "Jim Crow" but also by recent decisions and rationales of the Supreme Court concerning affirmative action. Harris is correct in arguing that whiteness serves as the basis of racialized privilege in which white racial identity provides the basis for allocating societal benefits in both public and private spheres. Whiteness as a property of status continues to assist in the reproduction of the existing system of racial classification and stratification that protects the socially entrenched white power elite. According to Harris, rejecting race-conscious remedial measures as unconstitutional under the Equal Protection Clause of the Fourteenth Amendment "is based on the Court's chronic refusal to dismantle the institutional protection of benefits for whites that have been based on white supremacy and maintained at the expense of Blacks" (1993, 1767).

Current legal definitions of race embrace the norm of colorblindness and thus disconnect race from social identity and race-consciousness. Within the discourse of colorblindness, blackness and whiteness are seen as neutral and apolitical descriptions reflecting skin color, and unrelated to social conditions of domination and subordination and to social attributes such as class, culture, language, and education. In other words, colorblindness is a concept that symmetrizes relations of power and privilege and flattens them out so that they appear symmetrical or equivalent. But blackness and whiteness exist symmetrically only as idealized oppositions; in the real world they exist as a dependent hierarchy, with whiteness constraining the social power of blackness.

According to Harris:

> To define race reductively as simply color, and therefore meaningless is as subordinating as defining race to be scientifically determinative of inherent deficiency. The old definition creates a false linkage between race and inferiority; the new definition denies the real linkage between race and oppression under systematic white supremacy. Distorting and denying reality, both definitions support race subordination. As Neil Gotanda has argued, colorblindness is a form of race subordination in that it denies the historical context of white domination and Black subordination. (1993, p. 1768)

Affirmation action needs to be understood not through privatizing social inequality through claims of bipolar corrective justice between black and white competitors but rather as an issue of distributive social justice and rights that focuses not on guilt or innocence but on entitlement and fairness.

Bennett's faltering rhetoric and specious logic speak directly to the current crisis of democracy that has deported the hopes and dreams of growing numbers of minority populations across the United States into an abyss of emptiness and despair. The crisis has exposed the infrastructure of American democracy to be made of Styrofoam, trembling spray-painted pillars of a Greek temple in an off-Broadway play. Democracy has been cut at the joints by events that are currently transpiring both locally and throughout the globe.

One of the tasks ahead for those of us who wish to reclaim the dignity offered by true justice, is to revivify democratic citizenship in an era of diminishing returns. It is to create critical citizens who are no longer content in occupying furtive spaces of private affirmation but who possess the will and the knowledge to turn these spaces into public spheres through the creation of new social movements and anticapitalist struggle.

The struggle in these new times is a daunting one. Record numbers of disaffected white youth are joining citizen militias and white supremacist organizations at a time when black churches are burning in the South, and when cross burnings are occuring at an alarming rate across the nation in Louisiana, Georgia, Pennsylvania, Oregon, Maine, Southern California, and elsewhere. As white youths search for identity in their lives, many are able to find meaning only in relation to their capacity to hate non-whites. While some postmodernists adventitiously assert that identities can be fluidly recomposed, rearranged, and reinvented toward a more progressive politics in these new "pluralistic" times, I maintain that this is a shortsighted and dangerous argument. It would take more than an army of Jacques Lacans to help us rearrange and suture the fusillade of interpolations and subject positions at play in our daily lives. My assertion that the contents of particular cultural differences and discourses are not as important as how such differences are embedded in and related to the larger social totality of economic, social, and political differences, may strike some listeners as extreme. Yet I think it is fundamentally necessary to stress this point.

We are not autonomous citizens that can fashionably choose whatever ethnic combinations we desire in order to reassemble our identity. While the borders of ethnicity overlap and shade into one another, it is dishonest to assert that pluralized, hybridized identities are options available to all citizens in the same way (Hicks, 1991). This is because class, race, and gender stratification and objective constraints and historical determinations restrict the choices of some groups over others. The division of labor linked to political organization and the politics of the marketplace regulate choices and often overdetermine their outcome (San Juan, 1996). Identity is more than the ideological trafficking between nationality and ethnicity, but rather the overlapping and mutual intereffectivity of discourses that are configured by the social relations of production. In other words, nationalism, ethnicity, and capitalist circuits of production can be seen moving into a shared orbit.

Rather than stressing the importance of diversity and inclusion, as do most multiculturalists, I think that significantly more emphasis should be placed on the social and political construction of white supremacy and the dispensation of white hegemony. The reality-distortion field know as "whiteness" needs to be identified as a cultural disposition and ideology linked to specific political, social, and historical arrangements. As Matt Wray and Annalee Newitz, editors of the recently published volume entitled *White Trash: Race and Class in America*, put it:

> It has been the invisibility (for whites) of whiteness that has enabled white Americans to stand as unmarked, normative bodies and social selves, the standard against which

all others are judged (and found wanting). As such, the invisibility of whiteness is an enabling condition for both white supremacy/privilege and race-based prejudice. Making whiteness visible to whites—exposing the discourses, the social and cultural practices, and the material conditions that cloak whiteness and hide its dominating effects—is a necessary part of any anti-racist project. (1997, 3–4).

A related theme that I would like to emphasize is the need to incorporate, yet move beyond, the politics of diversity and inclusion when discussing multicultural education. The discourse of diversity and inclusion is often predicated on hidden assumptions of assimilation and consensus that serve as supports for neo-liberal democratic models of identity.

Neo-liberal democracy, performing under the banner of diversity yet actually in the hidden service of capital accumulation, often reconfirms the racist stereotypes already prescribed by Euro-American nationalist myths of supremacy—stereotypes that one would think democracy is ostensibly committed to challenge. In the pluralizing move to become a society of diverse voices, neo-liberal democracy has often succumbed to a recolonization of multiculturalism by failing to challenge ideological assumptions surrounding difference that are installed in its current anti-affirmative action and welfare "reform" initiatives. In this sense people of color are still placed under the threshold of candidacy for inclusion into the universal right to self-determination, and interpolated as exiles from United States citizenship. After all, as a shrinking minority, whites are running scared, conscious of their own vulnerability, and frantically erecting fortresses of social regulation while they still have the power to do so. Todd Gitlin declares:

> The Republican tilt of white men is the most potent form of identity politics in our time: a huddling of men who resent (and exaggerate) their relative decline not only in parts of the labor movement but at home, in the bedroom and the kitchen, and in the culture. Their fear and loathing is, in part, a panic against the relative gains of women and minorities in an economy that people experience as a zero-sum game, in which the benefits accruing to one group seem to amount to subtractions from another. Talk about identity politics! These white men, claiming they deserve color-blind treatment, identify with their brethren more than their wives or sisters, or minorities. (1995, p. 233)

Of course, among whites one of the most hated groups of poor people in the Southland where I live is the Mexican migrant workers. Stereotyped as *crimmegrantes*, they have become the object of xenophobia par exellence. Ron Prince, one of the architects of Proposition 187, has remarked: "Illegal aliens are a category of criminal, not a category of ethnic group" (Gómez-Peña, 1996, p. 67). Gómez-Peña comments on the imbrication of borders as a perceived crisis-effect by white Americans:

> For many Americans, the border has failed to stop chaos and crisis from creeping in (the origin of crisis and chaos is somehow always located outside). Their worst nightmare is finally coming true: The United States is no longer a fictional extension of Europe, or the wholesome suburb imagined by the screenwriter of *Lassie*. It is rapidly

becoming a huge border zone, a hybrid society, a mestizo race, and worst of all, this process seems to be irreversible. America shrinks day by day, as the pungent smell of enchiladas fills the air and the volume of quebradita music rises. (1996, p. 67)

The process of "Mexicanization" has struck fear into the hearts of the Euro-American who views this inevitability as an obdurate political reality. And this fear is only exacerbated by the media and anti-immigration activists. As Gómez-Peña notes:

> Now, it is the "illegal aliens" who are to take the blame for everything that American citizens and their incompetent politicians have been unable (or unwilling) to solve. Undocumented immigrants are being stripped of their humanity and individuality, becoming blank screens for the projection of Americans' fear, anxiety, and rage. . . . Both the anti-immigration activists and the conservative media have utilized extremely charged metaphors to describe this process of "Mexicanization." It is described as a Christian nightmare ("hell at our doorsteps"); a natural disaster ("the brown wave"); a fatal disease or an incurable virus; a form of demographic rape; a cultural invasion; or the scary beginning of a process of secession or "Quebequization" of the entire Southwest. (1996, pp. 66, 67–68)

I remember the bestial hate mongering among whites after the anti-187 march in East Los Angeles in 1994. The size of the crowd—approximately one hundred thousand protesters by some estimates—instilled such a fear of a brown planet that many white Angelenos fervently took to the streets in anti-immigration demonstrations. Too much "difference-effect" resulting from the borderization phenomena has created among previously stable white constituencies a type of fibrillation of subjectivity—a discursive quivering that eventually leads to a state of identity collapse. Wreaking havoc on the social landscape by creating a spectacular demonology around African American and Latino gang members, "welfare queens," undocumented workers, and gays and lesbians, members of the professional-managerial class made up primarily of cosmopolitan whites have tried to convince white America that its identity is threatened and that white people now constitute the "new" oppressed. Can anyone take this claim seriously coming as it is from the most privileged group in history?

I believe that an emphasis on the construction of whiteness will help put a different and important focus on the problems surrounding identity formation at this particular juncture in our history. When North Americans talk about race, they inevitably refer to African Americans, Asians, Latinos, Native Americans, to the consistent exclusion of Euro-Americans. I want to challenge the prevailing assumption that in order to defeat racism we need to put our initiatives behind the inclusions of minoritarian populations—in other words, of non-whites. I want to argue instead that in addition to making an argument for diversity, we need to put more emphasis on the analysis of white ethnicity, and the destabilization of white identity, specifically white supremacist ideology and practice. As David Roediger notes:

> Whiteness describes, from Little Big Horn to Simi Valley, not a culture but precisely the absence of culture. It is the empty and therefore terrifying attempt to build an identity based on what one isn't and on whom one can hold back. (1994, p. 137)

Until my recent U.S. citizenship, I was a citizen of a country that supplies the United States with a substantial group of undocumented workers—Canada. But you don't see the U.S. government militarizing its Northern border. Canadians don't have to be too concerned about harassment from *la migra* if California's Propositions 187 or 209 someday take effect. Consider the vehemently racist comments directed against Mexican and other immigrants of color by Patrick Buchanan, a recent Republican candidate for the U.S. Presidency:

> If British subjects, fleeing a depression, were pouring into this country through Canada, there would be few alarms. The central objection to the present flood of illegals is they are not English-speaking white people from Western Europe; they are Spanish-speaking brown and black people from Mexico, Latin America, and the Caribbean. (Bradlee Jr., 1996: 1, 12)

I would ask you to consider Buchanan's remarks in light of United States history. I offer some comments made by Abraham Lincoln during a speech made in southern Illinois in 1858:

> "I am not," he told his audience, "nor ever have been, in favor of bringing about in any way the social or political equality of the white and black races. . . . I will say in addition that there is a physical difference between the white and black races which, I suppose, will forever forbid the two races living together upon terms of social and political equality; and in as much as they cannot so live, that while they do remain together there must be a position of the superiors and the inferiors; and that I, as much as any other man, am in favor of the superior being assigned to the white man." (Zinn, 1970, p. 148)

Another United States hero, Benjamin Franklin, wrote:

> Why increase the Sons of *Africa*, by planting them in *America*, where we have so fair an Opportunity, by excluding all Blacks and Tawneys, of increasing the lovely White and Red? (Cited in Perea, 1995, p. 973)

Or consider the views of Thomas Jefferson, who was concerned about the presence of Africans in America, whom he referred to as an impure "blot" on the purity of the land:

> . . . it is impossible not to look forward to distant times, when our rapid multiplication will expand itself . . . & cover the whole northern, if not the southern continent, with a people speaking the same language, governed in similar forms, & by similar laws; *nor can we contemplate with satisfaction either blot or mixture on that surface.* (Cited in Perea, 1995, p. 974)

Armed with Protestant Hebralism; an Augustinian conviction; a Spartan virtue of service; an antinomian iconoclasm; a classical republicanist image of independence; and models of classical character colored by Lycurgus, Cato the Elder, and Calvin,

Jefferson hid his racism under the higher calling of establishing God's New Jerusalem on the soil of America (Murphy, 1996). Not only was Thomas Jefferson a mean-spirited racist and slave owner but arguably he can be considered the central ideological founder of American apartheid. He advocated an approach to democracy that was inspired by a mystical reading of the French Revolution, that justified mass slaughter in the name of liberty and justice for whites only. It's perhaps no coincidence that when Timothy McVeigh was arrested driving away from Oklahoma City on the day the Federal Building was bombed, he was wearing a T-shirt that bore the celebrated words of Jefferson: "the tree of liberty must be refreshed from time to time by the blood of patriots and tyrants." While Jefferson was surely against the practice of slavery, he unhesitatingly called for the banishment of free blacks from the United States since he believed that "nature, habit, opinion has drawn indelible lines of distinction" between white people and black people such that they "cannot live in the same government" (O'Brien, p. 57).

Jefferson preached against racism yet he had one of his many slaves, James Hubbard, severely flogged for escaping. In addition, he proposed an amendment to the Virginia legal code that would ban free blacks from coming to Virginia of their own accord or taking up residence for more than a year. His amendment was rejected by his contemporaries as being too severe. Jefferson had even proposed that white women who had children by black fathers were to be ordered out of Virginia within a year of the child's birth. Failure to leave the state would place these women "out of the protection of the law" which meant, of course, that they could be lynched. Jefferson also suggested that the government purchase newborn slaves from their owners, and pay for their maintenance until the children could work off their debt up to their date of deportation to Santo Domingo (O'Brien, 1996). Fortunately, these other suggestions were also rejected by his contemporaries.

Not to be outdone in the racist department, we have Senator John Calhoun, speaking on the Senate floor in 1848, where he opposed annexation by the United States of land belonging to Mexico on the grounds of preserving a homogeneous white nation:

> I know further, sir, that we have never dreamt of incorporating into our Union any but the Caucasian race—the free white race. To incorporate Mexico, would be the very first instance of the kind of incorporating an Indian race; . . . I protest against such a union as that! *Ours, sir, is the Government of a white race.* (Cited in Perea, 1995, p. 976)

Compare the ideological logic behind California's Proposition 187 with the statements provided by Calhoun, Jefferson, Franklin, and Buchanan. Compare, too, Proposition 187's logic to its precursor—California's 1855 "Greaser Act." The "Greaser Act" was an antiloitering law that applied to "all persons who are commonly known as 'Greasers,' or the issue of Spanish and Indian blood . . . and who go armed and are not peaceable and quiet persons" (cited in López, p. 145).

This is the same racist logic that fueled David Duke's 1992 comments: ". . . that immigrants 'mongrelize' our culture and dilute our values" (Cited in López, p. 143).

Recent comments made by Duke during an appearance in California in 1996, were in support of Proposition 209, an anti-affirmative action effort at creating a "colorblind" society. This effort has been orchestrated by Ward Connerly, an African American, who is a University of California Regent and chairman of the Proposition 209 initiative. In addition to accusing minority men of raping white women "by the thousands" and claiming that black New Orleans police officers rape and kill local citizens, Duke remarked:

> I don't want California to look like Mexico . . . I don't want to have their pollution. I don't want the corruption. I don't want their disease. I don't want their superstition. I don't want us to look like that country. If we continue this alien invasion, we will be like Mexico. (Bernstein, 1996, A14)

Duke exhibits a perspective that hasn't changed since the days of the Zoot Suit massacre, Operation Wetback, and when public Los Angeles swimming pools were frequently drained by whites after they were used by Mexican Americans. It is a perspective also shared by the British extreme right, who sexualize racism in order to "generate fear among women and masculine protectiveness among men" in relation to the presence of black men in British inner-cities (Rattansi, 1994, p. 63). Such perspectives connote earlier ideas of the Empire as a dangerous place where white women need protection (Rattansi, p. 63). One example is a story that appeared in the National Front youth newspaper, *Bulldog*, which was titled: "Black pimps force White girls into prostitution" and which exhorted: "White Man! You have a Duty to Protect Your Race, Homeland and Family" (p. 63). Of course, this fear of the rape of the white woman is not projected solely onto the African American male. Underwriting Duke's comments on Mexico, for instance, was the image of the Mexican as rapist and beast. In his discussion of the relationship between San Diegans and Tijuanans, Ramón Gutiérrez describes how Tijuana—"as a place of unruly and transgressive bodies" (1996, p. 256)—has become fixed in the American psyche. He reports that "Tijuana first developed as an escape valve for the sexually repressed and regulated American Protestant social body of San Diego" (p. 255). He writes that "the international boundary between Mexico and the United States has long been imagined as a border that separates a pure from an impure body, a virtuous body from a sinful one, a monogamous conjugal body regulated by the law of marriage from a criminal body given to fornication, adultery, prostitution, bestiality, and sodomy" (p. 255–256).

While the United States is constructed as a country governed by nature and the law, such codes of civility that regulate kinship and the body are thought not to exist in Mexico, where only unregulated desire and criminality exist to menace all who come into contact with Mexicans. The image of the undocumented worker as an illegal alien, as a "migrant" living in squalor, spreading disease, raping white women, extorting lunch money from white school children, creating squatter communities, hanging out in shopping centers, forcing Anglo schools to adopt bilingual education programs in order to accommodate the offspring of criminals and to appease the foreigner living on U.S. soil, has served to identify Mexicans with dirt, filth, and unnatural acts, while symbolically constructing Euro-American citizens as pure, law-abiding, and living in harmony with God's natural law (Gutiérrez, 1996).

One of the nation's relatively unblemished heroes of history is Woodrow Wilson. Many U.S. citizens have little, if any, knowledge about Wilson's Palmer Raids against left-wing unions, his segregation of the federal government, and his military interventions in Mexico (eleven times beginning in 1914), Haiti in 1915, the Dominican Republic in 1916, Cuba in 1917, and Panama in 1918. Wilson also maintained forces in Nicaragua. Wilson was an unrepentant white supremacist who believed that black people were inferior to white people. In fact, Wilson ordered that black and white workers in federal government jobs be segregated. Wilson vetoed a clause on racial equality in the Covenant of the League of Nations. Wilson's wife told "darky" stories in cabinet meetings while Wilson's administration drafted a legislative program designed to curtail the civil rights of African Americans. Congress refused to pass it (Loewen, 1995). Wilson did manage to appoint southern whites to offices traditionally given to blacks. President Warren G. Harding was inducted into the Ku Klux Klan in a ceremony at the White House (Loewen, 1995). How many students can boast knowledge of this event? How can U.S. history books cover up these events, and hundreds of others, including the 1921 race riot in Tulsa, Oklahoma, in which whites dropped dynamite from an airplane onto a black community, destroying 1,100 homes and killing 75 people (Loewen, 1995)?

How can we forget the evils of slavery, including the 10,000 Native Americans shipped from Charleston, South Carolina, to the West Indies (in one year) in exchange for black slaves? Must we forget that the United States is a country conceived in slavery and baptized in racism?

The Protocols of the Learned Elders of Zion was a work that influenced another American hero—Henry Ford. His newspaper ran a series of anti-Semitic articles in the 1920s that were made available to the public in book form under the title, *The International Jew*. In this particular sense the United States is not "post-Fordist" at all. At least in the case of rightwing Christian movements, many who fervently believe that white people are the true Israelites, that blacks are subhuman, and that Jews are the issue of Satan. The organization known as Christian Identity is linked to British Israelism which began as a white supremacist Protestant organization in Victorian England. White Europeans were believed to be the twelve lost tribes of Israel. Like many post-millennial religions, Identity proclaims that God gave the Constitution of the United States to the white Christian Founding Fathers and only white Christian men can be true sovereign citizens of the Republic. Identity followers are set to destroy the "Beast"—the government of the United States, in order to hasten forth Armageddon (Southern Poverty Law Center, 1996). Some members of Pat Robertson's Christian Coalition are aligned with the Patriot movement. This movement wants to establish God's law on Earth, which in the view of some of the members of the movement, calls for the execution of homosexuals, adulterers, juvenile delinquents, and blasphemers (Southern Poverty Law Center, 1996). This not an attack on the Bible, but on some groups who profess ownership on its meanings.

Buchanan, Duke, Pete Wilson, and countless other conservative politicians currently enjoying considerable popularity among growing sectors of the United States population owe a great deal to the racist perspectives that they have inherited from historical figures such as Jefferson, Franklin, and Lincoln who have been sanctified and haigiographied in the larger political culture. It appears that it is as patriotic now for white people to proclaim racist sentiments as it was 150 years ago. Today, however, one has to camouflage one's racism in deceptive and sophisticated ways by hiding it in a call for family values, a common culture of decency, and a "colorblind" society, but the racist formations underwriting such a call are clearly in evidence to the discerning cultural critic.

The concept of "whiteness" became lodged in the discursive crucible of colonial identity by the early 1860s. Whiteness at that time had become a marker for measuring inferior and superior races. Interestingly, Genghis Khan, Attila the Hun, and Confucius were at this time considered as "white." "Blackness" was evaluated positively in European iconography from the twelfth to the fifteenth centuries, but after the seventeenth century and the rise of European colonialism, blackness became conveniently linked to inferiority (Cashmore, 1996). For instance, during the sixteenth and seventeenth centuries, blood purity (*limpieza de sangre*) became raised to a metaphysical—perhaps even sacerdotal—status, as it became a principle used to peripheralize Indians, Moors, and Jews.

Blackness was not immediately associated with slavery. In the United States, the humanistic image of Africans created by the abolitionist movement was soon countered by new types of racial signification in which white skin was identified with racial superiority. Poor Europeans were sometimes indentured and were in some sense *de facto* slaves. They occupied the same economic categories as African slaves and were held in equal contempt by the lords of the plantation and legislatures (Cashmore, 1996). However, poor Europeans were invited to align themselves with the plantocracy as "white" in order to avoid the most severe forms of bondage. This strategy helped plantation owners form a stronger social control apparatus as hegemony was achieved by offering "race privileges" to poor whites as acknowledgment of their loyalty to the colonial land (Cashmore, 1996).

By the early twentieth century, European maritime empires controlled over half of the land (72 million square kilometers) and a third of the world's population (560 million people). Seventy-five million Africans died during the centuries-long transatlantic slave trade (West, 1993). The logics of empire are still with us, bound to the cultural fabric of our daily being-in-the-world; woven into our posture toward others; connected to the lenses of our eyes; folded into the sinewy depths of our musculature; dipped in the chemical reactions that excite and calm us; structured into the language of our perceptions. We cannot easily will our racist logics away. We need to work hard to eradicate them. We need to struggle with a formidable resolve in order to overcome that which we are afraid to confirm exists, let alone confront, in the battleground of our souls.

According to Alex Callinicos (1993), racial differences are invented. Racism occurs when the characteristics that justify discrimination are held to be inherent in the oppressed group. This form of oppression is peculiar to capitalist societies; it arises in the circumstances surrounding industrial capitalism and the attempt to acquire a large labor force. Callinicos points to three main conditions for the existence of racism as outlined by Marx: economic competition between workers, the appeal of racist ideology to white workers, and efforts of the capitalist class to establish and maintain racial divisions among workers. Capitalism's constantly changing demands for different kinds of labor can only be met through immigration. Callinicos remarks that "racism offers for workers of the oppressing 'race' the imaginary compensation for the exploitation they suffer of belonging to the '*ruling* nation'" (1993, p. 39). Callinicos notes the way in which Marx grasped how racial divisions between "native" and immigrant workers could weaken the working class. United States politicians take advantage of this division, which the capitalist class understands and manipulates only too well. George Bush, Jesse Helms, Pat Buchanan, Phil Gramm, David Duke, and Pete Wilson have effectively used racism to divide the working class. At this point you might be asking yourselves: Doesn't racism pre-date capitalism? Here we agree with Callinicos that the heterophobia associated with pre-capitalist societies was not the same as modern racism. Pre-capitalist slave and feudal societies of classical Greece and Rome did not rely on racism to justify the use of slaves. The Greeks and Romans did not have theories of white superiority. If they did, that would have been unsettling news to Septimius Severus, Roman emperor from AD 193 to 211, who was, as many historians claim, a black man. Racism emerged during a key development of capitalism during the seventeenth and eighteenth centuries on colonial plantations in the New World where slave labor stolen from Africa was used to produce tobacco, sugar, and cotton for the global consumer market (Callinicos, 1993). Callinicos cites Eric Williams who remarks: "Slavery was not born of racism; rather, racism was the consequence of slavery" (cited in Callinicos, p. 24). Racism emerged as the ideology of the plantocracy. It began with the class of sugar–planters and slave merchants that dominated England's Caribbean colonies. Racism developed out of the "systemic slavery" of the New World. The "natural inferiority" of Africans was a way that whites justified enslaving them. According to Callinicos:

> Racism offers white workers the comfort of believing themselves part of the dominant group; it also provides, in times of crisis, a ready made scapegoat, in the shape of the oppressed group. Racism thus gives white workers a particular identity, and one moreover which unites them with white capitalists. We have here, then, a case of the kind of "imagined community" discussed by Benedict Anderson in his influential analysis of nationalism. (1993, p. 38)

To abolish racism, we need to abolish global capitalism. Callinicos is very clear on that point.

I do not maintain, as does Jean Baudrillard, that labor has been transformed simply into a sign among other signs, into a structure of obedience to a code. Furthermore, I do not believe that capitalism has passed from a phase where labor is exploited to one where it is only marketed and consumed. I do not want to reduce "being a worker" to its sign value or a practice of unequal gift exchange as Baudrillard suggests. The enemy of the worker is not the code so much as the social relations of production. Within much of the analysis by postmodernists, regimes of signification have been wrenched from their material location in narratives of human struggle. They are discovered hovering helter-skelter over the turmoil of the real. I do not believe, as do some postmodern theorists such as Baudrillard, that within postmodern cultures human needs are irrelevant. Indeed, material and symbolic needs are vitally important.

The development of a global postmodern culture has done little to undermine the pervasive destructive capacity for exploitation that accompanies capitalism. As critical educators, we must never deflect our glances from the global mode of production or the dangers of internationalized class domination.

The educational left has failed to address sufficiently the issue of whiteness and the insecurities that young whites harbor regarding their future during times of diminishing economic expectations. With their "racially coded and divisive rhetoric," neoconservatives may be able to enjoy tremendous success in helping insecure young white populations develop white identity along racist lines. Consider the comments by David Stowe who writes:

> The only people nowadays who profess any kind of loyality to whiteness *qua* whiteness (as opposed to whiteness as an incidental feature of some more specific identity) are Christian Identity types and Ayran Nation diehards. Anecdotal surveys reveal that few white Americans mention whiteness as a quality that they think much about or particularly value. In their day-to-day cultural preferences—food, music, clothing, sports, hairstyles—the great majority of American whites display no particular attachment to white things. There does seem to be a kind of emptiness at the core of whiteness. (1996, p. 74)

Cornel West has identified three white-supremacist logics: the Judeo-Christian racist logic; the scientific racist logic and the psychosexual racist logic. The Judeo-Christian racist logic is reflected in the Biblical story of Ham, Son of Noah, who, in failing to cover Noah's nakedness, had his progeny blackened by God. In this logic, unruly behaviour and chaotic rebellion are linked to racist practices. The "scientific" racist logic is identified with the evaluation of physical bodies in light of Greco-Roman standards. Within this logic, racist practices are identified with physical ugliness, cultural deficiency, and intellectual inferiority. The psychosexual racist logic identifies black people with Western sexual discourses associated with sexual prowess, lust, dirt, and subordination. A serious question is raised by West's typology in relation to the construction of whiteness: What are the historically concrete and sociologically specific ways that white supremacist discourses are guided by Western philosophies of identity and universality and capitalist relations of production and consumption? West has located racist practices in the commentaries by the church fathers on the Song of Solomon and the Ywain narratives in medieval Brittany, to name just a few historical sources. West has also observed that human bodies were classified according to skin color as early as 1684 (before the rise of modern capitalism) by French physician François Bernier. The famous eighteenth-century naturalist, Carolus Linnaeus, produced the first major written account of racial division in *Natural System* (1735). This is different from institutionalized racism within contemporary capitalism.

People don't discriminate against groups because they are different but rather the act of discrimination constructs categories of difference that hierarchically locate people as "superior" or "inferior" and then universalizes and naturalizes such differences. When I refer to whiteness or to the cultural logics of whiteness, I need to qualify what I mean. Here I adopt Ruth Frankenberg's injunction that cultural practices considered to be white need to be seen as contingent, historically produced, and transformable. White culture is not monolithic, and its borders must be understood as malleable and porous. It is the historically specific confluence of economic, geopolitical, and ethnocultural processes. According to Alastair Bonnett (1996), whiteness is neither a discrete entity nor a fixed, asocial category. Rather, it is an "immutable social construction" (1996, p. 98). White identity is an ensemble of discourses, contrapuntal and contradictory. Whiteness—and the meanings attributed to it—are always in a state of flux and fibrillation. Bonnett notes that "even if one ignores the transgressive youth or ethnic borderlands of Western identities, and focuses on the 'center' or 'heartlands' of 'whiteness,' one will discover racialized subjectivities that, far from being settled and confident, exhibit a constantly reformulated panic over the meaning of 'whiteness' and the defining presence of 'nonwhiteness' within it" (1996, p. 106). According to Frankenberg, white culture is a material and discursive space that

> is inflected by nationhood, such that whiteness and Americanness, though by no means coterminous, are profoundly shaped by one another. . . .
>
> . . . Similarly, whiteness, masculinity, and femininity are coproducers of one another, in ways that are, in their turn, crosscut by class and by the histories of racism and colonialism. (1993, p. 233)

Whiteness needs to be seen as *cultural*, as *processual*, and not ontologically different from processes that are non-white. It works, as Frankenberg notes, as "an unmarked marker of others' differentness—whiteness not so much void or formlessness as norm" (p. 198). Whiteness functions through social practices of assimilation and cultural homogenization; whiteness is linked to the expansion of capitalism in the sense that "whiteness signifies the production and consumption of commodities under capitalism" (p. 203). Yet capitalism in the United States needs to be understood as contingently white, since white people participate in maintaining the hegemony of institutions and practices of racial dominance in different ways and to greater or lesser degrees. Frankenberg identifies the key discursive repertoires of whiteness as follows:

> modes of naming culture and difference associated with west European colonial expansion; second, elements of "essentialist" racism . . . linked to European colonialism but also critical as rationale for Anglo settler colonialism and segregationism in what is now the USA; third, "assimilationist" or later "color- and power-evasive" strategies for thinking through race first articulated in the early decades of this century; and, fourth, . . . "race-cognizant" repertoires that emerged in the latter half of the twentieth century and were linked both to U.S. liberation movements and to broader global struggles for decolonization. (1993, p. 239)

Whiteness is a sociohistorical form of consciousness, given birth at the nexus of capitalism, colonial rule, and the emergent relationships among dominant and subordinate groups. Whiteness operates by means of its constitution as a universalizing authority by which the hegemonic white bourgeois subject appropriates the right to speak on behalf of everyone who is nonwhite, while denying voice and agency to these

Others in the name of civilized humankind. Whiteness constitutes and demarcates ideas, feelings, knowledges, social practices, cultural formations, and systems of intelligibility that are identified with or attributed to white people and which are invested in by white people as "white." Whiteness is also a refusal to acknowledge how white people are implicated in certain social relations of privilege and relations of domination and subordination. Whiteness, then, can be considered as a form of social amnesia associated with certain modes of subjectivity within particular social sites considered to be normative. As a lived domain of meaning, whiteness represents particular social and historical formations that are reproduced through specific discursive and material processes and circuits of desire and power. Whiteness can be considered to be a conflictual sociocultural, sociopolitical, and geopolitical process that animates commonsensical practical action in relationship to dominant social practices and normative ideological productions. Whiteness constitutes the selective tradition of dominant discourses about race, class, gender, and sexuality hegemonically reproduced. Whiteness has become the substance and limit of our common sense articulated as cultural consensus. As an ideological formation transformed into a principle of life, into an ensemble of social relations and practices, whiteness needs to be understood as conjunctural, as a composite social hieroglyph that shifts in denotative and connotative emphasis, depending upon how its elements are combined and upon the contexts in which it operates.

Whiteness is not a pre-given, unified ideological formation but is a multifaceted collective phenomenon resulting from the relationship between the self and the ideological discourses that are constructed out of the surrounding local and global cultural terrain. Whiteness is fundamentally Euro- or western-centric in its episteme, as it is articulated in complicity with the pervasively imperializing logic of empire.

Whiteness in the United States can be understood largely through the social consequences it provides for those who are considered to be nonwhite. Such consequences can be seen in the criminal justice system, in prisons, in schools, and in the board rooms of corporations such as Texaco. It can be defined in relation to immigration practices and social policies and practices of sexism, racism, and nationalism. It can be seen historically in widespread acts of imperialism and genocide and linked to an erotic economy of "excess." Eric Lott writes:

> In rationalized Western societies, becoming "white" and male seems to depend upon the remanding of enjoyment, the body, an aptitude for pleasure. It is the other who is always putatively "excessive" in this respect, whether through exotic food, strange and noisy music, outlandish bodily exhibitions, or unremitting sexual appetite. Whites in fact organize their own enjoyment through the other, Slavoj Zizek has written, and access pleasure precisely by fantasizing about the other's "special" pleasure. Hatred of the other arises from the necessary hatred of one's own excess; ascribing this excess to the "degraded" other *and indulging* it—by imagining, incorporating, or impersonating the other—one conveniently and surreptitiously takes and disavows pleasure at one and the same time. This is the mixed erotic economy, what Homi Bhabha terms the "ambivalence" of American whiteness. (1993: 482)

Whiteness is a type of articulatory practice that can be located in the convergence of colonialism, capitalism, and subject formation. It both fixes and sustains discursive regimes that represent self and "other"; that is, whiteness represents a regime of differences that produces and racializes an abject other. In other words, whiteness is a discursive regime that enables real effects to take place. Whiteness displaces blackness and brownness—specific forms of non-whiteness—into signifiers of deviance and criminality within social, cultural, cognitive, and political contexts. White subjects discursively construct identity through producing, naming, "bounding," and marginalizing a range of others (Frankenberg, 1993, p. 193).

Whiteness constitutes unmarked patriarchal, heterosexist, and Euro-American practices that have negative effects on and consequences for those who do not participate in them. Inflected by nationhood, whiteness can be considered an ensemble of discursive practices constantly in the process of being constructed, negotiated, and changed. Yet it functions to instantiate a structured exclusion of certain groups from social arenas of normativity. Coco Fusco remarks: "To raise the specter of racism in the here and now, to suggest that despite their political beliefs and sexual preferences, white people operate within, and benefit from, white supremacist social structures is still tantamount to a declaration of war" (1995, p. 76).

Whiteness is not only mythopoetical in the sense that it constructs a totality of illusions formed around the ontological superiority of the Euro-American subject, it is also metastructural in that it operates across specific differences; it solders fugitive, break-away discourses and re-hegemonizes them. Consumer utopias and global capital flows rearticulate whiteness by means of relational differences.

Whiteness is dialectically reinitiated across epistemological fissures, contradictions, and oppositions through new regimes of desire that connect the consumption of goods to the everyday logic of Western democracy. The cultural encoding of the typography of whiteness is achieved by remapping Western European identity onto economic transactions, by recementing desire to capitalist flows, by concretizing personal history into collective memory linked to place, to a myth of origin. Whiteness offers a safe "home" for those imperiled by the flux of change.

Whiteness can be considered as a conscription of the process of positive self-identification into the service of domination through inscribing identity into an onto-epistemological framework of "us" against "them." For those who are nonwhite, the seduction of whiteness can produce a self-definition that disconnects the subject from his or her history of oppression and struggle, exiling identity into the unmoored, chaotic realm of abject otherness (and tacitly accepts the positioned superiority of the Western subject). Whiteness provides the subject with a known boundary that places nothing "off limits," yet which provides a fantasy of belongingness. It's not that whiteness signifies preferentially one pole of the white–nonwhite binarism. Rather, whiteness seduces the subject to accept the idea of polarity itself as the limit-text of identity, as the constitutive foundation of subjectivity.

Whiteness offers coherency and stability in a world in which capital produces regimes of desire linked to commodity utopias where fantasies of omnipotence must find a stable home. Of course, the "them" is always located within the "us." The marginalized are always foundational to the stability of the central actors. The excluded in this case establish the condition of existence of the included. So we find that it is impossible to separate the identities of both oppressor and oppressed. They depend upon each other. To resist whiteness means developing a politics of difference.

Since we lack the full semantic availability to understand whiteness and to resist it, we need to rethink difference and identity outside of sets of binary oppositions. We need to view identity as coalitional, as collective, as processual, as grounded in the struggle for social justice.

While an entire range of discursive repertoires may come into play, jostling against, superseding, and working in conjunction with each other, white identity is constructed in relation to an individual's personal history, geopolitical situatedness, contextually specific practices, and his or her location in the materiality of the racial order. In other words, many factors determine which discursive configurations are at work and the operational modalities present.

Alastair Bonnett notes that a reified notion of whiteness "enables 'white' people to occupy a privileged location in antiracist debate; they are allowed the luxury of being passive observers, of being altruistically motivated, of knowing that their 'racial' identity might be reviled and lambasted but never actually made slippery, torn open, or, indeed, abolished" (1996, p. 98). Bonnett further notes:

> To dismantle "blackness" but leave the force it was founded to oppose unchallenged is to display both a political and theoretical naivety. To subvert "blackness" without subverting "whiteness" reproduces and reinforces the "racial" myths, and the "racial" dominance, associated with the latter. (1996, p. 99)

In his important volume, *Psychoanalytic Marxism* (1993) Eugene Victor Wolfenstein describes the whiteness of domination as the "one fixed point" of America's many racisms. He argues that whiteness is a social designation and a "history disguised as biology" (1993, p. 331). Whiteness is also an attribute of language. Wolfenstein claims that

> Languages have skin colors. There are white nouns and verbs, white grammar and white syntax. In the absence of challenges to linguistic hegemony, indeed, language is white. If you don't speak white you will not be heard, just as when you don't look white you will not be seen. (1993, p. 331)

Describing white racists as "virtuosos of denigration," Wolfenstein maintains that the language of white racism illustrates "a state of war" (p. 333). Yet the battles are fought through lies and deceit. One such lie is the idea of "colorblindness." Wolfenstein notes that colorblindness constitutes more than a matter of conscious deceit:

> White racism is rather a mental disorder, an ocular disease, an opacity of the soul that is articulated with unintended irony in the idea of "colorblindness." To be colorblind is the highest form of racial false consciousness, a denial of both difference and domination. But one doesn't have to be color blind to be blinded by white racism. . . . Black people see themselves in white mirrors, white people see black people as their own photographic negatives. (1993, p. 334)

Wolfenstein suggests two epistemological tasks be undertaken; black people need to look away from the white mirror; white people need to attempt to see black people as they see themselves and to see themselves as they are seen by other black people. Wolfenstein links white racism to what he terms "epidermal fetishism." Epidermal fetishism reduces people to their skin color and renders them invisible. It is a form of social character that is established within a process of exchange and circulation. As such, whiteness represents the super-ego (the standard of social value, self-worth, and morality). Since the ego is affirmatively reflected in the super-ego, it also must be white. Therefore blackness is repressed and "becomes identified with the unwanted or bad parts of the self" (p. 336). Wolfenstein writes:

> At the level of social character, white racism is self-limiting for white people, self-destructive for black people. White people alienate their sensuous potentialities from themselves. They are devitalized and sterilized. Blackness, officially devalued, comes to embody their estranged life and desire. They are able, however, to see themselves reflected in the mirrors of selfhood. But if black people have their selfhood structured by the whitened-out form of social character, they become fundamentally self-negating. Their blackness, hated and despised, must be hidden away. Hair straighteners and skin lighteners testify to the desire to go further and eradicate blackness altogether. (1993, p. 337)

The incorporeal luminescence of whiteness is achieved, according to Wolfenstein, by the subsumption of blackness within whiteness. What cannot be subsumed and digested is excreted. White people both despise and lust after blackness. White people need to recognize the discursive formations and material social relations that produce them as racialized subjects. This is crucial. It takes both courage and insight to accomplish this task. It is a commitment to understanding what society has made of us that we no longer wish to be part of us.

It is important to recognize that white racism is neither purely systemic nor purely individual. Rather, it is a complex interplay of collective interests and desires. White racism in this instance "becomes a rational means to collective ends" (p. 341) when viewed from the standpoint of ruling class interests. Yet for the white working class it is irrational and a form of false consciousness. White racism also circumscribes rational action for black people in that they are encouraged to act in terms of their racial rather than class interests.

Ian F. Haney López's book, *White by Law*, offers a view of white transparency and invisibility that is at odds with the thesis that whites are growing more conscious of their whiteness. López cites an incident at a feminist legal conference in which participants were asked to pick two or three words to describe themselves. All the women of color selected at least one racial term, but not one white woman selected a term referring to her race. This prompted Angela Harris to remark that only white people in this society have the luxury of having no color. An informal study conducted at Harvard Law School underscores Harris's remark. A student interviewer asked ten African Americans and ten white Americans how they identified themselves. Unlike the African Americans, most of the white Americans did not consciously factor in their "whiteness" as a crucial or even tangential part of their identity.

López argues that one is not born white but becomes white "by virtue of the social context in which one finds oneself, to be sure, but also by virtue of the choices one makes" (1996, p. 190). But how can one born into the culture of whiteness, who is defined as white, undo that whiteness? López addresses this question in his formulation of whiteness. López locates whiteness in the overlapping of *chance* (e.g., features and ancestry that we have no control over, morphology); *context* (context-specific meanings that are attached to race, the social setting in which races are recognized, constructed, and contested); and *choice* (conscious choices with regard to the morphology and ancestries of social actors) in order to "alter the readability of their identity" (1996, p. 191).

In other words, López maintains that chance and context are not racially determinative. López notes that:

> Racial choices must always be made from within specific contexts, where the context materially and ideologically circumscribes the range of available choices and also delimits the significance of the act. Nevertheless, these are racial choices, if sometimes only in their overtone or subtext, because they resonate in the complex of meanings associated with race. Given the thorough suffusion of race throughout society, in the daily dance of life we constantly make racially meaningful decisions. (1996, p. 193)

López's perspective offers new promise, it would seem, for abolishing racism since it refuses to locate whiteness only as antiracism's "other." I agree with Bonnett when he remarks that "to continue to cast 'whites' as antiracism's 'other,' as the eternally guilty and/or altruistic observers of 'race' equality work, is to maintain 'white' privilege and undermine the movement's intellectual and practical reach and utility" (1996, p. 107). In other words, whites need to ask themselves to what extent their identity is a function of their whiteness in the process of their ongoing daily lives and what choices they might make to escape whiteness. López outlines—productively in my view— three steps in dismantling whiteness. They are worth quoting in full:

> First, Whites must overcome the omnipresent effects of transparency and of the naturalization of race in order to recognize the many racial aspects of their identity, paying particular attention to the daily acts that draw upon and in turn confirm their whiteness. Second, they must recognize and accept the personal and social consequences of breaking out of a White identity. Third, they must embark on a daily process of choosing against Whiteness. (López, 1996, p. 193)

Of course, the difficulty of taking such steps is partly due to the fact that, as López notes, the unconscious acceptance of a racialized identity is predicated upon a circular definition of the self. It's hard to step outside of whiteness if you are white because of all the social, cultural and economic privileges that accompany whiteness. Yet, whiteness must be dismantled if the United States is to overcome racism. Lipsitz remarks:

> Those of us who are "white" can only become part of the solution if we recognize the degree to which we are already part of the problem—not because of our race, but because of our possessive investment in it. (1995, p. 384)

An editorial in the book, *Race Traitor*, puts it thus:

> The key to solving the social problems of our age is to abolish the white race. Until that task is accomplished, even partial reform will prove elusive, because white influence permeates every issue in U.S. society, whether domestic or foreign. . . . Race itself is a product of social discrimination; so long as the white race exists, all movements against racism are doomed to fail. (1996, p. 10)

I am acutely aware that people of color might find troubling the idea that white populations can simply reinvent themselves by making the simple choice of not being white. Of course, this is not what López and others appear to be saying. The choices one makes and the reinvention one aspires to as a race traitor are not "simple" nor are they easy choices for groups of whites to make. Yet from the perspective of some people of color, offering the choice to white people of opting out of their whiteness could seem to set up an easy path for those who don't want to assume responsibility for their privilege as white people. Indeed, there is certainly cause for concern. David Roediger captures some of this when he remarks: "Whites cannot fully renounce whiteness even if they want to" (1994, p. 16). Whites are, after all, still accorded the privileges of being white even as they ideologically renounce their whiteness, often with the best of intentions. Yet the possibility that whites might seriously consider nonwhiteness and antiwhite struggle is too important to ignore, to dismiss as wishful thinking, or to associate with a fashionable form of code-switching. Choosing not to be white is not an easy option for white people, like deciding to make a change in one's wardrobe. To understand the processes involved in the racialization of identity and to consistently choose nonwhiteness is a difficult act of apostasy, for it implies a heightened sense of social criticism and an unwavering commitment to social justice (Roediger, 1994). Of course, the question needs to be asked: If we can choose to be nonwhite, then can we choose to be black or brown? Insofar as blackness is a social construction (often "parasitic" on whiteness) then I would answer yes. Theologian James H. Cone, author of *A Black Theology of Liberation*, urges white folks to free themselves form the shackles of their whiteness. He writes:

> . . . if whites expect to be able to say anything relevant to the self-determination of the black community, it will be necessary for them to destroy their whiteness by becoming members of an oppressed community. Whites will be free only when they become new persons—when their white being has passed away and they are created anew in black being. When this happens, they are no longer white but free. . . . (1986, p. 97)

But again I would stress that becoming black or brown is not a "mere" choice but a self-consciously political choice, a spiritual choice, and a critical choice. To choose blackness or brownness merely as a way to escape the stigma of whiteness and to avoid responsibility for owning whiteness, is still very much an act of whiteness. To choose blackness or brownness as a way of politically disidentifying with white privilege and instead of identifying with and participating in the social struggles of nonwhite peoples is, on the other hand, an act of transgression, a traitorous act that reveals a fidelity to the struggle for justice. Lipsitz sums up the problems and the promise of the abolition of whiteness as follows:

> Neither conservative "free market" policies nor liberal social democratic reforms can solve the "white problem" in America because both of them reinforce the possessive investment in whiteness. But an explicitly antiracist pan-ethnic movement that acknowledges the existence and power of whiteness might make some important changes. Pan-ethnic, antiracist coalitions have a long history in the United States—in the political activism of John Brown, Soujourner Truth, and the Magon brothers, among others—but we also have a rich cultural tradition of pan-ethnic antiracism connected to civil rights activism . . . efforts by whites to fight racism, not out of sympathy for someone else but out of a sense of self-respect and simple justice, have never completely disappeared; they remain available as models for the present. (1995, p. 384)

Because ethnic identity is constructed diacritically, whiteness requires the denigration of blackness and browness (López). Therefore I do not argue for the construction of a positive white identity, no matter how well intentioned. Rather, I argue against celebrating whiteness in any form. To claim whiteness as an identity is to claim a social position of domination, no matter how you rationalize it. As López notes, whiteness retains its positive meanings only by denying itself. I call for the denial, disassembly, and destruction of whiteness as we know it and advocate its rearticulation as a form of critical agency dedicated to social struggle in the interests of the oppressed.

The work of critical multiculturalists attempts to unsettle both conservative assaults on multiculturalism and liberal paradigms of multiculturalism, the latter of which in my view simply repackage conservative and neo-liberal ideologies under a discursive mantle of diversity. In undertaking such a project, I have tried in a modest way to advance a critical pedagogy that will service a form of postcolonial hybridity.

It is true that the concept of hybridity has been used in a powerful way to counter essentialized attempts at creating monolithic and "authentic" forms of identity (McLaren, 1995; Hicks, 1991). However, Fusco rightly reminds us:

> Too often . . . the postcolonial celebration of hybridity has been interpreted as the sign that no further concern about the politics of representation and cultural exchange is needed. With ease, we lapse back into the integrationist rhetoric of the 1960s, and conflate hybridity with parity. (1995, p. 76)

Since not all hybridities are equal, we must attach to the term an ideological tacit nominal qualifier (Radhakrishnan, 1996). In making this assertion, Ragagopalan Radhakrishnan provides us with an important qualification. He maintains that we should distinguish between a metropolitan version of hybridity and postcolonial hybridity. Whereas the former is a ludic form of capricious self-styling, the latter is a critical identitarian mode. Metropolitan hybridity, notes Radhakrishnan, is "characterized by an intransitive and immanent sense of jouissance" while postcolonial hybridity is marked by a "frustrating search for constituency and a legitimate political identity" (1996, p. 159). Metropolitan hybridity is not "subjectless" or neutral but is a structure of identitarian thinking informed by the cultural logic of the dominant West. Postcolonial hybridity, on the other hand, seeks authenticity in "a third space that is complicitous neither with the deracinating imperatives of Westernization nor with theories of a static, natural, and single-minded autochthony" (p. 162). It is within such a perspective that educators are called to create *una pedagogia fronteriza.*

Critical multiculturalism as a point of intersection with critical pedagogy supports the struggle for a postcolonial hybridity. Gómez-Peña captures the concept of postcolonial hybridity when he conceptually maps what he calls the "New World Border":

> a great trans- and intercontinental border zone, a place in which no centers remain. It's all margins, meaning there are no "others," or better said, the only true "others" are those who resist fusion, *mestizaje,* and cross-cultural dialogue. In this utopian cartography, hybridity is the dominant culture; Spanish, Franglé, and Gringoñol are *linguas francas;* and monoculture is a culture of resistance practiced by a stubborn or scared minority. (1996, p. 7)

A revolutionary multiculturalism must engage what Enrique Dussel (1993) calls "the Reason of the Other." The debates over modernity and postmodernity have a different set of valences in Latinoamerica for *los olvidados,* for the peripheralized, for the marginalized, and for the wretched of the earth. Dussel writes about this distinction, from his own Latin American context:

> Unlike the postmodernists, we do not propose a critique of reason as such but we do accept their critique of a violent, coercive, genocidal reason. We do not deny the rational kernel of the universalist rationalism of the Enlightenment, only its irrational moment as sacrificial myth. We do not negate reason in other words, but the irrationality of the violence generated by the myth of modernity. Against postmodernist irrationalism, we affirm the "reason of the Other." (p. 55)

A revolutionary multiculturalism requires that we seek relationships of equality with peoples throughout the world. And this means coming to terms with our own history. It means having the courage to face the truth about the painful and often brutal realities of history. This means examining the horrors committed worldwide by those who have sought to justify their actions on various religious, political, racial, and nationalist grounds. It means condemning the genocide, torture, dispossession, and cruelty that have marked the history of many countries around the world. It also means examining our own past and present historical actions as a nation. We know from experience that one of the first casualties of war is truth, often followed by a motivated amnesia about the historical contexts surrounding conflicts in which we participate. While the United States is admired by many around the world, a significant number of people from other countries harbor a resentment towards this country. In many cases, such hatred has less to do with a jealousy of U.S. prosperity and freedom than with outrage at the ways in which the United States has treated oppressed peoples worldwide. Facing up to our shortcomings, as well as defending our considerable strengths as a nation, is a patriotic duty. In discussing our history we too often gloss over or ignore our own support of brutal dictatorships in Latin America, the Middle East, and elsewhere. In Latin America, for instance, the United States has supported regimes that are responsible for the torture and deaths of millions of peasants and indigenous peoples. The United States has condemned millions of innocent civilians to death through economic sanctions and embargos against Iraq, Afghanistan, and Cuba. Our assistance to repressive Arab and Islamic regimes has been shameful. Our support for Israel's 1982 invasion of Lebanon where 20,000 civilians lost their lives and where innocent victims fell prey to the massacres of Sabra and Shatila, and our refusal to protest the ongoing repressive practices against Palestinians in Israel, is a cause for much anger throughout the world. My point is pedagogical. More than ever, today we need to understand the world and our role in it from a global, internationalist perspective. Such an act is a necessary pedagogical condition in the struggle for a lasting world peace. To be critical about our own politics as well as the politics of other nations and groups is not an act of appeasing the enemies of the United States. Nor is it a justification for terrorism. Nobody deserves to be the victim of a terrorist attack. Terrorism is a horror that must be always condemned. Nor does this mean that a country does not have a moral and legal right to respond to terrorist actions or acts of war against them. It simply means that we must be prepared to take an honest look at the root causes of all wars in their broad historical specificity and to find ways to use the creative capacities of our citizens and the strength of our democracy in the best interests of the poor and the powerless both in the United States and throughout the world. To believe the flagwaving promotion of the role of the United States as the world's peacekeeper is to be misled by the dominant way of coding and mediating the public's perspectives on social reality; it is to mistake a shopworn and moth-infested myth as real, and to honor a belief that actually traduces the principles of what we regard as democracy and social justice.

There is pressure by powerful groups in the United States and the media to brand self-reflexive examinations of and critical introspection about U.S. complicity in the suffering of the poor and powerless in the so-called Third World as traitorous. To yield to such pressure will create a climate of repression within the United States similar to that which U.S. citizens have always associated with communist dictatorships. Current condemnations of leftist critique too often reflect the narrow and bigoted patrioteering found in the screeds of Limbaugh, Horowitz, Buchanan, and their vile ilk, who continue to serve as the custodians of a very racist and exploitative form of democratic life. It will take courage to persevere in such a reactionary climate. In his new book, *The Death of the West*, Pat Buchanan laments the falling population numbers of Western nations, and the supplanting of Western (white and Christian) populations with immigrants from Asia, Africa, and the Middle East. He implores Western women to assume their responsibility as racial breeders in order to prevent the Death of the West. Echoing the events of September 11, he argues that the foreign-born among us in the United States could very well be plotting to destroy America. Such pernicious nativism is growing in popularity.

We are called to work together as teachers and activists for a lasting democratic form of public life and to help in the struggle for world peace. Only when our struggle becomes collective will we have the means to change history. Our struggle must not stop at calling for better wages and living conditions for teachers and other workers but must anticipate an alternative to capitalism that will bring about a better chance for democracy to live up to its promise of freedom, prosperity, and social justice for all.

What I am advocating is a revolutionary multiculturalism that moves beyond the ludic, metrocentric focus on identities as hybrid and hyphenated assemblages of subjectivity that exist alongside or outside of the larger social totality. Revolutionary multiculturalism, as I am articulating the term, takes as its condition of possibility the capitalist world system; it moves beyond a monoculturalist multiculturalism that fails to address identity formation in a global context, and focuses instead on the idea that identities are shifting, changing, overlapping, and historically diverse (Shohat, 1995). Revolutionary multiculturalism is a politics of difference that is globally interdependent and raises questions about intercommunal alliances and coalitions. According to Ella Shohat, intercommunal coalitions are based on historically shaped affinities and the multicultural theory that underwrites such coalitionary politics needs "to avoid either falling into essentialist traps or being politically paralyzed by deconstructionist formulations" (1995, p. 177). Shohat articulates the challenge as follows:

> Rather than ask who can speak, then, we should ask how we can speak together, and more important, how we can move the dialog forward. How can diverse communities speak in concert? How might we interweave our voices, whether in chorus, in antiphony, in call and response, or in polyphony? What are the modes of collective speech? In this sense, it might be worthwhile to focus less on identity as something one "has," than on identification as something one "does." (1995, p. 177)

Revolutionary multiculturalism recognizes that the objective structures in which we live, the material relations tied to production in which we are situated, and the determinate conditions that produce us, are all reflected in our everyday lived experiences. In other words, lived experiences constitute more than subjective values, beliefs, and understandings; they are always mediated through ideological configurations of discourses, political economies of power and privilege, and the social division of labor. Revolutionary multiculturalism is a socialist-feminist multiculturalism that challenges the historically sedimented processes through which race, class, and gender identities are produced within capitalist society. Therefore, revolutionary multiculturalism is not limited to transforming attitudinal discrimination, but is dedicated to reconstituting the deep structures of political economy, culture, and power in contemporary social arrangements. It is not about reforming capitalist democracy but rather transforming it by cutting it at its joints and then rebuilding the social order from the vantage point of the oppressed.

Revolutionary multiculturalism must not only accommodate the idea of capitalism, it must also advocate a critique of capitalism and a struggle against it. The struggle for liberation on the basis of race and gender must not remain detached from the anticapitalist struggle. Often the call for diversity and pluralism by the apostles of postmodernism is a surrender to the ideological mystifications of capitalism. The fashionable apostasy of preaching difference from the citadels of postmodernist thought has dissolved resistance to the totalizing power of capitalist exploitation. In this regard, Ellen Meiksins Wood rightly warns:

> We should not confuse respect for the plurality of human experience and social struggles with a complete dissolution of historical causality, where there is nothing but diversity, difference and contingency, no unifying structures, no logic of process,

no capitalism and therefore no negation of it, no universal project of human emancipation. (1995, p. 263).

The challenge is to create at the level of everyday life a commitment to solidarity with the oppressed and an identification with past and present struggles against imperialism, against racism, against sexism, against homophobia, against all those practices of unfreedom associated with living in a white supremacist capitalist society. Participants in such a challenge become agents of history by living the moral commitment to freedom and justice, by maintaining a loyalty to the revolutionary domain of possibility, and by creating a collective voice out of the farthest reaching "we"—one that unites all those who suffer under capitalism, patriarchy, racism, and colonialism throughout the globe.

Living in Los Angeles is like being encysted in a surrealist hallucination. Yet as I look at the city from this cafe window, things don't seem that bad: Kid Frost pulsates through the airwaves; a 1964 Chevy Impala cruises the street in all its bravado lowrider beauty; the sun is shining bountifully on brown, black, and white skin (albeit prematurely aging the latter); my gas tank is full and the ocean is reachable before the heat gets too heavy and the streets get too packed. I'll take Olympic Boulevard toward Venice, searching for that glimmer of light in the eyes of strangers, seeking out that fertile space to connect, picking through that rag-and-bone shop of lost memories, and seizing that splinter of hope at the faultline of the impossible where the foundation of a new public sphere can be fashioned out of the rubble of concrete dreams. I dream with my fist stabbing the sun for a day when restitution of identity will not be brought about by revenge and violence but instead by a healing community; when labor-power will not have to be sold to a capitalist in order to pay for a day's meager rations; when factory seamstresses from Latin America no longer have to live in their cars or over-priced motel rooms; when there is no longer homelessness among full-time workers; when school policy and curricula are not driven by the corporate sector; when the notion of the white race is abolished without a trace and the capital-labor contradiction is replaced by freely associated labor and solidarity among races; and when the country is no longer run by morally bankrupt pro-business thugs but by workers themselves.

REFERENCES

Balibar, E., and Wallerstein, I. (1993). *Race, Nation, Class: Ambiguous Identities.* London and New York: Verso.

Balibar, E. (1996). "Is European Citizenship Possible?" *Public Culture*, No. 19, pp. 355–376.

Bannerji H. (1995). *Thinking Through.* Toronto, Canada: Women's Press.

Barrs, R. (1996). "The Real Story about How the Use of Crack Cocaine Exploded in South-Central." *New Times*, Sept. 12–18, Vol. 1, No. 4, p. 9.

Bauman, Z. (1992). *Mortality, Immortality and Other Life Strategies.* Stanford, CA: Stanford University Press.

Bauman, Z. (1996, May). "On Communitarians and Human Freedom, or, How to Square the Circle." *Theory, Culture and Society.* Vol. 13, No. 2, pp. 79–90.

Bennett, W. J. (1996). "Civil Rights Is the GOP Mission." *Los Angeles Times*, Monday, August 13, 1996. B5.

Bernstein, S. (1996). "Storm Rises over Ex-Klansman in Deabate." *Los Angeles Times*, Wednesday, September 11, A3, A14.

Bhabha, H. (1986). "Remembering Fanon." Foreword to Frantz Fanon, *Black Skin, White Masks*. London: Pluto Press.

Bhachu, P. (1996). "The Multiple Landscapes of Transnational Asian Women in the Diaspora." In Vered Amit-Talai and Caroline Knowles, eds., *Re-Situating Identities: The Politics of Race, Ethnicity, and Culture*. Peterborough, Canada and Essex, London: Broadview Press, pp. 283–303.

Boggs, C. (1995, Dec. 22–28). "The God Reborn: Pondering the Revival of Russian Communism." *Los Angeles View*, 10(20), 8.

Bonnett, A. (1996). "Anti-Racism and the Critique of White Identities." *New Community*, 22(1): 97–110.

Bradlee Jr., B. (1996). "The Buchanan Role: GOP Protagonist." *Boston Sunday Globe*, March 3, 1996, Vol. 249, No. 63, pp. 1, 12.

Buchanan, Patrick (2002). *The Death of the West: How Dying Populations and Immigrant Invasions Imperil Our Country and Civilization*. New York: St. Martin's.

Callinicos, A. 1993. *Race and Class*. London: Bookmarks.

Cashmore, E. (1996). *Dictionary of Race and Ethnic Relations* (fourth edition). London and New York: Routledge.

Chomsky, N. (1996). *Class Warfare: Interviews with David Barsamian*. Monroe, ME: Common Courage Press.

Cone, J. H. (1986). *A Black Theology of Liberation*. New York: Orbis Books.

Connell, R. (1996). "2,000 Protest Alleged U.S. Role in Crack Influx." *Los Angeles Times*, S. 29, p. B1, B4.

Connolly, W. (1995). *The Ethos of Pluralization*. Minneapolis, MN and London: University of Minnesota Press.

Cruz, J. (1996). "From Farce to Tragedy: Reflections on the Reification of Race at Century's End." In Avery Gordon and Christopher Newfield, eds., *Mapping Multiculturalism*. Minneapolis, MN and London: University of Minnesota Press, pp. 19–39.

Dussel, E. (1993). "Eurocentrism and Modernity." *Boundary 2* Vol. 20, No. 3, pp. 65–77.

Fanon, F. (1967). *Black Skin White Masks*. New York: Grove Press.

Feagin, J. R., and Vera, H. (1995). *White Racism*. London and New York: Routledge.

Frankenberg, R. (1993). *The Social Construction of Whiteness: White Women, Race Matters*. Minneapolis, MN: The University of Minnesota Press.

Fraser, N. (1993). "Clintonism, Welfare, and the Antisocial Wage: The Emergence of a Neoliberal Political Imaginary." *Rethinking Marxism*, Vol. 6, No. 1, pp. 9–23.

Fusco, C. (1995). *English Is Broken Here: Notes on Cultural Fusion in the Americas*. New York: The New Press.

Gallagher, C. A. (1994). "White Construction in the University." *Socialist Review*, Vol. 1, pp. 165–187.

Gardiner, M. (1996, May). "Alterity and Ethics: A Dialogical Perspective." *Theory, Culture and Society*, Vol. 13, No. 2, pp. 121–144.

Gatens, M. (1996). *Imaginary Bodies*. London and New York: Routledge.

Giroux, H. (1993). *Border Crossings*. London and New York: Routledge.

——— (1996). "Race and the Debate on Public Intellectuals." *International Journal of Educational Reform*, Vol. 5, No. 3, pp. 345–350.

Gitlin, T. (1995). *The Twilight of Common Dreams: Why America Is Wracked by Culture Wars*. New York: Metropolitan Books.

Goldberg, D. T. (1993). *Racist Culture: Philosophy and the Politics of Meaning*. Cambridge, MA and Oxford, England: Blackwell Publishers.

Gómez-Peña, G. (1996). *The New World Border*. San Francisco, CA: City Lights Bookstore.

Gutéerrez, R. (1996). "The Erotic Zone Sexual Transgression on the U.S.-Mexican Border." In Avery Gordon and Christopher Newfield, eds., *Mapping Multiculturalism*. Minneapolis, MN: University of Minnesota Press.

Harris, C. I. (1993). "Whiteness a Property." *Harvard Law Review*, Vol. 106, No. 8, pp. 1709–1791.

Hicks, E. (1991). *Border Writing*. Minneapolis, MN: University of Minnesota Press.

Holston, James, and Appadurai, A. (1996). "Cities and Citizenship." *Public Culture*, No. 19, pp. 187–204.

Ignatiev, N. (1995). *How the Irish Became White*. London and New York: Routledge.

Ignatiev, N. and Garvey, J. (1996). *Race Traitor*. New York and London: Routledge.

Kahn, J. S. (1995). *Culture, Multiculture, Postculture*. London, Thousand Oaks, CA and New Delhi: Sage Publications.

Kincheloe, J., and Steinberg, S. (In press). *Changing Multiculturalism: New Times. New Curriculum*. London: Open University Press.

Laclau, E. (1992). "Universalism, Particularism, and the Question of Identity." *October*, Vol. 61 (Summer), pp. 83–90.

Lash, S. (1996, May). "Postmodern Ethics: The Missing Ground." *Theory, Culture and Society*, Vol. 13, No. 2, pp. 91–104.

Lipsitz, G. (1995). "The Possessive Investment in Whiteness: Racialized Social Democracy and the 'White' Problem in American Studies." *American Quarterly*, Vol. 47, No. 3, pp. 369–387.

_____ (1996). "It's All Wrong, but Its All Right: Creative Misunderstandings in Intercultural Communication." In Avery Gordon and Christopher Newfield, eds., *Mapping Multiculturalism*. Minneapolis, MN and London: University of Minnesota Press, pp. 403–412.

López, I. E. Haney. (1996). *White by Law*. New York and London: New York University Press.

Loewen, J. W. (1995). *Lies My Teacher Told Me: Everything Your American History Textbook Got Wrong*. New York: Touchstone.

Lott, E. (1993). "White Like Me: Racial Cross-Dressing and the Construction of American Whiteness." In Amy Kaplan and Donald E. Pease, Eds., *Cultures of United States Imperialism*. Durham, NC and London: Duke University Press, pp. 474–498.

Luhrmann, T. M. (1996). *The Good Parsi*. Cambridge, MA and London, England: Harvard University Press.

Macedo, D., and Bartolome, L. (forthcoming). "Dancing with Bigotry: The Poisoning of Racial and Ethnic Identities." In Enrique Torres Trueba and Yali Zou, Eds., *Ethnic Identity and Power*. Albany, NY: State University of New York Press.

Martin-Barbero, J. (1993). *Communication, Culture, and Hegemony*. London, New Park, and New Delhi: Sage Publications.

McLaren, P. (1995). *Critical Pedagogy and Predatory Culture*. London and New York: Routledge.

_____ (in press). *Revolutionary Multiculturalism: Pedagogies of Dissent for the New Millennium*. Boulder, CO: Westview Press.

Miles, Robert (1982). *Racism and Migrant Labour: A Critical Text*. London: Routledge.

_____ (1993). *Racism After "Race Relations."* London: Routledge.

_____ (1994). "Explaining Racism in Contemporary Europ." In Ali Rattansi and Sallie Westwood, Eds., *Racism, Modernity and Identity*. Cambridge, MA and Cambridge, UK: Polity Press.

Miles, R., and Torres, R. (1996). "Does 'Race' Matter? Transatlantic Perspectives on Racism after 'Race Relations.'" In Vered Amit-Talai and Caroline Knowles (Eds.), *Re-Situating Identities*. Toronto, Canada: Broadview Press.

Moore, J., and Pachon, H. (1985). *Hispanics in the United States*. Englewood Cliffs, NJ: Prentice-Hall.

Moraes, M. (1996). *Bilingual Education: A Dialogue with the Bakhtin Circle*. Albany, NY: The State University of New York Press.

Novik, M. (1995). *White Lies, White Power: The Fight Against White Supremacy and Reactionary Violence*. Monroe, ME: Common Courage Press.

O'Brien, C. C. (1996). "Thomas Jefferson: Radical and Racist." The Atlantic Monthly, *October*, pp. 53–74.

Omi, M., and Winant, H. (1993). "The Los Angeles 'Race Riot' and Contemporary U.S. Politics." In Robert Gooding-Williams, Ed., *Reading Rodney King*. London and New York: Routledge, pp. 97–114.

Parenti, M. (1996). *Dirty Truths*. San Francisco, CA: City Lights Books.

Perea, J. F. (1995). "Los Olvidados: On the Making of Invisible People." *New York University Law Review*, Vol. 70, No. 4, pp. 965–991.

Radhakrishnan, R. (1996). *Diasporic Mediations.* Minneapolis, MN and London: University of Minnesota Press.

Rattansi, A. (1994). "'Western' Racisms, Ethnicities and Identities in a 'Postmodern' Frame." In Ali Rattansi and Sallie Westwood, Eds., *Racism, Modernity and Identity on the Western Front.* Cambridge, MA and Oxford, UK: Polity Press, pp. 403–412.

Ridgeway, J. (1995). *Blood in the Face.* New York: Thunder's Mouth Press.

Roediger, D. (1993). *The Wages of Whiteness.* London and New York: Verso.

_____ (1994). *Towards the Abolition of Whiteness.* London and New York: Verso.

Rugoff, R. (1995). *Circus Americanus.* London and New York: Verso.

Said, E. (1985). *Orientalism.* London: Penguin.

San J. E., Jr. (1995). *Hegemony and Strategies of Transgression.* Albany, NY: State University of New York Press.

Sarup, M. (1996). *Identity, Culture, and the Postmodern World.* Athens, GA: The University of Georgia Press.

Shohat, E., and Stam, R. (1994). *Unthinking Eurocentrism.* London and New York: Routledge.

Shohat, E. (1995). "The Struggle over Representation: Casting, Coalitions, and the Politics of Indentification." In Román de la Campa, E. Ann Kaplan, and Michael Sprinker, Eds., *Late Imperial Culture* (pp. 166–178). London and New York: Verso.

Simon, S. (1996). "Job Hunt's Wild Side in Russia." *Los Angeles Times,* January 2, pp. 1, 9.

Sleeter, C. E. (1996). "White Silence, White Solidarity" in Noel Ignatiev and John Gavey (eds.), *Race Traitor.* London and New York: Routledge.

Southern Poverty Law Center. (1996). *False Patriots: The Threat of Antigovernment Extremists.* Montgomery, AL: Southern Poverty Law Center.

Stowe, D. W. "Uncolored People: The Rise of Whiteness Studies." *Lingua Franca,* Vol. 6, No. 6, 1996, pp. 68–77.

The Boston Globe, January 26, 1990.

Time. "Banker to Mexico: 'Go get 'em.'" February 20, 1995, Vol. 145, No. 7, p. 9.

Trembath, P. (1996). "Aesthetics without Art or Culture: Toward an Alternative Sense of Materialist Agency." *Strategies,* Vol. 9/10, pp. 122–151.

Tsing, A. L. (1993). *In the Realm of the Diamond Queen.* Princeton, NJ: Princeton University Press.

Visweswaran, K. (1994). *Fictions of Feminist Ethnography.* Minneapolis, MN and London: University of Minnesota Press.

Wallace, A. (1996). "Less Diversity Seen as UC Preferences End." *Los Angeles Times,* Wednesday, October 2, Al, 18.

Webb, G. (1996). "Unholy Connection." *New Times,* Sept. 12–18, vol. 1, no. 4, pp. 10–24.

Welsch, W. (1996). "Aestheticization Processes: Phenomena, Distinctions and Prospects." *Theory, Culture and Society,* Vol. 13, No. 2, pp. 1–24.

West, C. (1993). *Keeping Faith: Philosophy and Race in America.* New York and London: Routledge.

Williams, R. (1974). *Politics and Letters.* London: Verso.

Winant, H. (1994). *Racial Conditions: Politics, Theory, Comparisons.* Minneapolis, MN and London: University of Minnesota Press.

_____ (1994). "Racial Formation and Hegemony: Global and Local Developments." In Ali Rattansi and Sallie Westwood, eds., *Racism, Modernity, and Identity on the Western Front.* Cambridge, MA and Oxford, U.K.: Polity Press, pp. 266–289.

Wolfenstein, E. V. (1993). *Psychoanalytic-Marxism: Groundwork.* New York and London: The Guildford Press.

Wood, E. M. (1995). *Democracy Against Capitalism: Renewing Historical Materialism.* Cambridge: Cambridge University Press.

Wray, M. and Newitz, A. (1997). *White Trash: Race and Clan in America.* New York: Routledge.

Yudice, G. (1995). "Neither Impugning nor Disavowing Whiteness Does a Viable Politics Make: The Limits of Identity Politics." In Christopher Newfield and Ronald Strickland, Eds., *After Political Correctness: The Humanities and Society in the 1990s.* pp. 255–285.

Zamichow, N. (1996). "Captains Courageous Enough Not to Fight." *Los Angeles Times.* January 2, pp. 1, 9–10.

Zinn, H. (1970). *The Politics of History.* Boston, MA: Beacon Press.

CHAPTER

11 Conclusion to Part Five

What I would like to emphasize in concluding this section of the fourth edition of *Life in Schools* is the importance of developing a pedagogy that brushes history against the grain of its enforced amnesia, that challenges the fabulous amalgamation of emptiness that constitutes our identities as citizens, that refuses to genuflect before the churchy advocates and praise-singers of the new world order. Teachers need to become warriors against certainty, to contest the interrogative monopoly of standardized tests and texts, and to intensify the obvious until it becomes strange while accelerating the unfamiliar until it becomes mundane.

This means that we must keep students connected to the power of the unacceptable, we must plague normalcy, and help to make students more comfortable with the unthinkable (*impensable*) possibilities of hope. We can do this, I believe, by stressing in our work the indissociability of language, power, and subjectivity and by emphasizing that all teaching constitutes a realm *not in, but of, politics*. We can achieve a pedagogy of transformation if we turn our teaching into an outrageous practice and a practice of outrage. If we can invent our pedagogies anew such that they are based on recovering dangerous memories from society's structural unconscious, from the Eurocentric archives of dead reason, then perhaps we can begin to build a project of recovering the lost particles of our dreams, dreams shattered in modernity's thralldom to the tight-fisted logic of consumer capitalism.

We need to teach dangerously, but to live with optimism. We need to be outrageous, but to temper our outrage with love and compassion. We need to be warriors for social justice, yes, but warriors whose ethical bearings and praxis are informed by the best that critical thought has to offer. Although the term "critical pedagogy" has admittedly become too vague, there are still crucial issues to be engaged in its vicinity. We need to remember that our students are not bodiless wraiths to be blown about the corridors by pedagogical rhetoric and sophistry; rather, students are complex historical agents and they need to be able to read the multiple texts of their own lives. That is, they need to read the languages and discourses in which they find themselves in order to reinvent themselves. Consequently, critical pedagogy must not become a "privileged space" for academics but must be forged amidst the daily struggle of the oppressed themselves. The spirit of the pedagogy I have been describing throughout this book can be summarized best by Paulo Freire who recently described his pedagogy of liberation in an interview with Moacir Gadotti as "a bohemian pedagogy of happiness . . . a pedagogy of laughter, of questioning, or curiosity, of seeing the future through the present, a pedagogy that believes in the possibility of the transformation of the world, that believes in history as a possibility."[1]

It is not an exercise to enhance the ability of citizens to survive in a world of market-driven logic. It is not designed to create loyal servants of tradition, beneficiaries of progress, and disciples of perpetual novelty in a world of endless commodities and renewable identities. Rather, critical pedagogy is designed to agitate overconfidence and ideological comfort, to establish roadblocks to modernity's search for the natural sublime, to render as unsuitable a consensus of ideas and practices that permit anyone to suffer needlessly. Critical pedagogy is at odds with inaction and disembodiment. It is a project that consitutes a rage against enforced silence and confrontation with indifference, a politics of hope set against the mindless Pepsi generation optimism and Coca Cola dreams of marketplace ideology.

Utopia must be linked to indictment; critique must be linked to possibility. Critical pedagogy does not traffic in the realization of endpoints, nor does it wallow in a cautious lethargy. On the contrary, it dares to gesture in the direction of hope. The struggle for liberation is not powered by high-tech blueprints for creating a just society but rather recognizes the importance of small victories on the picket lines, in the classroom, in public spaces, and during private encounters. Partial victories are never simply individual but rather arch toward a larger, collective struggle underwritten by the ontological quest to become more fully human. This quest is anchored in a self-reflexive process that uncoils the following questions: What am I to think? What are the terms and conditions of our belonging? How are power-based differences inscribed into our identity as social beings within a runaway capitalist hegemony? Critical pedagogy investigates the ontological import of such questions and explores what the contradictions between theory and practice encode.

But what is this gesture toward hope? Hearts gesturing toward hope create an arch of social dreaming; that is, such a gesture amounts to hope that is bolstered by critical reason and that turns on action; it is a hope bound to a vision of what could be possible, a vision fired by righteous anger. It is a vision that accounts for the totality of capitalist exploitation yet does not become totalizing in its own right. Consequently, this book has not proposed to solve the Sphinx's riddle of linking theory to an ultimate form of practice, vision to final action, desire to complete fulfillment. However, it does point to some provisional yet necessary directions for constructing a praxis of resistance and transformation and thereby encouraging democracy to live up to its promise. While we may look back nostalgically at the struggles of the volunteers who fought in the international brigades in Spain between 1936 and 1939, or wait with anticipation for the outcome of the Zapatista resistance in Chiapas, a growing recognition is dawning upon us like a sobering icy wind that current and future struggles for liberation will need to be rethought in the present conditions of global capitalism and the international division of labor. The class-unspecific efforts of the postmodernists on the academic left in attacking obscenely conspicuous consumption rather than scarcity has turned them into a legion of symbolic berserkers inflicting damage at points of consumption and the image—where alienation and despair run high—and destroying the symbols of capitalist triumph. Their efforts are welcomed, but woefully insufficient. We need transnational class struggles, but how to bring them about is not clear.

Our purposes may never be realized in our lifetime or in the lifetimes of our children or grandchildren. Yet we must never loosen our commitment to forging relations of solidarity with the oppressed or relinquish our continuing struggle against injustice. Dear educators and future educators, I end with a quotation attributed to the great Mexican revolutionary leader, Emiliano Zapata: *"Mejor morir de pie que vivir toda una vida arrodillados."* ("It is better to die on your feet than to live a lifetime on your knees.") The struggle is at hand and history has called on us to play a part in its making. Though the forces against us are increasing, our resolve remains strong. We, the teachers and students, have a voice and we will continue to struggle until it is collectively heard. *Hasta la victoria siempre.* It is because I believe that hope—in order to be liberating—must always be conjugated with class struggle that I will always remain committed to a revolutionary politics.

Some say that U.S. citizens have lost their collective memory, that they are confined to a space outside of history, condemned by hubris to live life in an eternal present. But how can U.S. citizens lose a knowledge of history that they have never possessed, that has been camouflaged from them by the corporate-driven media and their ideological allegiance to the state? For this reason, critical pedagogy cannot remain an isolated doctrine; it must etherealize itself by merging with our consciousness, our flesh, our emotions, our perceptions, and become a sensuous part of our being. It must also become concretized in our everyday actions and activities on and in the world. To be conscious of history is to be active in its making.

In travelling down the path of capitalist development, we have discovered, much to our alarm, that often it is the very political regimes that describe themselves as "free market democracies" that have become unremittingly resistant to self-criticism. The struggle to build a world free from exploitation is a daunting one, and requires that we take paths less traveled, that take us in directions less familiar, and toward destinations less certain. We make the path to freedom as we walk down it. And we remake ourselves in the process. Today, as in previous times when history has placed us at a dangerous crossroads, we face the ultimate choice between barbarism or socialism.

E N D N O T E

1. Moacir Gadotti, *Reading Paulo Freire: His Life and Work* (Albany, New York: State University of New York Press, 1994).

INDEX